Sashastra Seema Bal

Sub Inspector (SI) Recruitment Exam

Latest Edition
Practice Kit

10 Tests
10 Mock Test

Based On Real Exam Pattern

✓ Thoroughly Revised and Updated

✓ Detailed Analysis of all MCQs

<table>
<tr><td>Title</td><td>: Sashastra Seema Bal Sub Inspector (SI) Recruitment Exam</td></tr>
<tr><td>Author Name</td><td>: Mr. Rohit Manglik</td></tr>
<tr><td>Published By</td><td>: EduGorilla Community Pvt. Ltd.</td></tr>
<tr><td>Publishers Address</td><td>: 12/651, First Floor Opp. Arvindo Park, Near Jama Masjid,
Indira Nagar, Lucknow, Uttar Pradesh-226016, India</td></tr>
</table>

Copyright EduGorilla

Disclaimer EduGorilla

ROHIT MANGLIK
CEO, EduGorilla

Dear Applicants,

People say *"Success comes to those who work hard."* But I've seen people working hard for their exams day in and day out for marginal success. While others succeed in their examinations by putting in just half the work. So are they God Gifted? No! I believe that it's because they work *smart* and not just *hard*. Similarly, for your exams, you should strategize your preparation so as to increase the likelihood of success. Well with EduGorilla get ready to increase your *chances of selection* in your exam by *16x*.

EduGorilla helps you in not only working *hard* but also working in a *smart and strategic* manner. With EduGorilla's preparation package, you get a chance to make your exam preparation easy, and a fun learning path towards selection. Finding the right path to your preparations can be difficult if you don't know in which direction to head. Don't worry, we have you covered! EduGorilla will be your guide to success in your journey. With our Preparation Package, you can prepare strategically and beat the exam in just one attempt.

EduGorilla's Preparation Package includes-

• **Test Series**   • **Books**

Our preparation package is handcrafted as per the latest changes, expert opinions, and students' discretion. Thus, enabling you to get through each stage of the selection process for your exam.

Our Books are designed by the teachers and experts of the respective exam with a combined 150+ years of experience; to provide you with easy, efficient, and effective learning. Our books are smart, in the sense that not only do they give you the answers to the questions but also provide similar questions for practice.

EduGorilla's competent Test Series gives you real-time experience and confidence through which you can clear your offline or online exam in just one attempt. We currently host 83,000+ mock tests for 1,440+ competitive and academic exams.

Thus, EduGorilla misses no chance to assist you in your preparation and covers all stages of the exam, so that you don't have to look anywhere else.

We provide complete preparation packages for defense, banking, teaching, and other National & State-Level exams. Hence, it doesn't matter which exam you aspire to because you will reach your success.

ALL THE BEST !

Let EduGorilla be your Guide to Success.

Rohit Manglik,
Founder and CEO, EduGorilla

INTRODUCTION

EduGorilla focuses on guiding students to succeed in their examinations. With that in mind, our book, titled "Sashastra Seema Bal : Sub Inspector (SI) Recruitment Exam", has been drafted through the collective efforts of our distinguished experts with 150+ years of combined experience. This book consists of questions that are created following the latest changes in the syllabus and exam pattern. We compiled the book on the basis of questions that are most likely to appear in the SSB Sub-Inspector (SI). Through EduGorilla's "Sashastra Seema Bal : Sub Inspector (SI) Recruitment Exam" your chances of success will increase 16x.

EduGorilla does this through our Complete Preparation Package. This package consists of well-conceptualized and structured content in the form of questions that are tailor-made according to your needs and will help you practice for exams in a smart way by pinpointing all the necessary information. It also provides hints and solutions, along with a smart answer sheet for your self-evaluation. You can assess your shortcomings and work accordingly on areas that may require more of your attention.

EduGorilla promises to help you succeed in your examination and accomplish your dream goals. We believe in our aspirants and see them at the top of the merit list. And the first step towards the top is to start preparing with us. EduGorilla's "Sashastra Seema Bal : Sub Inspector (SI) Recruitment Exam" includes the following attributes.

➤ Well-Researched Content

➤ Top-Notch Quality

➤ Detailed Answers and Analysis

➤ Smart Answer Sheet

➤ Exam Relevant Questions

Therefore, EduGorilla fortifies your preparation and makes it durable enough to help you stand tall and beat the examination.

SSB Sub-Inspector (SI)
Scan QR code for Eligibility, Exam Pattern, Syllabus and more.

Book ID: 0846

TABLE OF CONTENTS

Q.1 Who has become the first Indian to win gold in the World Cadet Judo Championship 2022?
- **A.** Avtar Singh
- **B.** Linthoi Chanambam
- **C.** Poonam Chopra
- **D.** Kalpana Devi

Q.2 The Nobel Memorial Prize in Economic Sciences 2022 was awarded to three scientists for their research in which field?
- **A.** Behavioural Economics
- **B.** Global Poverty
- **C.** Banks and Financial Crises
- **D.** Quantitative Methods

Q.3 Which country's organisation in June 2022 signed an MoU with Bharat Electronics Limited (BEL) for the Supply of Airborne Defense Suite for Indian Air Force (IAF) helicopters?
- **A.** Japan
- **B.** United States of America
- **C.** Belarus
- **D.** France

Q.4 Which of the following has commissioned India's first 'Smart Managed' EV charging station?
- **A.** Tata Power Delhi Distribution
- **B.** Dakshin Gujarat Vij Company
- **C.** CESC Limited
- **D.** BSES Yamuna Power Limited

Ques (5-9):Direction: Study the information given below and answer the following question:

For a country, CO_2 emission (million metric tons) from various sectors are given in the following table.

CO₂ emissions (million metric tons)					
Sector	Power	Industry	Commercial	Agriculture	Domestic
2005	500	200	150	80	100
2006	600	300	200	90	110
2007	650	320	250	100	120
2008	700	400	300	150	150
2009	800	450	320	200	180

Q.5 What is the percentage $(\%)$ growth of CO_2 emissions from the power sector from 2005 to 2009?
- **A.** 60
- **B.** 50
- **C.** 40
- **D.** 80

Q.6 Which sector has recorded maximum growth in CO_2 emissions from 2005 to 2009?
- **A.** Power
- **B.** Industry
- **C.** Commercial
- **D.** Agriculture

Q.7 By what percentage $(\%)$, the total emissions of CO_2 have increased from 2005 to 2009?
- **A.** 89.32%
- **B.** 57.62%
- **C.** 40.32%
- **D.** 113.12%

Q.8 What is the average annual growth rate of power has increased from 2005 to 2009?
- **A.** 12.57%
- **B.** 16.87%
- **C.** 30.81%
- **D.** 50.25%

Q.9 What is the percentage contribution of the power sector to total CO_2 emissions in the year 2008?
- **A.** 30.82%
- **B.** 41.18%
- **C.** 51.38%
- **D.** 60.25%

Q.10 The ratio of numbers of girls and boys participating in sports of a school is 4:5. If the number of girls is 212, determine the number of boys participating in the sports.
- **A.** 256
- **B.** 265
- **C.** 251
- **D.** 263

Q.11 Cost of a dozen pens is Rs. 180 and cost of 8 ball pens is Rs. 56. Find the ratio of the cost of a pen to the cost of a ball pen.
- **A.** $\frac{15}{7}$
- **B.** $\frac{15}{8}$
- **C.** $\frac{17}{15}$
- **D.** $\frac{8}{15}$

Q.12 Azad invested Rs 55000 in a cosmetic shop for the whole year. After 4 months of Azad, Hind joined him and invested Rs 70000. Next year Azad invested Rs 10000 more and Hind withdrew Rs 10000 and at the end of two years profit earned by Azad is Rs 32375. Find the total profit if they distributed half of the total profit equally and rest in the capital ratio.
- **A.** Rs. 89600
- **B.** Rs. 75600
- **C.** Rs. 52800
- **D.** Rs. 62900

Q.13 Which of the following statement is true about the tropical convergence?
1. It is called ITCZ in short
2. It is a low-pressure zone between tropic of Cancer and tropic of Capricorn
3. Seasonal changes in position are found
- **A.** 1, 2 and 3
- **B.** 1 and 2
- **C.** 2 and 3
- **D.** 1 and 3

Q.14 'Amphan' made landfall in a part of West Bengal and Orissa in May 2020. It is an example of:
- **A.** Tropical cyclone
- **B.** Temperate cyclone
- **C.** Extra-tropical cyclone
- **D.** Anticyclone

Q.15 Arrange the layer of the atmosphere from top to bottom.
- **A.** Troposphere - Stratosphere - Mesosphere - Ionosphere
- **B.** Ionosphere - Troposphere - Stratosphere - Mesosphere

C. Ionosphere - Mesosphere - Stratosphere - Troposphere
D. Troposphere - Stratosphere - Ionosphere - Mesosphere

Q.16 Who is known as the father of neuroscience?
A. Santiago Ramón y Cajal
B. Alessandro Volta
C. Salim Ali
D. None of these

Q.17 Who invented the safety break, which stop the elevator from crashing?
A. Thomas Edison   **B.** Eli Whitney
C. Henry Ford   **D.** Elisha Otis

Q.18 An umbrella is made by stitching 10 triangular pieces of cloth of two different colours (see figure), each piece measuring 20 cm, 50 cm, and 50 cm. Now much cloth of each colour is required for the umbrella?

A. 5   **B.** 10   **C.** 15   **D.** 20

Q.19 A floral design on a floor is made up: of 16 tiles which are triangular, the sides of the triangle being 9 cm, 28 cm and 35 cm (see figure). Find the cost of polishing the tiles at the rate of 50p per cm2.

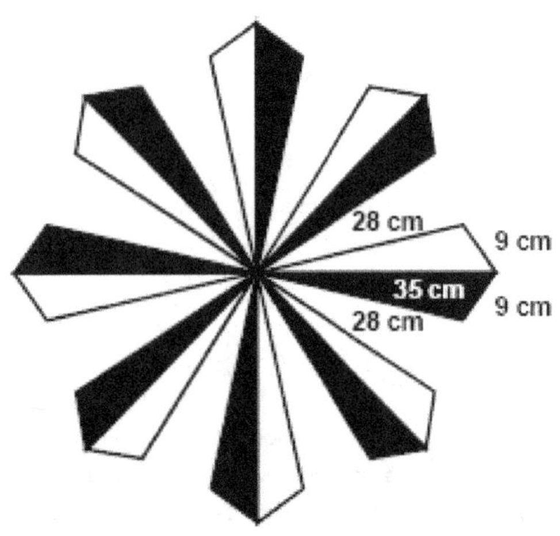

A. Rs. 700   **B.** Rs. 705.60
C. Rs. 709   **D.** Rs. 701

Q.20 One side of rectangular field is 15 m and one of its diagonals is 17 m find the area of the field?
A. 75 m²   **B.** 120 m²   **C.** 240 m²   **D.** 350 m²

Q.21 Direction: Answer the following question by selecting the most appropriate option.
In Diagnostic test in Mathematics, both background and performance of the students is needed for helping them in
A. Getting first position in the class
B. Crack competitive exam like JEE, NEET etc
C. Acquisition of intellectual habits and enhances learning
D. Become a politician

Q.22 The eight-year-old Tajamul Islam of Jammu and Kashmir is associated with which sport?
[Madhya Pradesh Public Service Commission (MPPSC), 2017]

A. Squash   **B.** Kickboxing
C. Swimming   **D.** Football

Q.23 Sultan Azlan Shah Cup is related to which among the following Sports?
A. Badminton   **B.** Hockey
C. Table Tennis   **D.** Golf

Q.24 In which district of Rajasthan 'JAKHAM' Multipurpose project is located?
[Rajasthan Police Sub Inspector, 2016]

A. Tonk   **B.** Banswara
C. Bharatpur   **D.** Pratapgarh

Q.25 The word 'Sociology' is made up of two words. These are-
A. Societies and Logy
B. Societia and Logistia
C. Socious and Logos
D. Socia and Logos

Q.26 Sociology emerged in:
A. America   **B.** Europe   **C.** Asia   **D.** Africa

Q.27 Find the value of ' ?' in the given equation:
$$72 \times 25 + 45 \times 20 = 15^3 - ?$$
A. 525   **B.** 675   **C.** 575   **D.** 625

Q.28 H.C.F of 493,527 and 697 is:
A. 27   **B.** 51   **C.** 17   **D.** 23

Q.29 Who was the first women prime minister of India?
A. Mrs. Unnnati Sharma
B. Mrs. Indira Gandhi
C. Sarojini Naidu
D. Rekha Saini

Q.30 Due to a shortage of labor in a factory, its production decreases by 25%. By how much% should the working period be increased so that production remains the same?
A. $53\frac{1}{3}\%$ **B.** $23\frac{1}{3}\%$ **C.** $40\frac{1}{3}\%$ **D.** $33\frac{1}{3}\%$

Q.31 In an examination, 40% of the students fail in Mathematics, 30% fail in English. 10% fail in both subjects. So, tell the% of students who passed in both the subjects.

A. 36% **B.** 20% **C.** 50% **D.** 40%

Q.32 In which year, the Government of India had set up the Sarkaria Commission on Centre-State relations?

A. 1980 **B.** 1983 **C.** 1987 **D.** 1992

Q.33 Which of the following statements is not correct about the Rajya Sabha?

A. Rajya Sabha is a permanent body.

B. It was duly constituted for the first time on April 3, 1952.

C. Twelve of Rajya Sabha members are nominated by the President.

D. One-third of its members retire every year.

Q.34 Which of the following is an indicator of mathematical reasoning?

[CTET Paper - I, 2019]

A. Ability to provide definitions of mathematical concepts

B. Ability to provide a justification for a mathematical procedure

C. Ability to calculate efficiently

D. Ability to recall the correct formulae in different situations

Q.35 In order to access the students' academic achievements of teaching environmental studies which of the following evaluation indicator should not be used?

A. Observation **B.** Discussion

C. Experimentation **D.** Remedial teaching

Q.36 Which of the following is the narrowest strait of the world?

[NCHM JEE (Hotel Mgmt & Catering), 2018]

A. Strait of Tartar

B. Bab-el-Mandeb

C. Strait of Dardanelles

D. Foveaux Strait

Q.37 Which among the following programmes is NOT being implemented in India with the assistance of the World Bank?

[NCHM JEE (Hotel Mgmt & Catering), 2018]

A. National Vector Borne Disease Control and Polio Eradication

B. National Rural Livelihoods Project

C. PMGSY Rural Roads Project

D. Delhi Mumbai Industrial Corridor Project

Q.38 The performance of a student is compared with another student in which type of testing?

[UGC NET Home Science, 2019]

A. Criterion-referenced testing

B. Diagnostic testing

C. Summative testing

D. Norm-referenced testing

Q.39 What is the main objective of formative evaluation?

A. To promote students to the next class

B. To enhance students' learning

C. To enhance co-operation in class

D. To understand the learning difficulties

Q.40 Yamini Krishnamurti is associated with which classical dance?

A. Bharatanatyam **B.** Kathakali

C. Odyssey **D.** Kuchipudi

Q.41 Leela Samson is associated with which classical dance form?

A. Bharatanatyam **B.** Kuchipudi

C. Odyssey **D.** Kathakali

Q.42 Direction: In the following question, some part of the sentence may have errors. Find out which part of the sentence has an error and select the appropriate option. If a sentence is free from error, select 'No Error' option.

In emerging economies, the private credit market (A)/ remains highly segmented and thus (B)/ weaken the power of monetary policy. (C)/ No error (D)

A. (A) **B.** (B) **C.** (C) **D.** No error

Q.43 The least number which should be added to 98243 so that the sum is exactly divisible by $3, 5, 7$ and 8 is?

A. 27 **B.** 33 **C.** 37 **D.** 47

Q.44 The English defeated the _____ in the battle of Wandiwash.

A. German **B.** French

C. Indians **D.** Americans

Q.45 Which of the following statements about National Research Foundation (NRF), proposed in National Education Policy (2020) is correct?

A. It does not fund research activities at state universities.

B. It provides funding to research projects in science as well as non-science disciplines.

C. It will be headed by the secretary of the Ministry of Education.

D. It aims to increase the expenditure of the government on Research and Development (R&D) to 2.5 percent of GDP by 2025.

Q.46 With respect to the insurance sector in India, consider the following statements:

1. FDI limit in the insurance sector has been raised to 74 percent in the 2021-22 budget.

2. Foreign ownership and control in agricultural insurance companies are not allowed.

Which of the statements given above is/are correct?

A. 1 only **B.** 2 only

C. Both 1 and 2 **D.** Neither 1 nor 2

Q.47 Which one of the following conditions is relevant for the presence of an organism on Mars?

A. Volcanic composition

B. Thermal states

C. Presence of Ice beams and ice water

D. Presence of ozone

Q.48 What is the age of RBC in human blood?

A. 30 days   **B.** 7 days   **C.** 120 days   **D.** 15 days

Q.49 What is the percentage of oxygen in $Al_2(SO_4)_3$?

[RRB/RRC Group D, 2018]

A. 57.7%   **B.** 56.1%   **C.** 53.1%   **D.** 52.6%

Q.50 ______ gas is used as illuminating gas.

[RRB/RRC Group D, 2018]

A. Methyl   **B.** Propane   **C.** Butene   **D.** Ethyne

Q.51 Which of the following is true with respect to diffraction?

A. Diffraction is the bending of light around the corners of a obstacle

B. Diffraction of light is of two types

C. For diffraction, the size of the obstacle should be comparable to wavelength of light

D. All of the above

Q.52 Why does the oil move up in the lamp?

A. Pressure difference   **B.** Capillary action
C. Low viscosity of oil   **D.** Light being hot

Q.53 Three spherical balls of radius 9 cm, 12 cm and 15 cm are melted to form a new spherical ball. What is the radius (in cm) of the new ball?

A. 17 cm   **B.** 28 cm   **C.** 18 cm   **D.** 16 cm

Ques (54-56):Direction: In the following question, sentences of a paragraph have been jumbled and labeled as A, B, C and D. You are required to rearrange the jumbled sentences of the paragraph and mark your response accordingly by selecting the correct option.

Q.54 A: This is where their senses of touch and smell come in.

B: The sense of smell is located in the antennae or feelers which are always moving.

C: Many kinds of ants are blind, so how they find their way home?

D: These senses are of big help to them.

A. ABCD   **B.** DCBA   **C.** CADB   **D.** BDAC

Q.55 A: Wars always give rise to patriotic feelings, however, in times of peace, they lie dormant.

B: They, rather, covertly urge society to work.

C: This does not mean they are absent.

D: After all, a good economy is also a deterrent to detrimental foreign forces so we should focus our energies on the holistic development of our nation.

A. CABD   **B.** DABC   **C.** BDCA   **D.** ACBD

Q.56 A: When we wish to do a great thing, we cannot expect success right away.

B: The Taj Mahal in Agra did not achieve its glory all of a sudden—it took several years to be recognized as a world heritage site.

C: We should carry on our work with patience and perseverance and the recognition and appreciation will follow soon.

D: The same is true of any great achievement.

A. ABCD   **B.** BDAC   **C.** DCBA   **D.** CABD

Ques (57-59):Direction: Each of the following items has a sentence with a blank space and four words or groups of words given after the sentence. Select whichever word or group of words you consider most appropriate for the blank space and indicate your response on the Answer Sheet accordingly.

Q.57 I only have a _________ of respect for her after she lied about her background.

A. Scintilla   **B.** Garrulous
C. Galore   **D.** Revile

Q.58 Instead of showing his mother his paper, the boy chose to ______ it up.

A. Refine   **B.** Crumble   **C.** Nurture   **D.** Flourish

Q.59 All I need is a _________ of money to pay for my basic needs.

A. Deviate   **B.** Modicum
C. Podium   **D.** Pandemonium

Q.60 Which one among the following is not a function of Mir Bakshi, the Head of the Military Department as well as of the nobility under the Mughal rule?

A. He was responsible for all incomes and expenditures and held control over Khalisa, Jagir and Inam lands.

B. He was responsible for the security of foreign travellers on the highways of the empire.

C. He made recommendations for appointment to Mansabs to the emperor.

D. He collected reports of intelligence and information agencies of the empire and presented them to the emperor at the court.

Q.61 The given Venn diagram shows which of the following options:

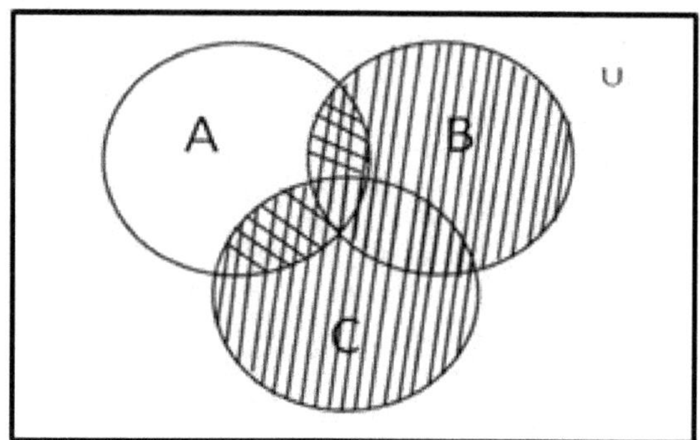

A. $A \cup (B \cap C)$ **B.** $A \cap (B \cup C)$
C. $(A \cap B) \cup C$ **D.** $(A \cup B) \cap C$

Q.62 Question 8 was solved by 67 examinees in an examination. Question 9 is 46 and Question 10 is 40. 28 examinees had solved both questions 8 and 9, 8 answered both questions 9 and 10, 26 both questions 8 and 10 and 2 solved all three questions, then how many had solved question 8, but questions 9 and not 10?

A. 16   **B.** 17   **C.** 15   **D.** 19

Ques (63-64):Direction: Each item in this section consists of a sentence with an underlined word followed by four options.

Select the option that is nearest in meaning to the underlined word.

Q.63 He is always <u>anxious</u>.

A. worried   **B.** dispassionate
C. sluggish   **D.** torpid

Q.64 The poems of Kabir are <u>ecstatic</u> in nature.

[UPSC NDA, 2019]

A. efficacious   **B.** eerie
C. rapturous   **D.** reverential

Q.65 Which one of the following Novels is not written by Shailesh Matiyani?

A. Kabutarkhana   **B.** Kameene
C. Jaymala   **D.** Mahabhoj

Q.66 Who among the following is known as the 'Gandhi of Uttarakhand'?

A. Govind Ballabh Pant
B. Hemwati Nandan Bahuguna
C. Indramani Badoni
D. Badri Dutt Pandey

Q.67 Who is known as the 'Encyclopaedia of Uttarakhand'?

A. Manglesh Dabral   **B.** Shiv Prasad Dabral
C. Viren Dangwal   **D.** Govind Chatak

Q.68 If $k(3 \text{ Median} - \text{Mode}) = \text{Mean}$ then k is?

A. 2   **B.** $\frac{1}{2}$ **C.** $\frac{1}{3}$ **D.** 3

Q.69 If x is the mean of data $6, x, 2$ and 4, then the mode is _______.

A. 6   **B.** 2   **C.** 4   **D.** 3

Q.70 A can do a work in 4 days and B can do the same work in 5 days. The contract for the work is Rs. 9000. What will be the share of B if they will work together?

A. 4000   **B.** 5000   **C.** 1000   **D.** 4500

Q.71 30 men can finish a work in 25 days. In how many days 15 men can finish the same work?

A. 50   **B.** 30   **C.** 20   **D.** 75

Q.72 In the given figure, lines PQ and ST intersect each other at O. If ∠ROQ = 90° and a : b = 4 : 5. What is the value of angle c?

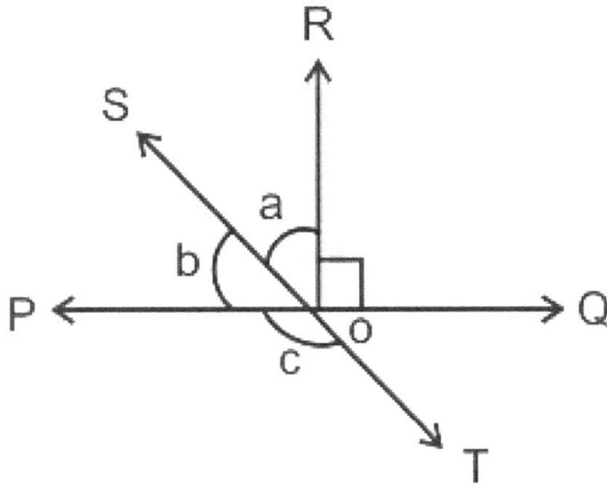

A. 120°   **B.** 100°   **C.** 130°   **D.** 145°

Q.73 Write four more rational numbers in the following pattern

$$\frac{1}{-6}, \frac{2}{-12}, \frac{3}{-18}, \frac{4}{-24}$$

[RRB/RRC Group D, 2018]

A. $\frac{5}{6}, \frac{7}{8}, \frac{9}{10}, \frac{11}{12}$

B. $\frac{5}{30}, \frac{6}{36}, \frac{7}{42}, \frac{8}{48}$

C. $\frac{5}{-6}, \frac{6}{-12}, \frac{7}{-18}, \frac{8}{-24}$

D. $\frac{5}{-30}, \frac{6}{-36}, \frac{7}{-42}, \frac{8}{-48}$

Ques (74-75):Direction: In the following question, a sentence has been given in Active/Passive Voice. Out of the four alternatives suggested, select the one which best expresses the same sentence in Passive/Active Voice.

Q.74 Students asked many questions to their teacher.

A. Many teachers were asked questions by the students.
B. The teacher was asked many questions by their students.
C. Their teacher was asked many questions by the students.
D. Their teachers were asked many questions by the students.

Q.75 Your mother called you many times.

A. You was called many times by your mother.
B. You were being called many times by your mother.
C. You called many times by your mother.
D. You were called many times by your mother.

Q.76 Which of the following day was observed as 'World Teachers Day'?

A. June, 24   **B.** May, 24
C. September, 5   **D.** October, 5

Q.77 Which of the following day was observed as the 'World Cancer Day' this year?

[KVS Trained Graduate Teacher, 2017]

A. February, 1   **B.** January, 26
C. February, 4   **D.** February, 14

Q.78 According to the cultural history of India 'Panchayatan' is:

A. An assembly of elders of the village
B. A religious sect
C. Temple construction style

D. Functionary of an administration

Q.79 A man sells an article at a 15% loss. If he had sold it for Rs. 450 more, he would have earned a profit of 10%. Find the cost price of this article.

A. 1800 **B.** 1600 **C.** 1700 **D.** 1500

Q.80 The selling price of glass is Rs 1965 and the loss percentage is 25%. If the selling price is Rs 3013, then what will be the profit percentage?

A. 13% **B.** 10% **C.** 15% **D.** 20%

Q.81 From a semi-circular sheet of diameter $28\ cm$, two squares are cut such that the sum of the lengths of their diagonals is $32\ cm$. If the product of the length of the diagonals of the squares is $252\ cm^2$, then find the area of the remaining sheet. Use $\pi = \dfrac{22}{7}$.

A. $48\ cm^2$ **B.** $56\ cm^2$ **C.** $64\ cm^2$ **D.** $72\ cm^2$

Q.82 In the figure given below, d_1 is the diameter of the outer circle, while d_2 is the diameter of the three semi-circles. If the area of the shaded region is $\dfrac{3}{8}$ of the area of the unshaded region, then find the ratio $d_1 : d_2$.

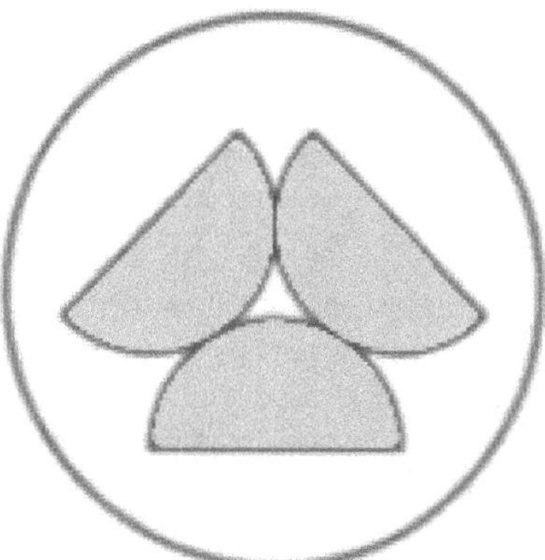

A. $\sqrt{5} : \sqrt{2}$ **B.** $\sqrt{8} : \sqrt{5}$
C. $\sqrt{11} : \sqrt{2}$ **D.** $\sqrt{11} : \sqrt{8}$

Q.83 If $a + b = 13$ and $ab = 42$, then find the value of $a^3 + b^3$?

A. 595 **B.** 565 **C.** 559 **D.** 556

Q.84 What is the difference between place value of 9 and actual value of 9 in number 569387?

[MPTET Paper I - Varg 3, 2012]

A. 8919 **B.** 8991 **C.** 1989 **D.** 9891

Q.85 The sum of the following numbers is:

1856, 3287, 8432, 9.999, 18.888

[MPTET Paper I - Varg 3, 2012]

A. 10453.887 **B.** 10435.887
C. 10435.878 **D.** 13603.887

Ques (86-90):Direction: For the following question, you have one brief passage with 15 question. Read the passage carefully and choose the best answer to each question out of the four alternatives.

Buddha was one of the world's great religious teachers. His real name was Gautam Siddharth. He was born in the year 500 B.C. He was born a prince. His father was the King of Kapilavastu. But he did not want to become a king. He wanted to find out the meaning of life. He left his place as a young man. He went out to seek the truth. For years he lived the hard life of poverty. He went to many teachers. But they could not help him. At least, the light came to him. He was thinking deeply under a Bodhi tree near Gaya. He became the 'Buddha' or the 'Enlightened One'.

Q.86 Who was Buddha?

[MPTET Paper I - Varg 3, 2012]

A. Buddha was God
B. Buddha was a saint
C. Buddha was a great religious teacher
D. Buddha was a great political leader

Q.87 What was the real name of Buddha?

[MPTET Paper I - Varg 3, 2012]

A. Gautam Siddhartha **B.** Mahatma Gautam
C. Hiuen Tsang **D.** Vardhaman

Q.88 Buddha was:

[MPTET Paper I - Varg 3, 2012]

A. Born a Muslim
B. Born in a poor family
C. Born a teacher
D. Born a prince

Q.89 Buddha was born:

[MPTET Paper I - Varg 3, 2012]

A. After the death of Christ
B. Before the birth of Christ
C. Two thousand years ago
D. At the same time as Mahavir

Q.90 The land of Buddha's birth is:

[MPTET Paper I - Varg 3, 2012]

A. Gaya **B.** India
C. The palace **D.** Kapilavastu

Q.91 World tourism day is celebrated on:

A. 25, September **B.** 26, September
C. 27, September **D.** 28, September

Q.92 What is the capital of Saudi Arabia?

[RBI Office Attendant, 2017]

A. Kabul **B.** Yerevan **C.** Riyadh **D.** Helsinki

Q.93 An article is listed at Rs. 7,600 and the discount offered for the unit is 10%. What additional discount must be given to bring the net selling price to Rs. 5,814?

A. 15%　　**B.** 12%　　**C.** 8%　　**D.** 10%

Q.94 Evaluate $\sqrt{41 - \sqrt{21 + \sqrt{19 - \sqrt{9}}}}$

A. 3　　**B.** 5　　**C.** 6　　**D.** 6.4

Q.95 If $x = 5$ and $y = x + 7$, then value of $\sqrt{x^2 + y^2} =$

A. 65　　**B.** 26　　**C.** 17　　**D.** 13

Q.96 Consider the following statements regarding Lok Devta:

1. Ramdev Ji started Kamadia Panth.
2. Dev Narayan composed 24 Vaniya.

Choose the correct one?

A. Only 1　　　　**B.** Only 2
C. Both 1 and 2　　**D.** None of these

Q.97 Select the most appropriate meaning of the given idiom.

A penny saved is a penny earned

[Delhi Forest Guard, 2021]

A. What you have is worth more than what you might have later
B. Better to show than tell
C. Money you save today you can spend later
D. Saving money for later

Q.98 Select the most appropriate meaning of the given idiom.

Birds of a feather flock together

[Delhi Forest Guard, 2021]

A. Comparing two things that cannot be compared
B. People with differences can also unite under something common
C. Believe what people do and not what they say
D. People who are alike are often friends

Q.99 A person borrows certain amount of money at the rate of 2.5% per month. If he pays Rs. 13110 after 6 months to clear his dues then find the amount of interest paid by the person.

A. Rs. 1840　　**B.** Rs. 1690　　**C.** Rs. 1710　　**D.** Rs. 1660

Q.100 A bank offers the business loan at simple interest, rate of interest for 1st 2 years is 8% for the next 3 years it is 10% and for the period beyond 5 years it is 12.5% per annum. If a person took the loan of Rs. $20\,L$ and paid Rs. $36.7\,L$ after some years. Find the number of years after which he repaid the loan:

A. 7 years　　**B.** 9 years　　**C.** 8 years　　**D.** 10 years

// Smart Answer Sheet //

Correct Percentage of students who answered correctly. **Skipped** Percentage of students who skipped.

Q.	Ans.	Correct / Skipped	Q.	Ans.	Correct / Skipped	Q.	Ans.	Correct / Skipped	Q.	Ans.	Correct / Skipped	Q.	Ans.	Correct / Skipped	Q.	Ans.	Correct / Skipped
1	B	51.89 % / 1.34 %	18	A	21.49 % / 4.49 %	35	D	69.33 % / 1.23 %	52	B	42.75 % / 1.81 %	69	C	46.81 % / 1.53 %	86	C	53.98 % / 1.18 %
2	C	59.27 % / 1.05 %	19	B	10.76 % / 4.61 %	36	A	56.7 % / 1.5 %	53	C	65.75 % / 1.3 %	70	A	85.11 % / 0.0 %	87	A	69.0 % / 1.08 %
3	C	62.31 % / 2.0 %	20	B	63.13 % / 1.1 %	37	D	60.62 % / 1.1 %	54	C	62.26 % / 1.53 %	71	A	87.98 % / 0.0 %	88	D	61.58 % / 1.72 %
4	D	61.78 % / 1.2 %	21	C	83.44 % / 0.0 %	38	D	64.58 % / 1.6 %	55	D	58.26 % / 1.06 %	72	C	58.08 % / 1.58 %	89	B	64.2 % / 1.64 %
5	A	50.85 % / 1.07 %	22	B	77.97 % / 0.0 %	39	B	41.35 % / 1.83 %	56	B	55.96 % / 1.51 %	73	D	85.82 % / 0.0 %	90	D	57.13 % / 1.8 %
6	D	54.51 % / 1.17 %	23	A	57.92 % / 1.6 %	40	D	47.0 % / 1.05 %	57	A	48.62 % / 1.68 %	74	C	45.7 % / 1.31 %	91	C	89.3 % / 0.0 %
7	A	41.89 % / 1.24 %	24	D	56.93 % / 1.21 %	41	A	66.93 % / 1.8 %	58	B	62.07 % / 1.21 %	75	D	58.91 % / 1.73 %	92	C	57.71 % / 1.75 %
8	A	65.24 % / 1.12 %	25	C	81.42 % / 0.0 %	42	C	84.91 % / 0.0 %	59	B	44.15 % / 1.83 %	76	D	80.34 % / 0.0 %	93	A	54.87 % / 1.18 %
9	B	56.52 % / 1.9 %	26	B	43.47 % / 1.31 %	43	C	81.56 % / 0.0 %	60	C	68.78 % / 1.65 %	77	C	46.01 % / 1.66 %	94	C	61.99 % / 1.58 %
10	B	52.05 % / 1.69 %	27	B	88.92 % / 0.0 %	44	B	78.78 % / 0.0 %	61	B	89.13 % / 0.0 %	78	C	85.01 % / 0.0 %	95	D	50.23 % / 1.27 %
11	A	41.15 % / 1.0 %	28	C	84.17 % / 0.0 %	45	B	55.88 % / 1.4 %	62	C	45.32 % / 1.23 %	79	A	55.25 % / 1.09 %	96	A	51.38 % / 1.33 %
12	D	23.19 % / 3.01 %	29	B	86.01 % / 0.0 %	46	A	46.91 % / 1.12 %	63	A	89.28 % / 0.0 %	80	C	45.14 % / 1.3 %	97	C	47.35 % / 1.83 %
13	A	59.52 % / 1.87 %	30	D	58.63 % / 1.14 %	47	C	55.06 % / 1.39 %	64	C	47.7 % / 1.34 %	81	A	88.45 % / 0.0 %	98	D	44.62 % / 1.61 %
14	A	48.65 % / 1.78 %	31	D	45.73 % / 1.59 %	48	C	65.76 % / 1.33 %	65	C	56.69 % / 1.93 %	82	C	59.2 % / 1.18 %	99	C	46.07 % / 1.86 %
15	C	78.7 % / 0.0 %	32	B	57.66 % / 1.49 %	49	B	66.24 % / 1.94 %	66	C	77.76 % / 0.0 %	83	C	14.95 % / 3.26 %	100	C	52.5 % / 1.32 %
16	A	46.85 % / 1.55 %	33	D	51.31 % / 1.11 %	50	B	77.1 % / 0.0 %	67	B	47.9 % / 1.26 %	84	B	83.49 % / 0.0 %			
17	D	45.27 % / 1.64 %	34	B	68.0 % / 1.26 %	51	D	86.41 % / 0.0 %	68	B	46.63 % / 1.48 %	85	D	76.36 % / 0.0 %			

//Hints and Solutions//

1. Indian judo player Linthoi Chanambam scripted history by winning a gold medal in the women's 57 kg category at the World Cadet Judo Championship 2022 in Sarajevo, Bosnia. 16-year-old Channambam has become the first Indian to win a gold medal at the World Judo Championships in any category.

Hence, the correct option is (B).

2. The Nobel Memorial Prize in Economic Sciences was awarded to Ben S Bernanke, the former chair of the US Federal Reserve, Douglas W Diamond and Philip H Dybvig of USA for research into banks and financial crises.

As per the committee, 'the laureates have provided a foundation for our modern understanding of why banks are needed, why they're vulnerable, and what to do about it'.

Hence, the correct option is (C).

3. Bharat Electronics Limited (BEL), a defence Public Sector Unit (PSU) under the Ministry of Defence (MoD), Government of India, has signed an MoU with Defense Initiatives (DI), Belarus, and Defense Initiatives Aero Pvt Ltd India, a subsidiary of DI Belarus. The MoU calls for the three companies to collaborate on the supply of Airborne Defense Suite (ADS) for Indian Air Force (IAF) helicopters. ADS is used for providing protection to helicopters.

Hence, the correct option is (C).

4. BSES Yamuna Power Limited (BYPL) has commissioned India's first 'Smart Managed' EV charging station.

- The charging station, which can charge five e-vehicles simultaneously, is co-located at BYPL's sub-station premise in Mayur Vihar Extension Phase I, New Delhi.
- BSES Yamuna Power Limited is a joint venture between Reliance Infrastructure and the NCT government of Delhi.

Hence, the correct option is (D).

5. Growth of CO_2 from power sector during 2005 to $2009 = 800 - 500 = 300$ (Just take values of 2009 and 2005 and subtract them)

$$\text{Percentage growth} = \left\{ \frac{(Value\ in\ 2009) - (Value\ in\ 2005)}{(Value\ in\ 2005)} \right\} \times 100\%$$

$$\text{Percentage growth} = \frac{(800 - 500)}{500} \times 100\%$$

$$= \frac{300}{500} \times 100 = 60\%$$

Hence, the correct option is (A).

6. Percentage Growth: $= \left\{ \frac{(Value\ in\ 2009) - (Value\ in\ 2005)}{(Value\ in\ 2005)} \right\} \times 100\%$

Power: $\% = \frac{(800 - 500)}{500} \times 100 = 60\%$

Industry: $\% = \frac{(450 - 200)}{200} \times 100 = 125\%$

Commercial: $\% = \frac{(320 - 150)}{150} \times 100 = 113\%$

Agriculture: $\% = \frac{(200 - 80)}{80} \times 100 = 150\%$

Domestic: $\% = \frac{(180 - 100)}{100} \times 100 = 80\%$

So, the maximum growth in CO_2 is Agriculture.

Hence, the correct option is (D).

7. Total emissions of CO_2 in $2005 = 500 + 200 + 150 + 80 + 100 = 1030$

Total emissions of CO_2 in $2009 = 800 + 450 + 320 + 200 + 180 = 1950$

$$\text{Percentage growth} = \left\{ \frac{(Value\ in\ 2009) - (Value\ in\ 2005)}{(Value\ in\ 2005)} \right\} \times 100\%$$

$$\% \text{ increased} = \frac{(1950 - 1030)}{1030} \times 100 = 89.32\%$$

Hence, the correct option is (A).

8. In 2005 to 2006: $\frac{100}{500} \times 100 = 20\%$

In 2006 to 2007: $\frac{50}{600} \times 100 = 8.33\%$

In 2007 to 2008: $\frac{50}{650} \times 100 = 7.69\%$

In 2008 to 2009: $\frac{100}{700} \times 100 = 14.28\%$

Average Annual growth rate $= \frac{50.30}{4} = 12.57\%$

Hence, the correct option is (A).

9. $\%$ contribution of the power sector to total CO_2 emissions in the year $2008 = \frac{700}{1700} \times 100 = 41.18\%$

Hence, the correct option is (B).

10. Given,

The ratio of girls and boys is 4:5 and the number of girls is 212.

Let, girls number is 4x and boys number is 5x.

Then according to question,

4x = 212

$x = \frac{212}{4}$

x = 53

Number of boys is 5x

Then,

$\Rightarrow 5 \times 53 = 265$

Hence, the correct option is (B).

11. Cost of a dozen pens = Rs. 180

Cost of 1 pen = $\dfrac{180}{12}$

= Rs 15

Cost of 8 ball pens = Rs 56

Cost of a ball pen = $\dfrac{56}{8}$

= Rs 7

Required ratio = $\dfrac{15}{7}$

Hence, the correct option is (A).

12. Azad invested Rs 55000 for a year and Rs 65000 for the next year.

Hind invested Rs 70000 for 8 months and Rs 60000 for the next year.

Capital Ratio = 55000 × 12 + 65000 × 12 : 70000 × 8 + 60000 × 12

= 660000 + 780000 : 560000 + 720000

= 1440000 : 1280000

= 9 : 8

Let total profit = Rs x

Azad's profit = x × 50% × 50% + x × 50% × $\dfrac{9}{17}$

$$32375 = \frac{x}{4} + \frac{9x}{34}$$

$$32375 = \frac{35x}{68}$$

x = 62900

Hence, the correct option is (D).

13. The southeast trade winds in the southern hemisphere and the northeast trade winds in the northern hemisphere meet each other near the equator. The meeting place of these winds is known as the Inter-Tropical Convergence Zone (ITCZ).

Characteristics features related to ITCZ:

- The Intertropical Convergence Zone (ITCZ) lies in the equatorial trough.
- It is a permanent low-pressure feature where surface trade winds, laden with heat and moisture, converge to form a zone of increased convection, cloudiness, and precipitation.
- It is a low-pressure zone between tropic of Cancer and tropic of Capricorn
- This is the region of ascending air, maximum clouds, and heavy rainfall.

- The location of ITCZ shifts north and south of the equator with the change of season.
- In the summer season, the sun shines vertically over the Tropic of Cancer, and the ITCZ shifts northwards.

Therefore, all the statements are correct about ITCZ or tropical convergence zone.

Hence, the correct option is (A).

14.

- 'Amphan' made landfall in a part of West Bengal and Orissa in May 2020. It is an example of a Tropical cyclone.
- A tropical cyclone is a rapidly rotating storm system characterized by a low-pressure center, a closed low-level atmospheric circulation, strong winds, and a spiral arrangement of thunderstorms that produce heavy rain and/or squalls.
- It caused widespread damage in Eastern India, specifically West Bengal, Odisha, and in Bangladesh in May 2020.

Hence, the correct option is (A).

15. The order of the layers of the atmosphere from top to bottom: Ionosphere - Mesosphere - Stratosphere - Troposphere

The space in which the air surrounds the earth is called the atmosphere.

The lower part of the atmosphere (which usually extends from four to eight miles) is called the troposphere, the upper part of it is called the stratosphere, and the part above it is called the mesosphere and the upper part from the mesosphere is called the ionosphere.

Hence, the correct option is (C).

16. Santiago Ramón y Cajal is known as the father of neuroscience and he won the Nobel Prize in 1906 for Physiology or Medicine for his neuron doctrine.

Neuroscience (or neurobiology) is the scientific study of the nervous system. It is a multidisciplinary science that combines physiology, anatomy, molecular biology, developmental biology, cytology, computer science and mathematical modeling to understand the fundamental and emergent properties of neurons and neural circuits.

Hence, the correct option is (A).

17. Otis invented the safety break, which would stop the elevator from crashing if it was activated by sudden falling when a rope broke.

Elevators also have electromagnetic brakes that engage when the car comes to a stop. The electromagnets actually keep the brakes in the open position, instead of closing them. With this design, the brakes will automatically clamp shut if the elevator loses power.

Hence, the correct option is (D).

18. Sides of each triangular piece are

a = 20 cm

b = 50 cm

c = 50 cm

$$\therefore s = \frac{a+b+c}{2}$$

$$= \frac{20+50+50}{2} \text{ cm}$$

$$= \frac{120}{2} \text{ cm}$$

= 60 cm

$\therefore$ Area of each triangular piece $=$

$$\sqrt{s(s-a)(s-b)(s-c)}$$

$$= \sqrt{60(60-20)(60-50)(60-50)} \text{ cm}^2$$

$$= \sqrt{60 \times 40 \times 10 \times 10} \text{ cm}^2$$

$$= \sqrt{6 \times 10 \times 10 \times 4 \times 10 \times 10} \text{ cm}^2$$

$$= \sqrt{6 \times 10^2 \times 2^2 \times 10^2} \text{ cm}^2$$

$$= 10 \times 2 \times 10\sqrt{6} \text{ cm}^2$$

$$= 200\sqrt{6} \text{ cm}^2$$

$\Rightarrow$ Area of 5 triangular pieces of one colour $= 5 \times 200\sqrt{6}$ cm²

$$= 1000\sqrt{6} \text{ cm}^2$$

Area of 5 triangular pieces of other colour = $1000\sqrt{6}$ cm²

Total triangular pieces are 10, i.e. five triangular pieces for each colour.

Hence, the correct option is (A).

19. There are 16 equal triangular tiles.

Sides of the triangle are

a = 9 cm

b = 28 cm

c = 35 cm

$$\therefore s = \frac{a+b+c}{2}$$

$$= \frac{9+28+35}{2} \ cm$$

$$= \frac{172}{2} \ cm$$

$$= 36 \ cm$$

Area of each triangle $= \sqrt{s(s-a)(s-b)(s-c)}$

$$= \sqrt{36(36-9)(36-28)(36-35)} cm^2$$

$$= \sqrt{36 \times 27 \times 8 \times 1} \ cm^2$$

$$= \sqrt{9 \times 4 \times 9 \times 3 \times 2 \times 4 \times 1} \ cm^2$$

$$= \sqrt{3^2 \times 2^2 \times 3^2 \times 3 \times 2 \times 2^2 \times 1} \ cm^2$$

$$= 3 \times 2 \times 3 \times 2\sqrt{3 \times 2} \ cm^2$$

$$= 36\sqrt{6} \ cm^2$$

$$= 36 \times 2.45 \ cm^2 (\text{approx.})$$

$$= 88.2 \ cm^2 (\text{approx})$$

Area of 16 triangles:

Total area of all the triangles-

= 16 × 88.2 cm² (approx.)

= 1411.2 cm² (approx.)

Cost of polishing the tiles-

Rate of polishing = Rs. 0.5 per cm²

$\therefore$ Cost of polishing all the tiles

= Rs. 0.5 × 1411.2

= Rs. 705.60 (approx.)

Hence, the correct option is (B).

20. Other side $= \sqrt{(17)^2 - (15)^2}$

$$\Rightarrow \sqrt{289 - 225}$$

$$\Rightarrow \sqrt{64} = 8 \ m$$

So,

Area $= (15 \times 8)m^2$

$$\Rightarrow 120 \ m^2$$

Hence, the correct option is (B).

21. In Diagnostic test, both background and performance of the students is needed for helping them in acquisition of intellectual habits and various powers as discipline. Diagnostic test in Mathematics are used by the teachers to detect the errors committed by the student during mathematical operations like addition, subtraction, multiplication, division. These tests are qualitative in nature not quantitative. These tests find the errors made by students and correct the so that help in their learning.

Hence, the correct option is (C).

22. Tajamul Islam of Jammu Kashmir won the world Kickboxing championship in Italy.

An eight-year-old Kashmiri girl, Tajamul Islam, created history by winning the gold medal in the under-8 world kickboxing championships. Islam won the gold after defeating her opponent from the USA in the final in Andria, Italy. Islam, representing India, became the first kickboxer from the war-torn Kashmir valley to complete this feat.

There were 90 countries participating in the tournament. Islam came into prominence on the kickboxing circuit after winning the gold medal in the national sub-junior category in New Delhi in 2015. "In five days, Tajamul Islam won six games," her coach Fasil Ali Dar was quoted as saying by The Hindu.

Hence, the correct option is (B).

23. The Sultan Azlan Shah Cup is an annual international men's field hockey tournament held in Malaysia. It began in 1983 as a biennial contest. The tournament became an annual event after 1998, following its growth and popularity. The tournament is named after the ninth Yang di-Pertuan Agong (King) of Malaysia, Sultan Azlan Shah, an avid fan of field hockey.

Hence, the correct option is (A).

24. 'JAKHAM' Multipurpose project is located in Pratapgarh.

Jakham Irrigation Project:

- The irrigation project comprises a storage dam on the river Jakham near village Anuppura in Dhariawad tehsil of district Pratapgarh.
- It was completed in the year 1986.
- It is constructed on river Jakham, which is a tributary of river Mahi.
- The project provides irrigation benefits to tribal people of the area consisting of 104 villages of Dhariawad Tehsil and 3 villages of Pratapgarh Tehsil.

Hence, the correct option is (D).

25. The word 'Sociology' is made up of two words. These are Socious and Logos.

A dictionary defines sociology as the systematic study of society and social interaction. The word "sociology" is derived from the Latin word socius (companion) and the Greek word logos (speech or reason), which together mean "reasoned speech about companionship".

Hence, the correct option is (C).

26. Sociology emerged in Europe.

The social, economic, political and intellectual background of the 18th century Europe facilitated the emergence of sociology. It emerged in European society corresponding to its socio-historical background which had its origin in the Enlightenment period.

Hence, the correct option is (B).

27. The given equation is:

$$72 \times 25 + 45 \times 20 = 15^3 - ?$$

By simplifying the above equation, we get,

$$1800 + 900 = 3375 - ?$$

$$\Rightarrow ? = 3375 - 2700$$

$$\Rightarrow ? = 675$$

Hence, the correct option is (B).

28. For H.C.F,

Factors of 493 = 17 × 29 = 1, 17, 29, 493

Factors of 527 = 17 × 31 = 1, 17, 31, 527

Factors of 697 = 17 × 41 = 1, 17, 41, 697

∴ H.C.F (493,527,697) = common factors of all three

= 17

Hence, the correct option is (C).

29. Mrs Indira Gandhi was the first women prime minister of India.

Indira Priyadarshini Gandhi (19 November 1917 – 31 October 1984) was an Indian politician and a central figure of the Indian National Congress. She was the 3rd prime minister of India and was also the first and, to date, only female prime minister of India.

Hence the correct option is (B).

30. Given,

Due to shortage of labor in a factory, its production decrease = 25%

Hence the working period $= \dfrac{25}{100-25} \times 100$

$$\Rightarrow 33\dfrac{1}{3}\%$$

Hence, the correct option is (D).

31. Given,

40% of the students in an exam fail in Mathematics,

30% fail in English,

10% fail in both subjects,

Total unsuccessful students = 40% + 30% - 10% = 60%

Hence, students passing in both the subjects = 100 - 60 = 40%

Hence, the correct option is (D).

32. Sarkaria Commission was set up in June 1983 by the central government to examine the relationship and balance of power between state and central governments in the country and suggest changes within the framework of Constitution of India. The Commission was so named as it was headed by Justice Rajinder Singh Sarkaria, a retired judge of the Supreme Court of India. The other two members of the committee were Shri B Sivaraman and Dr SR Sen.

Hence, the correct option is (B).

33. Option (D) is incorrect because one-third of its members retire every two years. Rajya Sabha is a permanent body. It was duly constituted for the first time on April 3, 1952. Twelve of Rajya Sabha members are nominated by the President.

Hence, the correct option is (D).

34. In mathematical reasoning, we determine the truth of the value of the given statement and justify all the parameters.

Mathematical reasoning is the ability to provide a justification for a mathematical procedure. It also involves the ability to think logically and systematically.

It plays an important role, both in solving problems and in conveying ideas when learning mathematics.

Reasoning supports students in learning mathematics.

In mathematical reasoning, there is no role in definitions and formulae.

Hence, from the above-mentioned points, it becomes clear that mathematical reasoning is the ability to provide a justification for a mathematical procedure.

Hence, the correct option is (B).

35. In order to access the students' academic achievements of teaching environmental studies remedial teaching evaluation indicator should not be used.

Remedial Teaching is a teaching method which is used for teaching the weaker section of previous lessons or teaching to specific students who has problems. Remedial teaching is done after the diagnosis of a problem.

Hence, the correct option is (D).

36. Strait of Tartar is the narrowest strait of the world.

Strait of Tartar is the narrowest Strait. It is 7.3 km wide at the narrowest point. It is a strait in the Pacific Ocean dividing the Russian island of Sakhalin from mainland Asia (South-East Russia), connecting the Sea of Okhotsk on the north with the Sea of Japan on the south.

Hence, the correct option is (A).

37. Delhi Mumbai Industrial Corridor Project programmes is NOT being implemented in India with the assistance of the World Bank.

The Delhi–Mumbai Industrial Corridor Project (DMIC) is a planned industrial development project between India's capital, Delhi and its financial hub, Mumbai. The DMIC project was launched in pursuance of an MOU signed between the Government of India and the Government of Japan in December 2006.

Hence, the correct option is (D).

38. Teachers are required to perform two important functions, i.e., teaching and testing. Testing is done to measure students' performance after teaching to find out whether learning has taken place. Students' performances are recorded in terms of grades and are interpreted.

Measures a student's performance in comparison to the performance of same-age students on the same assessment. The aim is to provide the relative rank or position of the students rather than assess them. attainment of specified curriculum objectives.

Hence, the correct option is (D).

39. Evaluation is a systematic way to assess learners' abilities, analyze performance, provide appropriate feedback to each learner and help them to progress. The formative evaluation assesses the performance of students, tests comprising various types of questions are constructed and administered during the period of instruction.

Purpose of formative evaluation:

Its main objective is to provide continuous feedback to both teacher and student concerning learning successes and failures while instruction is in process.

It is used to monitor the learning progress of students during the period of instruction.

Feedback to students reinforces successful learning and identifies the specific learning errors that need correction.

Feedback to the teacher provides information for max living instruction and for prescribing group and individual remedial work.

The formative evaluation depends on tests, quizzes homework, classwork, oral questions prepared for each segment of instruction.

This evaluation provides the student with feedback regarding his or her success or failure in attaining the instructional objectives.

Hence, the correct option is (B).

40. Kuchipudi is an indigenous dance form of Andhra Pradesh that originated and flourished in a village of the same name, its original name was Kuchelapuri or Kuchelapuram, a town in the Krishna district.

Hence, the correct option is (D).

41. It is a famous dance of classical dance. Bharatanatyam is one of the famous dances of India and belongs to the state of Tamil Nadu in South India. The name is derived from the word 'Bharata' and is related to 'Nritya Shastra'.

Hence, the correct option is (A).

42. Use 'weakens' in place of 'weaken'. The subject is singular so a singular verb is used.

Correct sentence: In emerging economies, the private credit market remains highly segmented and thus weakens the power of monetary policy.

Hence, the correct option is (C).

43. LCM of $3, 5, 7$ and $8 = 840$

$$98243 \div 840 = 116 \text{ remainder} = 803$$

So, the least number which should be added $= 840 - 803 = 37$

Hence, the correct option is (C).

44. The Battle of Wandiwash, 1760 was a local version of the Seven Years war in Europe. It put an end to the ambitions of the French to create a colonial empire in India.

The French forces were led by Comte De Lally. The British forces were led by Sir Eyre Coote. Britisher defeated the French in the Battle of Wandiwash in 1760.

Hence, the correct option is (B).

45. 'It provides funding to research projects in science as well as non-science disciplines' statement about National Research Foundation (NRF), proposed in National Education Policy (2020) is correct.

The primary activities of the NRF will be to:

- Fund competitive, peer-reviewed grant proposals of all types and across all disciplines. (It will fund research projects across four major disciplines –Sciences; Technology; Social Sciences; and Arts and Humanities).

- Seed, grow, and facilitate research at academic institutions, particularly at universities and colleges where research is currently in a nascent stage, through mentoring of such institutions;

- Act as a liaison between researchers and relevant branches of government as well as industry, so that research scholars are constantly made aware of the most urgent national research issues, and so that policymakers are constantly made aware of the latest research breakthroughs; so as to allow breakthroughs to be optimally brought into policy and/or implementation and recognize outstanding research and progress.

- In the budget 2021-22, NRF has been allocated 50,000 crores over the next 5 years.

Hence, the correct option is (B).

46. The insurance sector in India is well below its potential and in terms of insurance penetration and density, we are below the world average. To address this by way of competition and better insurance products, services, etc the government of India has been raising the FDI limit in the insurance sector.

In the budget 2021-22 government has raised the FDI limit in the insurance sector to 74 percent. So, statement 1 is correct.

Benefits of raising FDI in the insurance sector:

- It will lead to expansion of the insurance sector, increased penetration, a higher level of competition, and value for customers in terms of better products at a lower cost.

- The government in the budget 2021-22 has also allowed foreign ownership and control of insurance companies including agricultural insurance companies with certain safeguards. So, statement 2 is not correct.

Hence, the correct option is (A).

47. Mars is the only planet with similar day time temperatures and an atmosphere similar to earth. The most relevant condition for presence of life on Mars is occurrence of Ice beams and ice water.

Hence, the correct option is (C).

48. Human red blood cells are produced through a process named erythropoiesis, developing from committed stem cells to mature red blood cells in about 7 days. When matured, in a healthy individual these cells live in blood circulation for about 100 to 120 days (and 80 to 90 days in a full term infant).

Hence, the correct option is (C).

49. Given compound is Aluminium Sulphate $Al_2(SO_4)_3$.

The atomic mass of Aluminium $(Al) = 13 \times 2 = 26$

The atomic mass of Sulphur $(S) = 16 \times 2 = 32$

The atomic mass of oxygen $(O) = 8 \times 2 = 16$

Total molar mass of the compound is $(26 \times 2) + (32 \times 3) + (16 \times 12) = 342$ gm/mole

Molar Mass of the oxygen $= 12 \times 16 = 192$ gm/mole.

Percentage of oxygen in total compound $= \left(\frac{192}{342}\right) \times 100 = 56.140\%$

Therefore, the percentage of oxygen in Aluminium Sulphate is 56.1%.

Hence, the correct option is (B).

50.

- **Propane gas** is used as illuminating gas.
- The molecular formula Propane is C_3H_8.
- Propane is the gas normally used for cooking in the form of Liquified Natural Petroleum (LPG).

Compound	Molecular Formula
Methyl	CH_3
Butene	C_4H_8
Ethyne	C_2H_2

Hence, the correct option is (B).

51. Diffraction of light is the phenomenon of bending of light from the sharp corners of a slit or obstacle and spreading into the region of geometrical shadow. Diffraction can occur only when wavelength of light is comparable to the size of the obstacle or width of the slit.

Diffraction is of two types:

Fresnel Diffraction- It is the type of diffraction which occurs when the light source lies at a finite distance from the slit.

Fraunhofer Diffraction- It is the type of diffraction which occurs when a plane wavefront is incident on the slit and the wavefront emerging from the slit is also plane.

Hence, the correct option is (D).

52. Oil rises up to the wick in a lamp owing to the capillary action.

This effect is due to the surface tension of liquids. The wick here acts as a capillary tube.

Capillary action is the ability of a liquid to flow in narrow spaces without any assistance or even in opposition to external forces like gravity.

Hence, the correct option is (B).

53. Given:

Three spherical balls of radius 9 cm, 12 cm and 15 cm are melted to form a new spherical ball.

The volume of a sphere $= \dfrac{4}{3} \times \pi \times r^3$

Where r = radius of the sphere

The sum of the volume of the three balls $= \dfrac{4}{3} \times \pi \times \{(9)^3 + (12)^3 + (15)^3\}$

$\Rightarrow \dfrac{4}{3} \times \pi \times (3)^3 \{(3)^3 + (4)^3 + (5)^3\}$

$\Rightarrow \left(\dfrac{4\pi}{3}\right) \times 27 \times 216$

Let the radius of the new sphere be 'r'.

So, $\dfrac{4}{3} \times \pi \times r^3 = \left(\dfrac{4\pi}{3}\right) \times 27 \times 216$

$\Rightarrow r^3 = 27 \times 216$

$\Rightarrow r = 3 \times 6$ cm

$\Rightarrow r = 18$ cm

∴ The radius of the new ball 18 cm.

Hence, the correct option is (C).

54. C is the sentence that establishes the subject matter 'blind ants'. Hence, it will be the first sentence of the arrangement. A contextually follows C because it explains how they can go about even though they are blind. The third sentence is D as the phrase "these senses" refer to the 'sense of touch and smell'. B follows D because it connects with D by explaining where the sense of smell is located i.e. in their antennae.

Thus, the correct arrangement would be: CADB

Hence, the correct option is (C).

55. A is the sentence that establishes the subject matter- patriotic feelings. Hence, it will be the first sentence after rearrangement.

Sentence C is the logical successor of sentence A as it connects with it by stating that patriotic feelings are not absent in times of peace—they are only inactive. B follows C as it states what dormant patriotic feelings do—they urge people to work for the development of society in times of peace. D is the closing statement as it summarises the entire paragraph by talking about the 'focus on the overall development of the nation'.

Thus, the correct arrangement would be: ACBD

Hence, the correct option is (A).

56. B is the sentence that establishes the subject matter by giving an example of the Taj Mahal. Hence, it will be the first sentence after rearrangement. D contextually follows B as it compares an achievement to the Taj Mahal. A is the logical successor of D because it further explains D. Sentence C gives a suggestion and concludes the passage. It states that instead of being concerned with glory from the beginning, we should just work hard and glory will follow.

Thus, the correct arrangement would be: BDAC

Hence, the correct option is (B).

57. I only have a *scintilla* of respect for her after she lied about her background.

Scintilla means "a small amount" is the only option that fits in the given blank.

Hence, the correct option is (A).

58. Instead of showing his mother his paper, the boy chose to *crumble* it up.

Crumble means break or fall apart into small fragments, especially as part of a process of deterioration, it is the only option that fits in the given blank.

Hence, the correct option is (B).

59. All I need is a *modicum* of money to pay for my basic needs.

Modicum means a small amount of, it is the only option that fits in the given blank.

Hence, the correct option is (B).

60. Recommendation for appointment to Mansabs to the Emperor is not a function of Mir Bakshi, the head of the military department as well as of the nobility under the Mughal rule.

Hence, the correct option is (C).

61. The given Venn diagram shows $A \cap (B \cup C)$. Hence, the correct option is (B).

62. Let the set of examinees who solved Question 8 be A,

The set of candidates who solve Question 9 is B,

And the set of candidates who solve Question 10 is C, then

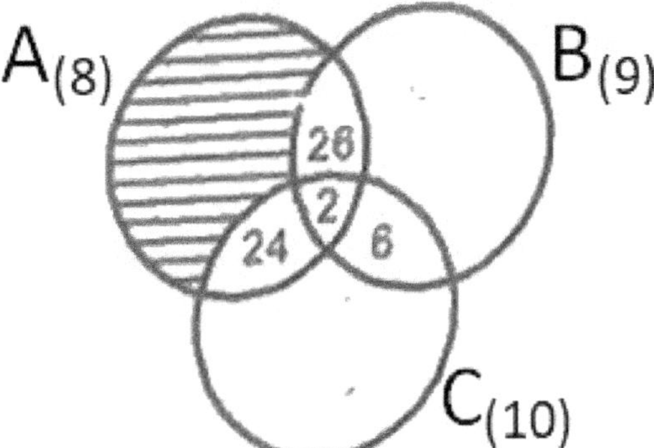

$n(A) = 67$
$n(B) = 46$
$n(C) = 40$
$n(A \cap B) = 28$
$n(B \cap C) = 8$
$n(A \cap C) = 26$
$n(A \cap B \cap C) = 2$

Number of examinees who solved question 8 but not questions 9 and 10 $= = 67 - (26 + 24 + 2)$

$= 67 - 52 = 15$

Hence, the correct option is (C).

63. Anxious means feeling or showing worry, nervousness, or unease about something.

Worried means anxious or troubled about actual or potential problems.

The option that is nearest in meaning to the underlined word 'anxious' is 'worried'.

Hence, the correct option is (A).

64. Ecstatic means feeling or expressing overwhelming happiness or joyful excitement.

Rapturous means characterized by, feeling, or expressing great pleasure or enthusiasm.

The option that is nearest in meaning to the underlined word ' ecstatic' is 'rapturous'.

Hence, the correct option is (C).

65. Jaymala is a novel written by the author Braj Kishore Dixit. He is also known as Brajesh.

Shailesh Matiyani is a famous Hindi writer and poet from the Indian state of Uttarakhand. He was born in the Almora district of Uttarakhand. 'Shailesh Matiyani Smriti Katha Puraskar' was started in Madhya Pradesh in his name. Kabutarkhana, Kameene, and Mahabhoj are novels written by Shailesh Matiyani.

Hence, the correct option is (C).

66. Indramani Badoni is a politician, freedom fighter and social activist from Uttarakhand.

- He was born on 25th December 1924 in the Akhodi village of Tehri Garhwal.
- He is best known for his leading role in the Uttarakhand statehood movement.
- He was the architect of the 1994 state movement.
- He is popularly called the 'Gandhi of Uttarakhand' due to his practice of non-violence and satyagraha.
- He was a founding member of the regional political party Uttarakhand Kranti Dal.
- He had started the movement to make Uttarakhand a separate state.
- He was honoured with the Uttarakhand Ratna award (posthumously) in 2016.

Hence, the correct option is (C).

67. Shiv Prasad Dabral is known as the 'Encyclopaedia of Uttarakhand'. The noted historian Shiv Prasad Dabral was born on 12th November 1912 in the Pauri Garhwal district of Uttarakhand. He is the author of the monumental history of Uttarakhand in 18 volumes, 2 collections of poetry, 9 plays, and several edited volumes in Hindi and Garhwali. His Uttarakhand ka Itihaas (History of Uttarakhand) is widely used by scholars as reference work.

Hence, the correct option is (B).

68. Relation Between Mean Median and Mode:

Mean – Mode = 3 (Mean – Median)

As we know,

Mean – Mode = 3 (Mean – Median)

$\Rightarrow$ Mean – Mode = 3Mean – 3Median

$\Rightarrow$ 3Median - Mode = 2Mean

$\Rightarrow \dfrac{1}{2}$ (3Median - Mode) = Mean

$\therefore k = \dfrac{1}{2}$

Hence, the correct option is (B).

69. Given data are $6, x, 2,$ and 4

$\therefore$ Mean $= \dfrac{\Sigma x_i}{N} = \dfrac{6+x+2+4}{4}$

$\Rightarrow x = \dfrac{12+x}{4}$

$\Rightarrow x = 4$

Now the data are: $2,4,4,6$

Mode $= 4$ ($\because 4$ occurs most frequently)

Hence, the correct option is (C).

70. Given,

Time taken by A = 4 days

Time taken by B = 5 days

Contract for work = Rs. 9000

As we know,

Total work = Efficiency × days

A's one-day work $= \dfrac{1}{4}$

B's one day work $= \dfrac{1}{5}$

$\therefore$ The ratio of their wages $= \dfrac{1}{4} : \dfrac{1}{5} = 5 : 4$

$\therefore$ B's share $= (9000) \times \dfrac{4}{9} = $ Rs. 4000

Hence, the correct option is (A).

71. Given,

Initially, 30 men can finish work in 25 days.

As we know,

$M_1 \times D_1 = M_2 \times D_2$

Where M_1 men can do work in D_1 days work and M_2 men can do the same work in D_2 days.

$M_1 = 30$

$M_2 = 15$

$D_1 = 25$

$(30 \times 25) = (15 \times D_2)$

$\Rightarrow D_2 = \dfrac{(750)}{15} = 50$

∴ 15 men can finish the same work in 50 days.

Hence, the correct option is (A).

72. Given:

$\angle ROQ = 90°$

$a : b = 4 : 5$

Calculations:

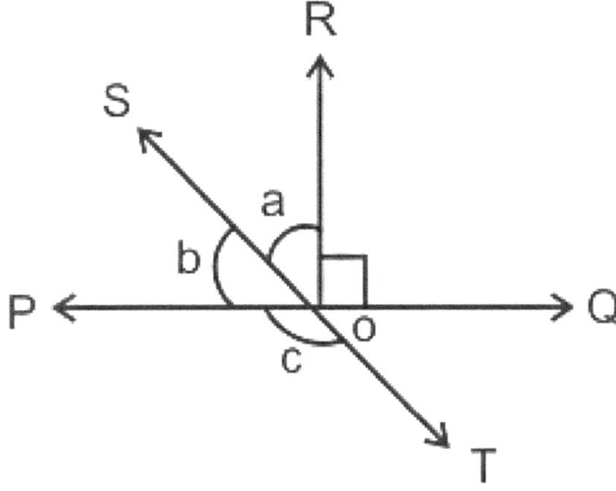

Let $\angle a$ and $\angle b$ be $4x$ and $5x$

According to the question, we have,

$\angle a + \angle b = 90°$ (The angle subtended at a straight line is 180° and $\angle ROQ = 90°$)

$\Rightarrow 4x + 5x = 90°$

$\Rightarrow 9x = 90°$

$\Rightarrow x = 10°$

$\angle b = 5x = 5 \times 10° = 50°$

Now,

$\angle b + \angle c = 180°$

$\Rightarrow 50° + \angle c = 180°$

$\Rightarrow \angle c = 130°$

∴ The value of $\angle c$ is 130°.

Hence, the correct option is (C).

73. $\dfrac{1}{-6}, \dfrac{2}{-12}, \dfrac{3}{-18}, \dfrac{4}{-24}, \dfrac{5}{-30}, \dfrac{6}{-36}, \dfrac{7}{-42}, \dfrac{8}{-48}$

Numerators are consecutive natural numbers and denominators are successive multiples of 6.

Hence, the correct option is (D).

74. Basic rules to be followed for Active/Passive conversions are:
1. The object of the active verb becomes the subject of the passive verb.
2. The finite form of the verb is changed (to be+ past participle).
3. The subject of the active sentence becomes the object of the passive sentence (or is dropped).
4. Preposition "by" is used before the object.
The given sentence is in the active form of simple past tense. The structures for active/passive voices are:

Active: Subject + verb (IInd form) + object.

Passive: Object + was/were + verb (IIIrd form) + by + subject.

So, with the help of the above structures, we can convert the given sentence into passive voice:

Their teacher was asked many questions by the students.

Hence, the correct option is (C).

75. The given sentence is in the active form of simple past tense. The structures for active/passive voices are:
Active: Subject + verb (IInd form) + object.

Passive: Object + was/were + verb (IIIrd form) + by + subject.

So, with the help of the above structures, we can convert the given sentence into passive voice:

You were called many times by your mother.

Hence, the correct option is (D).

76. World Teachers Day is celebrated on 5 October under the auspices of the United Nations. On this day teachers are honored in general and some working and retired teachers are honored for their special contribution.

It is celebrated by the United Nations to remember the joint meeting of UNESCO and the International Labor Organization in 1966, in which the situation of teachers was discussed and suggestions were presented for this.

Hence it is being celebrated every year in more than a hundred countries since 1994 and thus in the year 2019 it will be the 25th World Teachers' Day. An organization named Education International is going to celebrate this occasion with the slogan "Unite for Quality Education". Another organization is preparing to celebrate it with the theme of "Invest in the future, invest in teachers".

Hence, the correct option is (D).

77. World Cancer Day is observed on 4 February to raise awareness about cancer and encourage its prevention, detection and treatment. World Cancer Day is led by the Union for International Cancer Control (UICC) to support the goals of the World Cancer Declaration, written in 2008. The primary goal of World Cancer Day is to reduce deaths due to cancer and disease. Many people also resort to spirituality to overcome cancer.

Hence, the correct option is (C).

78. According to the cultural history of India 'Panchayatan' is temple construction style.

A temple Panchayatan has a main shrine at the centre which forms the base of the temple and is surrounded by four other shrines. It also has four subordinate shrines on each of the four corners.

Hence, the correct option is (C).

79. According to the question,

Man when sells the article at loss,

Loss percentage = x% = 15%

Cost Price = 100

Selling Price = 100 - x = 100 - 15 = 85

Now, if he sells the article to earn the profit of 10%,

Profit percentage = x% = 10%

Cost Price = 100

Selling Price = 100 + x = 100 + 10 = 110

The difference in Selling price = 110 - 85 = 25

And the sentence in the question says "if the product was sold for Rs. 450 more" which means the difference in amount is Rs. 450.

Therefore, 25% = 450

And we need to determine the Cost Price which is 100%, So

100% = ?

The equation for calculation becomes

$$\frac{450}{25} \times 100 = 1800 \text{ (Cost Price)}$$

This method can be remembered in the form of formula as:

$$\text{Cost} = \frac{\text{More gain} \times 100}{\text{Difference in percentage}}$$

Hence, the correct option is (A).

80. According to the question,

Selling price of glass = Rs. 1965

And loss = 25%

$$\therefore CP = \frac{1965}{75} \times 100 = \text{Rs. 2620}$$

If selling price = Rs. 3013

$$\therefore \text{Profit } \% = \frac{(3013 - 2620)}{2620} \times 100$$

$$= \frac{3930}{262} = 15\%$$

Hence, the correct option is (C).

81. Given,

Diameter of sheet = 28 cm

Sum of lengths of diagonals = 32 cm

Product of the length of diagonals = 252 cm^2

Let the sides of the two squares be x cm and y cm,

$\because$ Diagonal of square $= \sqrt{2} \times$ Side of square

Lengths of diagonals of the squares are $x\sqrt{2}\ cm$ and $y\sqrt{2}\ cm$.

Given, product of length of diagonals $= 252\ cm^2$

$$\Rightarrow x\sqrt{2} \times y\sqrt{2} = 252$$

$$\Rightarrow 2xy = 252 \text{........(1)}$$

Also, sum of lengths of diagonals = 32 cm

$$\Rightarrow x\sqrt{2} + y\sqrt{2} = 32$$

$$\Rightarrow x + y = \frac{32}{\sqrt{2}} = 16\sqrt{2}$$

Squaring both sides, we get

$$(x + y)^2 = \left(16\sqrt{2}\right)^2$$

$$x^2 + y^2 + 2xy = 512$$

Substituting from equation (1), we get

$$x^2 + y^2 = 512 - 252 = 260$$

As we know,

Area of square $= (\text{ side })^2$

Sum of areas of the squares $= x^2 + y^2 = 260\ cm^2$

Now,

Area of semi-circle $= \left(\frac{\pi}{8}\right) \times (\text{ diameter })^2$

$\Rightarrow$ Area of semi-circular sheet $= \frac{22}{7} \times \frac{1}{8} \times 28 \times 28 = 308\ cm^2$

$\therefore$ Area of remaining sheet $= 308 - 260 = 48\ cm^2$

Hence, the correct option is (A).

82. Given,

Area of the shaded region is $\frac{3}{8}$ of the area of the unshaded region.

Area of circle $= \frac{\pi}{4} \times (\text{ diameter })^2$

Area of outer circle $= \frac{\pi}{4} \times d_1^2$

Area of semi-circle $= \frac{\pi}{8} \times (\text{ diameter })^2$

Area of shaded region $=$ Area of three semi-circles $= 3 \times \frac{\pi}{8} \times d_2^2$

Now,

Area of shaded region $= \dfrac{3}{8} \times$ Area of unshaded region

Area of shaded region $= \dfrac{3}{8} \times ($Area of circle $-$ Area of shaded region$)$

$\Rightarrow \dfrac{11}{8} \times$ Area of shaded region $= \dfrac{3}{8} \times$ Area of circle

$\Rightarrow 11 \times$ Area of shaded region $= 3 \times$ Area of circle

$\Rightarrow 11 \times 3 \times \dfrac{\pi}{8} \times d_2^2 = 3 \times \dfrac{\pi}{4} \times d_1^2$

$\Rightarrow 11 d_2^2 = 2 d_1^2$

$\Rightarrow \dfrac{d_1^2}{d_2^2} = \dfrac{11}{2}$

$\Rightarrow \dfrac{d_1}{d_2} = \dfrac{\sqrt{11}}{\sqrt{2}}$

$\therefore d_1 : d_2 = \sqrt{11} : \sqrt{2}$

Hence, the correct option is (C).

83. Given:

a + b = 13

ab = 42

We know that,

$(a + b)^3 = a^3 + b^3 + 3ab(a + b)$

We have,

$(13)^3 = a^3 + b^3 + 3 \times 42 \times (13)$

$\Rightarrow a^3 + b^3 = (13)^3 - 3 \times 42 \times 13$

$\Rightarrow a^3 + b^3 = 2197 - 1638$

$\Rightarrow a^3 + b^3 = 2197 - 1638$

$\Rightarrow a^3 + b^3 = 559$

$\therefore$ The value of $a^3 + b^3$ is 559.

Hence, the correct option is (C).

84. Place value of 9 is = 9000

Actual value of 9 is = 9

Difference = 9000-9

= 8991

Hence, the correct option is (B).

85. Sum of 1856, 3287, 8432, 9.999, 18.888

= (1856 + 3287 + 8432 + 9.999 + 18.888)

= 13603.887

$\therefore$ The required answer = 13603.887

Hence, the correct option is (D).

86. The given passage is all about one of the world's great religious teachers- The Gautam Buddha.

The first line or sentence of the passage says "Buddha was one of the world's great religious teachers".

Hence, the correct option is (C).

87. Real name of Buddha was Gautam Siddhartha.

The second line or sentence of the passage says "His real name was Gautam Siddhartha". Here, the possessive pronoun 'his' is used for the 'Buddha'.

Hence, the correct option is (A).

88. Buddha was born a prince.

The fourth line or sentence of the passage says "He was born a prince". Here, the personal pronoun 'he' is used for the 'Buddha'.

Hence, the correct option is (D).

89. Buddha was born before the birth of Christ.

The third line or sentence of the passage says "He was born in the year 500 B.C". Here, the personal pronoun 'he' is used for the 'Buddha'.

In the sentence, the term "B.C" means "Before the birth of Jesus Christ".

Hence, the correct option is (B).

90. The land of Buddha's birth is Kapilavastu.

The fifth line or sentence of the passage says "His father was the King of Kapilavastu". Here, the possessive pronoun 'his' is used for the 'Buddha'.

Hence, the correct option is (D).

91. World Tourism Day, celebrated each year on 27 September, is the global observance day fostering awareness of tourism's social, cultural, political and economic value and the contribution that the sector can make towards reaching the Sustainable Development Goals. The colour of World Tourism Day is Blue.

There are three basic forms of tourism: domestic tourism, inbound tourism, and outbound tourism. These can be combined in various ways to derive the following additional forms of tourism: internal tourism, national tourism and international tourism.

Hence, the correct option is (C).

92. Riyadh is the capital of Saudi Arabia.

Riyadh is Saudi Arabia's largest city and country's administrative capital. The name Riyadh was derived from the plural form of the Arabic word "rawdah," meaning gardens or meadows. The city also serves as the capital of Riyadh Province and is situated near the center of the Arabian Peninsula. Riyadh rapidly grew from an enclosed desert village into a modern cosmopolitan city, and later became the capital of Saudi Arabia in 1932.

Hence, the correct option is (C).

93. The listed price that means the marked price of the article is Rs. 7600.

Discount = 10%.

After 10% discount price became = $(\frac{90}{100})$ × 7600 = 6840

The final selling price is 5814.

2nd discount = (6840 - 5814) =1026

The additional discount is given on the price Rs. 6840 = $(\frac{1026}{6840})$ × 100 = 15%

∴ 15% additional discount must be given to bring the net selling price to Rs. 5,814.

Hence, the correct option is (C).

94. According to the question,

$$\sqrt{41 - \sqrt{21 + \sqrt{19 - \sqrt{9}}}}$$

$$= \sqrt{41 - \sqrt{21 + \sqrt{19 - 3}}}$$

$$= \sqrt{41 - \sqrt{21 + \sqrt{16}}}$$

$$= \sqrt{41 - \sqrt{21 + 4}}$$

$$= \sqrt{41 - \sqrt{25}}$$

$$= \sqrt{41 - 5} = \sqrt{36} = 6$$

Hence, the correct option is (C).

95. Given, $x = 5$

Let's evaluate $y = x + 7 = 5 + 7 = 12$

Now for the given expression, its value at given $x = 5$ and $y = 12$ is, therefore,

$$= \sqrt{25 + 144}$$
$$= \sqrt{169}$$
$$= 13$$

Hence, the correct option is (D).

96. The following statements regarding Lok Devta are true:

- Ramdev Ji started Kamadia Panth.
- Ramdev Ji composed 24 Vaniya.
- As Symbol, His pagaliya (Footprints) are worshipped.
- Terah Taali dance is presented by kamadias.
- The fair of Ramdev Ji was held in Runicha (Jaisalmer), Bhadrapada Shukla Dwitiya to Ekadashi.

Thus, only statement 1 is correct.

Hence, the correct option is (A).

97. A penny saved is a penny earned means Money you save today you can spend later.

A penny saved is a penny earned This common phrase is used to encourage people to save money. It's as useful to save money that someone already has as it is to earn more money. Money spent is gone forever.

Hence, the correct option is (C).

98. The correct idiom is "Birds of feather flock together."

Flying is something birds do in groups or single units. Birds cannot dance and tweet together always. But when it comes to gathering, birds of the same species can generally be found in a group. Ornithologists deem there is safety in numbers for this avian species while on land if they flock together. The idiom was coined by William Turner in 1545.

Hence, the correct option is (D).

99. Given:

Rate of interest $= 2.5\%$ per month

Amount paid after 6 months $=$ Rs. 13110

Amount, $A = P + SI$

Simple interest, $SI = \frac{P \times R \times T}{100}$

Where $P \rightarrow$ Principal, $R \rightarrow$ rate of interest, $T \rightarrow$ time

Suppose the sum borrowed be Rs. x

$$SI = \frac{x \times 2.5 \times 6}{100} = 0.15x$$

$$A = x + 0.15x = 1.15x$$

$$1.15x = 13110$$

$$\Rightarrow x = 11400$$

$$\Rightarrow \text{Amount of interest} = 0.15 \times 11400$$

$$= \text{Rs. } 1710$$

Hence, the correct option is (C).

100. Given:

The rate of interest for 1st 2 years is 8%

For the next 3 years it is 10%

For the period beyond 5 years it is 12.5%

Principal $= Rs20L$

Amoun paid $= Rs\ 36.7L$

Amount $= P + SI$

Simple Interest, $SI = \frac{P \times R \times T}{100}$

Where $P \rightarrow$ Principal, $R \rightarrow$ rate of interest, $T \rightarrow$ time

Total $SI = A - P = 36.7L - 20L$

Total $SI = 16.7L$

SI for first 2 years $= 20L \times 2 \times \frac{8}{100} = 3.2L$

SI for next 3 years $= 20L \times 3 \times \frac{10}{100} = 6L$

So, total SI for the first 5 years $= 9.2L$

Then, the rest of the interest is obtained at the rate of 12.5%

Remaining interest $= 16.7\,L - 9.2L = 7.5L$

SI for next N years $= 20L \times N \times 12.5\% = 7.5L$

$N = 7.5L \times \dfrac{8}{20}L \quad (12.5\% \to \dfrac{1}{8}\,in\ \text{fraction})$

$N = 3$

That is, total years $= 2 + 3 + 3 = 8$ years.

Hence, the correct option is (C).

Q.1 Who has been named the 2022 Laureus Sportsman of the Year?

[Delhi Forest Guard, 2021]

A. Marcel Hug
B. Max Verstappen
C. Rafael Nadal
D. Robert Lewandowski

Q.2 Who clinched the gold medal in weightlifting at the ongoing Singapore International?

[Delhi Forest Guard, 2021]

A. Mirabai Chanu
B. Swati Singh
C. Kunjarani Devi
D. Karnam Malleswari

Q.3 Under which mission did INS Gharial arrived at Colombo to deliver critical lifesaving medicines on 29 April 2022?

A. MAITRI-22
B. DOSTI-IV
C. MISSION DOSTI
D. SAGAR IX

Q.4 Who has been appointed as the new the Chairperson of SEBI for a period of 3 years?

A. Arundhati Bhattacharya
B. Kalpana Morparia
C. Gita Gopinath
D. Madhabi Puri Buch

Q.5 Consider the following statement regarding to the Sattriya dance and select the correct code given below:

1. Sattriya is a fusion of dance, drama and music.
2. It follows the old living tradition of Vaishnavites of Assam.
3. It is based on various Ragas and Talas of devotional songs of Tulsidas, Kabir and Mirabai.

A. Only 3
B. Both 1 and 2
C. Both 1 and 3
D. All of the above

Q.6 With reference to the longitude of which of the following places is the India Standard Time determined?

A. Indore
B. Kanpur
C. Mirzapur
D. Varanasi

Q.7 The rings of Saturn are made up of:

A. Satellites
B. Hydrogen and helium
C. Small ice and rock particles
D. None of the above

Q.8 For which purpose magnetic compass is used?

A. For showing symbols
B. For finding the directions
C. For measuring distance
D. None of the above

Ques (9-11):Direction: Rearrange the following six sentences, (A), (B), (C), (D), (E) and (F), in a proper sequence to form a meaningful paragraph, then answer the questions that follow.

(A) While these disadvantages of biofuels are serious, there are numerous advantages as they are the only alternative energy source of future and the sooner we find solutions to these problems, the faster we will be able to solve the problems we are now facing with gasoline.

(B) This fuel can also help to stimulate jobs locally since they are also much safer to handle than gasoline and can thus have the potential to turnaround a global economy.

(C) These include dependence on fossil fuels for the machinery required to produce biofuel which ends up polluting as much as the burning of fossil fuels on roads and the exorbitant cost of biofuels which makes it very difficult for the common man to switch to this option.

(D) This turnaround can potentially help to bring world peace and end the need to depend on foreign countries for energy requirements.

(E) Biofuels are made from plant sources and since these sources are available in abundance and can be reproduced on a massive scale, they form an energy source that is potentially unlimited.

(F) However, everything is not as green with the biofuels as it seems as there are numerous disadvantages involved which at times overshadow their positive impact.

Q.9 Which of the following sentence should be the THIRD after rearrangement?

A. (A)   **B.** (B)   **C.** (C)   **D.** (D)

Q.10 Which of the following sentence should be the FIFTH after rearrangement?

A. (A)   **B.** (B)   **C.** (C)   **D.** (E)

Q.11 Which of the following sentence should be the SIXTH (LAST) after rearrangement?

A. (A)   **B.** (B)   **C.** (D)   **D.** (E)

Q.12 Which scientist/s proposed the theory of relativity?

A. Watson and Crick
B. Albert Einstein
C. Charles Darwin
D. John Dalton

Q.13 Who was the father of DNA fingerprinting?

A. James Watson
B. Hargobind Khurana
C. Alec Jeffreys
D. Nirenberg

Q.14 If $a = 0.1039$, then the value of $\sqrt{4a^2 - 4a + 1} + 3a$ is:

A. 0.1039   **B.** 0.2078   **C.** 1.1039   **D.** 2.1039

Q.15 In the equation $\dfrac{4050}{\sqrt{x}} = 450$, the value of x is $=$?

A. 81   **B.** 49   **C.** 9   **D.** 100

Q.16 Priyamvada Mohanty is associated with which classical dance form?

A. Kathakali   **B.** Bharatanatyam
C. Odissi   **D.** Koodiyattam

Q.17 Mrinalini Sarabhai is associated with which classical dance form?

A. Kathakali   **B.** Bharatanatyam
C. Koodiyattam   **D.** Kutti Attam

Q.18 On which date 'Mukhya Mantri Chiranjeevi Swasthya Bima Yojana' was launched:

A. 1st May 2021   **B.** 31st May 2021
C. 30 June 2021   **D.** 1st July 2021

Ques (19-20):Direction: In the following question, an idiomatic expression is followed by four alternatives. Choose the one which best expresses the meaning of the given idiom.

Q.19 A gentleman at large
[NCHM JEE (Hotel Mgmt & Catering), 2018]

A. a reliable person
B. a fat person
C. an unreliable person
D. a sophisticated person

Q.20 Like a fish out of water
[NCHM JEE (Hotel Mgmt & Catering), 2018]

A. in an easy situation
B. near a beach
C. in a dream state
D. in a very difficult and unsuitable situation

Q.21 Other than Venezuela, which among the following from the South American countries is a member of OPEC?
[NCHM JEE (Hotel Mgmt & Catering), 2018]

A. Argentina   **B.** Brazil
C. Ecuador   **D.** Bolivia

Q.22 Radisson Group of Hotels has its main headquarters in which country?
[NCHM JEE (Hotel Mgmt & Catering), 2018]

A. USA   **B.** Brazil   **C.** Australia   **D.** France

Ques (23-24):Direction: In the following question, a sentence has been given in Active/Passive Voice. Out of the four alternatives suggested, select the one which best expresses the same sentence in Passive/Active Voice.

Q.23 They broke the box.
A. Have the box broken?
B. Break the box.
C. The box was broken by them.
D. They have broken the box.

Q.24 The class was not attended by some students.
A. Some students do not attend the class.
B. Some students are not attending the class.
C. Some students was not attend the class.
D. Some students did not attend the class.

Q.25 If $f: R \rightarrow R$ and $g: R \rightarrow R$ are two fuctions defined as $f(x) = 2x$ and $g(x) = x^2 + 2$ then the value of (fog) 2 is:

A. 4   **B.** 6   **C.** 12   **D.** 10

Q.26 Find the value of $(\cos 2p\pi + i\sin 2p\pi)(\cos 2q\pi + i\sin 2q\pi)$?

A. 1   **B.** i   **C.** $\frac{1}{2}$ **D.** -1

Q.27 A traffic signal board, indicating 'SCHOOL AHEAD', is an equilateral triangle with side 'a'. Find the area of the signal board, using Heron's formula. If its perimeter is 180 cm, what will be the area of the signal board?

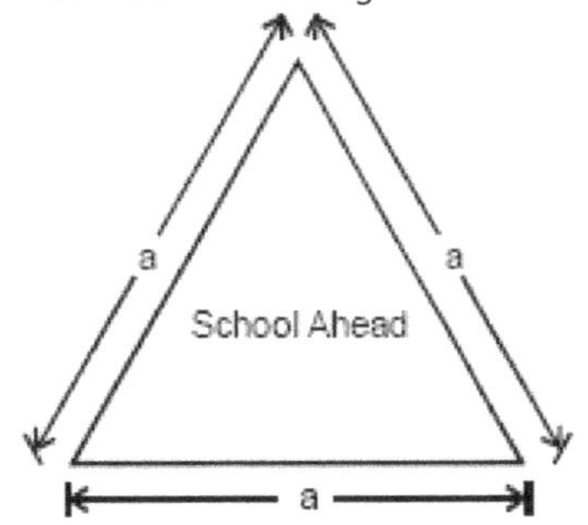

A. $900\sqrt{3}$ cm ^{2} **B.** $800\sqrt{3}$ cm ^{2}
C. $700\sqrt{3}$ cm ^{2} **D.** $600\sqrt{3}$ cm ^{2}

Q.28 The triangular side walls of a flyover have been used for advertisements. The sides of the walls are 122 m, 22 m and 120 m (see Fig.). The advertisements yield an earning of Rs. 5000 per m2 per year. A company hired one of its walls for 3 months. How much rent did it pay?

A. 14,50,000   **B.** 16,50,000
C. 13,50,000   **D.** 18,50,000

Q.29 Find the area of a triangle two sides of which are 18 cm and 10 cm and the perimeter is 42 cm.

A. $25\sqrt{11}$ cm ^{2} **B.** $21\sqrt{11}$ cm ^{2}
C. $24\sqrt{11}$ cm ^{2} **D.** $25\sqrt{11}$ cm ^{2}

Q.30 Which of the following types of assessment is conducted periodically with an eye on standards?
A. Formative assessment
B. Summative assessment
C. Portfolio assessment
D. Performance assessment

Q.31 Direction: Answer the following question by selecting the correct / most appropriate option.

The mathematics used by the Illiterate shopkeeper:

A. Should be discussed by the teachers in the classroom as an alternate strategy in solving related problems
B. Is not useful in the mathematics classroom
C. Is very useful in solving all mathematical problems
D. Has ambiguity and very low level of correctness in it

Q.32 How many groups and periods are there in the Modern Periodic Table?

[RRB/RRC Group D, 2018]

A. 7 groups and 18 periods
B. 7 groups and 7 periods
C. 18 groups and 7 periods
D. 18 groups and 18 periods

Q.33 What is the valency of copper in cuprous oxide?

[RRB/RRC Group D, 2018]

A. 4   **B.** 3   **C.** 2   **D.** 1

Q.34 Remedial teaching is helpful for:
A. Teaching the whole class
B. Recapitulating the lesson
C. Teaching in play-way method
D. Removing learning difficulties of weak students

Q.35 A test which is administered at the end of a language course for remedial teaching is:
A. Diagnostic test   **B.** Placement test
C. Achievement test   **D.** Memory test

Q.36 A sum of money was invested in a bank at 8% simple interest p.a. for 3 years. Had it been invested in mutual fund at 8.5% p.a. simple interest for 4 years, the earning would have been Rs. 500 more. What is the sum invested?
A. 5000   **B.** 5500   **C.** 5550   **D.** 4500

Q.37 A man wants to invest Rs. 8400 in his two sons bank account in such a way that when they become 18 years old they get equal interest. Present age of his 2 sons is 13 years and 15 years. If the Rate of simple interest. is 5% p.a. . Find the investment in younger son account?
A. 4050   **B.** 3650   **C.** 3150   **D.** 4500

Q.38 Which of the following is the organization of Remedial teaching in Mathematics?
A. Tutorial teaching
B. Auto-instructional teaching
C. Informal teaching
D. All of these

Q.39 Direction: In the following question, some part of the sentence may have errors. Find out which part of the sentence has an error and select the appropriate option. If the sentence is free from error, select 'No error'.

The question paper (A) comprised of many questions (B)/ which were out of the syllabus as reported by the students. (C)/ No error (D).

A. A   **B.** B   **C.** C   **D.** D

Q.40 Find the value of the expression $x^4 - 3x^3 + 4x^2 - 3x + 5$ at $x = 3$.
A. 12   **B.** 34   **C.** 32   **D.** 48

Ques (41-43):Direction: Fill in the blank with the appropriate option given below.

Q.41 She was beaten _______ a bat.

[NCHM JEE (Hotel Mgmt & Catering), 2019]

A. on   **B.** with   **C.** to   **D.** of

Q.42 The little girl was scared __________ crossing the busy road, alone.

[NCHM JEE (Hotel Mgmt & Catering), 2019]

A. on   **B.** in   **C.** at   **D.** of

Q.43 The little boy stood _____ the tree.

[NCHM JEE (Hotel Mgmt & Catering), 2019]

A. within   **B.** under   **C.** from   **D.** off

Q.44 The simplified value of $\left(\sqrt{3}+1\right)\left(10+\sqrt{12}\right)\left(\sqrt{12}-2\right)\left(5-\sqrt{3}\right)$ is-
A. 16   **B.** 88   **C.** 176   **D.** 132

Q.45 The value of '1856 - 3287 + 5432 - 679' is:

[MPTET Paper I - Varg 3, 2012]

A. 3132   **B.** 2233   **C.** 3322   **D.** 2244

Q.46 The value of $5 - [4 - \{3 - (3 - 3 - 6)\}]$ is:

[MPTET Paper I - Varg 3, 2012]

A. 11   **B.** 10   **C.** 9   **D.** 2

Ques (47-51):Direction: Read the passage carefully and choose the best answer to each question out of the four alternatives.

Buddha was one of the world's great religious teachers. His real name was Gautam Siddharth. He was born in the year 500 B.C. He was born a prince. His father was the King of Kapilavastu. But he did not want to become a king. He wanted to find out the meaning of life. He left his place as a young man. He went out to seek the truth. For years he lived the hard life of poverty. He went to many teachers. But they could not help him. At least, the light came to him. He was thinking deeply under a Bodhi tree near Gaya. He became the 'Buddha' or the 'Enlightened One'.

Q.47 Buddha left his home in the palace:

[MPTET Paper I - Varg 3, 2012]

A. To look for his mother
B. To get married
C. To find out the meaning of life
D. To help the people

Q.48 Most holy men have left their home to:

[MPTET Paper I - Varg 3, 2012]

A. Seek the truth

B. Start as Ashram

C. Start a religion

D. Be away from their family

Q.49 Another word for 'poverty' is:

[MPTET Paper I - Varg 3, 2012]

A. Prosperity　　　　**B.** Growth

C. Pennilessness　　　**D.** Luxury

Q.50 Another word for 'seek' is:

[MPTET Paper I - Varg 3, 2012]

A. To look around　　**B.** Neglect

C. Respect　　　　　**D.** Reply

Q.51 "At last light came to him." What does this 'light' mean?

[MPTET Paper I - Varg 3, 2012]

A. Electricity　　　　**B.** Knowledge

C. Candle　　　　　**D.** Ignorance

Q.52 Ashok Mehta Committee (1977) recommended:

A. Mandal Panchayat established

B. Established Nagar Panchayat

C. Panchayat Samiti established

D. Established Gram Panchayat

Q.53 In which year a new Ministry of Tribal Affairs was created?

A. 1999　　**B.** 2002　　**C.** 2005　　**D.** 2010

Q.54 The price of a football is Rs 2360 including the GST. If the rate of GST is 18% and the profit made by shopkeeper is 25%, then the cost price of football is?

A. Rs. 1750　**B.** Rs. 1800　**C.** Rs. 1600　**D.** Rs. 1500

Q.55 An article bought at 20% discount is sold at 25% profit. What is the profit or loss compared with the original price?

A. 10% profit　　　　**B.** 20% loss

C. 10% loss　　　　　**D.** No profit or loss

Q.56 $4^{61} + 4^{62} + 4^{63} + 4^{64}$ is divisible by

A. 17　　**B.** 3　　**C.** 11　　**D.** 13

Q.57 The volume of a sphere is $\frac{1}{4}$ times the volume of a right circular cylinder. The radius of sphere and cylinder are equal. The ratio of the diameter of the sphere to the height of the cylinder is:

A. 3 : 2　**B.** 8 : 3　**C.** 4 : 1　**D.** 3 : 8

Q.58 The area of circle X is 1036π cm^2 more than the area of a circle Y. If the sum of their diameters is 148 cm, then the circumference of circle X is how much more than the circumference of circle Y?

A. 66 cm　**B.** 77 cm　**C.** 88 cm　**D.** 99 cm

Q.59 ABCD is passes through a centre of three circles, AB = 2 cm and CD = 1 cm, if area of middle circle is average of the area of other two circle, then find BC.

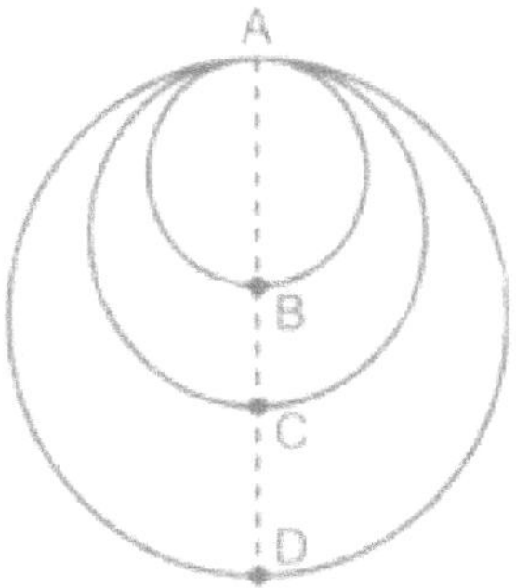

A. $\sqrt{6} - 1$ cm　　　　**B.** $\sqrt{6} + 1$ cm

C. $\sqrt{6} - 2$ cm　　　　**D.** $\sqrt{6} + 2$ cm

Q.60 Consider the following statements regarding the 'National Monetization Pipeline' (NMP) unveiled in the Union Budget 2021-22:

1. Potential brownfield infrastructure assets will be monetized under NMP.

2. Both domestic and foreign investors are eligible to invest under NMP.

3. Core infrastructure assets such as Dedicated Freight Corridors are not included under NMP.

Which of the statements given above is/are incorrect?

A. 3 only　　　　　**B.** 1 and 2 only

C. 1 and 3 only　　　**D.** 1, 2 and 3

Q.61 The proposed Agricultural Infrastructure and Development cess will be applicable on which of the following products?

A. Alcohol beverages　　**B.** Gold

C. Petrol and Diesel　　**D.** All of the above

Q.62 A certain amount of money is distributed between Anil, Sunil, and Mohan in such a way that Anil gets $\frac{3}{2}$ of Mohan, while Mohan gets 50% of Sunil. If the average money of all of them is Rs. 4,500 then, calculate the amount received by Anil.

A. Rs. 4,500　　　　**B.** Rs. 4,000

C. Rs. 3,500　　　　**D.** Rs. 3,000

Q.63 Consider the following statements about the Indian National Army (INA):

1. The idea of INA was first conceived by Mohan Singh, an officer of the British Indian army.

2. Recruits were sought only from Indian prisoners of war and ex-army men in British forces.

3. INA was headquartered in Calcutta.

Which of the statements given above is/are correct?

A. 1 and 2 only　　　**B.** 1 only

C. 2 and 3 only　　　**D.** 1, 2 and 3

Q.64 The greatest number of four digit which is divisible by 15, 25, 40 and 75?

A. 9000　　**B.** 9400　　**C.** 9600　　**D.** 9800

Q.65 Where is the capital of Zimbabwe?

[RBI Office Attendant, 2017]

A. Abuja   **B.** Makati   **C.** Nairobi   **D.** Harare

Q.66 Who is called as 'Hatimtai of Garhwal'?
A.   Kunwar Singh Negi
B.   Kripal Singh
C.   Govind Singh Rawat
D.   None of these

Q.67 Major Somnath Sharma who was honoured with Paramveer Chakra posthumously in 1947 belonged to
_________ .

A. Gorkha Rifle   **B.** Garhwal Rifle
C. Dogra Regiment   **D.** Kumaon Regiment

Q.68 Which of the following books is not written by Kalidasa?
[Madhya Pradesh Public Service Commission (MPPSC), 2017]

A. Meghdootam   **B.** Kumarasambhava
C. Uttararamacharitam   **D.** Ritusanharam

Q.69 'Society is the web of social relationships' whose definition is this?
A. MacIver   **B.** Aristotle
C. H. Maine   **D.** Pluto

Q.70 Kula exchange is associated with:
A. Tikopians   **B.** Trobriand Islanders
C. Krowe tribes   **D.** Azande tribes

Q.71 In the given figure, BC ∥ RS, ∠RAQ = ∠BAC, ∠SAD = 52°, then the value of x is:

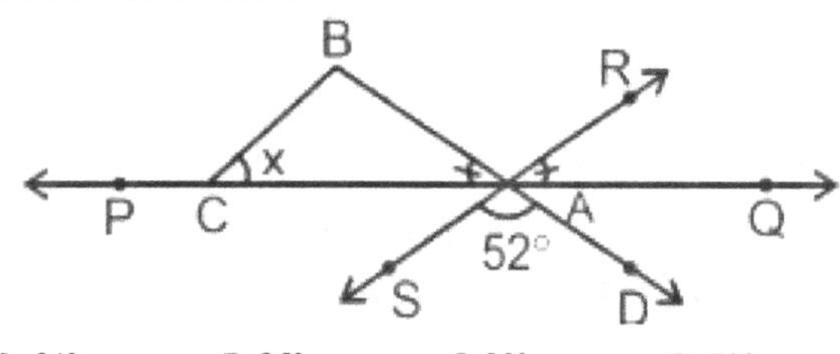

A. 64°   **B.** 26°   **C.** 38°   **D.** 52°

Q.72 'Bagh', a village in Gwalior is famous for:
A. Sculptures   **B.** Architecture
C. Cave Painting   **D.** All of the above

Ques (73-77):Direction: These are based on the tabulated data given below:

A company has 20 employees with their age (in years) and salary (in thousand rupees per month) mentioned against each of them.

S.No	Age in (years)	Salary (in thousand rupees per month)	S.No	Age in (years)	Salary (in thousand rupees per month)
1	44	35	11.	33	30
2	32	20	12.	31	35
3	54	45	13.	30	35
4	42	35	14.	37	40
5	31	20	15.	44	45
6	53	60	16.	36	35
7	42	50	17.	34	35
8	51	55	18.	49	50
9	34	25	19.	43	45
10	41	30	20.	45	50

Q.73 Classify the data of age of each employee in a class interval of 5 years. Which class interval of 5 years has the maximum average salary?
A. $35 - 40$ years   **B.** $40 - 45$ years
C. $45 - 50$ years   **D.** $50 - 55$ years

Q.74 What is the average age of the employees?
A. 40.3 years   **B.** 387.6 years
C. 47.2 years   **D.** 45.3 years

Q.75 What is the fraction $(\%)$ of employees getting a salary $\geq 40{,}000$ per month?
A. 45%   **B.** 50%   **C.** 35%   **D.** 32%

Q.76 What is the average salary (in thousand per month) in the age group $40 - 50$ years?
A. 35   **B.** 42.5   **C.** 40.5   **D.** 36.5

Q.77 What is the fraction of employees getting salary less than the average salary of all the employees?
A. 45%   **B.** 50%   **C.** 55%   **D.** 47%

Q.78 A can do a piece of work in 10 days and B can do it in 15 days. Number of days to complete the work if they work together is:
A. 6 days   **B.** 9 days   **C.** 7 days   **D.** 5 days

Q.79 A, B, and C can do a work in 24, 16 and 12 days respectively. How many days will it take them to complete the work, if the three of them decide to work together?
A. $5\frac{1}{3}$ days   **B.** $5\frac{2}{3}$ days   **C.** $5\frac{1}{2}$ days   **D.** $5\frac{3}{4}$ days

Q.80 A and B started a business, A invested Rs. 15000, and B invested Rs. 20000. If they got Rs. 8400 as profit at the end of one year then what is B profit?
A. Rs. 3600   **B.** Rs. 4800
C. Rs. 3000   **D.** Rs. 2400

Q.81 A person sold a horse at a gain of 15%. Had he bought it for 25% less and sold it for Rs. 600 less, he would have made a profit 32%. The cost price of the horse was:
A. Rs. 3,750   **B.** Rs. 3,250
C. Rs. 2,750   **D.** Rs. 2,250

Ques (82-83):Directions: Each item in this section consists of a sentence with an underlined word/words followed by four words. Select the option that is nearest in meaning to the underlined word and mark your response accordingly.

Q.82 She got the <u>divorce</u> within no time.

[UPSC NDA, 2020]

A. detachment

B. breaking down

C. annulment

D. punishment

Q.83 He was known for his <u>gentle</u> disposition.

[UPSC NDA, 2020]

A. harmful   **B.** amiable   **C.** cunning   **D.** adjusting

Q.84 The tradition of which sport started with the establishment of the Parsi Club?

[Madhya Pradesh Public Service Commission (MPPSC), 2017]

A. Hockey

B. Football

C. Cricket

D. Table Tennis

Q.85 Where is Roop Singh Stadium located?

[Madhya Pradesh Public Service Commission (MPPSC), 2017]

A. Gwalior   **B.** Indore   **C.** Bhopal   **D.** Jabalpur

Q.86 If $A:B = 7:3$, find the value of $\dfrac{AB+B^2}{A^2-B^2}$.

A. $\dfrac{3}{4}$ **B.** $\dfrac{4}{3}$ **C.** $\dfrac{7}{3}$ **D.** $\dfrac{3}{7}$

Q.87 If $X^2 + 4Y^2 = 4XY$, find the value of $X^3:Y^3$.

A. $27:1$ **B.** $1:64$ **C.** $8:1$ **D.** $1:8$

Q.88 _______ was the world's first female astronaut.

A. Svetlana Savitskaya

B. Valentina Tereshkova

C. Sally Ride

D. Judith Resnik

Q.89 Which of the following is the correct match of books and authors of 2017?

a.	First Love	i.	Sara Baume
b.	A Line Made by Walking	ii.	Gwendoline Riley
c.	The Heart's Inverisible Nguyen Furie	iii.	Viet-Thanh
d.	The Refugees	iv.	John Boyne

[KVS Trained Graduate Teacher, 2017]

A. a-iv b-iii c-ii d-i

B. a-ii b-iii c-i i d-v

C. a-ii b-i c-iv d-iii

D. a-i ii b-iii c-i d-v

Q.90 Which of the following day was observed on March 1st this year?

[KVS Trained Graduate Teacher, 2017]

A. Self Injury Awareness Day

B. Blood Cancer Awareness Day

C. Anti-terrorism Day

D. National Youth Day

Q.91 Which of the following day was observed as the International Day of Happiness in 2017?

[KVS Trained Graduate Teacher, 2017]

A. March, 25

B. February, 14

C. January, 1

D. March, 20

Q.92 Which of the following statements is/are applicable to Jain doctrine?

I. The surest way of annihilating Karma is to practice penance.

II. Every object, even the smallest particle has a soul.

III. Karma is the bane of the soul and must be ended.

Select the correct answer using the codes given below:

A. I only

B. II and III only

C. I and III only

D. I, II and III only

Q.93 Which of the following statements about a particular unit is true?

A. Centromere is found in animal cells which produces aster during cell division

B. The gene for producing insulin is present in every body cell

C. Nucleosome is formed of nucleotides

D. DNA consists of a core of eight histones

Q.94 Which of the following is now commercially manufactured by biotechnical processes?

A. Nicotine   **B.** Poppy   **C.** Quinine   **D.** Insulin

Q.95 What will come in place of the question mark in the following question?

$$120 \div 40 \text{ of } \frac{1}{4} + \frac{2}{5} \times 3\frac{1}{4} = ?$$

A. $13\frac{3}{10}$ **B.** $11\frac{1}{9}$ **C.** $3\frac{1}{10}$ **D.** $32\frac{3}{11}$

Q.96 Tapping is an operation:

A. External thread cutting

B. cutting of internal thread

C. Finishing of glued surface

D. Enlarge the last hole

Q.97 On whom is the ozone hole most formed?

A. Africa

B. India

C. Antarctica

D. Europe

Q.98 The successive discount of 15%, 20% and 25% on an article is equivalent to the single discount of:

A. 60%   **B.** 47%   **C.** 49%   **D.** 40%

Q.99 If $x_1, x_2, x_3,....., x_n$ are the observations of a given data. Then the mean of the observations will be:

A. Sum of observations/Total number of observations

B. Total number of observations/Sum of observations

C. Sum of observations+Total number of observations

D. None of the above

Q.100 If the mean of frequency distribution is 7.5 and $\sum f_i x_i = 120 + 3k$, $\sum f_i = 30$, then k is equal to:

A. 40   **B.** 35   **C.** 50   **D.** 45

// Smart Answer Sheet //

Correct — Percentage of students who answered correctly. **Skipped** — Percentage of students who skipped.

Q.	Ans.	Correct	Skipped	Q.	Ans.	Correct	Skipped	Q.	Ans.	Correct	Skipped	Q.	Ans.	Correct	Skipped	Q.	Ans.	Correct	Skipped	Q.	Ans.	Correct	Skipped
1	B	69.87 %	1.08 %	18	A	69.34 %	1.77 %	35	A	48.03 %	1.4 %	52	A	62.62 %	1.72 %	69	A	62.44 %	1.51 %	86	A	55.91 %	1.43 %
2	A	64.11 %	1.22 %	19	C	78.22 %	0.0 %	36	A	41.13 %	1.96 %	53	A	87.61 %	0.0 %	70	B	62.33 %	1.78 %	87	C	27.65 %	4.73 %
3	D	60.97 %	1.51 %	20	D	43.72 %	1.89 %	37	C	50.85 %	1.47 %	54	C	40.66 %	1.71 %	71	A	60.77 %	1.08 %	88	B	42.16 %	1.26 %
4	D	40.14 %	1.15 %	21	C	44.44 %	1.31 %	38	D	57.65 %	1.25 %	55	D	51.66 %	1.3 %	72	C	18.38 %	3.17 %	89	C	29.96 %	4.01 %
5	B	53.18 %	1.9 %	22	A	61.43 %	1.26 %	39	B	56.97 %	1.7 %	56	A	76.21 %	0.0 %	73	D	40.71 %	1.03 %	90	A	41.14 %	1.2 %
6	C	60.42 %	1.74 %	23	C	45.16 %	1.85 %	40	C	86.18 %	0.0 %	57	D	87.18 %	0.0 %	74	A	50.86 %	1.3 %	91	D	69.9 %	1.18 %
7	C	59.2 %	1.16 %	24	D	56.26 %	1.09 %	41	B	87.0 %	0.0 %	58	C	52.05 %	1.25 %	75	A	69.97 %	1.8 %	92	D	55.82 %	1.41 %
8	B	82.16 %	0.0 %	25	C	41.11 %	1.48 %	42	D	84.17 %	0.0 %	59	A	26.26 %	4.48 %	76	B	54.71 %	1.42 %	93	B	52.34 %	1.24 %
9	C	24.06 %	3.11 %	26	A	64.69 %	1.39 %	43	B	87.25 %	0.0 %	60	A	18.34 %	4.67 %	77	C	57.38 %	1.96 %	94	D	45.36 %	1.29 %
10	B	60.11 %	1.1 %	27	A	13.2 %	3.4 %	44	C	24.68 %	3.94 %	61	D	67.13 %	1.78 %	78	A	89.6 %	0.0 %	95	A	60.23 %	1.7 %
11	C	17.58 %	3.36 %	28	B	64.48 %	1.59 %	45	C	81.14 %	0.0 %	62	A	42.91 %	1.03 %	79	A	81.79 %	0.0 %	96	B	58.5 %	1.06 %
12	B	78.25 %	0.0 %	29	B	68.53 %	1.07 %	46	B	51.95 %	1.61 %	63	B	24.46 %	3.97 %	80	B	69.65 %	1.57 %	97	C	55.64 %	1.82 %
13	C	57.85 %	1.62 %	30	B	47.32 %	1.1 %	47	C	49.9 %	1.36 %	64	C	87.22 %	0.0 %	81	A	47.33 %	1.35 %	98	C	69.3 %	1.34 %
14	C	44.28 %	1.22 %	31	A	14.48 %	3.9 %	48	A	49.73 %	1.03 %	65	D	64.13 %	1.77 %	82	C	66.2 %	1.04 %	99	A	65.56 %	1.76 %
15	A	89.61 %	0.0 %	32	C	51.21 %	1.5 %	49	C	42.63 %	1.31 %	66	A	44.11 %	1.69 %	83	B	81.54 %	0.0 %	100	B	27.99 %	3.08 %
16	C	42.88 %	1.74 %	33	D	80.64 %	0.0 %	50	A	69.59 %	1.39 %	67	D	66.69 %	1.58 %	84	C	40.03 %	1.56 %				
17	A	60.21 %	1.46 %	34	D	68.45 %	1.89 %	51	B	12.71 %	4.67 %	68	C	69.41 %	1.69 %	85	A	84.0 %	0.0 %				

//Hints and Solutions//

1. F1 champion Max Verstappen has been named the 2022 Laureus Sportsman of the Year.

Jamaican Olympic sprinter Elaine Thompson-Herah has been named Sportswoman of the Year.

Hence, the correct option is (B).

2. Mirabai Chanu clinched the gold medal in weightlifting at the Singapore International.

The 2020 Tokyo Olympics silver medallist in weightlifting, Mirabai Chanu, clinched the gold medal at the ongoing Singapore International on 25 February 2022. This win also helped her secure a slot at the upcoming 2022 Commonwealth Games in Birmingham. Competing in a new weight category- 55 kg, Chanu lifted a total of 191 kg- 86 kg in Snatch and 105 kg in Clean and Jerk, to clinch the gold.

Hence, the correct option is (A).

3. INS Gharial, as part of Mission SAGAR IX, arrived at Colombo on 29 April 2022 and delivered over 760 kgs of 107 types of critical lifesaving medicines. The aim was to provide critical medical aid to Sri Lanka during the ongoing crisis. Since May 2020, the Indian Navy has successfully concluded eight such missions, deploying ten ships to 18 friendly foreign countries.

Hence, the correct option is (D).

4. Madhabi Puri Buch has been appointed as the new the Chairperson of SEBI for a period of 3 years.

The government has announced Madhabi Puri Buch as new the Chairperson of SEBI for a period of 3 years. Buch is a former whole-time member of SEBI. She will succeed Ajay Tyagi, whose five-year term comes to an end. This is the first time that a woman and a person from the private sector have been chosen for a key post with SEBI.

Hence, the correct option is (D).

5. Both statement 1 and 2 are correct.

The neo-Vaishnavite monasteries of the Majuli island keep the Sattriya dance form of Assam alive.This dance style is originated from Ankia Nat, or one-act play. Music, dance and drama are interlaced in it.

Hence, the correct option is (B).

6. The longitude passing through Royal Observatory Greenwich meridian is used as the standard time all over the world. Greenwich Mean Time in London is used as the standard time for all over the world as it has the standard meridian passing over it at 0°.

India Standard Time (IST) is 5:30 hours ahead of Coordinated universal time (UTC). This time zone is in use during Standard time in Asia. India Standard Time is a half-hour time zone. Its local time differs by 30 minutes instead of the normal whole hour. This time zone is often called India time. India lies in the east of the Prime Meridian, between 68°7' E and 97°25'E. The 82°30' East longitude is taken as the Standard Time Meridian of India, as it passes through the middle of India (Mirzapur in Uttar Pradesh).

Hence, the correct option is (C).

7. The rings of Saturn are made up of small ice and rock particles.

Saturn is called "The Jewel of the Solar System". It is a ringed planet. It is the second-largest planet after Jupiter. Its beautiful rings are not solid. They are made up of ice, dust, and rock. Its rings are huge but thin. They can be seen from the earth with the help of a telescope. It is very windy on Saturn. Winds around the equator can be 1800 kilometers per hour. On Earth, the fastest winds only get to about 400 kilometers per hour. Saturn goes around the Sun very slowly. A year on Saturn is more than 29 Earth years. But, it spins at its axis very fast i.e., 10 hours and 14 minutes a day.

Hence, the correct option is (C).

8. A magnetic compass, in navigation or surveying, an instrument. It is used for determining direction on the surface of Earth by means of a magnetic pointer that aligns itself with Earth's magnetic field. It functions as a pointer to "magnetic north", the local magnetic meridian. The magnetized needle at its heart aligns itself with the horizontal component of the Earth's magnetic field.

So it is clear that a Magnetic compass, in navigation or surveying, an instrument for determining direction on the surface of Earth by means of a magnetic pointer that aligns itself with Earth's magnetic field.

Hence, the correct option is (B).

9. While arranging sentences in a sequence, it is important to understand the theme of the passage so that the introductory and the following statements can be chosen accordingly. The passage central theme revolves around biofuels and their advantages -disadvantages. The first statement should be E as it introduces the topic 'biofuels' and mentions that they form an energy source that is potentially unlimited. Next should be statement F. It states a contradiction to the fact mentioned about biofuels in E that everything is good about the biofuels. It states that the biofuels have disadvantages too. Next should be statement C as it talks about the disadvantages of biofuels which have been introduced in the prior statement. Next should be statement A. It states that despite having disadvantages, biofuels have numerous advantages as well. It should be followed by statement B which talks about some other advantages as well. B mentions 'turnaround' which has also been mentioned in statement D making BD, a mandatory pair.

So, the correct logical order is EFCABD.

Hence, the correct option is (C).

10. While arranging sentences in a sequence, it is important to understand the theme of the passage so that the introductory and the following statements can be chosen accordingly. The passage central theme revolves around biofuels and their advantages -disadvantages. The first statement should be E as it introduces the topic 'biofuels' and mentions that they form an energy source that is potentially unlimited. Next should be statement F. It states a contradiction to the fact mentioned about biofuels in E that everything is good about the biofuels. It states that biofuels have disadvantages too. Next should be statement C as it talks about the disadvantages of biofuels which have been introduced in the prior statement. Next should be statement A. It states that despite having disadvantages, biofuels have numerous advantages as well. It should be followed by statement B which talks about some other advantages as well. B mentions 'turnaround' which has also been mentioned in statement D making BD, a mandatory pair.

So, the correct logical order is EFCABD.

Hence, the correct option is (B).

11. While arranging sentences in a sequence, it is important to understand the theme of the passage so that the introductory and the following statements can be chosen accordingly. The passage central theme revolves around biofuels and their advantages -disadvantages. The first statement should be E as it introduces the topic 'biofuels' and mentions that they form an energy source that is potentially unlimited. Next should be statement F. It states a contradiction to the fact mentioned about biofuels in E that everything is good about the biofuels. It states that the biofuels have disadvantages too. Next should be statement C as it talks about the disadvantages of biofuels which have been introduced in the prior statement. Next should be statement A. It states that despite having disadvantages, biofuels have numerous advantages as well. It should be followed by statement B which talks about some other advantages as well. B mentions 'turnaround' which has also been mentioned in statement D making BD, a mandatory pair.

So, the correct logical order is EFCABD.

Hence, the correct option is (C).

12. The theory of relativity was proposed by Albert Einstein.

It states that space and time are relative and all the motion must be relative to a frame of reference. It is a notion that states, laws of physics are the same everywhere. This theory is simple but hard to understand. It states there is no absolute reference frame on can measure velocity if the object or momentum is only in relation to other objects. The speed of light is constant irrespective of who measures it or how fast the person measuring it, is moving.

Hence, the correct option is (B).

13. DNA fingerprinting is a technique that shows the genetic makeup of living things.

The Father of DNA fingerprinting in the world is Sir Alec John Jeffreys. Sir Alec John Jeffreys is a British geneticist known for developing techniques for genetic fingerprinting and DNA profiling which are now used worldwide in forensic science to assist police detective work and to resolve paternity and immigration disputes.

Hence, the correct option is (C).

14. It is given that,

a = 0.1039

We have to find the value of,

$$\sqrt{4a^2 - 4a + 1} + 3a$$

$$= \sqrt{(1)^2 + (2a)^2 - 2 \times 1 \times 2a} + 3a$$

$$= \sqrt{(1 - 2a)^2} + 3a$$

$$= (1 - 2a) + 3a$$

$$= (1 + a)$$

$$= (1 + 0.1039)$$

$$= 1.1039$$

Hence, the correct option is (C).

15. It is given that,

$$\frac{4050}{\sqrt{x}} = 450$$

$$\Rightarrow \sqrt{x} = \frac{4050}{450}$$

$$\Rightarrow \sqrt{x} = 9$$

$$\Rightarrow x = (9)^2$$

$$\Rightarrow x = 81$$

Hence, the correct option is (A).

16. Priyamvada Mohanty is associated with Odissi classical dance form.

Priyambada Mohanty Hejmadi is an Indian classical dancer of Odissi, art writer, a biologist and a former vice chancellor of Sambalpur University. Odissi is considered to be one of the oldest surviving classical dance forms based on archaeological evidence. The traditional dance of Odisha, Odissi was born from the dance of the devadasis who danced in the temple.

Hence, the correct option is (C).

17. The tradition of Kathakali, a rich and thriving classical dance of the southwestern state of Kerala, is here. Kathakali means a story drama or a dance drama. Katha means story, here actors portray characters drawn from the Ramayana and Mahabharata epics and Puranas.

Hence, the correct option is (A).

18. Mukhya Mantri Chiranjeevi Swasthya Bima Yojana:

- Inaugurated on 1st May 2021.
- Every family in Rajasthan will be a beneficiary of Rs. 5 lakhs while paying an annual premium of just Rs. 850.
- Free medical care up to Rs. 5 lakh in 765 government and more than 330 private hospitals across Rajasthan.
- This scheme covers 1,576 types of medical procedures and treatment package including serious diseases like heart, cancer, Dialysis, and Covid-19.
- Beneficiaries can take advantage of free treatment facilities only when admitted in the hospital for 5 days

before being admitted and up to 15 days after discharge.

Hence, the correct option is (A).

19. The one best expresses meaning of given idiom **a gentleman at large** is **an unreliable person**.

A gentleman at large means has no serious occupation.

Example: He is **a gentleman at large**, you must not trust him.

Hence, the correct option is (C).

20. The best expresses the meaning of given idiom **like a fish out of water** is **in a very difficult and unsuitable situation**.

Like a fish out of water means one who does not feel comfortable in a new environment.

Example: When Carla transferred to a new school, she felt **like a fish out of water** because she didn't know anyone there.

Hence, the correct option is (D).

21. Other than Venezuela, Ecuador among the following from the South American countries is a member of OPEC.

Ecuador suspended its membership in December 1992, rejoined OPEC in October 2007, but decided to withdraw its membership of OPEC effective 1 January 2020. Indonesia suspended its membership in January 2009, reactivated it again in January 2016, but decided to suspend its membership once more at the 171st Meeting of the OPEC Conference on 30 November 2016. Gabon terminated its membership in January 1995. However, it rejoined the Organization in July 2016. Qatar terminated its membership on 1 January 2019.

Hence, the correct option is (C).

22. Radisson Group of Hotels has its main headquarters in USA.

Radisson Hotels is an international hotel chain headquartered in the United States. A division of the Radisson Hotel Group, it operates the brands Radisson Blu, Radisson Red, Radisson Collection, Country Inn & Suites, and Park Inn by Radisson among others.

Hence, the correct option is (A).

23. The given sentence is in active form of simple past tense. The structures for active/passive voices are:

Active: Subject + verb (IInd form) + object.

Passive: Object + was/were + verb (IIIrd form) + by + subject.

So, with the help of the above structures, we can convert the given sentence into passive voice.

The box was broken by them.

Hence, the correct option is (C).

24. The given sentence is the passive form of past negative indefinite tense. The structures for active/passive voices are:

Active: Subject + did not + verb (I^st form) + object

Passive: Object + was/were + not + verb (IIIrd form) + by + subject.

So, with the help of the above structures, we can convert the given sentence into active voice:

Some students did not attend the class.

Hence, the correct option is (D).

25. $(fog)2 = f\{g(x)\}$

$\because f(x) = 2x$

and $g(x) = x^2 + 2$

$\therefore f\{g(x)\} = f(x^2 + 2)$

$= 2(x^2 + 2$

$= f(x^2 + 2)$

$= 2(x^2 + 2)$

$= 2x^2 + 4$

Therefore, $(fog)2 = 2 \times (2)^2 + 4$

$= 2 \times 4 + 4 = 12$

Hence, the correct option is (C).

26. The given equation is,

$= (\cos 2p\pi + i\sin 2p\pi)(\cos 2q\pi + i\sin 2q\pi)$

$= \cos 2(p + q)\pi + i\sin 2(p + q)\pi$

$= (\cos\pi + i\sin\pi)^{2(p+q)}$

$= (-1 + 0)^{2(p+q)}$

$= (-1)^{2(p+q)} = 1$

Hence, the correct option is (A).

27. For an equilateral triangle with side 'a', area $\frac{\sqrt{3}}{4}a^2$

Each side of the triangle $= a + a + a = 180$ cm

$3a = 180$ cm

$a = \frac{180}{3} = 60$ cm

Now, $S = $ Semi-perimeter $= \frac{180}{2} = 90$ cm

Area of a triangle $= \sqrt{s(s - a)(s - b)(s - c)}$

Area of the given triangle

$\sqrt{90(90 - 60)(90 - 60)(90 - 60)}$ cm^2

$\sqrt{90 \times 30 \times 30 \times 30}$ cm^2

$= \sqrt{3 \times 30 \times 30 \times 30 \times 30}$ cm^2

$= \sqrt{3 \times (30)^2 \times (30)^2}$ cm^2

$= 30 \times 30 \times \sqrt{3}$ cm^2

Thus, the area of the given triangle

$$= 900\sqrt{3} \text{ cm}^2$$

Hence, the correct option is (A).

28. The sides of the triangular wall are $a = 122m, b = 120m, c = 22m$

$$\therefore s = \frac{a+b+c}{2}$$

$$= \frac{122+120+22}{2} \text{ m}$$

$$= \frac{264}{2} = 132$$

The area of a triangle is given by

$$\sqrt{s(s-a)(s-b)(s-c)}$$

$$= \sqrt{132(132-122)(132-120)(132-22)} \text{ m}^2$$

$$= \sqrt{132 \times 10 \times 12 \times 100^2}$$

$$= \sqrt{12 \times 11 \times 10 \times 12 \times 11 \times 10} \text{ m}^2$$

$$= \sqrt{12^2 \times 11^2 \times 10^2}$$

$$= \sqrt{(1320)^2} = 1320 \text{ m}^2$$

$\because$ Rent for 1 year (i.e. 12 months) per m^2 = Rs 5000

Rent for 3 months per m$^2 = 5000 \times \frac{3}{12}$

$\Rightarrow$ Rent for 3 months for 1320 m^2

$$= 5000 \times \frac{3}{12} \times 1320$$

$$= 5000 \times 3 \times 110$$

$$= \text{Rs } 16,50,000$$

Hence, the correct option is (B).

29. Let the sides of the triangle be $a = 18, b = 10$ and $c = ?$

$\therefore$ Perimeter $(2s) = 42$ cm

$$\Rightarrow s = \frac{42}{2} = 21 \text{ cm}$$

$$\therefore c = 42 - (18 + 10) = 14$$

$\therefore$ Area of a triangle $= \sqrt{s(s-a)(s-b)(s-c)}$

$\therefore$ Area of the given triangle $=$

$$\sqrt{21(21-18)(21-10)(21-14)} \text{ cm}^2$$

$$= \sqrt{21 \times 3 \times 11 \times 7}$$

$$= \sqrt{3 \times 7 \times 3 \times 11 \times 7}^2$$

$$= \sqrt{3^2 \times 7^2 \times 11} \text{ cm}^2$$

$$= 21\sqrt{11} \text{ cm}^2$$

Thus, the required area of the triangle $= 21\sqrt{11}$ cm^2

Hence, the correct option is (B).

30. Assessment is integral to the teaching-learning process which helps in facilitating student learning and improving instruction. It is a systematic way of collecting information to make a judgment about student learning.

It involves evaluating the final product and serve as an assessment of learning.

The purpose of this kind of evaluation is to grade, rank, classify, compare, and promote the students. They are conducted periodically to determine whether students have met the standards or learning objectives during a course of study.

Hence, the correct option is (B).

31. Observe a few illiterate adults doing arithmetic calculations: This is not very difficult you will find that many shopkeepers who have to do accounts and calculations have never been to school do the arithmetic calculations.

- Ask them questions about how they did the calculations. Compare their methods to the ones we usually use in schools for solving the same kinds of problems.

- Discussed by the teachers in the classroom as an alternate strategy in solving related problems.

- You may have to talk to a couple of people and find out their level of understanding before you hit upon any illiterate doing mathematics.

- Try and find out the process that she adopts to solve arithmetic problems.

Hence, the correct option is (A).

32.

- The periodic table is the tabular arrangement of chemical elements.

- The Modern Periodic table consists of 18 groups and 7 periods.

Group →	1	2	3	4	5	6	7	8	9	10	11	12	13	14	15	16	17	18
Period 1	H																	He
2	Li	Be											B	C	N	O	F	Ne
3	Na	Mg											Al	Si	P	S	Cl	Ar
4	K	Ca	Sc	Ti	V	Cr	Mn	Fe	Co	Ni	Cu	Zn	Ga	Ge	As	Se	Br	Kr
5	Rb	Sr	Y	Zr	Nb	Mo	Tc	Ru	Rh	Pd	Ag	Cd	In	Sn	Sb	Te	I	Xe
6	Cs	Ba	La	Hf	Ta	W	Re	Os	Ir	Pt	Au	Hg	Ti	Pb	Bi	Po	At	Rn
7	Fr	Ra	Ac	Rf	Db	Sg	Bh	Hs	Mt	Ds	Rg	Cn	Nh	Fl	Mc	Lv	Ts	Og

Lanthanides	La	Ce	Pr	Nd	Pm	Sm	Eu	Gd	Tb	Dy	Ho	Er	Tm	Yb
Actinides	Ac	Th	Pa	U	Np	Pu	Am	Cm	Bk	Cf	Es	Fm	Md	No

Hence, the correct option is (C).

33. The Valency of an element is defined as the capability to gain or lose its valence electrons in order to complete its valence shell.

Cuprous oxide or Cu₂O is one of the principle oxides of copper.

Its valency is 1.

Hence, the correct option is (D).

34. Remedial teaching refers to the teaching which is intended to improve the ability of slow learners to learn something.

It is an integral part of the teaching-learning program, also known as compensatory or corrective teaching. The objective of remedial teaching is to give additional help to learners who have fallen behind the rest of the class in any topic or subject. It is the process of identifying slow learners and providing them with the necessary help and guidance to overcome their problems.

Hence, the correct option is (D).

35. Tests are helpful in the teaching-learning process. It helps in the assessment of students and enhancing the performance of students. A test is a measurement device or technique used to quantify behaviour or aid in the undertaking and prediction of behaviour.

It is a comprehensive test that provides feedback to teachers and students on their strengths and weaknesses. It is specially conducted for removing the learning difficulties of learners. It is administered at the end of a language course for remedial teaching.

It helps the teacher to know the gaps in learner's understanding and then providing them with the necessary help and guidance to overcome.

Hence, the correct option is (A).

36. Given:

Initial Rate $= 8\%$

Time $= 3$ years

Rate in mutual fund $= 8.5\%$ and time $= 4$ years

Simple interest $= \dfrac{P \times R \times T}{100}$

Let the sum be Rs. x

S.I from the bank $= \dfrac{x \times 8 \times 3}{100}$

$\Rightarrow \dfrac{24x}{100}$

Earnings in the form of interest from mutual fund $= \dfrac{(x \times 8.5 \times 4)}{100}$

$\Rightarrow \dfrac{34x}{100}$

According to question:

$\dfrac{34x}{100} - \dfrac{24x}{100} = Rs.\,500$

$\Rightarrow 10x = 50000$ or $x = 5000$

∴ The sum invested $=$ Rs. 5000

Hence, the correct option is (A).

37. Let the amount invested be ' x ' on younger and ' y ' on elder son respectively.

When they will be of 18 years age, they will get equal amount

Time when age of son is 13 years $= 18 - 13 = 5$ years

Time when age of son is 15 years $= 18 - 15 = 3$ years

According to question:

$\dfrac{(x \times 5 \times 5)}{100} = \dfrac{(y \times 3 \times 5)}{100}$

$\Rightarrow \dfrac{25x}{100} = \dfrac{15y}{100}$

$\Rightarrow \dfrac{x}{y} = \dfrac{3}{5}$ or $x:y = 3:5$

Given that he invested total $(3 + 5) = 8$ unit $=$ Rs. 8400

∴ Younger son is 13 years and amount invested on him

$= \left(\dfrac{8400}{8}\right) \times 3$ unit

$=$ Rs. 3150

Hence, the correct option is (C).

38. All are the organizations of Remedial teaching in Mathematics. Tutorial teaching is a remedial teaching session given to one student or a small group of students.

Auto-instructional programs are educational material from which students learn by themselves. The teaching technique based on auto-instructional programs. Its purpose is to enable the learner to progress through a pre-arranged sequence of experiences to the acquisition of knowledge or skill.

Informal teaching encompasses student interests within a curriculum in a regular classroom but is not limited to that setting. It works through conversation and the exploration and enlargement of experience.

Hence, the correct option is (D).

39. The error lies in part (B) of the sentence. The verb "comprise" means to include or consists of. Since, it already includes the preposition "of" in its meanings, using "of" again with it is superfluous and therefore should be omitted from the sentence.

So, the correct sentence is- The question paper comprised many questions that were out of the syllabus as reported by the students.

Hence, the correct option is (B).

40. Given:

x⁴ - 3x³ + 4x² - 3x + 5 and x = 3

(3)⁴ - 3(3)³ + 4(3)² - 3(3) + 5

$\Rightarrow$ 81 - 81 + 36 - 9 + 5

$\Rightarrow$ 27 + 5

$\Rightarrow$ 32

Hence, the correct option is (C).

41. She was beaten <u>with</u> a bat.

With used to show the way in which somebody does something.

Example: He behaved **with** great dignity.

Hence, the correct option is (B).

42. The little girl was scared <u>of</u> crossing the busy road, alone.

Of means belonging to somebody relating to somebody.

Example: The love **of** a mother for her child.

Hence, the correct option is (D).

43. The little boy stood <u>under</u> the tree.

Under means directly below or at a lower level than something

Example: We took shelter **under** an oak tree.

Hence, the correct option is (B).

44. Given-

$$\left(\sqrt{3}+1\right)\left(10+\sqrt{12}\right)\left(\sqrt{12}-2\right)\left(5-\sqrt{3}\right)$$

$$=\left(\sqrt{3}+1\right)\left(10+2\sqrt{3}\right)\left(2\sqrt{3}-2\right)\left(5-\sqrt{3}\right)$$

$$=\left(\sqrt{3}+1\right)\times 2\left(5+\sqrt{3}\right)\times 2\left(\sqrt{3}-1\right)\left(5-\sqrt{3}\right)$$

$$=4\left(\sqrt{3}+1\right)\left(\sqrt{3}-1\right)\left(5-\sqrt{3}\right)\left(5+\sqrt{3}\right)$$

According the formula-

$$[(a+b)(a-b)=a^2-b^2]$$

$$=4(3-1)(25-3)$$

$$=4\times 2\times 22$$

$$=176$$

Hence, the correct option is (C).

45. 1856 – 3287 + 5432 – 679

= 7288 – 3966

= 3322

∴ The required value = 3322
Hence, the correct option is (C).

46. $5-[4-\{3-(3-3-6)\}]$

$=5-[4-\{3+6\}]$

$=5+5=10$

∴ The required value $=10$

Hence, the correct option is (B).

47. Buddha left his home in the palace to find out the meaning of life.

The seventh and the eighth sentence of the passage respectively says "He wanted to find out the meaning of life" and "He left his place as a young man". Here, the personal pronoun 'he' is used for the 'Buddha'.

Hence, the correct option is (C).

48. Most holy men have left their homes to seek the truth.

The ninth line or sentence of the passage says "He went out to seek the truth".

Hence, the correct option is (A).

49. The another word for poverty is pennilessness.

The word 'poverty' means the state of being inferior in quality or insufficient in amount.

Let us explore the given options:

- 'Prosperity' means the state of being prosperous (bringing wealth and success).

- 'Growth' means the process of increasing in amount, value, or importance.

- 'Pennilessness' means the state of a person having no money; very poor.

- 'Luxury' means a state of great comfort or elegance, especially when involving great expense.

Hence, the correct option is (C).

50. Another word for 'seek' is to look around.

Seek means to try to find or get something.

Let us explore the given options:

- 'To look around' means to try to find something that you want or need.

- 'Neglect' means fail to leave undone or unattended to especially through carelessness.

- 'Respect' means the state of being admired or respected.

- 'Reply' means to say something in response to something someone has said.

Hence, the correct option is (A).

51. Here light means knowledge.

Let us explore the given options:

- 'Electricity' is a form of energy resulting from the existence of charged particles (such as electrons or protons).

- 'Knowledge' means facts, information, and skills acquired through experience or education; the theoretical or practical understanding of a subject.

- 'Candle' is a cylinder or block of wax or tallow with a central wick which is lit to produce light as it burns.

- 'Ignorance' means a lack of knowledge or information.

Hence, the correct option is (B).

52. Ashok Mehta Committee (1977) recommended Mandal Panchayat established.

In December 1977, the Janata Government appointed a committee on Panchayati Raj institutions under the chairmanship of Ashoka Mehta. The committee submitted its report in August 1978 and made 132 recommendations to revive and strengthen the declining Panchayati Raj system in the country.

Hence, the correct option is (A).

53. In 1999 a new Ministry of Tribal Affairs was created.

A new Ministry of Tribal Affairs was created to provide a sharp focus to the welfare and development of the STs in the year 1999. Scheduled tribes are different from scheduled castes and their problems are also different from scheduled castes both geographically and culturally which this ministry was created to solve.

Hence, the correct option is (A).

54. $\Rightarrow$ Let the cost price of football be Rs P.

$\Rightarrow$ Then Selling price $= P \times 1.25 \times 1.18$

$\Rightarrow P \times 1.25 \times 1.18 = 2360$

$\Rightarrow P \times 1.25 = 2000$

$\therefore$ Cost price of football $= Rs\,1600$

Hence, the correct option is (C).

55. Let the marked price of the article be Rs. 100

$\Rightarrow$ Cost Price of the article

$= $ Rs. $\dfrac{100 \times 80}{100} = $ Rs. 80

$\Rightarrow$ Selling Price of the article

$= $ Rs. $\dfrac{80 \times 125}{100} = $ Rs. 100

$\therefore$ Now we can say, No profit or loss.

Hence, the correct option is (D).

56. $4^{61} + 4^{62} + 4^{63} + 4^{64} = 4^{61}(1 + 4 + 4^2 + 4^3)$
$= 4^{61}(1 + 4 + 4^2 + 4^3)$
$= 4^{61}(85) = 4^{61}(17 \times 5)$
Clearly 17 is a factor of $4^{61} + 4^{62} + 4^{63} + 4^{64}$
So, it will be divisible by 17.
Hence, the correct option is (A).

57. Given:

The volume of a sphere is $\dfrac{1}{4}$ times the volume of a right circular cylinder.

The radius of sphere and cylinder are equal.

Volume of the sphere $= \dfrac{4}{3} \times \pi \times r^3$

And, the volume of cylinder $= \pi \times r^2 \times h$

As per question,

$\dfrac{4}{3} \times \pi \times r^3 = \dfrac{1}{4} \times \pi \times r^2 \times h$

$\Rightarrow 16r = 3h$

$\Rightarrow h = \left(\dfrac{16}{3}\right)r$

$\therefore$ The ratio of the diameter of the sphere to the height of the cylinder $= 2r : \left(\dfrac{16}{3}\right)r$

$= 6 : 16 = 3 : 8$

Hence, the correct option is (D).

58. Given,

Area of circle X is 1036π cm ^{2} more than the area of a circle Y. Sum of their diameters is 148 cm.

Let the radii of circle X and Y be 'R' cm and 'r' cm respectively.

Sum of diameters $= 2R + 2r = 148$ cm

$\Rightarrow (R + r) = 74$ cm

Area of circle X – Area of circle Y = 1036π cm ^{2}

$\Rightarrow \pi R^2 - \pi r^2 = 1036\pi$

$\Rightarrow R^2 - r^2 = 1036$

$\Rightarrow (R + r)(R - r) = 1036$

$\Rightarrow (R - r) = \dfrac{1036}{74} = 14$ cm

Now,

Circumference of circle X- Circumference of circle Y $= 2\pi R - 2\pi r$

$= 2\pi(R - r)$

$= 2 \times \dfrac{22}{7} \times 14$

$= 88$ cm

$\therefore$ Circumference of circle X is 88 cm more than the circumference of circle Y.

Hence, the correct option is (C).

59. Given,

ABCD is passes through a centre of three circles, AB = 2 cm and CD = 1 cm.

Let the radius of middle circle be 'r' cm.

Area of circle of diameter $2\, cm = \pi \times 1^2$ cm ^{2}

Area of middle circle $= \pi \times r^2$ cm ^{2}

Diameter of bigger circle $= AB + BC + CD = 2r + 1$

Area of bigger circle $= \dfrac{\pi \times (2r+1)^2}{4}$ cm ^{2}

Area of middle circle is average of the area of other two circles.

$\pi \times r^2 = \dfrac{\left[\pi \times 1^2 + \dfrac{\pi \times (2r+1)^2}{4}\right]}{2}$

$\Rightarrow 2r^2 = 1 + r^2 + r + \dfrac{1}{4}$

$$\Rightarrow r^2 = r + \frac{5}{4}$$

$$\Rightarrow 4r^2 - 4r - 5 = 0$$

$$\Rightarrow r = \frac{(4 \pm 4\sqrt{6})}{8}$$

$$\Rightarrow 2r = \frac{(4 \pm 4\sqrt{6})}{4} = (1 \pm \sqrt{6})$$

$$\Rightarrow AC = 1 + \sqrt{6}$$

$(\because 1 - \sqrt{6}$ is negative $)$

$$\therefore BC = AC - AB$$

$$= 1 + \sqrt{6} - 2$$

$$= \sqrt{6} - 1 \text{ cm}$$

Hence, the correct option is (A).

60. To unlock the value of hitherto unutilized or underutilized public assets the central government has been focusing on asset monetization for some time. Many public sector assets are sub-optimally utilized and could be appropriately monetized to generate resources for financing new infrastructure.

In this direction, the central government in the Budget 2021-22 has proposed National Monetisation Pipeline (NMP) for potential brownfield infrastructure assets. Some of the core infrastructure assets that will be monetized under NMP include Dedicated Freight Corridor assets of Railways, Airports, NHAI Operational Toll Roads, Oil and Gas Pipelines of GAIL, etc.

- So, statement 1 is correct and statement 3 is not correct. (Brownfield infrastructure assets are those assets that are already in existence, unlike the Greenfield assets which are yet to be created.)

Both foreign and domestic investors are eligible for participating in National Monetisation Pipeline.

- So, statement 2 is correct.

Hence, the correct option is (A).

61. The proposed Agricultural Infrastructure and Development cess will be applicable on Alcohol beverages, Gold and Petrol and Diesel.

Agricultural Infrastructure and Development cess:

Union Budget 2021: The Minister proposed an Agriculture Infrastructure and Development Cess (AIDC) on a small number of items.

Items covered under Agricultural Infrastructure and Development cess are:

- Petrol, Diesel gold, silver, alcohol beverages, crude palm oil, crude soya bean and sunflower oil, apples, coal, lignite and peat specified fertilizers, peas, Kabuli chana, Bengal gram, lentil and cotton.

Hence, the correct option is (D).

62. Let the amount received by Anil, Sunil and Mohan be x, y and z respectively

According to the question, we have

Anil gets $\frac{3}{2}$ of Mohan

$x = \left(\dfrac{3}{2}\right) \times z$

$x = 1.5z$ ---(i)

Mohan gets 50% of Sunil

$z = 50\%$ of y

$z = \left(\dfrac{50}{100}\right) \times y$

$\dfrac{100z}{50} = y$

$y = 2z$ ---(ii)

The average amount received by Anil, Sunil and Mohan is

$\dfrac{(x + y + z)}{3} = 4{,}500$ ---(iii)

Substitute the values of x and z from (i) and (ii) in (iii), we get

$\Rightarrow \dfrac{(1.5z + 2z + z)}{3} = 4{,}500$

$4.5z = 4{,}500 \times 3$

$z = \dfrac{13{,}500}{4.5}$

$z = 3{,}000$

Now, The amount received by Anil is:

Put the value of z in (i), we get

$x = 1.5z$

$x = 1.5 \times 3{,}000$

$x = \text{Rs. } 4{,}500$

$\therefore$ The total amount received by Anil is Rs. 4,500.

Hence, the correct option is (A).

63. The idea of the Indian National Army (INA) was first conceived in Malaya by Mohan Singh, an Indian officer of the British Indian Army. Subhas Bose set up two INA headquarters, in Rangoon and in Singapore, and began to reorganize the INA. Recruits were sought from civilians, funds were gathered, and even a women's regiment called the Rani Jhansi regiment was formed.

Hence, the correct option is (B).

64. The greatest number of four-digit is 9999.

L.C.M. of 15, 25, 40 and 75 is 600.

On dividing 9999 by 600, we get the remainder of 399.

$\therefore$ Required number = (9999 - 399) = 9600

Hence, the correct option is (C).

65. Harare is the capital of Zimbabwe.

Harare, formerly Salisbury, capital of Zimbabwe, lying in the northeastern part of the country. The city was founded in 1890 at the spot where the British South Africa Company's Pioneer Column halted its march into Mashonaland; it was named for Lord Salisbury, then British prime minister.

Hence, the correct option is (D).

66. Kunwar Singh Negi was an Indian braille editor and social worker.

He was born in Pauri, Uttarakhand. He has transliterated 300 books into braille. His major works are Bhagwan Buddh Ka Updesh and Hazrat Mohammed Ki Vani. He was awarded Padma Shri (1981) and Padma Bhushan (1990). He is called 'Hatimtai of Garhwal'.

Hence, the correct option is (A).

67. Major Somnath Sharma who was honoured with Paramveer Chakra posthumously in 1947 belonged to Kumaon Regiment.

Major Somnath Sharma was born on 31 January 1923, to a Dogra Brahmin family at Dadh, Kangra, Punjab (present-day Himachal Pradesh). Major Somnath Sharma was commissioned into the 8th Battalion, 19th Hyderabad Regiment, of the British Indian Army. During World War II, he saw action against the Japanese in Burma during the Arakan Campaign. At that time he served under the command of Colonel K. S. Thimayya, who would later rise to the rank of general and become Chief of the Army Staff from 1957 to 1961. On 21 June 1950, Major Somnath Sharma's award of the Param Vir Chakra was gazetted for his actions on 3 November 1947 in defending the Srinagar airport.

Hence, the correct option is (D).

68. Uttararamacharitam is not written by Kalidasa. Uttararamacharitam is a famous Sanskrit play by Mahakavi Bhavabhuti.

Kalidasa was a classical Sanskrit author who is considered ancient India's greatest playwright. His plays and poetry are primarily based on the Vedas, the Ramayana, the Mahabharata and the Puranas.

Creations of Kalidasa:

- Ritusanharam
- Meghadutam
- Kumarasambhavam
- Raghuvansham
- Malavikagnimitram
- Vikramorvashiyam
- Abhijnanashakuntalam

Hence, the correct option is (C).

69. 'Society is the web of social relationships' MacIver definition is this.

As social beings, men not only live together, but they also continually interact. Thus, from one point of view, society is the "web of social relationships," as MacIver puts it.

The social web is a set of social relations that link people through the World Wide Web. The social web encompasses how websites and software are designed and developed in order to support and foster social interaction.

Hence, the correct option is (A).

70. Kula exchange is associated with Trobriand Islanders.

Kula, exchange system among the people of the Trobriand Islands of southeast Melanesia, in which permanent contractual partners trade traditional valuables following an established ceremonial pattern and trade route. ... The partnerships between men, involving mutual duties and obligations, were permanent and lifelong.

Hence, the correct option is (B).

71. Given:

BC || RS, ∠RAQ = ∠BAC, ∠SAD = 52°

Calculation:

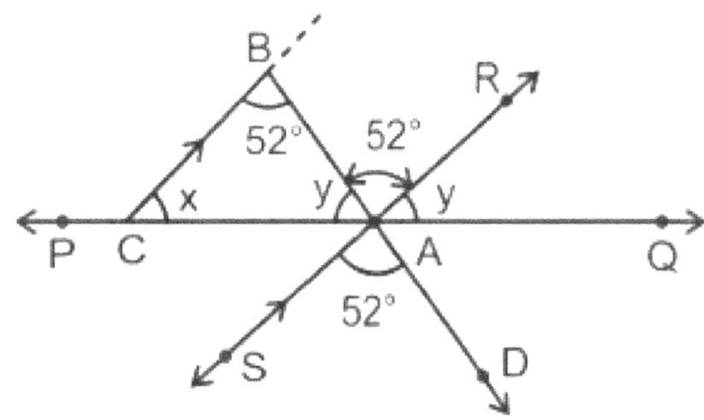

∠BAR = ∠SAD = 52° (Vertically opposite angle)

Let ∠ RAQ = ∠ BAC = y

52° + 2y = 180° (A straight line makes 180°)

⇒ 2y = 180° - 52°

⇒ y = 64°

In Δ ABC,

x + y + 52° = 180°

⇒ x + 64° + 52° = 180°

∴ x = 64°

Hence, the correct option is (A).

72. 'Bagh', a village in Gwalior is famous for Cave Painting.

The Bagh Caves are a group of nine rock-cut monuments, famous for Cave Painting, situated among the southern slopes of the Vindhyas in Bagh town of Dhar district in Madhya Pradesh state in central India. These monuments are located at a distance of 97 km from Dhar town.

Hence, the correct option is (C).

73. From the table,

In $30 - 35$ year:

Average salary $= \dfrac{(20+20+25+30+35+35+35)}{7} = 28.57$ (in thousand)

$= 28570$ per month

In $35-40$ years:

Average Salary $= \dfrac{(40+35)}{2} = 37.5$ (in thousand)

$= 37500$ per month

In $40-45$ years:

Average salary $\dfrac{35+35+50+30+45+45}{6}$

$= \dfrac{240}{6} = 40$ (in thousand)

$= 40000$ per month

In $45-50$ years:

Average salary $= \dfrac{50+50}{2}$

$= \dfrac{100}{2} = 50$ (in thousand)

50000 per month

In $50-55$ years:

Average salary $= \dfrac{45+60+55}{2} = 53.3$ (in thousand)

53300 per month

Hence, the correct option is (D).

74. From the table, total number of employess $= 20$

Average age of employees $= \dfrac{Sum\ of\ age}{Total\ number\ of\ employess}$

$= \dfrac{44+32+54+42+31+53+42+51+34+41+33+31+30+37+44+36+34+49+43+45}{20}$

$= \dfrac{806}{20} = 40.3$ years

Hence, the correct option is (A).

75. From the table,

Fraction $(\%)$ employees getting a salary $\geq$ of $40{,}000$ per month $= 9$

Total number of employees $= 20$

So, fraction $(\%)$ of employees getting $(\geq 40{,}000) =$
$\dfrac{9}{20} \times 100 = 45\%$

Hence, the correct option is (A).

76. From the table,

Number of employees, who age between 40 to 50 years $= 8$

The average salary in the age group $40-50$ years $= \dfrac{Sum\ of\ the\ salary\ (40\ to\ 50\ age\ group)}{Number\ of\ employees}$

$= \dfrac{35+35+50+30+45+45+50+50}{8} = \dfrac{340}{8}$

$= 42.5$ (in thousand)

Hence, the correct option is (B).

77. Average salary of employees $= \dfrac{Sum\ of\ salaries}{Number\ of\ employees}$

$= \dfrac{35+20+45+35+20+60+50+55+25+30+30+35+35+40+45+35+35+50+45+50}{20}$

$= \dfrac{775}{20} = 38.75$ (in thousand)

$= 38750$ per month

From the table,

11 employees have a salary less than $38{,}750$

Thus, $\dfrac{11}{20} = 55\%$

Hence, the correct option is (C).

78. Given,

A can do work in 10 days.

A's 1 day's work $= \dfrac{1}{10}$

B can do work in 15 days.

B's 1 day's work $= \dfrac{1}{15}$

(A + B)'s 1 day's work $= \dfrac{1}{10} + \dfrac{1}{15}$

$= \dfrac{(3+2)}{30}$

$= \dfrac{1}{6}$

$\therefore$ Together they can complete work in 6 days.

Hence, the correct option is (A).

79. Given,

A can do the work in 24 days.

B can do the work in 16 days.

C can do the work in 12 days.

Efficiency $= \dfrac{Total\ work}{Time\ taken}$

LCM of $24,16$ and $12 = 48 =$ Total work

Efficiency of $A = \dfrac{48}{24} = 2$ units/day

Efficiency of $B = \dfrac{48}{16} = 3$ units/day

Efficiency of $C = \dfrac{48}{12} = 4$ units/day

Total efficiency of A, B and C together $= (2 + 3 + 4) = 9$ units/day

Time taken by A, B and $C = \dfrac{48}{9} = \dfrac{16}{3} = 5\dfrac{1}{3}$ days

$\therefore$ Time taken if all of them work together is $5\dfrac{1}{3}$ days.

Hence, the correct option is (A).

80. Investment of A $=$ Rs. $15,000$

Investment of B $=$ Rs. $20,000$

Ratio $= 15,000 : 20,000$

$15 : 20$

Yearly profit $=$ Rs. $8,400$

B's profit $= \dfrac{20}{35} \times 8400 = Rs.\ 4800$

Hence, the correct option is (B).

81. Let the original $CP = Rs.\,x$

So, $SP = x + 15\%$ of x

$= \dfrac{115x}{100}$

$= Rs.\dfrac{23x}{20}$

New $CP = x - 25\%$ of x

$= \dfrac{75x}{100} = \dfrac{3x}{4}$

New $SP = \dfrac{3x}{4} + 32\%$ of $\dfrac{3x}{4}$

$= Rs.\dfrac{99x}{100}$

According to the question,

$\dfrac{23x}{20} - \dfrac{99x}{100} = 600$

Or, $\dfrac{115x - 99x}{100} = 600$

$16x = 600 \times 100$

$x = 600 \times \dfrac{100}{16}$

$= Rs.\,3750$

Hence, the correct option is (A).

82. The word 'divorce' means the action or an instance of legally dissolving a marriage.

The word 'annulment' means a judicial or ecclesiastical pronouncement declaring a marriage invalid.

Thus, we can say that 'annulment' is nearest in meaning to the given word.

Hence, the correct option is (C).

83. The word 'gentle' means having or showing a mild, kind, or tender temperament or character.

The word 'amiable' means having or displaying a friendly and pleasant manner.

Thus, we can say that 'amiable' is nearest in meaning to the given word.

Hence, the correct option is (B).

84. Cricket is the sport that started with the establishment of the Parsi club.

The first Indian cricket club was known as the Oriental cricket club founded in 1848 in Bombay by Parsees.

Hence, the correct option is (C).

85. Captain Roop Singh Stadium, is a cricket ground in Gwalior, Madhya Pradesh. The stadium has hosted 12 ODI matches, the first one was played between India and West Indies on 22 January 1988.

Hence, the correct option is (A).

86. Given-

$A:B = 7:3$

Let $A = 7k,\ B = 3k$.

On putting the values of A and B,

$\dfrac{AB + B^2}{A^2 - B^2}$

$= \dfrac{(7k \times 3k) + (3k)^2}{(7k)^2 - (3k)^2}$

$= \dfrac{21k^2 + 9k^2}{49k^2 - 9k^2}$

$= \dfrac{30k^2}{40k^2}$

$= \dfrac{3}{4}$

Hence, the correct option is (A).

87. Given-

$X^2 + 4Y^2 = 4XY$

$\Rightarrow X^2 + 4Y^2 - 4XY = 0$

$\Rightarrow (X - 2Y)^2 = 0$

$\Rightarrow X - 2Y = 0$

$$\Rightarrow X = 2Y$$

$$\Rightarrow \frac{X}{Y} = \frac{2}{1}$$

On cubing both the sides,

$$\Rightarrow \left(\frac{X}{Y}\right)^3 = \left(\frac{2}{1}\right)^3$$

$$\Rightarrow \frac{X^3}{Y^3} = \frac{8}{1}$$

$$\Rightarrow X^3 : Y^3 = 8 : 1$$

Hence, the correct option is (C).

88. On 16 June 1963, Soviet Cosmonaut Valentina Tereshkova became the first woman to travel into space.

By convention, an astronaut employed by the Russian Federal Space Agency (or its Soviet predecessor) is called a cosmonaut in English texts. Valentina Tereshkova was the first female cosmonaut and the first and youngest woman to have flown in space with a solo mission on the Vostok 6 in 1963.

On July 20, 1969, Neil Armstrong became the first human to step on the moon. He and Aldrin walked around for three hours.

Hence, the correct option is (B).

89.

Books	Authors
a. First Love	i. Gwendoline riley
b. A Line Made by Walking	ii. Sara Baume
c. The Heart's Inverisible Nguyen Furie	iii. John Boyne
d. The Refugees	iv. Viet-Thanh Nguyen

Hence, the correct option is (C).

90. Self-Injury Awareness Day (SIAD) (also known as Self-Harm Awareness Day) is a grassroots annual global awareness event/campaign on March 1, where on this day, and in the weeks leading up to and following In the U.S., some people prefer to be more open about their own harm, and awareness organizations make special efforts to raise awareness of self harm and self-injury. Some people wear an orange awareness ribbon, write "Love" on their arms, draw a butterfly on their wrists to raise awareness of the "Butterfly Project" wristbands or bead bracelets that encourage awareness of self-harm. The goal of people observing SIAD is to break common stereotypes surrounding self-harm and to educate medical professionals about the condition.

Hence, the correct option is (A).

91. 20 March: International Day of Happiness

The International Day of Happiness was celebrated on 20 March 2017 across the world. To mark the occasion, the United Nations released the World Happiness Report 2017, which ranked 155 countries by their happiness levels.

In the report, while Norway was adjudged as the happiest country in the world, India was ranked 122, much behind most of the SAARC nations including Pakistan and Nepal.

The General Assembly of the United Nations created the International Day of Happiness through a resolution on 12 July 2012. Consequently, the annual day was celebrated for the first time in 2013.

20 March was declared as the day of International Happiness following a Bhutanese concept that was coined by the fourth king of Bhutan Jigme Singye Wangchuck in 1970's.

Hence, the correct option is (D).

92. According to Jaina doctrine, the surest way of annihilating Karma is to practice penance and karma is the bane of the soul and must be ended. Every object, even the smallest particle has a soul.

Hence, the correct option is (D).

93. Insulin gene is found in every body cell but is not expressed in all cells. It is nucleosome which consists of a core of eight histones. DNA is composed of nucleotides. Centriole is found in animal cells, which i produces aster during cell division.

Hence, the correct option is (B).

94. Humulin is synthesized commercially by inserting the insulin gene into a suitable vector, the E. coli bacterial cell, to produce an insulin that is chemically identical to its naturally produced counterpart. This has been achieved using recombinant DNA technology.

Hence, the correct option is (D).

95. $? = 120 \div 40 \text{ of } \frac{1}{4} + \frac{2}{5} \times 3\frac{1}{4}$

$\Rightarrow ? = 120 \div 40 \times \frac{1}{4} + \frac{2}{5} \times \frac{13}{4}$

$\Rightarrow ? = 120 \div 10 + \frac{2}{5} \times \frac{13}{4}$

$\Rightarrow ? = 12 + \frac{13}{10}$

$\Rightarrow ? = 13\frac{3}{10}$

Hence, the correct option is (A).

96. Tapping is the process of cutting a thread inside a hole so that a cap screw or bolt can be threaded into the hole. Also, it is used to make thread on nuts. Tapping can be done on the lathe by power feed or by hand.
Hence, the correct option is (B).

97. On Antarctica is the ozone hole most formed.

The ozone hole occurs during the Antarctic spring, from September to early December, as strong westerly winds start to circulate around the continent and create an atmospheric container. Within this polar vortex, over 50 percent of the lower stratospheric ozone is destroyed during the Antarctic spring.

Hence, the correct option is (C).

98. Effective discount $\% = x + y - \frac{(xy)}{100}$

Where x and y are the success rates of discount

Therefore,

Effective discount on 15% and $20\% = 15 + 20 - \dfrac{(15\times20)}{100} = 32\%$

Now apply it on 25% and 32%

Effective discount on 25% and $32\% = 25 + 32 - \dfrac{(25\times32)}{100} = 49\%$

Hence, the correct option is (C).

99. The mean or average of observations will be equal to the ratio of sum of observations and total number of observations.

$$x_{\text{mean}} = \frac{x_1 + x_2 + x_3 + \cdots + x_n}{n}$$

Hence, the correct option is (A).

100. As per the given question,

$$x_{\text{mean}} = \frac{\sum fi\, xi}{\sum fi}$$

$$7.5 = \frac{(120 + 3k)}{30}$$

$225 = 120 + 3k$

$3k = 225 - 120$

$3k = 105$

$k = 35$

Hence, the correct option is (B).

Q.1 As on March 2018, which of the following is the India's fastest supercomputer?

[Super TET Paper - I, 2019]

A. Summit   **B.** Sierra   **C.** Mihir   **D.** Pratyush

Q.2 Who has been appointed as the Principal Director General of the Press Information Bureau (PIB) in August 2022?

A. Ravi Semwal   **B.** Anand Pandey
C. Priya Chaudhary   **D.** Satyendra Prakash

Q.3 Where has the only Genome Sequencing Lab in the Bihar started?

[Delhi Forest Guard, 2021]

A. Patna   **B.** Darbhanga
C. Gaya   **D.** Vaishali

Q.4 In which of the following city, the first-ever edition of the India Global Forum (IGF) was held in March 2022?

[Delhi Forest Guard, 2021]

A. Bengaluru   **B.** Panaji
C. Mumbai   **D.** Chennai

Ques (5-6):Direction: Select the option that conveys the meaning of the given idiom most appropriately.

Q.5 To be at one's finger's end

[Territorial Army Officer, 2017]

A. To be hopeless
B. To be highly perplexed
C. To be completely conversant with
D. To count things

Q.6 Elbow room

A. Opportunity for reconsideration
B. To give enough space to move or work in
C. Special room for the guest
D. To add a new room to the house

Q.7 Who was the first recipient of Paramvir Chakra from Kumaon Regiment?

A. Gen. B.C. Joshi
B. Major Shaitan Singh
C. Major Somnath Sharma
D. Hav. Chandri Chand

Q.8 What was the real name of the poet 'Gumani'?

A. Damodar Pant   **B.** Lokratna Pant
C. Mathura Dutt Pant   **D.** Gumani Pant

Q.9 What should come in place of both x in the equation $\dfrac{x}{\sqrt{128}} = \dfrac{\sqrt{162}}{x}$.

A. 12   **B.** 14   **C.** 144   **D.** 196

Q.10 Value of $\sqrt{10 + \sqrt{25 + \sqrt{121}}}$ in the following is?

A. 12   **B.** 14   **C.** 15   **D.** 4

Q.11 If the sum of n elements of the series $x_1, x_2, x_3 \dots , x_n$ is k, then find the mean of the series $ax_1, ax_2, ax_3 \dots , ax_n$ is:

A. ak **B.** $\dfrac{ak}{n}$ **C.** k **D.** $k + \dfrac{a}{n}$

Q.12 Find the mode if the median and mean are 7 and 5 respectively.

A. 10   **B.** 11   **C.** 12   **D.** 13

Q.13 In order to monitor students' progress and to modify teaching accordingly, the best method of evaluation is:

A. Formative evaluation
B. Summative evaluation
C. Qualitative evaluation
D. Objective-based evaluation

Q.14 Given below are two statements:

Statement I: Maximum performance tests are designed to assess the upper limits of the examinee's knowledge and abilities.

Statement II: Typical response tests are designed to measure the behaviour and characteristics of examinees.

In light of the above statements, choose the most appropriate answer from the options given below:

A. Both Statement I and Statement II are correct
B. Both Statement I and Statement II are incorrect
C. Statement I is correct but Statement II is incorrect
D. Statement I is incorrect but Statement II is correct

Q.15 The sum of $1 + 3 + 5 + 7 + \dots$ Upto n terms is:

A. $(n + 1)^2$ **B.** $(2n)^2$ **C.** n^2 **D.** $(n - 1)^2$

Q.16 What is the value of $\sqrt{625} + \sqrt{484}$?

A. 47   **B.** 56   **C.** 52   **D.** 35

Q.17 Consider the following statements about Congress Socialist Party:

1. It was founded by the efforts of Jayaprakash Narayan, Minoo Masaani and others.

2. It worked within the Congress Party and accepted Congress as the primary body leading the National Movement.

Which of the statements given above is/are correct?

A. 1 only   **B.** 2 only
C. Both 1 and 2   **D.** Neither 1 nor 2

Ques (18-19):Directions: Each item in this section consists of a sentence with an underlined word followed by four words. Select the option that is opposite in meaning to the underlined word and mark your response accordingly.

Q.18 He nodded <u>absently</u> throughout the meeting.

[UPSC NDA, 2020]

A. capably **B.** alertly
C. agitatedly **D.** dreamily

Q.19 I fully believe that the cornerstone of good policy is an electorate that is <u>educated</u> on national issues.

[UPSC NDA, 2020]

A. cerebral **B.** enlightened
C. ignorant **D.** erudite

Ques (20-22):Directions: Each of the following items in this section has a sentence with a missing preposition. Select the correct preposition from the given options and mark your response accordingly.

Q.20 Simulations of the 20th century by climate models that exclude the observed increase _______ greenhouse gases fail to simulate the increase in temperature over the second half of the 20th century.

[UPSC NDA, 2020]

A. of **B.** in **C.** by **D.** to

Q.21 In extremely poor societies, children can be put to work _______ a young age and are therefore a source of income.

[UPSC NDA, 2020]

A. in **B.** on **C.** by **D.** at

Q.22 People who are averse _____ hard work, generally do not succeed in life.

[UPSC NDA, 2020]

A. at **B.** to **C.** about **D.** on

Q.23 Direction: In the following question, some part of the sentence may have errors. Find out which part of the sentence has an error and select the appropriate option. If the sentence is free from error, select 'No error'.

These days it was not uncommon to see (A)/ practitioners prescribing multiple antibiotics (B)/ without any real indication or relevance for such a combination. (C)/ No error (D)

A. (A) **B.** (B) **C.** (C) **D.** (D)

Q.24 If both p and q belong to the set {1, 2, 3, 4}, then how many equations of the form $px^2 + qx + 1 = 0$ will have real roots?

[UPSC NDA, 2019]

A. 12 **B.** 10 **C.** 7 **D.** 6

Q.25 If $x = 3 + 2\sqrt{2}$, then the value of $\left(\sqrt{x} - \frac{1}{\sqrt{x}}\right)$ is?

A. 1 **B.** 2 **C.** $2\sqrt{2}$ **D.** $3\sqrt{3}$

Q.26 Which place is said to be the "Cathedral city of India"?
A. Banaras **B.** Kancheepuram
C. Madurai **D.** Bhubaneswar

Q.27 The terms 'Zat and Sawar' are related to which of the following administrative systems?
A. Iqtadari System **B.** Jotedari System
C. Mansabdari System **D.** Zamindari System

Q.28 Which one of the following is an important aspect of measurement of length?

[CTET Paper - I, 2016]

A. Using non-standard measures
B. Iteration
C. Conservation of length
D. Ability to use scale

Q.29 Which of the following is not a mathematical process?
A. Visualization **B.** Memorization
C. Estimation **D.** Transposition

Q.30 Which of the following is the winter capital of Ladakh?
A. Skardo **B.** Leh **C.** Kargil **D.** Hemis

Q.31 If 111111111 is divided by 111, then the quotient will be:
A. 111 **B.** 10101
C. 1001001 **D.** None of these

Q.32 The HCF of two numbers is 6 and their LCM is 432. If one of the numbers is 48, the other number is:
A. 52 **B.** 42 **C.** 27 **D.** 54

Q.33 'Golden Threshold' is a collection of poems written by:
A. Annie Besant **B.** Vijyalakshmi Pandit
C. Aruna Asaf Ali **D.** Sarojini Naidu

Q.34 Which of the following SAARC member has the highest population?
A. Bangladesh **B.** Pakistan
C. Nepal **D.** Afghanistan

Q.35 Where is the headquarters of the SAARC?
A. Manila **B.** Kathmandu
C. New Delhi **D.** Jakarta

Q.36 The diagonal of a square is $24\ cm$. What is its perimeter?
A. $46\sqrt{2}\ cm$ **B.** $28\ cm$
C. $48\sqrt{2}\ cm$ **D.** $36\sqrt{2}\ cm$

Q.37 An aluminium sheet $27\ cm$ long, $8\ cm$ broad and $1\ cm$ thick is melted into a cube. The difference in the surface areas of the two solids would be:
A. Nil **B.** $284\ cm^2$ **C.** $286\ cm^2$ **D.** $296\ cm^2$

Q.38 The volumes of two cubes are in the ratio $8:27$. The ratio of their surface areas is:
A. $2:3$ **B.** $4:9$
C. $12:9$ **D.** None of these

Q.39 An Rs. 100 shirt is offered at 10% discount and a Rs. 300 pair of trousers at 20% discount. If Pritam bought 1 shirt and 3 pairs of trousers, what is the effective discount (in %) he got?
A. 19 **B.** 18 **C.** 17 **D.** 16

Q.40 The reports of the Comptroller and Auditor-General of India relating to the accounts of the States are submitted to which among the following?

A. The President

B. The Governor

C. The Parliament

D. The Chief Minister

Q.41 Which among the following articles speaks about impeachment of the President of India?

A. Article 60

B. Article 61

C. Article 62

D. Article 63

Q.42 On which of the following dates is the **Martyr's Day** celebrated?

A. January 1

B. January 15

C. January 30

D. January 9

Q.43 On which date is the birthday of Nobel laureate Rabindranath Tagore celebrated?

A. 6 May   **B.** 7 May   **C.** 8 May   **D.** 9 May

Ques (44-48):Direction: Read the following passage and answer the question that follows.

An AC 3-Tier train ticket on the Delhi-Mumbai Rajdhani, under the Tatkal quota, is priced at around Rs. 2,900, where about a third — over Rs. 800 or 28 per cent — is charged as "dynamic pricing". It is such high pricing that majority of people probably referred to when they voted in Local Circles' citizens' poll.

Tatkal charges are extra charges levied for last minute booking by train passengers and form a part of dynamic charges in a ticket.

Tatkal fares have become "excessive", said almost three-fourth (74 per cent) of the 8,165 people who answered a query on their experience with Tatkal ticket fares on LocalCircles, a citizen interaction platform. Almost one-fifth polled found the charges "reasonable". Five per cent even found the charges "quite low".

Almost 80 per cent of people found the ticket cancellation charges high, and desired that such charges on Tatkal tickets be lowered. For seven questions, Local Circles received votes from over 27,000 participants from over 200 districts. "Railway travellers from Vadodara to Bhubaneswar and from Jammu Tavi to Tirunelveli participated in this survey," said Sachin Taparia, Founder, Local Circles.

Almost half of the people who voted were from tier-1 cities, 30 per cent from tier-2 cities and 22 per cent from tier-3 and rural locations. Almost 40 per cent of people who participated in the poll were females.

From the 7,739 people who voted on the question "how has cleanliness of trains and railway stations improved in last 12 months", about four-fifth felt there was an improvement. Specifically, 39 per cent felt there was marginal improvement, 38 per cent voted for "significant improvement". Over a fifth (23 per cent) of train customers felt there was no improvement, including five per cent who felt the cleanliness of trains and stations have worsened.

Almost 46 per cent of 8,000-odd people found the food served in trains edible though not delicious, while four per cent found the food catered delicious. 31 per cent said the food was unhygienic or inedible, while 19 per cent were "unsure" about judging the quality of food.

On punctuality of trains, 66 per cent of 8,122 people who took the poll during the last 12 months said the trains were delayed by upto one hour.

There is scope to make the India Railway Catering and Tourism Corporation Web site more consumer-oriented and scope to improve food hygiene standards.

Q.44 Which among the following is correct regarding the gender-based participation in the survey conducted by Local Circles regarding the railway services?

A. There was no participation from females in the survey conducted for giving opinion regarding railway services in India.

B. There was no participation from males in the survey conducted regarding the services catered by Indian Railways.

C. There is equal participation from males and females in the survey conducted.

D. The number of females participating in the survey is less than that of the males who have given response via the survey.

Q.45 Which among the following is correct regarding the result of the survey regarding the punctuality of trains run by Indian Railways in the country?

A. The survey found out that trains are mainly running before time with no margin for being late.

B. The survey found out that the trains are not running late but they are being made to run late due to certain issues.

C. The survey found out that the trains are very well on time but only in the foggy days of the year.

D. The survey found that the trains are not running on time at all especially in the recent months.

Q.46 Which among the following is correct regarding the cleanliness in trains run by the Indian Railways, as described in the passage?

A. Most of the passengers are of the opinion that the cleanliness in trains has deteriorated in the last few months.

B. Most of the passengers are of the opinion that the cleanliness in trains has improved significantly in the last few months.

C. Most of the passengers are of the opinion that they cannot comment publicly regarding the cleanliness of trains in India.

D. Most of the passengers are of the opinion that some kind of improvement has been observed in the level of cleanliness in the trains in the past year.

Q.47 Which among the following is correct regarding the percentage of people who are of the view that the tatkal fares are actually low?

A. Nobody has given the opinion that the tatkal fares are quite low.

B. Majority of the people is of the view that the tatkal fares are quite low as compared to other countries.

C. The people are of the opinion that the tatkal fares are very low as compared to the international community but it is high with respect to the society at large.

D. Hardly 5% people are of the view that the tatkal fares are actually quite low.

Q.48 Which among the following is similar in meaning to the word **Dynamic** as used in the passage?

A. Changing
B. Energetic
C. Compelling
D. Vigorous

Q.49 Rajinder Singh was the _________ recipient of Mahavir Chakra.

A. First
B. Second
C. Third
D. Fourth

Q.50 Consider the following statements with reference to the One Nation-One Ration Card (ONORC) Scheme.

1. It was started as inter-State portability of ration cards by the Ministry of Consumer Affairs, Food and Public Distribution in 2019.

2. It allows any National Food Security Act (NFSA), 2013 beneficiaries to lift their entitled quota of food grains from any Fair Price Shop (FPS) of their choice anywhere in the country.

3. A migrant will be allowed to buy a maximum of 75% of the family quota from the PDS store.

Which of the statements given above is/are correct?

A. 1 and 2 only
B. 2 and 3 only
C. 1 and 3 only
D. 1, 2 and 3

Q.51 Which of the following seaweed species are commercially exploited in India?

1. Kappaphycus alvarezii

2. Gracilaria edulis

3. Gelidiella acerosa

4. Sargassum spp

Select correct code:

A. 1 and 2 only
B. 2, 3 and 4
C. 1, 3 and 4
D. 1, 2, 3 and 4

Q.52 A work can be completed by A, B and C alone in 9 days,12 days and 18 days respectively. If A, B and C are working together, then in how many days they can complete the work?

A. 12 days
B. 9 days
C. 7 days
D. 4 days

Q.53 If A can complete a work in 60 days and B can complete the same work in 15 days. Then in how many days A and B together can complete the whole work.

A. 12 days
B. 15 days
C. 8 days
D. 18 days

Q.54 If $x^2 - 2x + 1 = 0$, find the value of $x^3 + (\frac{1}{x^3})$.

A. 2
B. -2
C. -3
D. 3

Q.55 Simplify: $\left(\dfrac{\frac{3}{2+\sqrt{3}} - \frac{2}{2-\sqrt{3}}}{2-5\sqrt{3}} \right) = ?$

A. $\frac{1}{2} - 5\sqrt{3}$
B. $2 - 5\sqrt{3}$
C. 1
D. 0

Q.56 In a business, A, B and C invested Rs 380, Rs 400, and Rs 420 respectively. Divide a net profit of Rs 180 among the partners.

A. $A = 45, B = 56, C = 76$
B. $A = 57, B = 60, C = 63$
C. $A = 12, B = 23, C = 34$
D. $A = 18, B = 34, C = 56$

Q.57 Which Veda is the primary source of classical music?

A. Rigveda
B. Yajurveda
C. Samveda
D. Atharvaveda

Q.58 When is 'Raag Bhairav' or 'Raag Bhairavi' sung?

A. First stroke of the night
B. Second stroke of night
C. Night's third stroke
D. Morning

Q.59 In the given figure AH ∥ BG ∥ CF, ∠DCH = 55°. Find the value of ∠AED : ∠BDE.

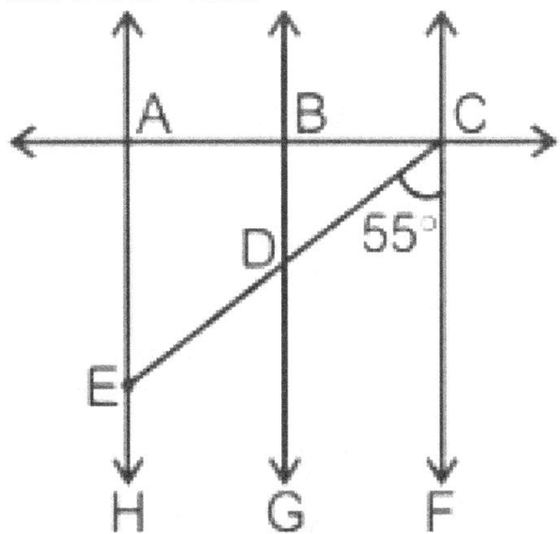

A. 11 : 25
B. 12 : 25
C. 13 : 25
D. 14 : 25

Q.60 Shreyas and Tejas are friends. Each has some money. If Shreyas gives Rs. 20 to Tejas, then Tejas Will have twice the money left with Shreyas. But, if Tejas gives Rs. 15 to Shreyas, then Shreyas will have thrice as much as is left with Tejas. How much money does each have?

A. Rs. 48, Rs. 36
B. Rs. 60, Rs. 20
C. Rs. 170, Rs. 124
D. Rs. 43, Rs. 26

Q.61 Vishnu sells an article at 25% profit. Had he sold it for Rs. 51 more, he would have gained 28%. The cost price of the article will be:

A. 1500
B. 1700
C. 2100
D. 2500

Q.62 A number is first decreased by 20% and then increased by 10%. The number so obtained is 12 less than the original number. The original number is:

A. 200
B. 100
C. 400
D. 80

Q.63 In two successive years, 100 and 200 students of a school appeared at the final examination. Respectively 80% and 60% of them passed. Find the cumulative passing percentage in 2 years.

A. 50%
B. 60%
C. 66.67%
D. 65%

Q.64 What is the SI unit of power?

A. Watt
B. Joule
C. Ampere
D. Volt

Q.65 In which unit is capacitance measured for day to day applications?

A. Farad

B. Microfarad

C. Megafarad

D. None of the above

Q.66 If $\dfrac{1}{1+\dfrac{1}{1+\dfrac{1}{1+\dfrac{1}{y}}}} = \dfrac{7}{11}$, then what is the value of y?

A. 2   **B.** 1   **C.** 4   **D.** 3

Q.67 National Mission for Sustainable Agriculture consists of which of the following sub-mission?

[Rajasthan Police Sub Inspector, 2016]

A. Animal husbandry

B. Health Management

C. Cooperative agriculture

D. Soil Health Management

Q.68 The principal amount of Rs. 27000 is invested in the ratio of 4 : 5 in simple interest at the rate of interest 20% and 24% respectively for 4 years. Find the total simple interest.

A. Rs. 25000

B. Rs. 20000

C. Rs. 17000

D. Rs. 24000

Q.69 At what rate percent compounded yearly will Rs. 44,000 amounts to Rs. 48,510 in 2 years?

A. 5% p.a.   **B.** 6% p.a.   **C.** 10% p.a.   **D.** 9% p.a.

Q.70 A solid sphere of diameter 60 mm is melted to stretch into a wire of length 144 cm. What is the diameter of the wire?

A. 0.5 cm   **B.** 1 cm   **C.** 1.5 cm   **D.** 2 cm

Q.71 The man created by the lines used to join the equal values is known as:

A. Dot map

B. Isopleth map

C. Choropleth map

D. None of the above

Q.72 The 'Tropic of Cancer' has not crossed which one of the following Indian states?

A. Gujarat

B. Mizoram

C. West Bengal

D. Uttar Pradesh

Q.73 Which one of the following has longest duration in the Earths history?

A. Period   **B.** Eon   **C.** Era   **D.** Epoch

Q.74 What are 'the camel', 'the mongoose', 'kaboom' and 'aluminum' that have been in news recently?

A. Cricket bats

B. Military codes

C. Squadrons

D. Chess moves

Q.75 Which country is to play host to the ICC Under -19 World Cup 2020 tournament?

A. England

B. New Zealand

C. South Africa

D. Zimbabwe

Q.76 The average of the daily incomes of A, B and C is Rs. 250. If B earns Rs. 30 more than C and A earns double of C. What is the daily income of C?

A. Rs. 195   **B.** Rs. 190   **C.** Rs. 180   **D.** Rs. 185

Q.77 If 210 is to be divided into 4 parts proportional to 6, 7, 5 and 3, what is the largest part?

A. 70   **B.** 60   **C.** 80   **D.** 30

Q.78 Who is considered the first real founder of Jainism?

A. Parshwanath

B. Rishabhdeva

C. Neminath

D. Arishtanemi

Q.79 When glycerol is mixed with a high amount of HI, it produces:

A. 2-iodopropane

B. Allyl iodide

C. Propene

D. Glycerol triiodide

Q.80 The charge / size ratio of a cation determines its polarization power. Which of the following sequences represents the increasing order of polarization strength of the cation species, $K^+, Ca^{2+}, Mg^{2+}, Be^{2+}$?

A. $Mg^{2+} < Be^{2+} < K^+ < Ca^{2+}$

B. $Be^{2+} < K^+ < Ca^{2+} < M^{2+}$

C. $K^+ < Ca^{2+} < Mg^{2+} < Be^{2+}$

D. $Ca^{2+} < Mg^{2+} < Be^{2+} < K^+$

Q.81 Which one of the following pairs is/are not correctly matched?

Name of the author	Title of the Book
1. R.C. Dutt	Economic History of India
2. Bal Gangadhar Tilak	The Drain of Wealth and Indian Nationalism at the turn of the century
3. W. Digly	Prosperous British India
4. V. Anstey	The Economic Development of India

A. 1 and 2 only

B. 2 only

C. 1 and 3 only

D. 2 and 3 only

Q.82 Who discovered the nucleus?

A. Thomson

B. Ernest Rutherford

C. James Chadwick

D. James Rutherford

Q.83 The Herpes disease is caused by _______.

A. Bacteria   **B.** Protozoa   **C.** Fungus   **D.** Virus

Q.84 The first Railway engine was invented by________?

A. James Watt

B. Isaac Newton

C. Richard Trevithick

D. George Stephenson

Q.85 Who invented the ballpoint pen?

A. Biro Brothers

B. Waterman Brothers

C. Bicc Brothers

D. Write Brothers

Ques (86-87):Direction: In the following question, a sentence has been given in Active/Passive Voice. Out of the four alternatives suggested, select the one which best expresses the same sentence in Passive/Active Voice.

Q.86 This bottle contains milk.

A. Milk is contained in this bottle

B. Milk is contained by this bottle

C. Milk was contained in this bottle

D. Milk is contained for this bottle

Q.87 Rabindranath Tagore wrote the 'Gitanjali'.

A. The 'Gitanjali' was written by Rabindranath Tagore
B. The 'Gitanjali' is written by Rabindranath Tagore
C. The 'Gitanjali' is being written by Rabindranath Tagore
D. The 'Gitanjali' has been written by Rabindranath Tagore

Q.88 In the figure given below, R is the diameter of each of the larger circle. What is the diameter of the shaded circle?

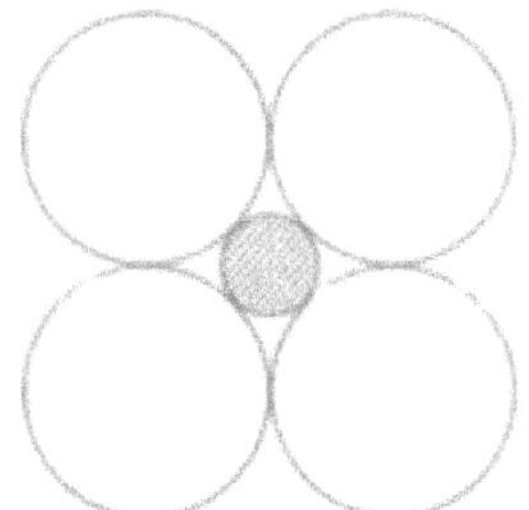

A. $R(2 - \sqrt{2})$ **B.** $R\sqrt{2}$
C. $R(\sqrt{2} + 1)$ **D.** $R(\sqrt{2} - 1)$

Q.89 In the figure, O is the centre of the circle. Find the diameter of the circle if the area of shaded region is 112 cm^2.

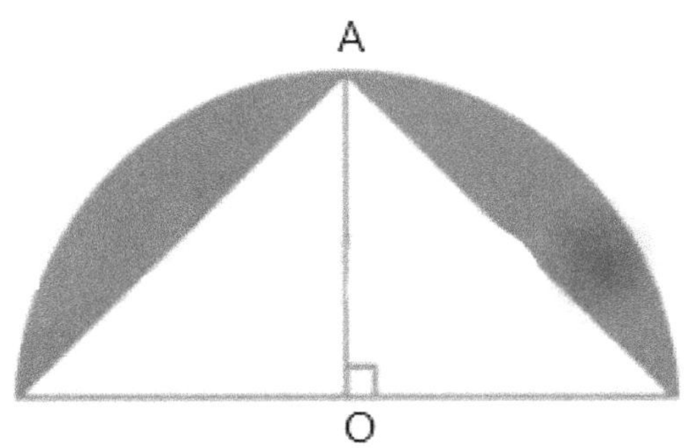

A. 21 cm   **B.** 28 cm   **C.** 14 cm   **D.** 7 cm

Ques (90-92):Direction: There are four jumbled sentences given below. Select the option that gives their correct order.

Q.90 A: This quantity, called the Long Period Average (LPA), is a mean of monsoon rainfall from 1961-2010.

B: The India Meteorological Department (IMD) has forecast a 'normal' monsoon for this year.

C: The IMD, for over 20 years now, follows a two-stage monsoon forecast system. After the prognosis in April, it gives an updated estimate in late May or early June.

D: In the agency's parlance, normal implies that the country will get 96% to 104% of the 88 cm that it gets from June-September.

[NCHM JEE (Hotel Mgmt & Catering), 2016]

A. CADB   **B.** BDAC   **C.** CBAD   **D.** BCAD

Q.91 A: The lion was struggling to get out and started to whimper.

B: They tied him up against a tree.

C: Soon, the mouse walked and noticed the lion in trouble and he helped him.

D: One day, a few hunters came into the forest and took the lion with them.

[NCHM JEE (Hotel Mgmt & Catering), 2016]

A. DBAC   **B.** DCBA   **C.** BACD   **D.** DABC

Q.92 A: It is responsible for the issue and supply of the Indian rupee and the regulation of the Indian banking system.

B: RBI is India's central bank and regulatory body under the jurisdiction of Ministry of Finance , Government of India.

C: Its top official is designated as Governor who is a civil servant of the IAS or IES or ISS cadre.

D: It also manages the country's main payment systems and works to promote its economic development.

[NCHM JEE (Hotel Mgmt & Catering), 2016]

A. BCDA   **B.** BDAC   **C.** DCBA   **D.** BADC

Q.93 Functional theory of stratification propounded by

______________.

A. Davis and Parsons   **B.** Parsons and Ross
C. Davis and Moore   **D.** Goode and Hatt

Q.94 What is meant by sex-ratio?

A. The ratio between number of female and number of male in a population
B. The ratio between the number of adult male and adult females in a population
C. The relation between male and female
D. The number of females per 1000 males in a population

Q.95 The Indian INSET system was established in:
A. 1981   **B.** 1982   **C.** 1983   **D.** 1984

Ques (96-100):Direction: Read the following bar graph carefully and answer the following question.

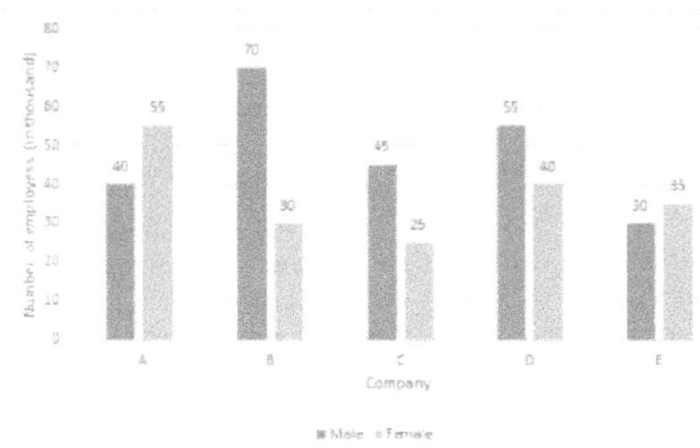

Q.96 Find the difference between the number of male employees and female employees of five companies.
A. 50000   **B.** 61000   **C.** 51000   **D.** 55000

Q.97 Find the male employees of company D are approximately what percent of total male employees of five companies?
A. 29%   **B.** 28%   **C.** 30%   **D.** 23%

Q.98 Find the average number of employees in the five companies.
A. 88000   **B.** 85000   **C.** 81000   **D.** 80000

Q.99 Find the number of female employees of a company E is approximately what percent less than the total employees of the same company?
A. 46%   **B.** 49%   **C.** 41%   **D.** 40%

Q.100 Find the ratio between the number of total employees of company B and C.

A. 1 : 5   **B.** 7 : 3   **C.** 5 : 4   **D.** 10 : 7

// Smart Answer Sheet //

Correct — Percentage of students who answered correctly.   **Skipped** — Percentage of students who skipped.

Q.	Ans.	Correct / Skipped	Q.	Ans.	Correct / Skipped	Q.	Ans.	Correct / Skipped	Q.	Ans.	Correct / Skipped	Q.	Ans.	Correct / Skipped	Q.	Ans.	Correct / Skipped
1	D	66.77 % / 1.44 %	18	B	76.52 % / 0.0 %	35	B	45.77 % / 1.81 %	52	D	61.91 % / 1.71 %	69	A	30.93 % / 4.69 %	86	A	66.41 % / 1.79 %
2	D	31.86 % / 3.54 %	19	C	79.04 % / 0.0 %	36	C	86.18 % / 0.0 %	53	A	83.61 % / 0.0 %	70	B	78.85 % / 0.0 %	87	A	86.66 % / 0.0 %
3	A	63.02 % / 1.68 %	20	B	50.15 % / 1.87 %	37	C	69.93 % / 1.45 %	54	A	61.07 % / 1.85 %	71	B	88.46 % / 0.0 %	88	D	43.59 % / 1.71 %
4	A	56.58 % / 1.12 %	21	D	63.49 % / 1.29 %	38	B	79.98 % / 0.0 %	55	C	89.0 % / 0.0 %	72	D	84.3 % / 0.0 %	89	B	43.91 % / 1.45 %
5	C	11.68 % / 4.78 %	22	B	86.1 % / 0.0 %	39	A	27.0 % / 4.59 %	56	B	64.78 % / 1.25 %	73	B	89.68 % / 0.0 %	90	B	46.21 % / 1.31 %
6	B	68.61 % / 1.55 %	23	A	64.67 % / 1.56 %	40	B	66.84 % / 1.53 %	57	A	58.64 % / 1.26 %	74	A	66.12 % / 1.65 %	91	A	69.45 % / 1.1 %
7	C	66.0 % / 1.58 %	24	C	19.14 % / 3.44 %	41	B	82.83 % / 0.0 %	58	D	41.2 % / 1.14 %	75	C	45.79 % / 1.11 %	92	D	64.14 % / 1.46 %
8	D	41.19 % / 1.52 %	25	B	47.79 % / 1.0 %	42	C	83.94 % / 0.0 %	59	A	51.36 % / 1.8 %	76	C	47.06 % / 1.25 %	93	C	40.11 % / 1.27 %
9	A	77.55 % / 0.0 %	26	D	57.86 % / 1.65 %	43	B	86.19 % / 0.0 %	60	A	63.88 % / 1.04 %	77	A	45.0 % / 1.7 %	94	D	80.37 % / 0.0 %
10	D	79.86 % / 0.0 %	27	C	62.08 % / 1.88 %	44	D	16.27 % / 4.34 %	61	B	55.93 % / 1.44 %	78	B	68.78 % / 1.71 %	95	C	53.41 % / 1.69 %
11	B	56.68 % / 1.12 %	28	D	86.88 % / 0.0 %	45	D	25.44 % / 3.58 %	62	B	88.99 % / 0.0 %	79	A	56.45 % / 1.59 %	96	D	88.0 % / 0.0 %
12	B	82.23 % / 0.0 %	29	B	84.16 % / 0.0 %	46	D	23.8 % / 4.26 %	63	C	89.1 % / 0.0 %	80	C	60.32 % / 1.5 %	97	D	64.13 % / 1.1 %
13	A	68.76 % / 1.29 %	30	A	54.95 % / 1.35 %	47	D	24.93 % / 3.03 %	64	A	83.88 % / 0.0 %	81	B	68.58 % / 1.51 %	98	B	51.12 % / 1.95 %
14	A	12.68 % / 4.97 %	31	C	65.43 % / 1.25 %	48	A	28.78 % / 4.31 %	65	B	86.02 % / 0.0 %	82	B	83.87 % / 0.0 %	99	A	41.78 % / 1.95 %
15	C	82.64 % / 0.0 %	32	D	85.29 % / 0.0 %	49	A	41.25 % / 1.49 %	66	D	47.98 % / 1.4 %	83	D	55.1 % / 1.83 %	100	D	52.98 % / 1.39 %
16	A	78.29 % / 0.0 %	33	D	45.67 % / 1.37 %	50	A	22.4 % / 3.07 %	67	D	63.09 % / 1.33 %	84	C	60.06 % / 1.35 %			
17	C	10.07 % / 3.62 %	34	B	57.65 % / 1.34 %	51	D	48.74 % / 1.15 %	68	D	86.67 % / 0.0 %	85	A	48.05 % / 1.29 %			

//Hints and Solutions//

1. As on March 2018, Pratyush is the India's fastest supercomputer.

Pratyush is set up at the Indian Institute of Tropical Meteorology (IITM) in Pune and is used for weather and climate predictions.

India's most powerful supercomputer Pratyush, the first multi-petaflop device in the country which is being used to improve weather and climate predictions, has made it to the 39th spot on the Top 500 List of supercomputers in the world.

- The 4 petaflop supercomputer has improved India's ranking in the list from high 300s to under 50 for the first time.
- One petaflop is a million billion floating-point operations per second and is a reflection of the computing capacity of a system
- Pratyush will be used to do more accurate weather and climate forecasting, including the all-important monsoon predictions.

Hence, the correct option is (D).

2. Satyendra Prakash has been appointed as the Principal Director General of the Press Information Bureau (PIB) in August 2022.

He is an Indian Information Service officer of the 1988 batch. He succeeded Jaideep Bhatnagar who superannuated on 31 July 2022. Prior to this, Mr Prakash held the position of Principal DG, Central Bureau of Communication.

Hence, the correct option is (D).

3. Patna has the only Genome Sequencing Lab of the state started. Bihar's first and only genome-sequencing facility at Patna-based Indira Gandhi Institute of Medical Sciences (IGIMS), has become non-operational since last week due to a lack of reagents. No samples are being tested in the state at the moment to ascertain the omicron variant of COVID- 19.

Hence, the correct option is (A).

4. The India Global Forum (IGF) at Bengaluru was held on 7th and 8th March 2022.

IGF is the agenda-setting forum for international business and global leaders.

Minister of State for Skill Development and Entrepreneurship Mr Rajeev Chandrasekhar will be taking part in it.

This is the first ever edition of IGF at Bengaluru. The previous editions were hosted at Dubai and UK.

Hence, the correct option is (A).

5. The meaning of the given idiom **to be at one's finger's end** is **to be completely conversant with.**

To be at one's finger's end means within one's range of skills or knowledge.

Example: Every solution should **be at one's finger's end** to qualify for this exam.

Hence, the correct option is (C).

6. The meaning of the given idiom **elbow room** is **to give enough space to move or work in**.

Elbow room means adequate space to move or work in.

Example: At first the management gave the new director plenty of **elbow room**.

Hence, the correct option is (B).

7. Major Somnath Sharma was the first recipient of Paramvir Chakra from the 44th Battalion Kumaon Regiment.

The Param Vir Chakra is India's highest wartime gallantry award. The medal of the Param Vir Chakra was designed by Savitri Khanolkar. The Param Vir Chakra is India's highest military decoration, awarded for displaying distinguished acts of valour during wartime. Param Vir Chakra was introduced on 26th January 1950 and with effect from 15 August 1947.

Hence, the correct option is (C).

8. The real name of the poet 'Gumani' was Gumani Pant.

Gumani Pant was a poet in the court of Kashipur, knowledgeable in the Sanskrit and Hindi poems. He was also known as the first poet of Kumaoni and Nepali. He was also considered to be the first poet to recite or write poems in Khadi Boli. He was the one who started the tradition of Khadi Boli poems and introduce Kumaoni poem in the central plains proving him to be an ancient Kurmanchal poet.

Hence, the correct option is (D).

9. Given:

$$\frac{x}{\sqrt{128}} = \frac{\sqrt{162}}{x}$$

Then $x^2 = \sqrt{128 \times 162}$

$$= \sqrt{64 \times 2 \times 18 \times 9}$$

$$= \sqrt{8^2 \times 6^2 \times 3^2}$$

$$= 8 \times 6 \times 3$$

$$= 144$$

$$\therefore \quad x = \sqrt{144} = 12$$

Hence, the correct option is (A).

10. Given:

$$\sqrt{10 + \sqrt{25 + \sqrt{121}}}$$

$$= \sqrt{10 + \sqrt{15 + 11}}$$

$$= \sqrt{10 + 6} = \sqrt{16} = 4$$

Hence, the correct option is (D).

11. Mean of n elements $= \dfrac{\text{Sum of all } n \text{ elements}}{\text{Total number of elements (n)}}$

Sum of the series $x_1, x_2, x_3 \ldots \ldots, x_n$ is given $= k$

$$x_1 + x_2 + x_3 \ldots \ldots + x_n = k$$

Sum of the series $ax_1, ax_2, ax_3 \ldots \ldots, ax_n$

$$S = ax_1 + ax_2 + ax_3 \ldots \ldots + ax_n$$

$$\Rightarrow S = a(x_1 + x_2 + x_3 \ldots \ldots + x_n)$$

$$\Rightarrow S = ak$$

Now the mean of the series $ax_1, ax_2, ax_3 \ldots \ldots, ax_n$

$$M = \frac{S}{n}$$

$$\Rightarrow M = \frac{ak}{n}$$

Hence, the correct option is (B).

12. Given:

Median = 7 and Mean = 5

Mode = 3(Median) − 2(Mean)

Mode = 3 × 7 − 2 × 5

= 11

∴ The mode is 11.

Hence, the correct option is (B).

13. Evaluation refers to a process of making value judgments based on both qualitative and quantitative data collected over a period of time. CCE describes two different types of evaluation which include 'formative' and 'summative' evaluation.

'Formative evaluation' is a type of evaluation which refers to monitor the child's progress throughout the teaching-learning process. Oral testing, anecdotal records, portfolios, class test, etc are the tools of formative evaluation.

Hence, the correct option is (A).

14. Cronbach classified personnel selection tests into two broad categories, **tests of maximum and tests of typical performance**. Organizations will run performance, tests in order to identify performance-related bottlenecks.

Statement I: Maximum performance tests are designed to assess the upper limits of the examinee's knowledge and abilities.

Maximum performance is how one performs when exerting as much effort as possible. The distinguishing feature of maximum performance tests is that they seek to assess how much or how well people can perform at their best. Hence, candidates are encouraged to do well in order to earn the best score, they can.

Maximum job performance occurs when people know that their performance is being evaluated when they receive instructions to exert great effort, and when the duration of the assessment is short enough to enable performers to remain focused on the task. Thus, maximum performance tests are designed to assess the upper limits of the examinee's knowledge and abilities.

Hence, the correct option is (A).

15. The sum of n terms of an AP with first term a and common difference d is given by:

$$S_n = \frac{n}{2} \times [2a + (n-1)d]$$

Given: 1 + 3 + 5 + 7 + ...

The series is an AP series.

For the given AP series first term is a = 1 and the common difference is d = 2.

As we know that,

$$S_n = \frac{n}{2} \times [2a + (n-1)d]$$

By substituting a = 1 and d = 2 in the above equation we get

$$\Rightarrow S_n = \frac{n}{2}[2 \times 1 + (n-1) \times 2]$$

$$\therefore S_n = \frac{n}{2}[2 + 2n - 2] = \frac{n}{2} \times 2n = n^2$$

Hence, the correct option is (C).

16. As we know, root of 625 = 25 and root of 484 = 22

So, $\sqrt{625} + \sqrt{484}$

$\Rightarrow$ 25 + 22

$\Rightarrow$ 47

Hence, the correct option is (A).

17. It was founded in 1934, in Bombay, by Jaiprakash Narayan, Minoo Masaani, Ram Manohar Lohia and Acharya Narendra Dev. From the beginning, all the Congress Socialists were agreed upon basic propositions:

That the primary struggle in India was the national struggle for freedom and that nationalism was a necessary stage on the way to socialism, that socialists must work inside the National Congress because it was the primary body leading the national struggle. That to achieve this objective they must organize the workers and peasants in their class organizations, wage struggles for their economic demands and make them the social base of the national struggle.

Hence, the correct option is (C).

18. The word 'absently' means lost in thought and unaware of one's surroundings or actions.

The word 'alertly' means the state of being constantly attentive and responsive to signs of opportunity, activity, or danger.

Thus, we can say that 'alertly' is the opposite in meaning to the given word.

Hence, the correct option is (B).

19. The word 'educated' means having or displaying advanced knowledge or education.

The word 'ignorant' means lacking knowledge or awareness in general; uneducated or unsophisticated.

Thus, we can say that 'ignorant' is the opposite in meaning to the given word.

Hence, the correct option is (C).

20. The preposition 'in' is used for showing when something happens.

Complete Sentence: Simulations of the 20th century by climate models that exclude the observed increase in greenhouse gases fail to simulate the increase in temperature over the second half of the 20th century.

Hence, the correct option is (B).

21. The preposition 'at' is used while referring to someone's age.

Complete Sentence: In extremely poor societies, children can be put to work at a young age and are therefore a source of income.

Hence, the correct option is (D).

22. The preposition 'to' is used when someone is affected by something.

Complete Sentence: People who are averse to hard work, generally do not succeed in life.

Hence, the correct option is (B).

23. The error is in part (A) of the sentence. "These days" indicates that the sentence is about the present situation, therefore, the sentence should be written in the present tense.

Replace "was" by "is" Or change "these days" to "those days" if want to keep the sentence in the past tense.

Hence, the correct option is (A).

24. It is given that,

Both p and q belong to the set {1, 2, 3, 4} and the quadratic equation of the form, $px^2 + qx + 1 = 0$ has real roots.

By comparing the quadratic equation of the form, $px^2 + qx + 1 = 0$ with the standard quadratic equation $ax^2 + bx + c = 0$. We get, $a = p, b = q$ and $c = 1$.

Now, we know that.

Discriminant (D) = $b^2 - 4ac$

Therefore, according to the question,

$D = q^2 - 4p$

∵ The roots are real.

⇒ $D \geq 0 \Rightarrow q^2 - 4p \geq 0$

⇒ $q^2 \geq 4p$

∵ p and q belong to the set {1, 2, 3, 4}

Case -1:

If p = 1 then $q^2 \geq 4 \Rightarrow q \in$ {2, 3, 4}

Hence, for p = 1, q can take 3 values.

So, three quadratic equation of the form, $px^2 + qx + 1 = 0$ can be formed for p = 1.

Case -2:

If p = 2 then $q^2 \geq 8 \Rightarrow q \in$ {3, 4}

Hence, for p = 2, q can take 2 values

So, two quadratic equation of the form, $px^2 + qx + 1 = 0$ can be formed for p = 2.

Case -3:

If p = 3 then $q^2 \geq 12 \Rightarrow q \in$ {4}

Hence, for p =1, q can take 1 value

So, only one quadratic equation of the form, $px^2 + qx + 1 = 0$ can be formed for p = 3.

Case -4:

If p = 4 then $q^2 \geq 16 \Rightarrow q \in$ {4}

Hence, for p =4 , q can take 1 value

So, only one quadratic equation of the form, $px^2 + qx + 1 = 0$ can be formed for p = 4.

So, in total we get, 3 + 2 + 1 + 1 = 7 possible quadratic equations of the form $px^2 + qx + 1 = 0$ that can be formed such that both p and q belong to the set {1, 2, 3, 4} and have real roots.

Hence, the correct option is (C).

25. Given,

$$x = 3 + 2\sqrt{2}$$

$$\Rightarrow x = 2 + 1 + 2\sqrt{2}$$

$$\Rightarrow x = \left(\sqrt{2} + 1\right)^2$$

$$\Rightarrow \sqrt{x} = \sqrt{2} + 1$$

$$\Rightarrow \frac{1}{\sqrt{x}} = \frac{1}{\sqrt{2}+1}$$

$$\Rightarrow \frac{1}{\sqrt{x}} = \frac{1}{\sqrt{2}+1} \times \frac{\sqrt{2}-1}{\sqrt{2}-1}$$

$$\Rightarrow \frac{1}{\sqrt{x}} = \sqrt{2} - 1$$

$$\therefore \sqrt{x} - \frac{1}{\sqrt{x}}$$

$$= \sqrt{2} + 1 - \left(\sqrt{2} - 1\right)$$

$$= \sqrt{2} + 1 - \sqrt{2} + 1$$

$$= 2$$

Hence, the correct option is (B).

26. The "Cathedral city of India" as Bhubaneswar is known, was once the capital of an ancient Kalinga kingdom.

The modern capital of Orissa is Bhubaneswar, which means "Lord of the Universe." Tribuhuvaneswara, or "Lord of the Three Worlds," is Shiva's name here, and the city gets its name from him. Bhubaneswar used to be home to over 7,000 shrines. Along with the holy city of Puri and Konark, the city is an important part of the Golden Triangle.

Hence, the correct option is (D).

27. Zat and Sawar are related to the Mansabdari administrative system.

Mansabdar was a military unit introduced by Akbar. It means position or rank. The mansab had dual representation, one was cavalry rank called sawar, while the other was personal rank called zat.

Hence, the correct option is (C).

28. Measurement of an object is done to quantify its shape, size, perimeter, area, etc. to get an exact idea about its attributes.

The teacher should first introduce the non-standardized measures at the primary level as children to some extent are familiar with them and can relate to them easily.

Hence, the correct option is (D).

29. Mathematics is the study of numbers, shape, quantity, and patterns. The nature of mathematics is logical and it relies on logic and connects learning with children day to day life.

Hence, the correct option is (B).

30. Skardo is the winter capital of Ladakh.

Skardo is a place in the Gilgit - Baltistan region(Currently occupied by Pakistan) It serves as an important gateway to the eight-thousanders of Karakoram mountain range The term "Skardo" refers to "a low land between two high places." The area of this district is 77 Km sq The region has a cold semi-arid climate. The Skardo fort was built by King Ali Sher Khan Anchan. The fort is also called as "Kharphocho fort". The fort has a similar design as of Leh Palace.

Hence, the correct option is (A).

31. $1111111111 = 111000000 + 111000 + 111$

$$= \frac{111111111}{111}$$

$$= \frac{111000000}{111} + \frac{111000}{111} + \frac{111}{111}$$

$$= 1000000 + 1000 + 1$$

$$= 1001001$$

Hence, the correct option is (C).

32. Given:

The HCF of two numbers is 6 and their LCM is 432.

Formula Used:

product of the numbers = LCM $\times$ HCF

Let the other number be 'x'

$\Rightarrow 6 \times 432 = 48 \times x$

$\Rightarrow x = 54$

$\therefore$ the other number is 54.

Hence, the correct option is (D).

33. 'Golden Threshold' is a collection of poems written by Sarojini Naidu.

The heritage home was named 'Golden Threshold' after Sarojini Naidu's debut eponymous book of poetry published in 1905. The Golden Threshold is an off-campus annexe of the University of Hyderabad. It is named after the renowned Indian poet and political leader Sarojini Naidu's eponymous first collection of poems.

Hence, the correct option is (D).

34. India is the most populous country among the SAARC nations but as per the options given in the question, Pakistan is the most populous country which has population of 200,813,818 in 2018.

Hence, the correct option is (B).

35. Kathmandu is the headquarters of the SAARC.

SAARC was founded in Dhaka on 8 December 1985. Its secretariat is based in Kathmandu (Nepal). The SAARC Secretariat was established in Kathmandu on 16 January 1987 and was inaugurated by Late King Birendra Bir Bikram Shah of Nepal.

Hence, the correct option is (B).

36. The diagonal of a square $=$ side $\times \sqrt{2}$

$\Rightarrow 24 =$ side $\times \sqrt{2}$

$\Rightarrow$ Side $= 12\sqrt{2}\ cm$

Perimeter of the square $= 4 \times$ side $= 4 \times 12\sqrt{2} = 48\sqrt{2}\ cm$

$\therefore$ The perimeter of the square is $48\sqrt{2}\ cm.$

Hence, the correct option is (C).

37. Volume of cube $=$ Volume of sheet $= (27 \times 8 \times 1)cm^3 = 216\ cm^3$

Edge of cube:

$\sqrt[3]{216}\ cm = 6\ cm$

Surface area of sheet:

$= 2(lb + bh + lh)$

$= 2(27 \times 8 + 8 \times 1 + 27 \times 1)cm^2$

$= (216 + 8 + 27)cm^2$

$= 502\ cm^2$

Surface area of cube:

$= 6a^2$

$= (6 \times 6^2)cm^2$

$= 216\ cm^2$

∴ Required difference,

$$= (502 - 216)cm^2$$

$$= 286 \ cm^2$$

Hence, the correct option is (C).

38. Let their edges be a and b Then, $\dfrac{a^3}{b^3} = \dfrac{8}{27}$

$$\Rightarrow \left(\dfrac{a}{b}\right)^3 = \left(\dfrac{2}{3}\right)^3$$

$$\Rightarrow \dfrac{a}{b} = \dfrac{2}{3}$$

$$\Rightarrow \dfrac{a^2}{b^2} = \dfrac{4}{9}$$

$$\Rightarrow \dfrac{6a^2}{6b^2} = \dfrac{4}{9} \text{ Or } 4:9$$

Hence, the correct option is (B).

39. Given,

Marked price of shirt = Rs. 100

discount $= 10\%$ of marked price

$$= \dfrac{10}{100} \times 100$$

$$= \text{Rs. } 10$$

Marked price of trouser $= \text{Rs. } 300$

discount on trouser $= 20\%$ of marked price

$$= \dfrac{20}{100} \times 300$$

$$= \text{Rs. } 60$$

The Marked price of 3 trouser $= \text{Rs. } 900$

So, total discount on trouser $= \text{Rs. } 180$

total Marked price $= (900 + 100)$

$$= 1000$$

Hence, total Discount $= (180 + 10)$

So, discount $\% = \dfrac{190}{1000} \times 100$

$$= 19\%$$

Therefore, the effective discount will be 19%.

Hence, the correct option is (A).

40. Article 151 Audit Reports:

(1) The reports of the Comptroller and Auditor-General of India relating to the accounts of the Union shall be submitted to the president, who shall cause them to be laid before each House of Parliament.

(2) The reports of the Comptroller and Auditor-General of India relating to the accounts of a State shall be submitted to the Governor of the State, who shall cause them to be laid before the Legislature of the State.

Hence, the correct option is (B).

41. Article 61 article speaks about impeachment of the President of India.

As per Article 61, President of India can be impeached on ground of violation of the Constitution. However what amounts to violation of the Constitution has not been defined. The process of impeachment can begin in any of Lok Sabha or Rajya Sabha. The charges for impeachment should be signed by 1/4 members of the house in which the process begins and a notice of 14 days should be given to the President. The impeachment bill has to be passed by majority of not less than two-thirds of the total membership of the House (special majority). One passed in that house, the bill reaches to another house, which shall investigate the charges. President has right to appear and be represented in case of such investigations. If other house also sustains those charges, then it would again need to pass the bill by special majority and thus president stands removed from the office on which the bill is passed in other house. Since it is a bill for removal of president himself, no presidential assent is needed here.

Hence, the correct option is (B).

42. Martyr's Day is celebrated on January 30.

Martyrs' Day is celebrated in India to honor the victims who fought for freedom. Fifteen countries in the world including India, celebrate **Martyr's Day** to pay homage to their freedom fighters.

Hence, the correct option is (C).

43. 7 May is celebrated as the birthday of Nobel laureate Rabindranath Tagore.

Every year May 7 is celebrated as Rabindranath Tagore Jayanti, the day falling on the 25th day of the Bengali month of Baisakh. The great Indian Bahugya (man) was born on this day on 7 May 1861 and was a Bengali polymath - poet, writer, playwright, musician, philosopher, social reformer and painter.

Hence, the correct option is (B).

44. "Almost 40 percent of people who participated in the poll were females."

It is clear that the participation of females is less than that of the males in the survey conducted by Local Circles to find out the opinion of the passengers regarding the railways services in the country.

Among the given options, option (A) is not correct since it does not follow from the passage whereas options (B) and (C) can be eliminated based on the same logic. Only option (D) is correct with reference to the participation of the females in the said survey.

Hence, the correct option is (D).

45. "On punctuality of trains, 66 percent of 8,122 people who took the poll during the last 12 months said the trains were delayed by upto one hour."

It is clear from the above lines that according to the results of the said survey, the trains are now running late as observed and experienced by the passengers.

Among the given options, option (D) is only correct since others do not follow from the given passage.

Hence, the correct option is (D).

46. "From the 7,739 people who voted on the question "how has cleanliness of trains and railway stations improved in last 12 months", about four-fifth felt there was an improvement. Specifically, 39 per cent felt there was marginal improvement, 38 per cent voted for "significant improvement". Over a fifth (23 percent) of train customers felt there was no improvement, including five per cent who felt the cleanliness of trains and stations have worsened."

It is clear from the above lines that most of the people who voted in the survey felt that there is a sense of improvement in the level of cleanliness in the trains run by the Indian Railways whereas very few felt that there was no improvement in the level of cleanliness, rather the same had deteriorated in the past year.

Among the given options, it is very clear that only option (D) can be considered since it describes the proper results of voting with regard to the cleanliness in the trains run by Indian Railways.

Hence, the correct option is (D).

47. "Tatkal fares have become "excessive", said almost three-fourth (74 per cent) of the 8,165 people who answered a query on their experience with Tatkal ticket fares on Local Circles, a citizen interaction platform. Almost one-fifth polled found the charges "reasonable". Five per cent even found the charges "quite low".

It is quite clear that only 5% candidates have given the opinion that the tatkal fares in the railways are very low.

Among the given options, only option (D) is correct since it gives the correct data regarding the results of the survey.

Hence, the correct option is (D).

48. The word **dynamic** has been used in order to imply that there is a changing component in the pricing of tickets in case of tatkal tickets in the Indian Railways. This forms that changing part of the ticket price.

Among the given options, changing means the same as the word used in the passage whereas others are similar in meaning to the given word but not for this given context. Therefore they can be eliminated.

Hence, the correct option is (A).

49. On 30 December 1949, he became independent India's first recipient of the Mahavir Chakra.

On 21st October 1947, the Jammu & Kashmir State Forces were ordered to fight and push back thousands of Pakistani raiders all along its borders. The small troop with limited ammunitions sans

any road communication, they fought the raiders tenaciously. Kohla-Domel garrison fell to the invaders the following day. Brigadier Singh, the Chief of Military Staff, lead a column to fight the invaders. Maharaja Hari Singh, meanwhile, ordered a further troop of 100 to assist Brigadier Singh. He had to hold off the raiders till help came after 4 days. He defended and saved the Uri-Rampur sector with the help of the Indian Army, but not without sacrificing his life in the process.

Hence, the correct option is (A).

50. One Nation-One Ration Card (ONORC) Scheme:

- 'One Nation, One Ration Card' scheme of the Union Government is being implemented by 32 States and Union Territories, reaching about 69 crore beneficiaries, said Finance Minister Nirmala Sitharaman in a Budget speech.

- It was started as inter-State portability of ration cards by the Ministry of Consumer Affairs, Food and Public Distribution in 2019. So, statement 1 is correct.

- It allows any National Food Security Act (NFSA), 2013 beneficiaries to lift their entitled quota of food grains from any Fair Price Shop (FPS) of their choice anywhere in the country. Hence, statement 2 is correct.

- This can be done by using their existing ration card with Aadhaar based authentication.

- A migrant will be allowed to buy a maximum of 50% of the family quota from the PDS store. So, statement 3 is incorrect.

- It will bring more transparency and efficiency in the distribution of foodgrains.

- The scheme will ensure the food security of migrant labourers who move to other states to seek better job opportunities.

- This will help achieve the target set under Sustainable Developmental Goals (SDG) 2 of ending hunger by 2030.

Hence, the correct option is (A).

51. Seaweed Farming:

In Budget 2021, the Finance Minister has proposed to set up a multi-purpose seaweed park in Tamil Nadu. It will be a part of the Seaweed Farming promotion in India.

Seaweed: It is the name given to the many species of marine algae and plants. These species grow in water bodies such as rivers, seas and oceans. The practice of cultivating and harvesting seaweed is known as Seaweed Farming.

Seaweed Species in India: The commercially exploited seaweed species in India mainly include Kappaphycus alvarezii, Gracilaria edulis, Gelidiella acerosa, Sargassum spp. and Turbinaria spp. So, statements 1, 2, 3 and 4 are correct.

Hence, the correct option is (D).

52. As we know,

If someone completes a work in n days.

Then, work done in one day $= \left(\frac{1}{n}\right)$ part of the whole work

Work done by A in one day $= \left(\frac{1}{9}\right)$

Work done by B in one day $= \left(\frac{1}{12}\right)$

And, Work done by C in one day $= \left(\frac{1}{18}\right)$

So, work done by $(A + B + C)$ in one day $=$ $\left(\frac{1}{9} + \frac{1}{12} + \frac{1}{18}\right)$

$= \frac{4+3+2}{36} = \frac{9}{36}$

Time taken by A, B and C to complete the work $=$

$$\frac{1}{\text{work done by } (A+B+C) \text{ in one day}}$$

$= \frac{1}{\left(\frac{9}{36}\right)}$ days

$= \frac{36}{9}$ days

$= 4$ days

$\therefore A, B$ and C together can complete the work in 4 days.

Hence, the correct option is (D).

53. Given,

A can complete a work in 60 days.

B can complete the same work in 15 days.

As we know,

If someone completes a work in n days.

then work done in one day $= \frac{1}{n}$ part of the total work

Work done by A in one day $= \left(\frac{1}{60}\right)$ part of the work

Work done by B in one day $= \left(\frac{1}{15}\right)$ part of the work

So, work done by $(A + B)$ in one day $= [\left(\frac{1}{40}\right) + \left(\frac{1}{15}\right) =$ $\frac{(1+4)}{60} = \frac{5}{60}]$ part of the work

Time taken by both A, B to complete the work $= \left(\frac{1}{(A+B)}\right)$ days

$= \frac{1}{\left(\frac{5}{60}\right)}$

$= \frac{60}{5}$

$= 12$ days

$\therefore A$ and B together can complete the work in 12 days.

Hence, the correct option is (A).

54. Given equation is $x^2 - 2x + 1 = 0$

$(a + b)^3 = a^3 + b^3 + 3ab(a + b)$

According to the question, we have

$$x^2 - 2x + 1 = 0$$

After dividing equation by x, we get

$\Rightarrow x - 2 + \left(\frac{1}{x}\right) = 0$

$\Rightarrow x + \left(\frac{1}{x}\right) = 2$

After cubing both sides, we get

$\Rightarrow \left\{x + \left(\frac{1}{x}\right)\right\}^3 = (2)^3$

$\Rightarrow x^3 + \left(\frac{1}{x^3}\right) + 3x\left(\frac{1}{x}\right)\left\{x + \left(\frac{1}{x}\right)\right\} = 8$

$\Rightarrow x^3 + \left(\frac{1}{x^3}\right) + 3\left\{x + \left(\frac{1}{x}\right)\right\} = 8$

$\Rightarrow x^3 + \left(\frac{1}{x^3}\right) + 3(2) = 8$

$\Rightarrow x^3 + \left(\frac{1}{x^3}\right) = 8 - 6$

$\Rightarrow x^3 + \left(\frac{1}{x^3}\right) = 2$

$\therefore$ The value of $x^3 + \left(\frac{1}{x^3}\right)$ is 2.

Hence, the correct option is (A).

55. Given,

$= \dfrac{\frac{3}{2+\sqrt{3}} - \frac{2}{2-\sqrt{3}}}{2-5\sqrt{3}}$

$= \dfrac{\frac{3(2-\sqrt{3})-2(2+\sqrt{3})}{(2+\sqrt{3})(2-\sqrt{3})}}{2-5\sqrt{3}}$

$= \dfrac{6-3\sqrt{3}-4-2\sqrt{3}}{(2+\sqrt{3})(2-\sqrt{3})(2-5\sqrt{3})}$

$= \dfrac{2-5\sqrt{3}}{2-5\sqrt{3}}$

$= 1$

Hence, the correct option is (C).

56. The ratio of investments corresponds to the ratio of profits:

A's profit: B's profit: C's profit

$= A : B : C$

$= 380 : 400 : 420$

$= 19 : 20 : 21$

Profit share of $A = \frac{19}{60} \times 180 =$ Rs. 57

Profit share of $B = \frac{20}{60} \times 180 =$ Rs. 60

Profit share of $C = \dfrac{21}{60} \times 180 =$ Rs. 63

Hence, the correct option is (B).

57. The Rigveda is the source of Sanatana Dharma or Hinduism. There are 1028 suktas in which the deities are praised. In this scripture, there are mantras to invoke the Gods in the Yajna. This is the first Veda. The Rigveda is considered by all historians of the world to be the first creation of the Indo-European language-family.

Hence, the correct option is (A).

58. The origin of 'Raag Bhairav' or 'Raag Bhairavi' is believed to be from Chic Bhairavi. In this Re, Ga, Dha, and Ni seem soft and M is considered as a vadi and Sa is a conversational tone. Singing time is morning.

Hence, the correct option is (D).

59. Given:

AH ∥ BG ∥ CF

∠DCH = 55°

Calculation:

CF ∥ AH

⇒ ∠FCD = ∠AED = 55° (Alternate angle)

∠FCD + ∠CDG = 180° (Two parallel lines intersected by transversal line, the sum of interior angle is 180°)

⇒ ∠CDG = 180° - 55°

⇒ ∠CDG = 125°

⇒ ∠CDG = ∠BDE = 125° (Vertical opposite angle)

∠AED : ∠BDE = 55° : 125°

∴ ∠AED : ∠BDE = 11 : 25

Hence, the correct option is (A).

60. Let Tejas has Rs. y and Shreyas has Rs. x.

From given data, we get

⇒ 2 (x - 20) = y + 20

⇒ 2x - 40 = y + 20

⇒ 2x - y = 60   ----(1)

And also x + 15 = 3 (y - 15)

⇒ x - 3 y + 15 + 45 = 0

⇒ x - 3y = - 60

⇒ 2x - 6y = - 120   ----(2)

From equation 1 and equation 2, we get

⇒ x = 48 and y = 36

∴ Shreyas has Rs. 48 and Tejas has Rs. 36

Hence, the correct option is (A).

61. Given

On selling article for Rs 51 more, Vishnu is getting 3% more profit.

Formula

Selling price = Cost price × $\left[\dfrac{(100 + Profit\%)}{100}\right]$

Let CP be 100x.

SP₁ = 100x × $\left(\dfrac{125}{100}\right)$ = 125x

SP₂ = 100x × $\left(\dfrac{128}{100}\right)$ = 128x

According to question

128x - 125x = 51

⇒ 3x = 51

⇒ x = 17

∴ Cost price = 100x = 100 × 17 = 1700.

Hence, the correct option is (B).

62. Given

A number is first decreased by 20% and then increased by 10%. The number so obtained is 12 less than the original number.

Formula used:

X% of Y = Y × $\dfrac{X}{100}$

Suppose the number = X

So,

X × 0.8 × 1.1 = X - 12

⇒ 0.12 × X = 12

⇒ X = 100

Hence, the correct option is (B).

63. Given:

In two successive years, 100 and 200 students of a school appeared at the final examination. Respectively 80% and 60% of them passed.

Formula used:

X% of Y = Y × $\dfrac{X}{100}$

Total number of students appeared in 2 years = 100 + 200 = 300

And

Total number of passed students in 2 years = 100 × 0.8 + 200 × 0.6

= 80 + 120

= 200

So,

Required percentage = $\left[\dfrac{200}{300}\right]$ × 100 = 66.67%

Hence, the correct option is (C).

64. The SI unit of power is Watt.

Power is generally expressed in kilowatts (kW).

Joule - Energy, Ampere - Current, Volt - Potential difference.

Hence, the correct option is (A).

65. Microfarad unit is capacitance measured for day to day applications.

This is because the value of 1 farad is too large to be stored in common capacitors.

Hence, to avoid decimal calculations, Microfarad is more commonly used.

Hence, the correct option is (B).

66. Given that,

$$\dfrac{1}{1+\dfrac{1}{1+\dfrac{1}{1+\dfrac{1}{y}}}} = \dfrac{7}{11}$$

Assuming from options,

Assuming $y = 3$,

$$\Rightarrow \dfrac{1}{1+\dfrac{1}{1+\dfrac{1}{1+\frac{1}{3}}}}$$

$$= \dfrac{1}{1+\dfrac{1}{1+\frac{1}{3}}}$$

$$= \dfrac{1}{1+\frac{1}{4}}$$

$$= \dfrac{1}{1+\frac{4}{7}} = \dfrac{7}{11}$$

$$\therefore y = 3$$

Alternative solution:

$$\Rightarrow \dfrac{1}{1+\dfrac{1}{1+\frac{y}{y+1}}} = \dfrac{7}{11}$$

$$\Rightarrow \dfrac{1}{1+\frac{y+1}{2y+1}} = \dfrac{7}{11}$$

$$\Rightarrow \dfrac{2y+1}{3y+2} = \dfrac{7}{11}$$

$$\Rightarrow 22y + 11 = 21y + 14$$

$$\therefore y = 3$$

Hence, the correct option is (D).

67. National Mission for Sustainable Agriculture consists of Soil Health Management as one of the sub-missions.

National Mission for Sustainable Agriculture (NMSA):

It is one of the major missions of the National Action Plan on Climate Change (NAPCC). Change in agricultural practices also plays a crucial role in the mitigation of climate change effects. This mission tries to comprehensively revamp the agricultural practices so that the desired objectives of the Nationally Determined Contributions (NDC's) can be achieved.

Hence, the correct option is (D).

68. Let P = principal, R = rate of interest and N = time

Simple Interest $= \dfrac{PNR}{100}$

Given,

$$P = 27000$$

Two sums,

$$27000 \times \dfrac{4}{9} = \text{Rs. } 12000$$

and $27000 \times \dfrac{5}{9} = \text{Rs. } 15000$

Total simple interest earned

$$= \dfrac{(12000 \times 20 \times 4)}{100} + \dfrac{(15000 \times 24 \times 4)}{100}$$

$$= Rs.\, 24000$$

Hence, the correct option is (D).

69. Given:

Principal = Rs. 44,000

Amounts = Rs. 48,510

Time = 2 years

Formula Used:

$$A = P\left[1 + \dfrac{R}{100}\right]^n$$

$$\Rightarrow 48,510 = 44,000\left[1 + \dfrac{R}{100}\right]^2$$

$$\Rightarrow \dfrac{48510}{44000} = \left[\dfrac{(100+R)}{100}\right]^2$$

$$\Rightarrow \dfrac{441}{400} = \left[\dfrac{(100+R)}{100}\right]^2$$

$$\Rightarrow \dfrac{21}{20} = \dfrac{(100+R)}{100}$$

$$\Rightarrow 2,100 = 2,000 + 20R$$

$$\Rightarrow 2100 - 2000 = 20R$$

$$\Rightarrow 100 = 20R$$

$$\therefore R = 5\% \text{ p.a.}$$

Hence, the correct option is (A).

70. Given:

Radius of sphere $= \dfrac{60}{2}$ = 30 mm = 3 cm

Volume of sphere $= \frac{4}{3} \times \pi \times r^3$

Volume of solid sphere $= \frac{4}{3} \times \pi \times 3^3 = 36\pi$ cm³

$\Rightarrow 36\pi = \pi \times r^2 \times 144$

$\Rightarrow$ r = 0.5 cm

Radius of wire = 0.5 cm

∴ Diameter of wire = 2 × 0.5 = 1 cm

Hence, the correct option is (B).

71. Isopleth maps simplify information about a region by showing areas with continuous distribution. Isopleth maps may use lines to show areas where elevation, temperature, rainfall, or some other quality is the same, values between lines can be interpolated.

Hence, the correct option is (B).

72.

- An imaginary line is called as tropic of cancer.
- The tropic of cancer does not pass-through Uttar Pradesh.
- It makes an angle of 23.50 degrees.
- At the north of the equator, there is the tropic of cancer.
- It passes through the middle of the country.
- Through 17 countries, the tropic of cancer passes.
- In India, the tropic of cancer passes through the 8 states.
- The states are- Gujarat, Rajasthan, Madhya Pradesh, Chhattisgarh, Jharkhand, West Bengal, Tripura, and Mizoram.
- Through Mahi River, the River crosses twice.

Hence, the correct option is (D).

73. Eon is the longest duration of geological time.

- Eons are divided into eras, which are in turn divided into periods, epochs, and ages.
- The first three eons (i.e., every eon but the Phanerozoic) can be referred to collectively as the Precambrian supereon.
- Earth's history is characterized by four eons, in order from oldest to youngest, these are the Hadeon, Archean, Proterozoic, and Phanerozoic.
- Collectively, the Hadean, Archean, and Proterozoic are sometimes informally referred to as the "Precambrian."

Hence, the correct option is (B).

74. These terms were mentioned in the news recently to indicate the different the cricket bats used. "The Camel" bat was recently used by Afghanistan's Rashid Khan. Mangoose, Kaboom and Aluminium are some of the other names used to describe different cricket bats.

Hence, the correct option is (A).

75. The ICC Under-19 World Cup 2020 tournament will be hosted by South Africa. Indian U-19 Cricket Team is led by Priyam Garg. India is the defending champion of the U-19 World cup and winner of the championship for four times.

Many IPL 2020-fame players are to play for India, including Yashasvi Jaiswal and Ravi Bishnoi. India's first match is against Sri Lanka on January 19. India is placed in Group A with Sri Lanka, Japan and New Zealand. Recently the India U-19 team has won the U-19 Asia Cup and a Tri-Nations Tournament with Bangladesh and England.

Hence, the correct option is (C).

76. Let the income of A = a

Let the income of B = b

Let the income of C = c

Now according to question,

b = 30 + c _______ (i)

a = 2c _______ (ii)

Average of income of A, B & C according to question = 250

$$\text{Average} = \frac{(\text{Sum total of individual value of n things})}{(\text{total no of things i.e. n})}$$

Here the formula transforms accordingly to

$$\text{Average} = \frac{(sum\ of\ incomes\ of\ A, B, C)}{3}$$

$$250 = \frac{(a+b+c)}{3}$$

$\Rightarrow$ a + b + c = 750 _______ (iii)

Using equations (i), (ii), (iii)

(2c) + (c + 30) + c = 750

$\Rightarrow$ 4c = 720

$\Rightarrow$ c = 180

Daily income of C = 180

Hence, the correct option is (C).

77. According to the information given in the problem, the 4 parts are in the ratio 6 : 7 : 5 : 3, let the four parts be 6x, 7x, 5x and 3x respectively.

∴ 6x + 7x + 5x + 3x = 210

$\Rightarrow$ 21x = 210

$\Rightarrow$ x = $\frac{210}{21}$ = 10

∴ Largest part = 7x = 7 × 10 = 70

Hence, the correct option is (A).

78. Rishabhdeva is considered the first real founder of Jainism.

He is the first Tirthankara in Jainism and is also said to have lived a million years ago.

Hence, the correct option is (B).

79. When glycerol is treated with an excess of HI, it produces 2-iodopropane.

In the first step, a molecule of glycerol reacts with 3 HI molecules to form unstable 1,2,3-triiodopropane. This loses a molecule of iodine to form allyl iodide.

Allyl iodide adds a molecule of HI to obtain an unstable molecule which loses a molecule of iodine to form propene.

A molecule of HI is added to propene to form 2-iodopropane.

Hence, the correct option is (A).

80. The charge size ratio of a cation determines its polarizing power. Higher is the charge and lower is the size, higher will be the charge to size ration and higher will be the polarizing power of the cation. The charge of Kion is $+1$ whereas that of other ions is $+2$.

Thus, K^+ has the lowest polarizing power.

For the remaining ions, the decreasing order of the size is $Ca^{2+} > Mg^{2+} > Be^{2+}$.

Hence, the increasing order of polarizing power is $Ca^{2+} < Mg^{2+} < Be^{2+}$.

Hence, the increasing order of the polarizing power of the cationic species is $K^+ < Ca^{2+} < Mg^{2+} < Be^{2+}$.

Hence, the correct option is (C).

81.

Name of the author	Title of the Book
R.C. Dutt	• Romesh Chandra Dutt, a retired ICS officer, published The Economic History of India at the beginning of the 20th century in which he examined in minute detail the entire economic record of colonial rule since 1757.
Dadabhai Naoroji	• Poverty and Unbritish Rule in India book was written by Dadabhai Naoroji.
W. Digly	• 'Prosperous' British India, more completely titled Prosperous' British India: A Revelation from Official Records, was a book published in 1901 by British author William Digby that described the economic conditions prevailing in British India in the latter half of the nineteenth century under British rule.
V. Anstey	• The Economic Development of India by V. Anstey lucidly explains the journey of the Indian economy pre and post-independence and its gradual transition to a relatively market-friendly economy today.

Hence, the correct option is (B).

82. The atomic nucleus is the small, dense region consisting of protons and neutrons at the center of an atom, discovered in 1911 by Ernest Rutherford based on the 1909 Geiger–Marsden gold foil experiment.

Hence, the correct option is (B).

83. Herpes is an infection caused by the Herpes Simplex Virus.

Herpes can appear in various parts of the body, most commonly on the genitals or mouth. It is a contagious disease that can be passed from person to person through direct contact.

Hence, the correct option is (D).

84. The first railway engine was invented by Richard Trevithick.

In 1802, Richard Trevithick patented a "high-pressure engine" and created the first steam-powered locomotive engine on rails. Trevithick wrote on February 21, 1804, after the trial of his High-Pressure Tram-Engine, that carried ten tons of Iron, five wagons, and seventy Men.

Hence, the correct option is (C).

85. The Hungarian brothers, Laszlo and George Biro made the first ballpoint pen in 1894. It followed the first workable fountain pen which was invented by L.E. Waterman in 1884.

Hence, the correct option is (A).

86. The given sentence is in the active voice. It is a simple to form of present tense. The structures for active/passive voices are:

Active: Subject + verb ("s" or "es" with singular noun) + object

Passive: Object + Is/are/am + verb (IIIrd form) + by + subject

So, based on the above structures, we can convert the given sentence into passive voice:

Milk is contained in this bottle.

Please note that here the verb "contained" will be followed by the preposition "in" and not "by".

Hence, the correct option is (A).

87. The 'Gitanjali' was written by Rabindranath Tagore.

Given sentence is in the simple past tense and it is in active voice, we need to change it into passive voice.

Rule:

Subject + (was / were) + V^3 + Optional Agents.

Hence, the correct option is (A).

88. Suppose 'r' is the diameter of shaded circle;

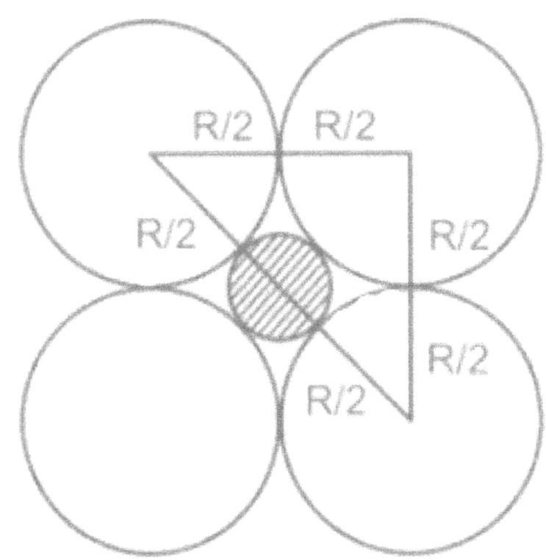

In the figure, O is the centre of the shaded circle;

Observing triangle;

$$\Rightarrow R^2 + R^2 = (R + r)^2$$

$$\Rightarrow 2R^2 = (R + r)^2$$

$$\Rightarrow \sqrt{2}R = (R + r)$$

$$\Rightarrow r = \sqrt{2}R - R$$

$$\Rightarrow r = R(\sqrt{2} - 1)$$

$\therefore$ Diameter of the shaded circle $= R(\sqrt{2} - 1)$

Hence, the correct option is (D).

89.

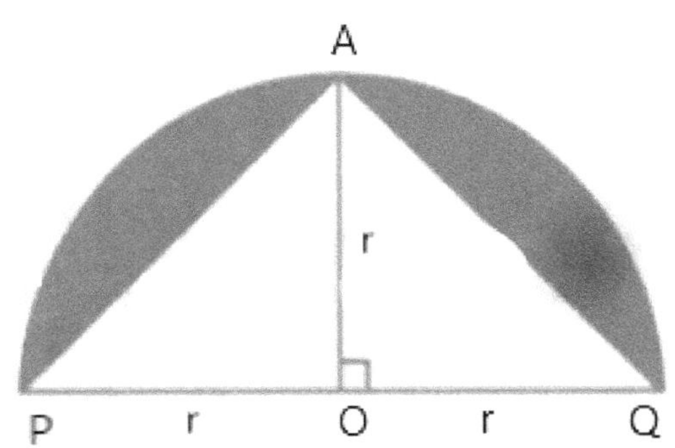

Since O is the centre, PQ must be the diameter.

Area of the semicircle $= \dfrac{\pi r^2}{2}$

As we know,

Area of a triangle $= \dfrac{1}{2} \times$ Height $\times$ Base

From the figure, we can write:

Base, PQ = r + r = 2r

Height, OA = r

Area of the $\triangle PAQ = \dfrac{1}{2} \times$ r $\times$ 2r

$= r^2$

Since the area of shaded region is 112 cm ^{2}.

$$\therefore \frac{\pi r^2}{2} - r^2 = 112$$

$$\Rightarrow \frac{22r^2}{14} - r^2 = 112$$

$$\Rightarrow r = 14$$

$\therefore$ Diameter of the circle $= 28$ cm

Hence, the correct option is (B).

90. Sentence B will be placed at first as it starts the information about IMD, so with it, we can start the paragraph.

Sentence D will be placed at second as it is giving the next information about the forecast of monsoon.

Sentence A follows D, so it will be placed at third as it is giving more information about the previous sentence.

Sentence C will be placed at the last as it is the only sentence of the paragraph.

Thus, the sequence becomes:

B: The India Meteorological Department (IMD) has forecast a 'normal' monsoon for this year.

D: In the agency's parlance, normal implies that the country will get 96% to 104% of the 88 cm that it gets from June-September.

A: This quantity, called the Long Period Average (LPA), is a mean of monsoon rainfall from 1961-2010.

C: The IMD, for over 20 years now, follows a two-stage monsoon forecast system. After the prognosis in April, it gives an updated estimate in late May or early June.

Hence, the correct option is (B).

91. Sentence D will be placed at first as it is independent and starts the story. With it, we can start the paragraph.

Sentence B will be placed at second as it is giving the next information about the paragraph in a chronological way.

Sentence A follows B, so it will be placed at third as it is developing the story of the paragraph.

Sentence C will be placed at the last as it is the conclusion of the paragraph.

Thus, the sequence becomes:

D: One day, a few hunters came into the forest and took the lion with them.

B: They tied him up against a tree.

A: The lion was struggling to get out and started to whimper.

C: Soon, the mouse walked and noticed the lion in trouble and he helped him.

Hence, the correct option is (A).

92. Sentence B will be placed at first as it starts the story. With it, we can start the paragraph.

Sentence A will be placed at second as it is giving the next information about the paragraph.

Sentence D follows A, so it will be placed at third as it is giving further information about the paragraph.

Sentence C will be placed at the last.

Thus, the sequence becomes:

B: RBI is India's central bank and regulatory body under the jurisdiction of Ministry of Finance , Government of India.

A: It is responsible for the issue and supply of the Indian rupee and the regulation of the Indian banking system.

D: It also manages the country's main payment systems and works to promote its economic development.

C: Its top official is designated as Governor who is a civil servant of the IAS or IES or ISS cadre.

Hence, the correct option is (D).

93. Functional theory of stratification propounded by Davis and Moore.

The functional theory of stratification provided by Kingsley Davis and Wilbert Moore suggests that social inequalities are functional for society because they provide an incentive for the most talented individuals to occupy jobs that are essential to the orderly maintenance of a society.

Hence, the correct option is (C).

94. The number of females per 1000 males in a population is known as sex ratio.

Sex ratio defined here as the number of females per 1000 males in the population, is an important social indicator to measure the extent of prevailing equity between males and females in a society at a given point of time.

Hence, the correct option is (D).

95. The Indian INSET system was established in 1983. INSET stands for in-service training.

To assess the adequacy of training inputs including the process of planning, preparation, and content of modules and materials used in training programs. To study the impact of training in terms of change in classroom practices of teachers. To study perceptions of the teachers about the relevance and usefulness of in-service training. To find out the constraints or problems, if any, in using training inputs in classroom transactions. To analyze the opinion of other functionaries such as BRC/CRC coordinators on the impact of teacher training on classroom processes.

Hence, the correct option is (C).

96. Total number of female employees of companies = 55000 + 30000 + 25000 + 40000 + 35000 = 185000

Total number of male employees of companies = 40000 + 70000 + 45000 + 55000 + 30000 = 240000

Required difference = 240000 - 185000 = 55000

Hence, the correct option is (D).

97. Total number of male employees of companies = 40000 + 70000 + 45000 + 55000 + 30000 = 240000

Male employees of a company D = 55000

Required percentage = $\dfrac{55000}{240000} \times 100$

22.91% ≈ 23%

∴ The required percentage is 23%.

Hence, the correct option is (D).

98. Total number of female employees of companies = 55000 + 30000 + 25000 + 40000 + 35000 = 185000

Total number of male employees of companies = 40000 + 70000 + 45000 + 55000 + 30000 = 240000

Total employees in five companies = 185000 + 240000 = 425000

Required average = $\dfrac{425000}{5}$ = 85000

∴ The required average is 85000.

Hence, the correct option is (B).

99. Total employees in a company E = 30000 + 35000 = 65000

Total female employees of a company E = 35000

Required percentage = $\left(\dfrac{65000-35000}{65000}\right) \times 100$

$= \left(\dfrac{30000}{65000}\right) \times 100$

$= \dfrac{30}{65} \times 100$

$= 46.15\% \approx 46\%$

Hence, the correct option is (A).

100. Total number of employees of a company B = 70000 + 30000 = 100000

Total number of employees of a company C = 45000 + 25000 = 70000

Required ratio = 100000 : 70000 = 10 : 7

∴ The ratio between the number of total employees of company B and C is 10 : 7.

Hence, the correct option is (D).

Q.1 The International Financial Services Centres Authority (IFSCA) and __________ has signed an MoU in April 2022.

A. Bajaj Finance Limited

B. Aditya Birla Finance Ltd

C. Muthoot Finance Ltd

D. GVFL Limited

Q.2 The first train was successfully test-fired between which country's railway link from Bihar's Madhubani district?

A. Nepal   **B.** Bhopal

C. Bihar   **D.** Allahabad

Q.3 The winner of US Open Tennis Tournament, 2018 (Women's Singles) was:

[Delhi Forest Guard, 2020], [Super TET Paper - I, 2019]

A. Caroline Wozniacki   **B.** Simona Halep

C. Naomi Osaka   **D.** Serena Williams

Q.4 Which city has been chosen by the Union of European Football Associations (UEFA) as a replacement of St Petersburg for the Champions League 2022 ?

[Delhi Forest Guard, 2021]

A. Paris   **B.** Brussels   **C.** London   **D.** Munich

Q.5 The Panchayats (Extension to Scheduled Areas) Act (PESA) does not authorize the States give the Gram Sabhas power to regulate and restrict which of the following?

A. Sale/consumption of liquor

B. Minor Forest Produce

C. Identify the beneficiary of the schemes

D. Manage mineral resources

Q.6 The Chairman of the Finance Commission is the ex-officio Chairman of:

    1.   Monetary Policy Committee

    2.   Tax Policy Council

    3.   Tax Policy Research Unit (TPRU)

Select the correct answer from options given below:

A. 1 & 3 Only   **B.** 2 Only

C. 2 & 3 Only   **D.** None of the above

Q.7 The difference between SI and CI on an amount of Rs. 20,000 for 2 years is Rs. 150. What is the rate of interest?

A. 7%   **B.** 8%   **C.** 8.66%   **D.** 8.33%

Q.8 All teachers are encouraged to use precise mathematical vocabulary and to promote the use of mathematical vocabulary among pupils. This vocabulary is known as:

[Rajasthan Teachers Eligibility Test - Level 1 Primary Level (RTET), 2017]

A. Language in Mathematics Education

B. Values in Mathematics Education

C. Correlation in Mathematics Education

D. Tools in Mathematics Education

Q.9 Which of the following is NOT true with respect to the learning of Mathematics?

[CTET Paper - I, 2019]

A. Ability to perform and excel in Mathematics is innate

B. Teachers' beliefs about learners have powerful impact on learning outcomes

C. Students' socio-economic background impacts their performance in Mathematics

D. School's language of instruction can impact a child's performance in Mathematics

Ques (10-13):Direction: Given below in the table is the decadal data of Population and Electrical Power Production of a country.

Year	Population (million)	Electrical Power Production (GW)*
1951	20	10
1961	21	20
1971	24	25
1981	27	40
1991	30	50
2001	32	80
2011	35	100
		*1GW=1000 million watt

Q.10 The average decadal growth rate (%) of the population is (approx.):

A. 12.21%   **B.** 9.82%   **C.** 6.73%   **D.** 5%

Q.11 Based on the average decadal growth rate, what will be the population in the year 2021?

A. 40.34 *million*   **B.** 38.44 *million*

C. 37.28 *million*   **D.** 3662 *million*

Q.12 In the year 1951, what was the power availability per person?

A. 100 W **B.** 200 W **C.** 400 W **D.** 500 W

Q.13 In which decade, the average power availability per person was maximum?

A. 1991 **B.** 2001 **C.** 2011 **D.** 1981

Q.14 A, B and C invested Rs. 12600, Rs. 10800 and Rs. 16200 respectively in a business. They invested the respective amount for the same time period. Out of the total profit earned in the business, C received Rs. 16200 as his share. Find the difference between the profits of A and B.

A. Rs. 1500 **B.** Rs. 1800

C. Rs. 2400 **D.** Rs. 2700

Ques (15-17):Direction: In the following question has a sentence with a blank space and four words or groups of words given after the sentence. Select whichever word or group of words you consider most appropriate for the blank space and indicate your response on the Answer Sheet accordingly.

Q.15 The records give us an _________ of how people saw the world.

A. Potent **B.** Omen **C.** Inkling **D.** Alchemy

Q.16 The __________ of a dynasty have been found in an architecture excavation.

A. Sundry **B.** Fluffy **C.** Futile **D.** Remains

Q.17 The necklace I received from my late husband is a loving ______ from my time spent with him.

A. Memento **B.** Momentous
C. Murky **D.** Amorphous

Q.18 Which of the following statements about the Gupta Empire under Samudragupta is not correct?

A. Prayag Prashasti of Samudragupta composed by his court poet Harisena is engraved on an Ashokan pillar at Allahabad.

B. Samudragupta was the first Gupta ruler to have exercised direct administrative control over western and Southern India.

C. Samudragupta carved out an extensive empire which is evident from the fact that he had performed an Asvamedha sacrifice.

D. None of the above

Q.19 Which of the following is a erosional feature by river?

A. Loess **B.** U-shaped valley
C. V-shaped valley **D.** Natural levee

Q.20 Which of the following is true about the Indian ocean currents:

1. It is mostly driven by the monsoon wind
2. Seasonal reversal is found in the northern part
3. Agulhas is a cold current near the east African coast

A. 1,2 and 3 **B.** 1 and 2
C. 2 and 3 **D.** 1and 3

Q.21 The invisible line joins the North pole to the South Pole is called:

A. Meridian **B.** Latitude
C. Equator **D.** Axial plane

Q.22 Three number are in the ratio of 3 : 4 : 5 and their L.C.M. is 2400. Their H.C.F. is:

[NCHM JEE (Hotel Mgmt & Catering), 2019]

A. 40 **B.** 80 **C.** 120 **D.** 200

Q.23 The total number of prime numbers up to 100 is:

A. 25 **B.** 26 **C.** 27 **D.** 28

Q.24 Let P is a prime number such that $P^2 + 7$ are also a prime number then how many such values of P are possible?

A. One **B.** Two **C.** Four **D.** Seven

Q.25 Which one of the following quantities does not have a unit?

A. Velocity **B.** Density
C. Specific Gravity **D.** Stress

Q.26 The substances which have infinite electrical resistance are called ______.

A. Insulators **B.** Condensers
C. Conductors **D.** Resistors

Q.27 Where was 'Kheer Bhavani Mela' 2019 celebrated in India?

A. Manipur
B. West Bengal
C. Jammu and Kashmir
D. Jharkhand

Q.28 Bathukamma Utsav, 2019 was held in which state of India?

A. Arunachal Pradesh **B.** Himachal Pradesh
C. Meghalaya **D.** Telangana

Q.29 Which of the following is NOT correctly matched?

A. Indira Gandhi – Bharat Ratna
B. Mother Teresa – Nobel Laureate
C. Kiran Bedi – Magsaysay Award
D. Ela Bhatt – Pulitzer Prize

Q.30 Who of the following had defined society as union in itself?

A. Giddings **B.** A.W. Green
C. R.M. Maclver **D.** John F. Cuber

Q.31 Direction: In the following question, some part of the sentence may have errors. Find out which part of the sentence has an error and select the appropriate option. If a sentence is free from error, select 'No Error'.

He was too tired that he could not (1) / cross the street even with (2) / the help of a supporter. (3) / No error (4)

A. 1 **B.** 2 **C.** 3 **D.** 4

Q.32 A sold a horse to B for Rs. 3600 by losing 10%. B sold it to C at a price which would have given A a profit of 12%. B's gain is:

A. Rs. 180 **B.** Rs. 190 **C.** Rs. 200 **D.** Rs. 880

Q.33 A car was sold at a gain of 20%. Had it been sold for Rs. $50,000$ more, the gain would have been 25%. The cost price of the car is:

A. Rs. 10 lacs **B.** Rs. 15 lacs
C. Rs. 5 lacs **D.** Rs. 2.5 lacs

Q.34 World Tsunami Awareness Day being observed on _________.

A. 5th november **B.** 6th November
C. 4th November **D.** 3th November

Q.35 When is World Bio-fuel Day (International Biodiesel Day) celebrated every year?

A. August 10 **B.** August 11
C. August 12 **D.** August 13

Q.36 What will come in place of the question mark (?) in the following question?

$$(12)^4 \times (144)^8 \div (24)^3 = (?)^{17} \times 2^{(-3)}$$

A. 18   **B.** 12   **C.** 24   **D.** 6

Q.37 Which of the following was/were the provisions of the Government of India Act, 1935?

1. It proposed an All India Federation.
2. It provided for the abolition of dyarchy at the provincial level.
3. It provided residuary powers to the Viceroy.

Select the correct answer using the code given below.

A. 1 and 2 only   **B.** 2 and 3 only
C. 1 and 3 only   **D.** 1, 2 and 3

Q.38 Which of the following is the Japanese currency?

A. Taka   **B.** Lira   **C.** Mark   **D.** Yen

Q.39 The ratio of managers to management trainees is $3:5$. When 21 new management trainees are recruited the ratio will become $3:8$. How many managers will there be in the group?

A. 27
B. 24
C. 21
D. Cannot be determined

Q.40 A and B together have Rs. $2,448$. If 25% of $A's$ amount is equal to 35% of $B's$ amount, then find the amount with A.

A. Rs. 1,020   **B.** Rs. 1,462
C. Rs. 1,468   **D.** Rs. 1,428

Q.41 The famous Rock Garden is located in which city?

A. Jaipur   **B.** Shimla
C. Lucknow   **D.** Chandigarh

Q.42 Find a quarter of 40% of the square of 40.

[UP Police Constable, 2019]

A. 120   **B.** 140   **C.** 160   **D.** 180

Q.43 A man spends 75% of his income. If his income increases by 28% and his expenditure increases by 20%, then what is the increase or decrease percentage in his savings?

[SSC Sub Inspector (CPO), 2020]

A. 13% increase   **B.** 52% decrease
C. 13% decrease   **D.** 52% increase

Q.44 The roots of the equation $3x^2 - 2x + 4 = 0$ are,

A. Real and equal   **B.** Imaginary
C. Real and unequal   **D.** None of these

Q.45 If α and β are the roots of the equation $ax^2 + 2bx + c = 0$ then find the value of $\dfrac{\alpha}{\beta} + \dfrac{\beta}{\alpha}$

A. $\dfrac{4b^2 - 2ac}{ac}$ **B.** $\dfrac{4b^2 + 2ac}{ac}$ **C.** $b^2 - 4ac$ **D.** $b^2 + 4ac$

Q.46 Which of the following statement with reference to the Rural Infrastructure Development Fund (RIDF) is incorrect?

A. The Government of India set up RIDF in 1995-96, for financing ongoing rural infrastructure projects.
B. The funds released under RIDF are maintained by the Reserve Bank of India.
C. These funds are provided on a year-to-year basis by the Government of India.
D. Union Budget of 2021 enhanced RIDF to Rs. 40,000 crore from Rs. 30,000 crore.

Q.47 What is Operation Green?

A. It is a scheme which aims to develop 200 Urban Forests across the country in the next five years.
B. It is a drive of the Maharashtra State Government with a target of planting 50 crore trees across the state.
C. It is a mission of the Indian Airforce in Mauritius for assistance in dealing with the environmental crisis due to oil spill.
D. It is a price fixation scheme that aims to ensure farmers are given the right price for their produce.

Q.48 If the length and breadth of a rectangle are 25cm and 10cm, respectively, then its area is:

A. 100 sq.cm   **B.** 250 sq.cm
C. 115 sq.cm   **D.** 200 sq.cm

Q.49 The area of a rhombus whose diagonals are of lengths 100 cm and 8.2 cm is:

A. 410 cm²   **B.** 82 cm²   **C.** 41 cm²   **D.** 820 cm²

Q.50 The area of a trapezium is 480 cm², the distance between two parallel sides is 15 cm and one of the parallel side is 20 cm. The other parallel side is:

A. 20 cm   **B.** 34 cm   **C.** 44 cm   **D.** 50 cm

Ques (51-52):Direction: Each item in this section consists of a sentence with an underlined word followed by four options. Select the option that is nearest in meaning to the underlined word.

Q.51 Some people complain when they <u>encounter</u> a small misfortune in the course of their thoroughly happy life

[UPSC NDA, 2019]

A. run into   **B.** run away
C. run down   **D.** run with

Q.52 This world is full of <u>miseries</u>

[UPSC NDA, 2019]

A. indifferent love
B. perfect happiness
C. great suffering
D. moderate sympathies

Q.53 What is the value of $\sqrt{(269) - \sqrt{169}}$

A. 17   **B.** 15   **C.** 16   **D.** 22

Q.54 What is the square root of 0.09?

A. 0.003   **B.** $\dfrac{3}{100}$ **C.** 0.03   **D.** 0.3

Q.55 What is the bond formed due to the electrostatic attraction known as?

A. Covalent bond
B. Electrovalent bond
C. Electromagnetic bond
D. Polar bond

Q.56 What is the boiling point for Ethanol?

A. 100 °C   **B.** 78.3 °C   **C.** 62 °C   **D.** 46 °C

Q.57 The marked price of an article is Rs.1000. Three successive discounts of 10%, 20% and 30% are given. Find the selling price of the article.

A. Rs. 564   **B.** Rs. 404   **C.** Rs. 544   **D.** Rs. 504

Q.58 Who among the following has not been an editor of 'Almora Akhbar'?

A. Buddhi Ballabh Pant
B. Munshi Imtiyaz Ali
C. Jeeva Nand Joshi
D. Sri Dev Suman

Q.59 The main objective of co-curricular activities in the school is:

A. To get a sense of adjustment in the personality of the students.
B. Escape from the day-to-day activities of the classroom.
C. Introducing students to the world of revision work.
D. To meet the substitute satisfaction needs of students.

Q.60 Assessment of performance done by students frequently at the end of the unit using criterion-referenced tests and employing multiple techniques of evaluation is known as what type of evaluation.

[Haryana Primary Teacher (PRT), 2019]

A. Continual of evaluation
B. Periodicity of evaluation
C. Above (A) & (B) both
D. Neither (A) nor (B) above

Q.61 Kalinga war was fought in which year?

A. 269 BC   **B.** 263 BC   **C.** 260 BC   **D.** 261 BC

Q.62 Who was the first woman Central Minister of India?

A. Indira Gandhi
B. Rajkumari Amrit Kaur
C. Laxmi Bai
D. Razia Sultan

Q.63 Which Bharat Ratna recipient's birthday is celebrated as Engineer's Day?

A. Abdul Kalam Azad   **B.** J R D Tata
C. M Visvesvaraya   **D.** C V Raman

Q.64 Who was the first Indian to go into space?

A. Rakesh Sharma   **B.** Ramesh Sharma
C. Suresh Sharma   **D.** Mahesh Sharma

Ques (65-67):Direction: In this question, each item consists of six sentences of passage. The first and sixth sentences are given in the beginning as SI and S6. The middle four-sentence in each have been jumbled up and labelled as P, Q, R and S. You are required to find the proper sequence of the four sentences.

Q.65 S1: The British rule in India has brought about the moral, material, cultural and spiritual ruination of this great country.

S6: We are not to kill anybody but it is our dharma to see that the curse of this Government is blotted out.

P: I regard this rule as a curse.

Q: Sedition has become my religion

R: Ours is a non-violent battle

S: I am out to destroy this system of Government.

[UPSC NDA, 2019]

A. S P R Q   **B.** P S Q R   **C.** Q R P S   **D.** S R P Q

Q.66 S1: Mr. Sherlock Holmes and Doctor Watson were spending a weekend in a University town.

S6: It was clear that something very unusual happened.

P: One evening they received a visit from an acquaintance, Mr. Hilton Soames.

Q: On that occasion, he was in a state of great agitation.

R: They were staying in furnished rooms, close to the library.

S: Mr. Soames was a tall, thin man of a nervous and excitable nature.

The proper sequence should be

A. P R S Q   **B.** R P S Q   **C.** P Q R S   **D.** R P Q S

Q.67 S1: The machines that drive modern civilisation derive their power from coal and oil.

S6: Nuclear energy may also be effectively used in this respect.

P: But they are not inexhaustible.

Q: These sources may not be exhausted very soon.

R: A time may come when some other sources have to be tapped and utilised.

S: Power may, of course, be obtained in future from forests, water, wind and withered vegetables.

The proper sequence should be

A. P Q R S   **B.** Q P R S   **C.** S R Q P   **D.** S P Q R

Q.68 A person spends $\frac{2}{7}$th of his salary on rent, $\frac{1}{4}$th of the salary on education, and the remaining on food. If he spends Rs. 2800 on his rent then what is the amount he spends on food?

A. 4550   **B.** 4200   **C.** 4500   **D.** 4000

Q.69 Which state has launched Mask Abhiyan?

A. Kerala   **B.** Odisha
C. Maharashtra   **D.** Uttar Pradesh

Q.70 A solid sphere of radius 13 cm is melted and its some part is used to cast a hollow sphere whose internal radius is 5 cm. What will be the thickness of the sphere if the surface area of solid sphere is equal to the total surface area of hollow sphere?

A. 6 cm   **B.** 7 cm   **C.** 8 cm   **D.** 9 cm

Ques (71-72):Direction: In the following question, out of the four alternatives, select the alternative which best expresses the meaning of the Idiom/Phrase.

Q.71 Sow wild oats.

A. To make someone fool

B. To make space to red

C. To take revenge

D. To waste time by doing foolish things

Q.72 Method to my madness.

A. No manners.

B. There's a reason for someone's strange behavior.

C. Crazy, demented, out of one's mind, in a confused or befuddled state of mind, senile.

D. This means to deceive someone into thinking well of them.

Q.73 Why do birds not feel trouble breathing while flying at very high altitudes?

A. Their lungs are very big

B. They fly passively

C. They have extra air sacs

D. They use less oxygen

Q.74 Dinosaurs are:

A. Cyanozoic reptile   **B.** Mesozoic Reptiles

C. Mesozoic bird   **D.** None of these

Q.75 For which year has the Asian Football Confederation awarded the hosting rights of Women's Asian Cup to India for the first time since 1979?

A. 2021   **B.** 2022   **C.** 2023   **D.** 2024

Q.76 _____ was the first Chairman and Commissioner of the Indian Premier League.

A. Rajeev Shukla   **B.** Sourav Ganguly

C. Ranjib Biswal   **D.** Lalit Modi

Q.77 Buddhist site Tabo Monastery is located in which of the following state of India?

A. Arunachal Pradesh   **B.** Himachal Pradesh

C. Sikkim   **D.** Assam

Q.78 If $a^3 + b^3 + c^3 = 3abc$. Find the value of $a + b + c$?

A. 4   **B.** 6   **C.** 2   **D.** 0

Q.79 Which country released a commemorative postage stamp on 75th anniversary of UN?

A. USA   **B.** India   **C.** Russia   **D.** China

Q.80 Headquarters of UNO are situated at:

A. New York, USA

B. Hague (Netherlands)

C. Geneva

D. Paris

Q.81 The First Indian satellite is:

A. Aryabhata spacecraft

B. Bhaskara-1

C. Rohini RS-1

D. INSAT-1A

Q.82 Who discovered X-Ray?

A. Wilhelm Conrad Rontgen

B. William Lee

C. X Rollswick

D. I. Thompson

Q.83 What is the basis of remedial teaching?

A. Diagnosis

B. Weakness of the student

C. Individual difference

D. All of the above

Q.84 Which one of the following statement is incorrect regarding errors and mistakes?

A. Mistakes occur, but errors are made.

B. Errors can simply happen, but mistakes involve human actions.

C. An error is a deviation from accuracy or correctness.

D. A mistake is an error caused by a fault

Q.85 Find the area of sector of a circle with radius 4 cm and $\angle 30°$. Find the area of corresponding major sector. $(\pi = 3.14)$

A. 50.24 cm ^{2} **B.** 50.25 cm ^{2}

C. 60.24 cm ^{2} **D.** 80.24 cm ^{2}

Q.86 In the below figure,QR is the diameter of the circle with the center O having the value of 10 cm. It contain two parallel chords named as PQ and RS having the length of 6 cm. Find the vertical distance between the two chords.

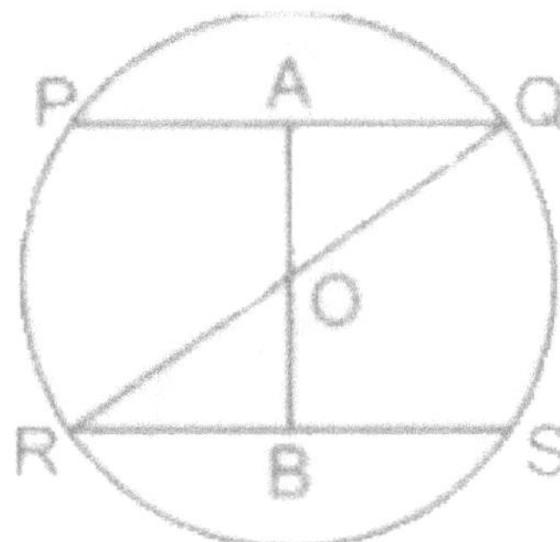

A. 6 cm   **B.** 7 cm   **C.** 8 cm   **D.** 5.5 cm

Q.87 3 men or 5 women can complete the work in 12 days then in how many days 3 men and 7 women will complete the same work?

A. 5 days   **B.** 8 days   **C.** 10 days   **D.** 15 days

Q.88 A man and a woman received Rs. 1500 as wages for 20 days for the work they did together. If the efficiency of the man is double the women, then find daily wages of woman.

A. Rs. 25   **B.** Rs. 50   **C.** Rs. 500   **D.** Rs. 100

Ques (89-90):Direction: In the following question, a sentence has been given in Active/Passive Voice. Out of the four alternatives suggested, select the one which best expresses the same sentence in Passive/Active Voice.

Q.89 He was not given the information he needed.
A. Somebody was not given the information he needed.
B. The information he needed wasn't given to him.
C. He needed the information he wasn't given.
D. They didn't give him the information he needed.

Q.90 Bipin was not told about the meeting.
A. Somebody did not tell Bipin about the meeting.
B. There was nobody who could tell Bipin about the meeting.
C. Nobody told Bipin about the meeting.
D. The meeting was not told about Bipin.

Q.91 Refer the below data table and answer the following question.

Items	Yearly expense in Rs. lakhs
Raw Materials	4
Labour	3
Rent	4
Interest	6
Taxes	1

Raw Materials and Interest are what percent of total expenses?
A. 48.31 percent
B. 41.06 percent
C. 62.81 percent
D. 55.56 percent

Q.92 The mean of 10 observations is 5. If 2 is added to each observation and then multiplied by 3, then what will be the new mean?
A. 5
B. 7
C. 15
D. 21

Q.93 $44 - 6 + 43 \times 2 - 87 = ?$
A. 37
B. 38
C. 73
D. 83

Q.94 The side BC of a triangle ABC is produced to D. If $\angle ACD = 112°$ and $\angle CBA = \frac{3}{4} \angle BAC$, then the measure of $\angle CBA$ is:
A. 30°
B. 48°
C. 45°
D. 64°

Q.95 Providing learning support to pupils who lag far behind their counterparts in school performance includes:
A. Giving more activities for language practice
B. Providing extra notes and coaching
C. Allowing them to complete assignments without time limits
D. Initially adapting school curriculum and teaching strategies

Ques (96-100):Direction: Read the following passage carefully and answer the questions given below it.

The yearly festival was close at hand. The store room was packed with silk fabrics, gold ornaments, clay bowls full of sweet curd and platefuls of sweetmeats. The orders had been placed with shops well in advance. The mother was sending out gifts to everyone.

The eldest son, a government servant, lived with his wife and children in far off lands. The second son had left home at an early age. As a merchant he travelled all over the world. The other sons had split up over petty squabbles, and they now lived in homes of their own. The relatives were spread all across the world. They rarely visited. The youngest son, left in the company of a servant, was soon bored, left her and stood at the door all day long, waiting and watching. His mother, thrilled and excited, loaded the presents on trays and plates, covered them with colourful kerchiefs, and sent them off with maids and servants. The neighbours looked on.

The day came to an end. All the presents had been sent off.

The child came back into the house and **dejectedly** said to his mother, "Maa, you gave a present to everyone, but you didn't give me anything !"

His mother laughed, "I have given all the gifts away to everyone, now see what's **left** for you." She kissed him on the forehead.

The child said in a tearful voice, "Don't I get a gift ?"

"You'll get it when you go far away."

"But when I am close to you, don't I get something from your own hands ?"

His mother reached out her arms and drew him to her. "This is all I have in my own hands. It is the most precious of all."

Q.96 Why did the woman's second son travel?
A. He was restless by nature
B. He did not want to stay at home
C. He was rich and could afford to travel
D. His job was such that he had to travel

Q.97 Why did the woman's eldest son not attend the festival?
A. He was not on good terms with his youngest brother who lived at home
B. He had quarrelled with his mother
C. His wife did not allow him to return home
D. None of these

Q.98 How did the woman prepare for the festival?
I. She bought expensive gifts for her children and neighbours.
II. She ordered her servants to prepare sweets and food well in advance.
III. She made sure that her youngest child was looked after well so that he wouldn't be bored.
A. None
B. Only I
C. Only II
D. Both I and II

Q.99 What did the youngest child do while his mother was busy ?
I. He waited for a chance to steal some sweetmeats.
II. He pestered his mother to give him a present.
III. He stood at the door waiting and watching.
A. Only I
B. Only II
C. Both I and III
D. Only III

Q.100 Which of the following can be said about the woman ?
A. She was a widow who had brought up her children single handedly
B. She was not a good mother since her children had left home at an early age

C. She enjoyed sending her family gifts at festival time

D. She gave expensive presents to show that she was wealthy

// Smart Answer Sheet //

Correct — Percentage of students who answered correctly. **Skipped** — Percentage of students who skipped.

Q.	Ans.	Correct / Skipped	Q.	Ans.	Correct / Skipped	Q.	Ans.	Correct / Skipped	Q.	Ans.	Correct / Skipped	Q.	Ans.	Correct / Skipped	Q.	Ans.	Correct / Skipped
1	D	48.8 % / 1.69 %	18	B	63.39 % / 1.12 %	35	A	78.41 % / 0.0 %	52	C	48.93 % / 1.41 %	69	B	67.79 % / 1.2 %	86	C	41.82 % / 1.41 %
2	A	59.88 % / 1.15 %	19	C	45.46 % / 1.48 %	36	B	18.79 % / 4.52 %	53	C	79.1 % / 0.0 %	70	B	16.58 % / 4.9 %	87	A	86.19 % / 0.0 %
3	C	49.54 % / 1.74 %	20	B	40.32 % / 1.36 %	37	D	86.61 % / 0.0 %	54	D	86.44 % / 0.0 %	71	D	42.23 % / 1.42 %	88	A	41.64 % / 1.58 %
4	A	63.61 % / 1.05 %	21	A	56.41 % / 1.37 %	38	D	50.43 % / 1.58 %	55	B	40.23 % / 1.45 %	72	B	55.84 % / 1.47 %	89	D	13.98 % / 4.16 %
5	A	64.04 % / 1.73 %	22	A	49.95 % / 1.18 %	39	C	45.24 % / 1.73 %	56	B	24.81 % / 3.51 %	73	C	61.15 % / 1.97 %	90	C	27.05 % / 3.32 %
6	D	29.26 % / 4.75 %	23	A	56.49 % / 1.08 %	40	D	54.33 % / 1.32 %	57	D	64.14 % / 1.13 %	74	B	46.01 % / 1.0 %	91	D	49.95 % / 1.96 %
7	C	51.86 % / 1.49 %	24	A	57.28 % / 1.87 %	41	D	77.56 % / 0.0 %	58	D	12.47 % / 3.15 %	75	B	30.21 % / 3.57 %	92	D	55.82 % / 1.6 %
8	A	49.11 % / 1.38 %	25	C	28.46 % / 4.93 %	42	C	85.15 % / 0.0 %	59	A	44.82 % / 1.81 %	76	D	49.22 % / 1.17 %	93	A	85.94 % / 0.0 %
9	A	51.43 % / 1.52 %	26	A	76.5 % / 0.0 %	43	D	62.82 % / 1.54 %	60	B	42.65 % / 1.94 %	77	B	66.43 % / 1.66 %	94	B	53.59 % / 1.01 %
10	B	47.85 % / 1.34 %	27	C	87.25 % / 0.0 %	44	B	46.08 % / 1.21 %	61	D	26.53 % / 4.02 %	78	D	86.19 % / 0.0 %	95	D	66.46 % / 1.19 %
11	B	62.82 % / 1.93 %	28	D	87.7 % / 0.0 %	45	A	59.87 % / 1.33 %	62	B	68.16 % / 1.67 %	79	B	21.8 % / 4.67 %	96	D	68.51 % / 2.0 %
12	D	69.8 % / 1.17 %	29	D	60.61 % / 1.2 %	46	B	56.42 % / 1.2 %	63	C	61.16 % / 1.99 %	80	A	56.61 % / 1.92 %	97	D	77.49 % / 0.0 %
13	C	67.62 % / 1.74 %	30	A	46.41 % / 1.94 %	47	D	50.75 % / 1.94 %	64	A	59.98 % / 1.88 %	81	A	60.42 % / 1.97 %	98	A	57.04 % / 1.21 %
14	B	46.86 % / 1.27 %	31	A	85.04 % / 0.0 %	48	B	89.36 % / 0.0 %	65	B	67.67 % / 1.09 %	82	A	82.78 % / 0.0 %	99	D	67.58 % / 1.95 %
15	C	66.74 % / 1.83 %	32	D	55.21 % / 1.85 %	49	A	54.06 % / 1.84 %	66	B	14.51 % / 4.7 %	83	D	65.16 % / 1.79 %	100	C	60.27 % / 1.69 %
16	D	66.03 % / 1.58 %	33	A	56.71 % / 1.5 %	50	C	57.96 % / 1.3 %	67	B	49.0 % / 1.99 %	84	A	60.93 % / 1.13 %			
17	A	49.17 % / 1.44 %	34	A	49.22 % / 1.6 %	51	A	85.74 % / 0.0 %	68	A	51.32 % / 1.63 %	85	A	41.87 % / 1.24 %			

//Hints and Solutions//

1. The International Financial Services Centres Authority (IFSCA) and GVFL Limited signed an MoU at IFSCA's office at Gift City, Gujarat.

It has been signed for cooperation and collaboration to support and facilitate the FinTech ecosystem in GIFT IFSC. IFSCA is a unified regulator responsible for the development and regulation of financial products, financial services and institutions in the IFSCs.

Hence, the correct option is (D).

2. The first train was successfully test-fired between Nepal country's railway link from Bihar's Madhubani district.

Train service between Jainagar in Bihar and Kurtha in Nepal is expected to start soon after the speed test of the train. Rajesh Kumar, Chief Public Relations Officer of East-Central Railway (ECR) said that the speed trial was successfully carried out by locomotive at a speed of 110 km per hour on the kilometer-long newly-gauge converted railway section between Jaynagar of Samastipur division and Kurtha in Nepal. During this senior high officials of IRCON and Nepal Railways were present.

Hence, the correct option is (A).

3. The winner of US Open Tennis Tournament, 2018 (Women's Singles) was Naomi Osaka.

- Naomi Osaka beats Serena Williams in the dramatic U.S Open final.
- She became the first Japanese woman to win a Grand Slam title.
- She registered an emphatic 6-2, 6-4 win over Serena Williams in the finals.

Hence, the correct option is (C).

4. Russia was stripped of hosting the Champions League final by UEFA on 25 Feb 2022 with St. Petersburg replaced by Paris after Russia's invasion of Ukraine. France last hosted the Champions League final 16 years ago, when Barcelona beat Arsenal in the 2006 final.

Hence, the correct option is (A).

5. The Panchayats (Extension to Scheduled Areas) Act (PESA) does not authorize the States give the Gram Sabhas power to regulate and restrict Sale/consumption of liquor.

Panchayats (Extension to Scheduled Areas) Act (PESA) authorizes the States give the Gram Sabhas power to regulate and restrict sale/consumption of liquor; ownership of minor forest produce; power to prevent alienation of land and restore alienated land; power to manage village markets, control money lending to STs and power to manage village markets, control money lending to STs and Mandatory executive functions to approve plans of the Village Panchayats, identify beneficiaries for schemes, issue certificates of utilization of funds.

Hence, the correct option is (A).

6. Union Finance Minister is the Chairman of Tax Policy Council. RBI Governor is the ex-officio Chairperson of the newly constituted Monetary Policy Committee. Tax Policy Research Unit is headed by an officer of the level of Chief Commissioner at functional level alternatively from CBDT and CBEC for a fixed tenure, who will directly report to Revenue Secretary.

Hence, the correct option is (D).

7. Given,

Difference of CI and SI amount $=$ Rs. 150

Time $(T) = 2$ years

Principal(P) = Rs. 20000

As we know,

Difference of CI and $SI = P \times \left(\frac{R}{100}\right)^2$

Where $R =$ Rate of interest.

As per the formula,

$$CI - SI = 20000 \left(\frac{R}{100}\right)^2$$

$$\Rightarrow 150 = 20000 \left(\frac{R}{100}\right)^2$$

$$\Rightarrow \frac{3}{400} = \left(\frac{R}{100}\right)^2$$

$$\Rightarrow R = 8.66\%$$

$\therefore$ Rate of interest is 8.66%.

Hence, the correct option is (C).

8. Language of mathematics is a vast term that includes a large number of symbols, notations, equations, mathematical expression and mathematical phrases too.

- Values in Mathematics Education:- There are ten values in mathematics
- Practical value of mathematics:- e.g. learning by doing, counting
- Intellectual value of mathematics:- e.g. imagination, memorization
- Social value of mathematics:- co-operation, objectivity
- Moral value of mathematics:- Honesty, Justice
- Disciplinary value of mathematics:- Simplicity, accuracy
- Cultural value of mathematics:- e.g. singing, dancing
- International value of mathematics:- researches, journals
- Artistic value of mathematics:- Drawing, sketching
- Vocational value of mathematics:- e.g. Tailoring, carpentry
- Psychological value of mathematics:- kindness, happiness

Hence, the correct option is (A).

9. Mathematics is a branch of science which deals with counting, calculating, and studying numbers, shapes, and structures. It is the study of numbers, shape, quantity, and patterns. It relies on logic and connects learning with children's day to day life.

Hence, the correct option is (A).

10. Average decadal growth rate $\%$ of population is 9.82% (approx.)

$$\text{Average} = \frac{\text{sum of observations}}{\text{total no. of observations}}$$

$1951 - 1961$	$\frac{1}{20} \times 100 = 5\%$
$1961 - 1971$	$\frac{3}{21} \times 100 = 14.28\%$
$1971 - 1981$	$\frac{3}{24} \times 100 = 12.5\%$
$1981 - 1991$	$\frac{3}{27} \times 100 = 11.11\%$
$1991 - 2001$	$\frac{2}{30} \times 100 = 6.67\%$
$2001 - 2011$	$\frac{3}{32} \times 100 = 9.37\%$

total of growth $\% = (5 + 14.28 + 12.50 + 11.11 + 6.67 + 9.37)\% = 58.93\%$

total no. of decades $= 6$

$$\text{Average} = \frac{58.93\%}{6} = 9.82\%$$

Hence, the correct option is (B)

11. Based on the average decadal growth rate,

The population in the year is

$$35 + \frac{35 \times 9.28}{100} = 38.44 \ million$$

The population in the year 2021 will be $38.44 \ million$

Hence, the correct option is (B).

12. In the year 1951, the power availability per person was $500 \ W$

$1GW = 1000$ million watt

$10GW = 10000$ million watt

$$\text{The power availability per person} = \frac{\text{Electrical Power Production}}{\text{Population}}$$

$$\Rightarrow \frac{10000}{20} = 500 \ W$$

Hence, the correct option is (D).

13. The average power availability per person was maximum in 2011

$$\text{The power availability per person} = \frac{\text{Electrical Power Production}}{\text{Population}}$$

1951	$\frac{10000}{20} = 500 \ W$
1961	$\frac{20000}{21} = 952.38 \ W$
1971	$\frac{25000}{24} = 1041.67 \ W$
1981	$\frac{40000}{27} = 1481.48 \ W$
1991	$\frac{50000}{30} = 1666.67 \ W$
2001	$\frac{80000}{32} = 2500 \ W$
2011	$\frac{100000}{35} = 2857 \ W$

Hence, the correct option is (C).

14. Given,

Ratio of investments of A, B and C

$= 12600 : 10800 : 16200$

$= 126 : 108 : 162$

$= 63 : 54 : 81$

$= 7 : 6 : 9$

Let the total profit $= x$

Then, C's share $= \left[\frac{9}{(7+6+9)}\right] x = 16200$

$\Rightarrow \left(\frac{9}{22}\right) x = 16200$

$\Rightarrow x = $ Rs. 39600

Therefore, difference in profit of A and $B = \left[\frac{(7-6)}{22}\right] x$

$= \left(\frac{1}{22}\right) \times 39600 = $ Rs. 1800

Hence, the correct option is (B).

15. The records give us an *inkling* of how people saw the world.

Inkling means a little knowledge or suspicion about something, it is the only option that fits in the given blank.

Hence, the correct option is (C).

16. The *remains* of a dynasty have been found in an architecture excavation.

Remains means the parts left over after other parts have been removed, used, or destroyed, it is the only option that fits in the given blank.

Hence, the correct option is (D).

17. The necklace I received from my late husband is a loving *memento* from my time spent with him.

Memento means an object kept as a reminder of a person or event, it is the only option that fits in the given blank.

Hence, the correct option is (A).

18. Samudragupta was the fourth ruler of the Gupta Empire and the son and successor of Chandragupta I. The main source of Samudragupta's history is an inscription engraved on the

Allahabad pillar known as Prayag Prashasti and composed by his court poet Harisena. He also performed an Asvamedha sacrifice.

Hence, the correct option is (B).

19. The landscape is being continuously worn away by two processes – weathering and erosion. Erosion is the wearing away of the landscape by different agents like water, wind, and ice.

- At higher gradients, downward, vertical erosion is more dominant. This produces V-shaped valleys
- The V-shaped valley is typical of one that has been carved by flowing water.
- The erosion is more pronounced when the water flow is a heavy one, and the water carries suspended particles (sedimentary load).

Hence, the correct option is (C).

20. The ocean current is a general movement of a mass of water in a fairly defined direction over great distances. Base on the temperature characteristics it can be categorized as warm and cold current. It can be broadly categorized into Atlantic ocean current, Pacific ocean current, and Indian ocean current. The currents in the northern portion of the Indian Ocean differ entirely from the general pattern of circulation.

- The currents in the northern portion of the Indian Ocean differ entirely from the general pattern of circulation.
- They change their direction from season to season in response to the seasonal rhythm of the monsoons.
- In the northern section of the Indian Ocean, there is a clear reversal of currents between winter and summer.
- In winter, the north equatorial current and the south equatorial current flow from east to west.
- The northeast monsoons drive the water along the coast of the Bay of Bengal to circulate in an anti-clockwise direction.
- Similarly, along the coasts of the lands bordering the Arabian Sea, an anticlockwise circulation of currents develops.

Therefore, statements 1 and 2 are correct.

Hence, the correct option is (B).

21. Both longitude and latitude are angles measured with the center of the earth as an origin. Longitude is an angle from the prime meridian, measured to the east (longitudes to the west are negative). Latitudes measure an angle up from the equator (latitudes to the south are negative).

- The line joining the north and south pole is called Prime Meridian.
- A (geographic) meridian (or line of longitude) is half of an imaginary great circle on the Earth's surface.
- It is a coordinate line terminated by the North Pole and the South Pole, connecting points of equal longitude, as measured in angular degrees east or west of the Prime Meridian.

Hence, the correct option is (A).

22. Let the numbers be 3x, 4x and 5x.

Then, their L.C.M. = 60x

So, 60x = 2400 or x = 40

∴ The numbers are (3 x 40), (4 x 40) and (5 x 40)

Hence, required H.C.F. = 40

Hence, the correct option is (A).

23. Given:

Prime numbers up to 100.

There is no formula to calculate the number of prime numbers. We have to count each and every one.

The prime numbers are:

2, 3, 5, 7 ,11, 13, 17, 19, 23, 29, 31, 37, 41, 43, 47, 53, 59, 61, 67, 71, 73, 79, 83, 89, 97.

∴ There are 25 prime numbers below 100.

Hence, the correct option is (A).

24. Given:

P is a prime number and $P^2 + 7$ is also gives a Prime number.

The numbers having exactly two factors, one and the number itself is called prime numbers.

Let the $P^2 + 7$ is equal to x

∴ X should be a prime number.

If P is 2

∴ $X = P^2 + 7 = (2)^2 + 7 = 11$, where 11 is a prime number.

If P is 3

∴ $X = P^2 + 7 = (3)^2 + 7 = 16$, where 16 is even number.

If P is 5

∴ $X = P^2 + 7 = (5)^2 + 7 = 32$, where 32 is even number.

So, all the values of P other than 2 give the values of X as the even number.

∴ Only one value of P is possible which gives the X as a prime number.

Hence, the correct option is (A).

25. Specific gravity is defined as the ratio of the density of any solid or liquid object to the density of pure water.

Specific gravity = density of object/density of pure water

SI unit of density of object / SI unit of density of pure water

= kg per volume / kg per volume

No unit

Therefore, Specific Gravity has no unit.

Quantities	Unit
Velocity	m/Sec

Density	kg/m³
Stress	Nm⁻²

Hence, the correct option is (C).

26.

- The substances which have infinitely high electrical resistance are called insulators.
- An insulator does not allow electricity to flow through it.
- Rubber, wood and paper are the good insulators of electricity.

Hence, the correct option is (A).

27. Kheer Bhavani Mela is a popular fair held in Jammu and Kashmir. This Mela is one of the biggest religious festivals of Kashmiri Pandits, it is held annually on Jyeshtha Ashtami.

Hence, the correct option is (C).

28. Bathukamma Utsav, 2019 was held in the Telangana state of India.

This festival celebrated in the state of Telangana between 28 September to 6 October 2019 is also known as the 'Festival of Flowers'. The brightly painted figures of Telangana men and women are Thota Vaikuntam's signature style, he exaggerated contoured of reconstructed form, with highly stylized folk features and perspective mark his paintings.

Hence, the correct option is (D).

29. Ela Bhatt – Pulitzer Prize is NOT correctly matched.

Ela Bhatt was the recipient of several honorary degrees and international and Indian awards, including the Ramon Magsaysay Award for Community Leadership (1977), the Right Livelihood Award for Changing the Human Environment (1984), and the Padma Shri (1985) and Padma Bhushan (1986), two of India's highest civilian honours.

Hence, the correct option is (D).

30. Giddings had defined society as union in itself.

According to Giddings, Society is the union itself, the organisation, the 'sum of formal relations' in which associating 'individuals are bound together'. Society is part of the system where people live together and form a community or a union. It is a way of living together and creating a relationship with each other.

Hence, the correct option is (A).

31. Here, the error is in part 1. 'Too' should be replaced with so, because the correct conjunction pair is so that, and too is always paired with to i.e. too to.

Correct sentence: He was so tired that he could not cross the street even with the help of a supporter.

Hence, the correct option is (A).

32. Given,

For A,

Cost price of horse $= \left(3600 \times \frac{100}{90}\right) =$ Rs. 4000

For B,

Selling price of horse $=$ Rs. $\left(4000 \times \frac{112}{100}\right) =$ Rs. 4480

$\therefore B's$ gain $= 4480 - 3600 =$ Rs. 880

Hence, the correct option is (D).

33. Let CP of car be x

SP at 20% gain $= x + 0.20x = 1.2x$

SP at 25% gain $= x + 0.25x = 1.25x$

According to question,

$$1.25x - 1.2x = 50000$$

$$\Rightarrow 0.05x = 50000$$

$$\Rightarrow x = \frac{50000}{0.05}$$

$$x = Rs.\,10,00,000$$

Hence, the correct option is (A).

34. World Tsunami Awareness Day is observed on 5th November around the world, including Pakistan, with the aim of reducing the number of people affected by disasters worldwide.

World Tsunami Awareness Day encourages the development of national and community-level, local disaster risk reduction strategies to save more lives against disasters. This year's observance promotes the " Sendai Seven Campaign ," target (e).

Hence, the correct option is (A).

35. Ministry of Petroleum and Natural Gas celebrates World Biofuel Day on August 10 every year. On the occasion, the ministry also organized the webinar with the theme "Biofuels towards Atmanirbhar Bharat".

Biofuels are fuels such as ethanol and biodiesel that are made from biomass materials that are, plant or algae material or animal waste. Small Industry Day is observed on 30 August every year to support and promote small scale industries. The country celebrates September 15 as National Engineer's Day to appreciate the contributions of Mokshagundam Visvesvaraya. World Suicide Prevention Day is observed on 10 September every year to raise awareness to prevent cases of suicide.

Hence, the correct option is (A).

36. Given,

$$= (12)^4 \times (144)^8 \div (24)^3 = (?)^{17} \times 2^{(-3)}$$

$$= 12^4 \times (12^2)^8 \div (12 \times 2)^3 = (?)^{17} \times 2^{(-3)}$$

$$= 12^{20} \div (12^3 \times 2^3) = (?)^{17} \times 2^{(-3)}$$

$$= 12^{17} \div 2^3 = (?)^{17} \times 2^{(-3)}$$

$$= 12^{17} \times 2^{(-3)} = (?)^{17} \times 2^{(-3)}$$

$$\therefore 12$$

Hence, the correct option is (B).

37. The Act provided for the establishment of an All-India Federation to be based on the union of the British Indian provinces and the Princely States. Dyarchy which was introduced at the provincial level in the Government of India Act of, 1919 was abolished. The Act divided the powers between the Centre and Units in terms of 3 lists: Federal List (for Centre, with 59 items), Provincial List (for provinces, with 54 items), and the Concurrent List (for both, with 36 items). Residuary powers were given to the Viceroy.

Hence, the correct option is (D).

38. The Japanese Yen is the official currency of Japan. It is the third most traded currency in the foreign exchange market after the United States dollar and the Euro. It is also widely used as a reserve currency after the U.S. Dollar, the Euro and the Pound sterling.

Hence, the correct option is (D).

39. Let the number of manager and management trainees be $3x$ and $5x$ respectively.

According to the question,

$$\frac{3x}{5x+21} = \frac{3}{8}$$

$$24x = 15x + 63$$

$$9x = 63$$

$$x = 7$$

Number of managers $= 3x = 3 \times 7 = 21$

Hence, the correct option is (C).

40. According to Question-

$$25\% \text{ of } A = 35\% \text{ of } B$$

$$\Rightarrow \frac{25}{100} \times A = \frac{35}{100} \times B$$

$$\Rightarrow \frac{A}{B} = \frac{35}{25} = \frac{7}{5}$$

Required Amount $= \frac{7}{12} \times 2448 =$ Rs. $1,428$

Hence, the correct option is (D).

41. The famous Rock Garden is located in the city of Chandigarh.

The famous Rock Garden which is also known as Nek Chand's Rock Garden after its founder Nek Chand. The Rock Garden of Chandigarh is a sculpture garden in Chandigarh, India.

This beautiful garden was established in 1957. Spread across an area of 40 ac, this garden is also famous for being one of the most eco-friendly gardens in the country, as it is has been built solely by home-waste and other industrial items.

Hence, the correct option is (D).

42. Calculations :

Square of 40 = $(40)^2$

$= 1600$

A quarter of 40% of 1600 = 25% of 40% of 1600

$$\left(\frac{1}{4}\right) \times \left(\frac{2}{5}\right) \times 1600$$

$$\Rightarrow 1600 \times \left(\frac{2}{20}\right)$$

$$\Rightarrow 160$$

$\therefore$ The result will be 160

Hence, the correct option is (C).

43. Given:

Man spends 75% of his income.

Income increases by 28%

Expenditure increases by 20%

Formula Used:

Saving = Income – Expenditure

Calculation:

Let the Income of a man = 100

Expenditure = 75% of 100

$$\Rightarrow \left(\frac{75}{100}\right) \times 100 = 75$$

Saving = Income – Expenditure

Initial Saving $\Rightarrow$ 100 – 75 = 25   ----(1)

Now as per the question,

His income increased by 28%

His new income = Old income + 28% of Old income

$$\Rightarrow \text{His new income} = \left(\frac{128}{100}\right) \times 100 = 128$$

Similarly, his expenditure increased by 20%

$$\text{His new expenditure} = \left(\frac{120}{100}\right) \times 75$$

$$\Rightarrow \text{His new expenditure} = 90$$

Saving(new) = Income(new) – Expenditure(new)

Saving(new) = 128 - 90 = 38 ----(2)

Now, % increase in savings = $\left\{\dfrac{(38-25)}{25}\right\} \times 100$ ----(from 1 and 2)

$$\Rightarrow 13 \times 4 = 52\%$$

$\therefore$ The % increase in saving is 52%

Hence, the correct option is (D).

44. The given equation is,

$$3x^2 - 2x + 4 = 0$$

On comparing the above equation with $ax^2 + bx + c = 0,$

$$a = 3, b = -2, c = 4$$

Discriminant,

$$b^2 - 4ac = (-2)^2 - 4 \times 3 \times 4$$

$$= 4 - 48$$

$$= -44 \text{ (Negative)}$$

So, the roots are imaginary.
Hence, the correct option is (B).

45. The given equation is,

$$ax^2 + 2bx + c = 0$$

Here, addition of roots $= \alpha + \beta = \dfrac{-2b}{a}$

Multiplication of roots $= \alpha\beta = \dfrac{c}{a}$

$$\Rightarrow \dfrac{\alpha}{\beta} + \dfrac{\beta}{\alpha} = \dfrac{\alpha^2 + \beta^2}{\alpha\beta}$$

$$= \dfrac{(\alpha+\beta)^2 - 2\alpha\beta}{\alpha\beta}$$

$$= \dfrac{\frac{4b^2}{a^2} - 2\frac{c}{a}}{\frac{c}{a}}$$

$$= \dfrac{4b^2 - 2ac}{ac}$$

Hence, the correct option is (A).

46. Rural Infrastructure Development Fund (RIDF):

- The government of India created the RIDF in NABARD in 1995-96, with an initial corpus of Rs. 2,000 crore.
- Objective: To provide loans to State Governments and State-owned corporations to enable them to complete ongoing rural infrastructure projects.
- The funds released under RIDF are maintained by the National Bank for Agriculture and Rural Development (NABARD). So, statement 2 is incorrect.
- Union Budget of 2021 enhanced RIDF to Rs. 40,000 crore from Rs. 30,000 crore.
- These funds are provided on a year-to-year basis by the Government of India.

Hence, the correct option is (B).

47. Operation Green:

- Union Budget 2021: 'Operation Green Scheme' to be extended to 22 perishable products, to boost value addition in agriculture and allied products.

- It is a price fixation scheme that aims to ensure farmers are given the right price for their produce. Hence, statement 4 is correct.
- It aims to promote Farmer Producers Organizations (FPO), Agri-logistics, processing facilities and professional management of agri-produce.
- It focuses on organized marketing of Tomatoes, Onions and Potatoes (TOP vegetables) by connecting farmers with consumers.
- State Agriculture and other Marketing Federations, Farmer Producer Organizations (FPO), cooperatives, companies, Self-help groups, food processors, etc. can avail the financial assistance under it.

Hence, the correct option is (D).

48. Given,

Length = 25 cm

And breadth = 10 cm

Area of rectangle = Length x breadth

= 25 x 10

= 250 sq.cm
Hence, the correct option is (B).

49. Given,

Lenth = 100 cm, breath = 8.2 cm

Area of rhombus $= \dfrac{1}{2} d_1 d_2$

$$A = \dfrac{1}{2} \times 100 \times 8.2$$

$$A = 410 \text{ cm }^2$$

Hence, the correct option is (A).

50. Given,

$$a = 20 \ cm, \ h = 15 \ cm, \text{ Area } = 480 \text{ sq.cm}$$

Area of trapezium $= \dfrac{1}{2} h(a + b)$

$$480 = \dfrac{1}{2}(15)(20 + b)$$

$$20 + b = \dfrac{(480 \times 2)}{15}$$

$$20 + b = 64$$

$$b = 44 \text{ cm}$$

Hence, the correct option is (C).

51. Encounter means unexpectedly be faced with or experience (something hostile or difficult).

Run into means start to experience a difficult or unpleasant situation.

Run away means escape from a place, person, or situation.

Run down means reduce (or become reduced) in size, numbers, or resources.

Run with means associate habitually with (someone).

The option that is nearest in meaning to the underlined word 'encounter' is 'run into'.

Hence, the correct option is (A).

52. Miseries means a state or feeling of great physical or mental distress or discomfort.

Great suffering means distress, unhappiness, misery.

Indifferent love means not caring what the other person does in a relationship.

Perfect happiness is a feeling of contentment and joy.

Moderate sympathies means feeling sadness for other people.

The option that is nearest in meaning to the underlined word 'miseries' is 'great suffering'.

Hence, the correct option is (C).

53. Given that,

$$\sqrt{(269) - \sqrt{169}}$$

$$\Rightarrow \sqrt{269 - 13}$$

$$\Rightarrow \sqrt{256} = 16$$

Hence, the correct option is (C).

54. Given:

$$\sqrt{0.09}$$

$$\Rightarrow \sqrt{\frac{9}{100}}$$

$$\Rightarrow \frac{3}{10}$$

$$\Rightarrow 0.3$$

Hence, the correct option is (D).

55. The bond formed, as a result of the electrostatic attraction between the positive and negative ions is termed as Electrovalent bond. It is also known as Ionic bond.

Hence, the correct option is (B).

56. Ethanol, with a molecular weight (MW) of 46, has a boiling point of 78 °C (173 °F), whereas propane (MW 44) has a boiling point of -42 °C (-44 °F).

Hence, the correct option is (B).

57. Given-

Marked price of the article $(MP) =$ Rs. 1000

First discount ($D_1) = 10\%$

Second discount ($D_2) = 20\%$

Third discount ($D_3) = 30\%$

According to the formula-

$$SP = MP(1 - D_1\%)(1 - D_2\%)(1 - D_3\%)$$

[where SP is selling price of the article]

$$\Rightarrow SP = 1000(1 - 10\%)(1 - 20\%)(1 - 30\%)$$

$$\Rightarrow SP = 1000\left(1 - \frac{10}{100}\right)\left(1 - \frac{20}{100}\right)\left(1 - \frac{30}{100}\right)$$

$$\Rightarrow SP = 1000 \times \frac{90}{100} \times \frac{80}{100} \times \frac{70}{100}$$

$$\Rightarrow SP = 504$$

The selling price of the article is Rs. 504.

Hence, the correct option is (D).

58. Sri Dev Suman has not been an editor of 'Almora Akhbar'. He was a social activist from the Tehri District of Uttarakhand. He was born at Jaul village patti Bamund of Tehri Garhwal.

- Almora Akhbar was the first and the only letter of Kumaon to be published continuously from 1871 to 1918.
- Almora newspaper was a contemporary of the leading English newspaper 'Pioneer'.
- During the long lifespan of 48 years, Almora newspaper was edited by Budhi Ballabh Pant, Munshi Imtiyaz Ali, Jeeva Nand Joshi, Sadanand Sanwal, Vishnu Dutt Joshi, and after 1913 Badridatta Pandey.
- After Badridatta Pandey became the editor of Almora newspaper in the year 1913, the circulation of the newspaper increased.
- The credit of linking Almora newspaper with the freedom movement also goes to Badridutt Pandey.

Hence, the correct option is (D).

59. The teaching-learning process consists of curricular activities (related to academic subjects) and co-curricular activities (organized outside the classroom).

Both curricular and co-curricular activities are complementary to each other and deserve equal weight and emphasis white planning the total school program during a full session.

Hence, the correct option is (A).

60. Evaluation is a systematic process of collecting, analyzing, and interpreting evidence of students' progress and achievement.

Evaluation needs to be integrated with the process of teaching and learning. There are different type of evaluation process that ensures meaningful learning.

Hence, the correct option is (B).

61.

- Kalinga war was fought between the Mauryan empire and the Kalinga empire in 261 BC.

- This war was one of the largest and bloodiest battles in history.

- The heavy casualty in this war prompted Ashoka to give up war and adopt Buddhism.

Hence, the correct option is (D).

62. Rajkumari Amrit Kaur was the first women Central Minister of India.

Rajkumari Bibiji Amrit Kaur Ahluwalia was an Indian activist and politician. Following her long-lasting association with the Indian independence movement, she was appointed the first Health Minister of India in 1947 and remained in office until 1957.

Hence, the correct option is (B).

63. Engineers day is observed on September 15 to commemorate the birth anniversary of M Visvesvaraya.

Under his able Dewanship, the state of Mysore saw a major transformation in the realms of Agriculture, Irrigation, Industrialization, Education, Banking, and Commerce.

Hence, the correct option is (C).

64. In 1984, Indian Air Force pilot Rakesh Sharma made history by becoming the first Indian to travel to space.

Mr. Sharma was part of the Soviet Union's Soyuz T-11 expedition, which was launched on April 2, 1984.

He spent nearly eight days orbiting Earth.

Hence, the correct option is (A).

65. The passage is in points about how the British rule has ruined the country.

The first line tells us that the rule is a curse as it destroys. It then explains about our non-violent battle and the intention of destroying the government. The last line sarcastically explains that our dharma is to see that the curse of this Government is blotted out.

The correct sequence is:

S1: The British rule in India has brought about moral, material, cultural and spiritual ruination of this great country.

P: I regard this rule as a curse.

S: I am out to destroy this system of Government.

Q: Sedition has become my religion.

R: Ours is a non-violent battle.

S6: We are not to kill anybody but it is our dharma to see that the curse of this Government is blotted out.

Hence, the correct option is (B).

66. Since the introductory part is already there, R will be the 1st statement as it takes the story forward by talking about the place where Mr. Sherlock Holmes and Doctor Watson were staying.

The next statement will be P as tells us about the visit by someone who was known to them.

Now the statement P must be followed by S as it narrates how Mr. Soames looked like.

And the concluding statement will be Q.

So the correct order will be: R-P-S-Q.

Hence, the correct option is (B).

67. Since the introductory part is already there, Q will be the 1st statement as it tells us more about the idea of exhaustion of sources of power.

The next statement will be P as it further states that the sources are exhaustible.

Now the statement P must be followed by R as it makes us explore other sources of power as well.

And the concluding statement will be S.

So the correct order will be: Q-P-R-S.

Hence, the correct option is (B).

68. Let the total salary be x

Given that, salary spent on rent $= \dfrac{2x}{7}$

According to the question,

$$\dfrac{27}{x} = 2800$$

$$x = 9800$$

The portion of salary spent on food $= x - \left(\dfrac{2x}{7}\right) - \dfrac{x}{4}$

$$= x - \left(\dfrac{15x}{28}\right)$$

$$= \dfrac{13x}{28} \quad .....(i)$$

Putting the value of x in equation (i)

$$= \dfrac{13}{28} \times 9800$$

$$= 4550$$

Hence, the correct option is (A).

69. Odisha state has launched Mask Abhiyan.

The aim of Mask Abhiyan is to prevent the spread of COVID-19. The main objective of the Mask Abhiyan is to turn the use of masks into a habit. The fines charged for violators of the rule increased from Rs 1000 to Rs 2000.

Hence, the correct option is (B).

70. Given:

Radius of sphere = 13 cm

Surface area of solid sphere is equal to the total surface area of hollow sphere.

Surface area of sphere $= 4 \times \pi \times$ (radius)^2

Internal radius of the sphere = 5 cm

Let the thickness of the sphere be x cm.

External radius of the sphere = (5 + x) cm

Surface area of the solid sphere = Total surface area of the hollow sphere

$$4 \times \pi \times (13)^2 = 4 \times \pi \times [(5)^2 + (5 + x)^2]$$

$$\Rightarrow 169 = (25 + 25 + x^2 + 10x)$$

$$\Rightarrow x^2 + 10x = 119$$

x = 7 cm

So, the thickness of the hollow sphere = x = 7 cm

Hence, the correct option is (B).

71. The idiom "sow wild oats" is used for young people who waste their time doing stupid or idle things

OR

to have many sexual relationships particularly when one is young.

Example: They look upon his indiscretions as just his sowing his wild oats.

Hence, the correct option is (D).

72. Phrase: 'method to my madness' means that there is often a reason behind someone's mysterious behavior; There's a reason for someone's strange behavior.

Example: "At the start of his presentation, it seemed that he's out of his mind, but when he finished, we saw that there's a method in his madness."

Hence, the correct option is (B).

73. Birds do not feel breathing trouble when flying at very high altitudes because they have extra air sacs. Birds have hollow bones which are very light and strong. Their wings are light and the shape of their wings is perfect for catching wind.

Hence, the correct option is (C).

74. Dinosaurs, which means large lizards in the Greek language, were Earth's most important terrestrial vertebrate organisms for about 16 million years. It existed from the end of the Triassic period (about 23 million years ago) to the Cretaceous period (about 6.5 million years ago), after which most of them became extinct as a result of the Cretaceous – Trilogy extinction event.

Hence, the correct option is (B).

75. The Asian Football Confederation has awarded the hosting rights of the 2022 Women's Asian Cup to India for the first time since 1979.

The decision was taken at the AFC Women's Football Committee meeting.

In February 2020, the AFC Women's Football Committee had recommended India to be hosts.

The tournament will likely be held in the second half of 2020.

AFC: Headquarters - Kuala Lumpur, Malaysia.

Hence, the correct option is (B).

76. Lalit Modi was the founder & first Chairman and Commissioner of the Indian Premier League (IPL), and ran the tournament for three years until 2010.

In 2010 he was announced as the second most powerful person in Indian Sports by Sports Illustrated.

Brijesh Patel is the present Chairman of the Indian Premier League in the year 2020.

There have been thirteen seasons of the IPL tournament. The current IPL title holders are the Mumbai Indians, who won the 2020 season.

Hence, the correct option is (D).

77. Buddhist site Tabo Monastery is located in Himachal Pradesh state of India.

Tabo Monatery was founded in 996 CE in the Tibetan year by the king of the western Himalayan kingdom of Guge namely Buddhist Lotsawa Rinchen Zangpo. It is located in the Tabo village of Spiti Valley, Himachal Pradesh, Northern India.

Hence, the correct option is (B).

78. Given:

$$a^3 + b^3 + c^3 = 3abc$$

$$a^3 + b^3 + c^3 - 3abc = 0$$

We know that,

$$a^3 + b^3 + c^3 - 3abc = (a + b + c)$$
$$(a^2 + b^2 + c^2 - ab - bc - ca)$$

$$\Rightarrow (a + b + c)(a^2 + b^2 + c^2 - ab - bc - ca) = 0$$

So,

$$(a^2 + b^2 + c^2 - ab - bc - ca) = 0$$

And,

$$a + b + c = 0$$

$\therefore$ The value of $a + b + c$ is 0.

Hence, the correct option is (D).

79. The Indian government released a commemorative postage stamp on the 75th anniversary of the United Nations. S Jaishankar, External Affairs Minister was the chief guest at the event. "As a founding member of the United Nations, India is invested with its heart and soul, right from the crafting of the principles of the UN Charter to being in the forefront of keeping its peace," the external affairs minister said.

Hence, the correct option is (B).

80. The headquarters of the United Nations is a distinctive complex in New York City (USA). The United Nations has three additional, subsidiary, regional headquarters or headquarter districts. These are located in Geneva (Switzerland), Vienna (Austria), and Nairobi (Kenya).

Hence, the correct option is (A).

81. Aryabhata spacecraft was India's first satellite, named after the famous Indian astronomer of the same name. Contents Aryabhatta, which was launched by the Soviet Union on 19 April 1975.

Hence, the correct option is (A).

82. Wilhelm Conrad Rontgen discovered X-rays. Rontgen's discovery occurred accidentally when he was testing whether cathode rays could pass through glass when he noticed a glow coming from a nearby chemically coated screen. X-rays are electromagnetic energy waves that act similarly to light rays but at wavelengths approximately 1,000 times shorter than those of light.

Hence, the correct option is (A).

83. Remedial teaching refers to the method of teaching that helps the teacher to provide learners with the necessary help and guidance to overcome the problems which are determined through diagnosing them.

Hence, the correct option is (D).

84. If students have not learned something, you cannot expect them to correct themselves. Students make mistakes when they try to do something which they are not yet able to do.

Hence, the correct option is (A).

85. Let the radius of circle $r = 4$ cm

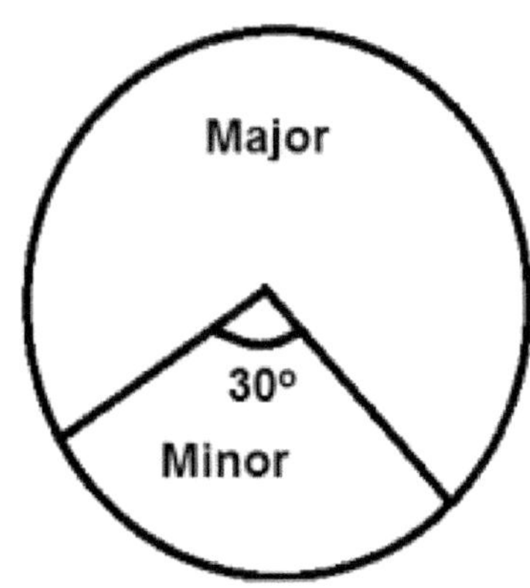

$\angle \theta = 30°$

Area of sector of circle $= \dfrac{\theta}{360°} \times \pi r^2$

$= \dfrac{30°}{360°} \times \pi \times 4 \times 4$

$= \dfrac{\pi}{12} \times 16$

$= \dfrac{4\pi}{3}$

$= \dfrac{4}{3} \times 3.14$

$= 4.186$ cm^2

Area of major sector = Area of circle-area of minor sector

$= \pi r^2 - 4.186$

$= 3.14 \times 4 \times 4 - 4.186$

$= 3.14 \times 16 - 4.186$

$= 50.24$ cm^2

Hence, the correct option is (A).

86. From the figure, it is clear that there are two right angle triangle named as AOQ and ORB.

Here, A is the center of the chordPQ and B is the center of the chord RS.

So, PA = AQ = RB = SB = $\dfrac{6}{2}$ = 3 cm

O is the center of the diameter QR,

So, OQ = QR = $\dfrac{10}{2}$ = 5 cm

In triangle AOQ, applying Pythagoras theorem,

$OQ^2 = AQ^2 + AO^2$

$25 = 9 + AO^2$

$AO^2 = 16$

$AO = 4$

In triangle AOQ and ORB,

$\angle A = \angle B$

$\angle Q = \angle R$

So, by AA congruency,

$\triangle\, AOQ \rightarrow ORB$

So, $AO = OR = 4$

Vertical distance $= 8$ cm

Hence, the correct option is (C).

87. Given,

3 men or 5 women can complete the work in 12 days.

Work done by 3 men = Work done by 5 women

1 men $= \dfrac{5}{3} \times$ women

Now, 3 men $+7$ women $= 3 \times \left(\dfrac{5}{3}\right) + 7$ women $= 12$ women

As we know,

$W1 \times D1 = W2 \times D2$

$\therefore 5 \times 12 = 12 \times D2$

$\Rightarrow D2 = 5$ days

Hence, the correct option is (A).

88. Given,

Wages of 20 days of 1 man and 1 woman = Rs. 1500

Let efficiency of 1 woman be 1 unit/day

Efficiency of 1 man $= 2$ unit/day

According to the question,

$2 + 1 = 3$ unit

$\Rightarrow 3$ unit $= 1500$

$\Rightarrow 1$ unit $= \dfrac{1500}{3} = 500$

20 day's wages of 1 woman = Rs. 500

Daily wages of 1 woman $= \dfrac{500}{20} = $ Rs. 25

Hence, the correct option is (A).

89. The given sentence is in passive form and its structure is:

Passive: Object + was/were (not) + verb (IIIrd form) + (by + subject).

Its active structure would be:

Active: Subject + did not + verb (Ist form) + object.

It is optional to include the part (By + subject) in the passive voice. In sentences where the subject is hidden or not given, we need to create a subject accordingly.

The active form of the given sentence would be:

They didn't give him the information he needed.

Hence, the correct option is (D).

90. The sentence is in passive form and needs to be changed into active voice. The structure for passive/active voice has been shown below:

Passive: Object + was/were + verb (IIIrd form) + (by + subject).

Active: Subject + verb (IInd form) + object.

So, according to the above structure, the active voice of the given sentence would be:

Nobody told Bipin about the meeting.

Hence, the correct option is (C).

91. Total expenses = 4 + 3 + 4 + 6 + 1

$= 18$ lakh

Total raw materials and interest expenses = 4 + 6

$= 10$ lakh

% raw materials and interest expenses $= \dfrac{10}{18} \times 100$

$= 55.56\%$

Hence, the correct option is (D).

92. Here, mean = 5, and number of observation = 10

$$\text{Mean} = \dfrac{Sum\ of\ observation}{Number\ of\ observations}$$

$\therefore$ Sum of observations = 5 × 10

$= 50$

Now 2 added to each observation

$\therefore$ Sum = 50 + (10×2)

$= 70$

Now each observation multiplied by 3

$\therefore$ New sum = 70 × 3 = 210

$$\text{New mean} = \dfrac{New\ sum}{Number\ of\ observations}$$

$= \dfrac{210}{10}$

$= 21$

Hence, the correct option is (D).

93. $= 44 - 6 + 43 \times 2 - 87$
$= 44 - 6 + 86 - 87$
$= 130 - 93$
$= 37$

Hence, the correct option is (A).

94. Given:

$\angle ACD = 112°$ and $\angle CBA = \dfrac{3}{4} \angle BAC,$

Calculation:

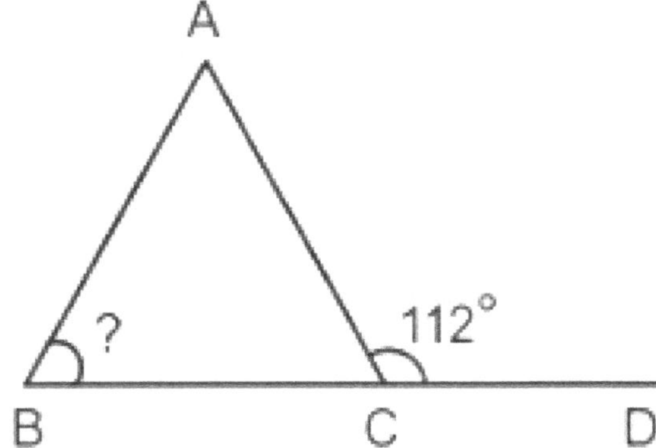

$\angle ACD + \angle ACB = 180°$ (The sum of linear pair angles is 180°)

$\Rightarrow \angle ACB = 180° - 112°$

$\Rightarrow \angle ACB = 68°$

Now we have,

$\angle CBA = \left(\dfrac{3}{4}\right) \angle BAC$

$\Rightarrow \angle BAC = \left(\dfrac{4}{3}\right) \angle CBA$

In Δ ABC,

$\angle BAC + \angle CBA + \angle ACB = 180°$ (The sum measures of all three angles of a triangle are 180°)

$\Rightarrow \left(\dfrac{4}{3}\right) \angle CBA + \angle CBA + 68° = 180°$

$\Rightarrow \left(\dfrac{7}{3}\right) \angle CBA = 180° - 68°$

$\Rightarrow \left(\dfrac{7}{3}\right) \angle CBA = 112°$

$\Rightarrow \angle CBA = 16 \times 3 = 48°$

$\therefore \angle CBA = 48°$.

Hence, the correct option is (B).

95. Providing learning support to pupils who lag far behind their counterparts in school performance includes initially adapting school curriculum and teaching strategies.

During learning, a child makes mistakes willingly-unwillingly or due to some alternative conceptions. It is the job of a teacher to help students to correct those mistakes after diagnosing them. Remedy means to provide instructional correctives. The method so followed is known as remedial teaching. The following are its characteristics:

It can be used for improving the required skills.

It favours providing learning support to pupils who lag far behind their counterparts in school) performance by initially adapting school curriculum and teaching strategies.

Hence, the correct option is (D).

96. The eldest son, a government servant, lived with his wife and children in far off lands. **The second son had left home at an early age. As a merchant he travelled all over the world.**

Kindly refer to the 2nd and 3rd sentences of the 2nd paragraph. The 3rd sentence clearly states that he travelled all over the world because he was a merchant.

Hence, the correct option is (D).

97. The eldest son, a government servant, lived with his wife and children in far off lands.

The above reference has been taken from the 1st sentence of the 2nd paragraph and nothing has been mentioned here as to why the eldest son had not attended the festival.

Hence, the correct option is (D).

98. From the last sentence of the 2nd paragraph '**...The neighbours looked on.**' it is clearly inferred that the mother did not buy gifts for her neighbours. The statement I hence is not correct.

The second last sentence of the 1st paragraph says, '**... The orders had been placed with shops well in advance.**' which

means the mother did not order any of the servants to prepare sweets or food. The statement II is also false here.

The third last sentence of the 2nd paragraph which states, '**... The youngest son, left in the company of a servant, was soon bored, left her and stood at the door all day long, waiting and watching.**' clearly contradicts what's being stated in the statement III. The statement III hence is not true as well.

Hence, the correct option is (A).

99. In the third last sentence of the 2nd paragprah, '**... The youngest son, left in the company of a servant, was soon bored, left her and stood at the door all day long, waiting and watching.**' it is clearly stated that the youngest son stood at the door while his mother was busy.

The other two given statements are nowhere mentioned in the passage.

Hence, the correct option is (D).

100. His mother, <u>thrilled and excited</u>, loaded the presents on trays and plates, covered them with colourful kerchiefs, and sent them off with maids and servants.

We can clearly infer from the above sentence taken from the 2nd paragraph of the passage that the mother really enjoyed sending gifts to her family members at festival time.

Hence, the correct option is (C).

Q.1 Who among the following was appointed as the Chief Information Commissioner (CIC) in March 2020?

[SSC MTS, 2021]

A. Ajay Bhushan Pandey
B. Satish Kumar Sharma
C. Amita Pandove
D. Bimal Julka

Q.2 Who among the followings has been elected as the 15 th President of India in July 2022 ?

A. Nirmala Sitharaman
B. Swati Piramal
C. Hima Kohli
D. Droupadi Murmu

Q.3 Who among the following has won the French Presidential Election-2017?

[UPPSC Staff Nurse, 2017]

A. Marine Le Pen
B. Francois Hollande
C. Emmanuel Macron
D. Jean-Luc Mélenchon

Q.4 What is the contribution of India to the UN Women Core budget in 2022?

[Delhi Forest Guard, 2021], [HSSC Canal Patwari, 2021]

A. USD 10,000
B. USD 50,000
C. USD 100,000
D. USD 500,000

Q.5 Who discovered the ruins of Harappa?
A. Sir John Hubert Marshall
B. Dr. Sahni
C. M. Wheeler
D. M.S. Vats

Q.6 In which time is the raga des sung?
A. Dead of night
B. Morning
C. First stroke of the night
D. Second stroke of night

Q.7 Which of the following is well-known in singing?
A. Shobhana Narayan
B. Pandit Yuraj
C. M. S. Gopalakrishnan
D. M. S. Subbulakshmi

Q.8 If A: B=2: 5, B: C=4: 3 and C: D=2: 1, then what is value of A: C: D ?
A. 6: 5: 2
B. 7: 20: 10
C. 8: 30: 15
D. 16: 30: 15

Q.9 The duplicate ratio of $x + 3 : x + 7$ is $4 : 9$ then find the value of x.
A. 5
B. 3
C. 2
D. 4

Q.10 The solution to the inequality $-x^2 + 5x - 6 > 0$ is:
A. $(-2,3]$
B. $[3,2)$
C. $(2,3)$
D. $(0,0)$

Q.11 The sum of all odd numbers of two terms will be-
A. 2475
B. 2530
C. 4905
D. 5049

Q.12 After giving a discount of 10%, a trader earns 20% profit on an item. Find the profit percentage when he gives no discount.
A. 30%
B. 33%
C. 25%
D. 20%

Q.13 Who is the author of the book Azadi- Freedom, Fascism or Fiction?
A. Maroof Raza
B. Shashi Tharoor
C. Anupam Kher
D. Arundhati Roy

Ques (14-15):Direction: In the following question, sentences of a paragraph have been jumbled and labeled as A, B, C and D. You are required to rearrange the jumbled sentences of the paragraph and mark your response accordingly by selecting the correct option.

Q.14 A: It was a Sunday morning and, like every other Sunday, Rose Kunis was headed to work.

B: She worked as a pastor at a local church.

C: After reaching the church, she hunted for an empty spot to park her car.

D: But that was not the only thing that made her unique—she was the only female pastor in the entire country.

A. ABDC
B. DBCA
C. BADC
D. ADBC

Q.15 A: Some of them have entrances decorated with flowers and trees.

B: Others have painted the interiors with soft colors.

C: Nowadays many have started to install special lights so that the customers can click wonderful pictures.

D: In order to attract and keep their customers, restaurants have tried to look as pleasing as possible.

A. DABC
B. ACDB
C. BDCA
D. CABD

Q.16 Evaluate- $\left(\dfrac{x^a}{x^b}\right)^{a+b} \cdot \left(\dfrac{x^b}{x^c}\right)^{b+c} \cdot \left(\dfrac{x^c}{x^a}\right)^{c+a}$
A. 1
B. 0
C. x
D. $x^{2(a^3+b^3+c^3)}$

Q.17 A sum of money becomes 27 times in 3 years. Find the rate of interest at which the money is lent at compound interest charged annually.
A. 250%
B. 200%
C. 261%
D. 245%

Q.18 Calculate the principal, if an amount of Rs. 605 is received in compound interest at the rate of 10% per annum after 2 years.
A. 413
B. 500
C. 5500
D. 454

Q.19 Consider the following organizations:

1. East India Association
2. The Bombay Presidency Association
3. Poona Sarvajanik Sabha

Which of the following is the correct chronological sequence of the formation of the above organizations?

A. 1-3-2   **B.** 3-2-1   **C.** 2-1-3   **D.** 3-1-2

Q.20 'Jonas Salk' invented the vaccine for ________.

A. Typhoid   **B.** Cholera   **C.** Hepatitis   **D.** Polio

Q.21 Who is known as the father of Artificial Intelligence?

A. Vint Cerf   **B.** Ray Tomlinson
C. Tim Berners-Lee   **D.** John McCarthy

Q.22 In this figure PQ ⊥ RS and RT ∥ PQ. if ∠PST = 68° then find reflexive ∠RTS.

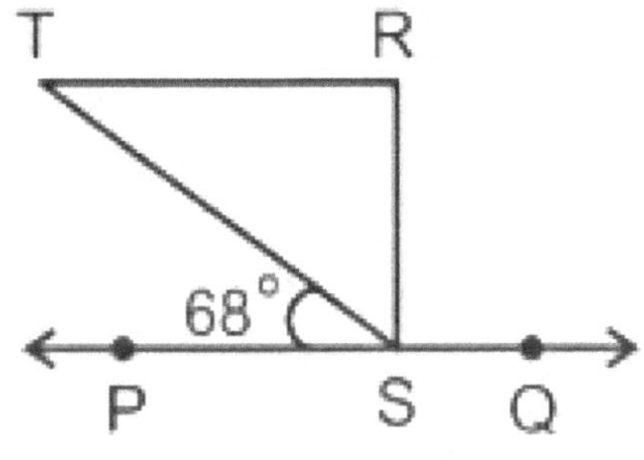

A. 134°   **B.** 292°   **C.** 234°   **D.** 102°

Q.23 Which among the following waves are most commonly used in the Night Vision Devices?

A. Ultra Violet Rays   **B.** Gamma Rays
C. Infra-Red Rays   **D.** X Rays

Q.24 The apparatus used in submarines to give a clear view of the objects on the surface of the ocean or ground is known as________.

A. Periscope   **B.** Vernier Caliper
C. Telescope   **D.** Stereoscope

Q.25 What is the value of $\sqrt{7\sqrt{7\sqrt{7\sqrt{7\ldots\ldots}}}}$?

A. 49   **B.** $\sqrt{7}$
C. 7   **D.** None of these

Q.26 A rectangular field has an area of $120\ m^2$ and a perimeter of $46\ m$. What is the maximum length of the pole that can be placed in the field?

A. 16 m   **B.** 19 m
C. 17 m   **D.** Can't be determined

Q.27 The radius of the two cylinders is in the ratio of 3 : 2 and their heights are in the ratio 3 : 7. The ratio of their volumes is :

A. 4 : 7   **B.** 7 : 4   **C.** 28 : 27   **D.** 27 : 28

Q.28 The radius of a cylinder is 5 cm and height is 8 cm. The number of centimetres that may be subtracted either from the radius or from the height to get the same decrease in the volume of cylinder is

A. 0 cm   **B.** 1 cm   **C.** 20 cm   **D.** 40 cm

Q.29 The largest and the oldest museum of India is located in the state/union territory of:

A. New Delhi   **B.** West Bengal
C. Uttar Pradesh   **D.** Andhra Pradesh

Q.30 What is the unit digit of the sum of first 222 whole numbers?

A. 4   **B.** 6   **C.** 1   **D.** 0

Q.31 One of the factor of $\left(8^{2k} + 5^{2k}\right)$, where k is an odd number, is:

A. 89   **B.** 86   **C.** 13   **D.** 40

Q.32 What percent of 1 day is 37 minutes 45 sec?

A. 2.62%   **B.** 2.1%   **C.** 2.69%   **D.** 0.25%

Q.33 40 litres of 60% concentration of acid solution is added to 35 litres of 80% concentration of acid solution. What is the concentration of acid in the new solution?

A. 66%   **B.** $66\frac{2}{3}\%$ **C.** $69\frac{1}{3}\%$ **D.** 69%

Ques (34-35):Direction: In the following question, out of the four given alternatives, select the alternative which best expresses the meaning of the Idiom/Phrase.

Q.34 Ever and anon

A. Always   **B.** Occasionally
C. Continuously   **D.** Never

Q.35 Backbite

A. Scold gently
B. Thrash someone badly
C. Praise highly of someone
D. Slander someone in his/her absence

Q.36 World Environment Day is observed globally on ________ every year.

A. 9th June   **B.** 3rd June   **C.** 5th June   **D.** 8th June

Q.37 The United Nations General Assembly had decided to observe an International Democracy day every year. On which date is it celebrated?

A. September 5   **B.** September 10
C. September 15   **D.** September 20

Ques (38-39):Direction: Each item in this section consists of a sentence with an underlined word followed by four options. Select the option that is opposite in meaning to the underlined word.

Q.38 Ramesh is a very dubious character.

[UPSC NDA, 2019]

A. shady   **B.** suspicious
C. trustworthy   **D.** doubtful

Q.39 Do not indulge in unmindful activities, please.

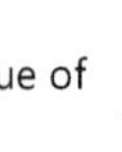

[UPSC NDA, 2019]

A. vigilant   **B.** careless   **C.** stupid   **D.** fatuous

Q.40 The curved surface area of sphere X is 96% more than that of sphere Y, while the curved surface area of sphere Z is 44% more than that of sphere Y. Find the ratio of the volumes of sphere X and sphere Z?

A. 125 : 64   **B.** 216 : 125
C. 343 : 216   **D.** 512 : 343

Q.41 Consider the following statements with reference to SWAMITVA Scheme:

1. The Ministry of Rural Development (MoRD) is the Nodal Ministry for THE implementation of the scheme.

2. The scheme will help in streamlining planning and revenue collection in rural areas and ensuring clarity on property rights.

3. The scheme will enable the creation of better-quality Gram Panchayat Development Plans (GPDPs).

Which of the statements given above is/are correct?

A. 1 only   **B.** 2 and 3   **C.** 2 only   **D.** 1 and 3

Q.42 Consider the following statements with reference to the Limited Liability Partnership (LLP):

1. In an LLP, each partner is not responsible or liable for another partner's misconduct or negligence.

2. The internal governance structure of a company and LLP both are regulated by statute, Companies Act, 2013.

Which of the statements given above is/are correct?

A. 1 only   **B.** 2 only
C. Both 1 and 2   **D.** Neither 1 nor 2

Q.43 Which one of the following layers is the thinnest of all?

A. Crust   **B.** Mantle
C. Core   **D.** None of the above

Q.44 Which of the following agent can shape a rock-like Mushroom?

A. Glacier   **B.** Wind
C. River   **D.** Sea wave

Q.45 Match the following,

List I (Wind)	List II (Type)
a. Monsoon	i. Local wind
b. Trade wind	ii. Seasonal wind
c. Blizzard	iii. Permanent wind

Choose the correct option from the following,

A. a - i, b - ii, c - iii   **B.** a - ii, b - iii, c - i
C. a - ii, b - i, c - iii   **D.** a - iii, b - i, c - ii

Ques (46-48):Directions: Each of the following items in this section has a sentence with a missing preposition. Select the correct preposition from the given options and mark your response accordingly.

Q.46 I have known her ______ a long time.

[UPSC NDA, 2020]

A. since   **B.** for   **C.** at   **D.** before

Q.47 I accepted the offer ______ certain conditions.

[UPSC NDA, 2020]

A. on   **B.** in   **C.** by   **D.** within

Q.48 She is a woman ______ humble origin.

[UPSC NDA, 2020]

A. off   **B.** of   **C.** from   **D.** within

Q.49 The LCM and HCF of polynomial $P(x)$ and $Q(x)$ are $56(x^4 + x)$ and $4(x^2 - x + 1)$ respectively. If the polynomial $P(x) = 28(x^3 + 1)$ then $Q(x) =$?

[Joint Entrance Examination (Polytechnic), 2018]

A. $8x(x^2 - x + 1)$ **B.** $6x(x^2 + x - 1)$
C. $4x(x^2 - x + 1)$ **D.** None of these

Q.50 In the figure given below, AB is a line of length 4a, with M as midpoint. Semi - circles are drawn on one side with AM and MB as diameters. A circle with centre O and radius r is drawn such that this circle touches all the three semi - circles. What is the value of r?

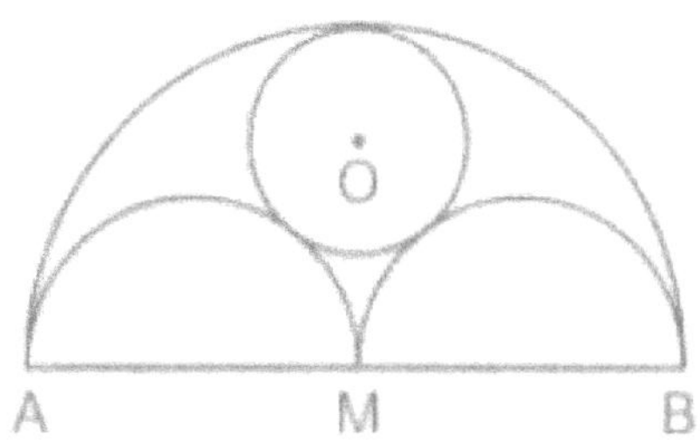

A. $\frac{a}{3}$ **B.** $\frac{2a}{3}$ **C.** $\frac{a}{4}$ **D.** $\frac{3a}{4}$

Q.51 A circular wire of radius 49 cm is bent in the form of a rectangle whose sides are in the ratio of 9: 5. The smaller side of the rectangle is: (Take $\pi = \frac{22}{7}$)

A. 55 cm   **B.** 45 cm   **C.** 25 cm   **D.** 35 cm

Ques (52-53):Direction: In the following question, a sentence has been given in Active/Passive Voice. Out of the four alternatives suggested, select the one which best expresses the same sentence in Passive/Active Voice.

Q.52 You have misspelt the word.
A.   The words have been misspelt by you
B.   The word had been misspelt by you
C.   The word has been misspelt by you
D.   Misspelling of the word has been done by you

Q.53 What was your drawing on the blackboard?
A.   What is being drawn on the blackboard?
B.   What was being drawn on the blackboard by you?
C.   What had been drawn on the blackboard by you?
D.   What was to be drawn on the blackboard by you?

Q.54 If $4b^2 + \frac{1}{b^2} = 2$, then the value of $8b^3 + \frac{1}{b^3}$ is:
A. 0   **B.** 1   **C.** 2   **D.** 5

Q.55 The Capital of Argentina is ________.

A. Havana   **B.** Canberra
C. Buenos Aires   **D.** Ottawa

Q.56 The first medieval ruler to propound the divine theory of kingship was:

A. Qutabuddin Aibak   **B.** Iltutmish
C. Balban   **D.** Alauddin Khilji

Q.57 The first woman in the world to climb Mount Everest twice is __________.

A. Sherpa Tenzing   **B.** Edmund Hillary
C. Premlata Agarwal   **D.** Santosh Yadav

Q.58 Which one of the following manuscript is included in the UNESCO's Memory of World Register?

A. Rig Veda   **B.** Ramayana
C. Mahabharata   **D.** None of the above

Q.59 KUSUM scheme is related to:

A. Solar pumps
B. Woman empowerment
C. Woman security fund
D. Bus service for women

Q.60 Who among the following introduced the concept of 'imaginary reference group'?

A. New Comb   **B.** Merton
C. Klinberg   **D.** Hyman

Q.61 According to Weber, the three types of leadership are:

A. Rational, feudal and capitalistic
B. Legal, traditional and charismatic
C. Feudal, traditional and charismatic
D. None of these

Q.62 What substance do bacteria on your teeth produce and create spots in the teeth?

A. Gum disease   **B.** Plaque
C. Gingivitis   **D.** None of these

Q.63 Blood sugar level can be decreased by:

A. Insulin given from mouth
B. Glucagon given through mouth
C. Intravenous injection of insulin
D. Intravenous injection of glucagon

Ques (64-68):Read the passage given below and answer the question that follow by selecting the most appropriate option.

One day in 1924, five men who were camping in the Cascade Mountains of Washington saw a group of huge apelike creatures coming out of the woods. They hurried back to their cabin and locked themselves inside. While they were in, the creatures attacked them by throwing rocks against the walls of the cabin. After several hours, these strange hairy giants went back into the woods. After this incident the men returned to the town and told the people of their adventure. However, only a few people accepted their story. These were the people who remembered hearing tales about footprints of an animal that walked like a human being. The five men, however, were not the first people to have seen these creatures called Bigfoot. Long before their experience, local Native Americans were certain that a race of apelike animals had been living in the neighboring mountain for centuries. They called these creatures Sasquatch. In 1958, workmen, who were building a road through the jungles of Northern California often found huge footprints in the earth around their camp. Then in 1967, Roger Patterson, a man who was interested in finding Bigfoot went into the northern California jungles with a friend. While riding, they were suddenly thrown off from their horses. Patterson saw a tall apelike animal standing not far away. He managed to shoot seven rolls of film of the hairy creature before the animal disappeared in the hushes. When Patterson's film was shown to the public, not many people believed his story. In another incident, Richard Brown, a music teacher and also an experience hunter spotted a similar creature. He saw the animal clearly through the telescopic lens of his rifle. He said the creature looked more like a human than an animal. Later many other people also found deep footprints in the same area. In spite of regular reports of sightings and footprints, most experts still do not believe that Bigfoot really exists.

Q.64 What did the five campers do when they saw a group of apelike creatures?

A. They ran into the woods and hid there for several hours.
B. They quickly ran back into their cabin and locked the cabin door.
C. They threw rocks against the walls of their cabin to frighten the creatures away.
D. They attacked the creatures by throwing rocks at them.

Q.65 Did the town people believe the story of the five men about their meeting with Bigfoot ?

A. No, not everyone believed their story.
B. Only those who had heard the same tale the second time believed them
C. Some said the five men were making up their own story.
D. All the people believed what they said..

Q.66 Who were the first people to have seen these apelike creatures before the five campers?

A. The workers who built the road in the jungles of Northern California.
B. Roger Patterson and his friend.
C. The local Native Americans.
D. Richard Brown, a music teacher and a hunter.

Q.67 The word neighbouring would BEST be replaced with

A. Far-off   **B.** Nearby
C. Remote   **D.** Far-away

Q.68 Who gave the name 'Sasquatch' to the apelike creatures?

A. The five campers
B. Roger Patterson
C. The local Native Americans
D. Richard Brown

Q.69 What will come in place of the question mark '?' in the following question?

$(0.1 \times 0.004) + (0.02 \times 0.3) - (0.04 \times 0.03) = ?$

A. 0.0022   **B.** 0.0034   **C.** 0.0046   **D.** 0.0052

Q.70 How many elements have been known so far?

A. 102   **B.** 106   **C.** 104   **D.** 118

Q.71 Which of the following is the element with the last permanent nucleus of the periodic table?

A. Uranium   **B.** Radan   **C.** Bismuth   **D.** Radium

Q.72 A shopkeeper sold 6 cold-drink bottles at the cost price of 8. What percentage of profit did he make?

A. $33\frac{1}{3}\%$ **B.** $33\frac{2}{3}\%$ **C.** $35\frac{1}{3}\%$ **D.** $35\frac{2}{3}\%$

Q.73 A man bought watermelons at the rate of 54 for Rs. 2700 and sold them at rate of 4 for Rs. 280. How many watermelons should be sold to earn a profit of Rs. 1200?

A. 54   **B.** 60   **C.** 20   **D.** 80

Q.74 The median of the observations 22, 24, 33, 37, x + 1, x + 3, 46, 47, 57, 58 in ascending order is 42. What are the values of 5th and 6th observations respectively?

[UPSC NDA, 2019]

A. 42, 45   **B.** 41, 43   **C.** 43, 46   **D.** 40, 40

Q.75 Arithmetic mean of 10 observations is 60 and sum of squares of deviations from 50 is 5000. What is the standard deviation of the observations?

[UPSC NDA, 2019]

A. 20   **B.** 21   **C.** 22.36   **D.** 24.70

Q.76 Which of the following statements relating to the International Labor Organisation (ILO) is incorrect?

A. Social security was one of the agendas of ILO when it was found.

B. In 2003, ILO launched a Global Campaign on "Social Security and Coverage for All".

C. Due to a lack of consensus, social security was not included as one of the human rights under the Universal Declaration of Human Rights (UDHR), 1948.

D. ILO mandate of extension of social security measures was restated in 1944 in the Declaration of Philadelphia to provide a basic income to all in need of such protection and comprehensive medical care.

Q.77 The International Monetary Fund (IMF) works to foster which of the following?

1. Global monetary cooperation
2. Secure financial stability
3. Facilitate international trade
4. Reduction of poverty around the world

Select the correct answer using the code given below:

A. 1 and 2 only   **B.** 2 and 3 only
C. 1, 2 and 4 only   **D.** 1, 2, 3 and 4

Q.78 'Playing It My Way' is the autobiography of which Cricketer?

[NCHM JEE (Hotel Mgmt & Catering), 2018]

A. M.S. Dhoni   **B.** Sachin Tendulkar
C. Virat Kohli   **D.** Yuvraj Singh

Q.79 Which of the following personalities has never served as the Prime Minister of India?

[NCHM JEE (Hotel Mgmt & Catering), 2018]

A. Zakir Hussain   **B.** Lal Bahadur Shastri
C. Indira Gandhi   **D.** Inder Kumar Gujral

Q.80 Direction: In the following question, some part of the sentence may have errors. Find out which part of the sentence has an error and select the appropriate option. If the sentence is free from error, select 'No error'.

I purchased (A)/ this ball yesterday (B)/ and have given it to my friend. (C)/ No error (D)

A. A   **B.** B   **C.** C   **D.** D

Q.81 Direction: In this question, each item consists of six sentences of passage. The first and sixth sentences are given in the beginning as SI and S6. The middle four-sentence in each have been jumbled up and labelled as P, Q, R and S. You are required to find the proper sequence of the four sentences.

S1: The body can never stop.

S6: It comes from food.

P: To support this endless activity, the body needs all the fuel for action.

Q: Sometimes it is more active than at other times, but it is always moving.

R: Even in the deepest sleep we must breathe.

S: The fuel must come from somewhere.

The proper sequence should be

A. P Q R S   **B.** P R Q S   **C.** Q R P S   **D.** S R Q P

Q.82 A, B, C started a business with their investments in the ratio $1:4:6$. After 6 months, A invested the same amount as before, and B, as well as C, withdrew half of their investments. The ratio of their profits at the end of the year is:

A. $1:2:3$ **B.** $3:4:15$
C. $3:5:10$ **D.** $3:6:8$

Q.83 Which of the fractions given below, when added to $\frac{5}{7}$ give 1?

A. $\frac{6}{21}$ **B.** $\frac{4}{2}$ **C.** $\frac{6}{14}$ **D.** $\frac{5}{3}$

Q.84 With which game is Amitabh Vijayvargiya associated?

[Madhya Pradesh Public Service Commission (MPPSC), 2017]

A. Hockey   **B.** Football
C. Cricket   **D.** None of these

Q.85 What was the name of the cricket world cup played in 1987?

[Madhya Pradesh Public Service Commission (MPPSC), 2017]

A. Reliance Cup

B. Benson & Hedges Cup

C. Wills cup

D. None of these

Q.86 If 3 men or 6 women can harvest a field in 40 days. How long will 2 men and 6 women take to harvest it?

A. 24 days   **B.** 32 days   **C.** 16 days   **D.** 28 days

Q.87 50 men earn Rs. 45,000 in 5 days, then how much 30 men earn in 25 days.

A. Rs. 1,35,000   **B.** Rs. 17,20,000
C. Rs. 60,000   **D.** Rs. 75,000

Q.88 Which one of the following is not a feature of ideology?
A. A political belief system
B. An action-oriented set of political ideas
C. The world view of a particular social class or social group
D. The political ideas that do not embody or articulate class or social interests

Q.89 Which of the following is called as the leader of Lok Sabha?
A. Speaker   **B.** President
C. Prime Minister   **D.** Deputy Speaker

Q.90 In Remedial teaching concentration on trouble spots is best done by:
A. Arranging intensive practice
B. Arranging medicine
C. Arranging trouble
D. Arranging bubble spot

Ques (91-92):Direction: Select the correct one-word for the given group of words.

Q.91 A collection of historical documents or records providing information about a place, institution, or group of people is known as:
A. Arena   **B.** Arsenal   **C.** Asylum   **D.** Archives

Q.92 A person who abstains from all kinds of alcoholic drinks is known as:
A. Tenant   **B.** Teetotaller
C. Drunkard   **D.** Truant

Q.93 What is the smallest number by which 392 must be multiplied so that the product is a perfect cube?
A. 7   **B.** 8   **C.** 6   **D.** 5

Ques (94-96):Direction: The following table gives the percentage of marks obtained by seven students in six different subjects in an examination.

The Numbers in the Brackets give the Maximum Marks in Each Subject.

Student	Subject (Max. Marks)					
	Maths	Chemistry	Physics	Geography	History	Computer Science
	(150)	(130)	(120)	(100)	(60)	(40)
Ayush	90	50	90	60	70	80
Aman	100	80	80	40	80	70
Sajal	90	60	70	70	90	70
Rohit	80	65	80	80	60	60
Muskan	80	65	85	95	50	90
Tanvi	70	75	65	85	40	60
Tarun	65	35	50	77	80	80

Q.94
What are the average marks obtained by all the seven students in Physics? (rounded off to two-digit after the decimal)
A. 77.26   **B.** 89.14   **C.** 91.37   **D.** 96.11

Q.95
What was the aggregate of marks obtained by Sajal in all six subjects?
A. 409   **B.** 419   **C.** 429   **D.** 449

Q.96
In which subject is the overall percentage the best?
[NCHM JEE (Hotel Mgmt & Catering), 2016]

A. Maths   **B.** Chemistry
C. Physics   **D.** History

Q.97 If the difference between a number and 37.5% of the number is 45, find the number.
A. 60   **B.** 66   **C.** 72   **D.** 78

Q.98 $9\frac{3}{4} \div \left[2\frac{1}{6} \div \left\{ 4\frac{1}{3} - \left(2\frac{1}{2} + \frac{3}{4} \right) \right\} \right]$ is equal to:

A. 3   **B.** $\frac{39}{8}$ **C.** 4   **D.** $\frac{15}{4}$

Q.99 A, B, C subscribe Rs. 50000 for a business. A subscribes Rs. 4000 more than B and B Rs. 5000 more than C. Out of a total profit of Rs. 35000, A receives:
A. Rs. 8400   **B.** Rs. 11900
C. Rs. 13600   **D.** Rs. 14700

Q.100 Simple interest on Rs. 24000 at $8\frac{1}{2}\%$ per annum for 8 months is:
A. Rs. 1560   **B.** Rs. 1620   **C.** Rs. 1480   **D.** Rs. 1360

// Smart Answer Sheet //

Correct — Percentage of students who answered correctly. **Skipped** — Percentage of students who skipped.

Q.	Ans.	Correct / Skipped	Q.	Ans.	Correct / Skipped	Q.	Ans.	Correct / Skipped	Q.	Ans.	Correct / Skipped	Q.	Ans.	Correct / Skipped	Q.	Ans.	Correct / Skipped
1	D	21.77 % / 3.36 %	18	B	47.95 % / 1.62 %	35	D	78.31 % / 0.0 %	52	C	46.61 % / 1.93 %	69	D	47.9 % / 1.97 %	86	A	52.62 % / 1.66 %
2	D	88.0 % / 0.0 %	19	A	55.1 % / 1.81 %	36	C	67.09 % / 1.96 %	53	B	64.47 % / 1.78 %	70	D	86.89 % / 0.0 %	87	A	88.35 % / 0.0 %
3	C	43.35 % / 1.55 %	20	D	21.54 % / 4.71 %	37	C	89.1 % / 0.0 %	54	A	10.28 % / 3.76 %	71	C	41.05 % / 1.63 %	88	D	68.2 % / 1.97 %
4	D	83.16 % / 0.0 %	21	D	45.78 % / 1.79 %	38	C	85.88 % / 0.0 %	55	C	80.3 % / 0.0 %	72	A	20.07 % / 3.69 %	89	C	78.0 % / 0.0 %
5	A	64.51 % / 1.42 %	22	B	87.77 % / 0.0 %	39	A	51.81 % / 1.49 %	56	C	45.72 % / 1.08 %	73	B	69.35 % / 1.5 %	90	A	43.11 % / 1.34 %
6	D	59.0 % / 1.55 %	23	C	11.7 % / 4.97 %	40	C	29.77 % / 4.87 %	57	D	30.7 % / 4.75 %	74	B	48.58 % / 1.68 %	91	D	52.17 % / 1.87 %
7	D	64.46 % / 1.74 %	24	A	55.24 % / 1.77 %	41	B	42.68 % / 1.17 %	58	A	59.56 % / 1.11 %	75	A	22.2 % / 4.53 %	92	B	65.24 % / 1.59 %
8	D	78.26 % / 0.0 %	25	C	22.32 % / 4.53 %	42	A	65.88 % / 1.68 %	59	A	42.91 % / 1.65 %	76	C	15.49 % / 3.87 %	93	A	65.01 % / 1.65 %
9	A	79.08 % / 0.0 %	26	C	69.53 % / 1.41 %	43	A	76.7 % / 0.0 %	60	C	77.38 % / 0.0 %	77	D	60.27 % / 1.78 %	94	B	61.93 % / 1.44 %
10	C	86.76 % / 0.0 %	27	D	26.48 % / 4.93 %	44	B	48.15 % / 1.56 %	61	B	47.92 % / 1.34 %	78	B	50.18 % / 1.12 %	95	D	54.46 % / 1.47 %
11	A	46.15 % / 1.24 %	28	A	40.5 % / 1.83 %	45	B	25.04 % / 3.62 %	62	B	62.31 % / 1.03 %	79	A	66.0 % / 1.75 %	96	A	56.36 % / 1.97 %
12	B	57.33 % / 1.48 %	29	B	80.13 % / 0.0 %	46	B	84.82 % / 0.0 %	63	C	83.29 % / 0.0 %	80	C	79.65 % / 0.0 %	97	C	65.58 % / 1.81 %
13	D	46.75 % / 1.08 %	30	C	83.82 % / 0.0 %	47	A	86.59 % / 0.0 %	64	B	89.65 % / 0.0 %	81	C	68.79 % / 1.34 %	98	B	48.86 % / 1.21 %
14	A	53.88 % / 1.8 %	31	A	79.87 % / 0.0 %	48	B	83.86 % / 0.0 %	65	A	42.37 % / 1.68 %	82	A	80.35 % / 0.0 %	99	D	54.42 % / 1.91 %
15	A	49.24 % / 1.3 %	32	A	64.3 % / 1.78 %	49	A	41.66 % / 1.45 %	66	C	81.46 % / 0.0 %	83	A	40.41 % / 1.46 %	100	D	63.68 % / 1.15 %
16	A	15.02 % / 4.41 %	33	C	77.05 % / 0.0 %	50	B	55.57 % / 1.72 %	67	B	79.44 % / 0.0 %	84	C	58.75 % / 1.82 %			
17	B	42.96 % / 1.61 %	34	B	67.44 % / 1.73 %	51	A	48.8 % / 1.25 %	68	C	60.51 % / 1.65 %	85	A	22.27 % / 4.13 %			

//Hints and Solutions//

1. Bimal Julka was appointed as the Chief Information Commissioner (CIC) in March 2020.

Information Commissioner Bimal Julka was appointed as the Chief Information Commissioner (CIC), according to a Rashtrapati Bhavan communique. President Ram Nath Kovind administered the oath of office to Julka as the CIC in the Central Information Commission at a ceremony held at the Rashtrapati Bhavan, it said.

The transparency watchdog has been functioning without a chief after Sudhir Bhargava retired on January 11 and is at a reduced strength of six information commissioners, against the sanctioned strength of 11 (including the CIC).

Hence, the correct option is (D).

2. Former Jharkhand Governor and National Democratic Alliance candidate Droupadi Murmu has been elected as the 15th President of India on 21 July 2022.

She is the first tribal woman to be elected to the position & the youngest as well.

She defeated opposition candidate Yashwant Sinha by bagging 64.03% of the electoral college votes.

Hence, the correct option is (D).

3. Emmanuel Macron has won the French Presidential Election-2017.

On 7 May 2017, Macron was elected President of France with 66.1% of the vote compared to Marine Le Pen's 33.9%. The election had record abstention at 25.4% and 8% of ballots being blank or spoilt.

Hence, the correct option is (C).

4. India has contributed USD 500,000 to the UN Women, the United Nations agency for gender equality and women empowerment for their core budget.

India's Permanent Representative to the United Nations T.S.Tirumurti announced that India reaffirmed its partnership of women-led development and gender parity. UN Women Executive Director, Sima Bahous thanked India for its contribution.

Hence, the correct option is (D).

5. Sir John Hubert Marshall led an excavation campaign in 1921-1922, during which he discovered the ruins of the city of Harappa. By 1931, the Mohenjo-Daro site had been mostly excavated by Marshall and Sir Mortimer Wheeler. By 1999, over 1,056 cities and settlements of the Indus Civilization were located.

Hence, the correct option is (A).

6. The raga des is sung in the second stroke of night.

The raga des originates from Kafithat.

All the vowels are made in its descent. Playing time is considered to be the second hour of the night.

Hence, the correct option is (D).

7. 'Madurai Shanmukhavadivu Subbulakshmi' or M.S. Subbulakshmi is considered synonymous with Carnatic music and was the first singer in India to be awarded the highest civilian award of Bharat Ratna. His sung songs, especially bhajans, are still very popular among the people.

Hence, the correct option is (D).

8. A : B = 2 : 5

B : C = 4 : 3

B is the common terms so first of all the value of B should be made equal.

LCM of 4 and 5 is 20.

$A:B = 2:5$ (multiply by 4)

$B:C = 4:3$ (multiply by 5)

So, A : B : C = 8 : 20 : 15

Now, A: B: C = 8 : 20 : 15

And C : D = 2 : 1

Cis common so its value should be made equal.

LCM of 15 and 2 is 30.

A : B : C = 8 : 20 : 15 (multiply by 2)

C : D = 2 : 1 (multiply by 15)

Now, $A:B:C:D = 16:40:30:15$

Therefore, $A:C:D = 16:30:15$

Hence, the correct option is (D).

9. Duplicate ratio $= x + 3 : x + 7$ is $4:9$

i.e. $\left(\frac{x+3}{x+7}\right)^2 = \frac{4}{9}$

$\Rightarrow \frac{x+3}{x+7} = \frac{2}{3}$

$\Rightarrow 3x + 9 = 2x + 14$

$\Rightarrow x = 5$

$\therefore$ The value of $x = 5$

Hence, the correct option is (A).

10. The given equation is-

$-x^2 + 5x - 6 > 0$

$\Rightarrow x^2 - 5x + 6 < 0$

$\Rightarrow x^2 - 3x - 2x + 6 < 0$

$\Rightarrow x(x - 3) - 2(x - 3) < 0$

$\Rightarrow (x - 3)(x - 2) < 0$

So, (2,3) is the solution to the given inequality.
Hence, the correct option is (C).

11. Series is $\quad 11 + 13 + 15 + \cdots \ldots .99$

nth term $\quad = a + (n-1)d$

$99 = 11 + (n-1)2$
$99 = 11 + 2n - 2$
$99 = 9 + 2n$
$99 - 9 = 2n$
$\qquad 90 = 2n$

$90 = 2n$
$n = \dfrac{90}{2} = 45$

$$\begin{aligned} S_n \quad &= \frac{n}{2}[a + l] \\ &= \frac{45}{2}[11 + 99] \\ &= \frac{45}{2}[110] \\ &= 45 \times 55 \\ &= 2475 \end{aligned}$$

Hence, the correct option is (A).

12. Given,

Let the marked price of an item be Rs. a and cost price be Rs. b.

When it offers discount,

Selling price $= \dfrac{9a}{10}$

Profit percentage $= 20\%$

$\Rightarrow \dfrac{9a}{10} = b \times \dfrac{120}{100}$

$\Rightarrow a = \dfrac{4b}{3}$

When he gives no discount,

Selling price $= a$

Profit percentage $= \dfrac{(a-b)}{b} \times 100$

$\Rightarrow \dfrac{\left(\frac{4b}{3} - b\right)}{b} \times 100$

$\Rightarrow 33.33\%$

Hence, the correct option is (B).

13. The fiction book Azadi: Freedom, Fascism or Fiction is written by Arundhati Roy.

Azadi is a collection of nine essays, some written for magazines and periodicals, and some delivered as public lectures between 2018 and 2020. The pieces offer strong criticism of Prime Minister Narendra Modi and the network of forces associated with his regime.

Hence, the correct option is (D).

14. A is the sentence that introduces 'Rose Kunis'. Hence, it will be the first sentence after rearrangement. B follows A as it further gives detailed information about Rose. D follows B and states what else made her unique. The last sentence is C as it states what she did after reaching the church.

Thus, the correct arrangement would be: ABDC

Hence, the correct option is (A).

15. D is the sentence that establishes the subject matter. Therefore, it will be the first sentence after rearrangement. The next sentence will be A because it starts with "some of them" and refers to the restaurants mentioned in D. The third sentence will be B as it starts with "others" and talks about the interiors of the restaurants and the concluding sentence will be C because it talks about a current trend.

Thus, the correct arrangement would be: DABC

Hence, the correct option is (A).

16. Given-

$$\left(\frac{x^a}{x^b}\right)^{a+b} \cdot \left(\frac{x^b}{x^c}\right)^{b+c} \cdot \left(\frac{x^c}{x^a}\right)^{c+a}$$

$$= \left(x^{a-b}\right)^{a+b} \cdot \left(x^{b-c}\right)^{b+c} \cdot (x^{c-a})^{c+a}$$

$$= x^{(a-b)(a+b)} \cdot x^{(b-c)(b+c)} \cdot x^{(c-a)(c+a)}$$

$$= x^{a^2 - b^2} \cdot x^{b^2 - c^2} \cdot x^{c^2 - a^2}$$

$$= x^{a^2 - b^2 + b^2 - c^2 + c^2 - a^2}$$

$$= x^0$$

$$= 1$$

Hence, the correct option is (A).

17. Given:
A sum of money becomes 27 times in 3 years,
Concept used,
Compound interest,
Calculation:
Ratio of principal to Amount

$$P:A = \sqrt[3]{1}:\sqrt[3]{27}$$
$$P:A = 1:3$$

AS we know,

$$\text{Rate} = \frac{\text{Difference}}{\text{Original}} \times 100$$

$$\Rightarrow \text{Rate} = \frac{2}{1} \times 100$$

$$\Rightarrow \text{Rate} = 200\%$$

Hence, the correct option is (B).

18. Given:
Amount = Rs. 605
Rate $= 10\%$
Time $= 2$ years
Formula used

Amount = Principal$[1 + r\%]^t$

Where r and t are rate and time respectively

Calculation:

According to question,

$$605 = P\left[1 + \left(\frac{10}{100}\right)\right]^2$$

$$\Rightarrow 605 = P\left(\frac{110}{100}\right)^2$$

$$\Rightarrow 605 = P\left(\frac{11}{10}\right) \times \left(\frac{11}{10}\right)$$

$$\Rightarrow P = \left(605 \times \frac{100}{121}\right)$$

$$\Rightarrow P = \text{Rs. } 500$$

$\therefore$ Principal is Rs. 500.

Hence, the correct option is (B).

19. The East India Association was founded by Dadabhai Naoroji in 1866, in collaboration with Indians and retired British officials in London.

The Bombay Presidency Association was started by Badruddin Tyabji, Pherozshah Mehta, and K.T. Telang in 1885.

The Poona Sarvajanik Sabha was founded in 1867 by Mahadeo Govind Ranade and others, with the object of serving as a bridge between the government and the people.

Hence, the correct option is (A).

20. 'Jonas Salk' invented the vaccine for polio.

- He used the dead polioviruses as a vaccine and their entry into any organism lead to the formation of useful antibodies.
- These antibodies are effective for all counter-attacks against viral attacks.

Hence, the correct option is (D).

21. John McCarthy is known as the father of Artificial Intelligence.

Artificial intelligence is a branch of computer science that aims to create intelligent machines that can work and react like humans.

Hence, the correct option is (D).

22. Given,

PQ ⊥ RS

RT ∥ PQ

∠PST = 68°

RT ∥ PS

⇒ ∠PST = ∠RTS = 68° (Alternative angles)

Reflexive ∠RTS = 360° - ∠RTS

⇒ 360° - 68° = 292°

∴ Reflexive ∠RTS is 292°

Hence, the correct option is (B).

23. Infrared is used in night vision equipment when there is insufficient visible light to see. Night vision devices operate through a process involving the conversion of ambient light photons into electrons that are then amplified by a chemical and electrical process and then converted back into visible light.

Hence, the correct option is (C).

24. The apparatus used in submarines to give a clear view of the objects on the surface of the ocean or ground is known as a periscope.

- Periscope is a device like a long tube, containing mirrors that allow you to see over the top of something, used especially in a submarine to see above the surface of the sea.
- The Vernier Caliper is a precision instrument that can be used to measure internal and external distances extremely accurately.
- The Telescope is an optical instrument for making distant objects appear larger and therefore nearer.
- A stereoscope is a device for viewing a stereoscopic pair of separate images.

Hence, the correct option is (A).

25. Let $x = \sqrt{7\sqrt{7\sqrt{7\sqrt{7}\ldots\ldots}}}$

On squaring both sides, we get

$$x^2 = \sqrt{7\sqrt{7\sqrt{7\sqrt{7}\ldots\ldots}}}$$

$$\Rightarrow 7x = x^2$$

$$\Rightarrow x^2 - 7x = 0$$

$$\Rightarrow x(x - 7) = 0$$

$$\Rightarrow x = 0,7$$

It not possible that $x = 0$.

So, $x = 7$

Hence, the correct option is (C).

26. Let the length and breadth of the field be a and b meters respectively.

Therefore,

$$ab = 120$$

And,

$$2(a + b) = 46$$

$$\Rightarrow a + b = 23$$

The maximum length of the pole is equal to the diagonal of the rectangular field.

As we know that diagonal ^{2} = length ^{2} + breadth ^{2}

It means we have to calculate the value of $a^2 + b^2$.

As we know that,

$$(a + b)^2 = a^2 + b^2 + 2ab$$

$$\Rightarrow a^2 + b^2 = (a + b)^2 - 2ab = 23^2 - 2 \times 120 = 289$$

So, diagonal $^2 = 289$

Diagonal $= 17\,m$

Hence, the correct option is (C).

27. Given,

The radius of two cylinders are in the ratio of 3 : 2

Their heights are in the ratio 3 : 7.

Volume of cylinder $= \pi r^2 h$

Radius $= r$ and Height $= h$

Let the radii of two cylinders be $3x$ and $2x$ respectively.

Let the heights of two cylinders be $3y$ and $7y$ respectively.

We know that volume of cylinder $= \pi r^2 h$

$$\frac{v_1}{v_2} = \frac{\pi r_1^2 \, h_1}{\pi r r_2{}^2 \, h_2}$$

$$\Rightarrow \frac{v_1}{v_2} = \frac{[\pi \times (3x)^2 \times 3y]}{[\pi \times (2x)^2 \times 7y]}$$

$$= \frac{27}{28}$$

$$\Rightarrow v_1 : v_2 = 27 : 28$$

$\therefore$ The ratio of their volumes is $27 : 28$.

Hence, the correct option is (D).

28. Let height be decreased by $x\,cm$, now volume of cylinder $= \pi \times 5^2 \times (8 - x)$

Let radius be decreased by $x\,cm$, now volume of cylinder $= \pi (5 - x)^2 \times 8$

$$\Rightarrow \pi (5 - x)^2 \times 8 = \pi (5)^2 \times (8 - x)$$

$$\Rightarrow (5 - x)^2 \times 8 = 25 \times (8 - x)$$

$$\Rightarrow (25 - 10x + x^2) \times 8 = 200 - 25x$$

$$\Rightarrow 200 - 80x + 8x^2 = 200 - 25x$$

$$\Rightarrow 8x^2 - 55x = 0$$

$$x = 6.875 \text{ or } 0$$

We have both 6.875 and 0 in the options but we will use 0 as the correct option because we can't reduce 6.875 from the radius which is only $5\,cm$.

Hence, the correct option is (A).

29. The largest and the oldest museum of India is Indian Museum of West Bengal. It has rare collection of artefacts, fossils, mummies and mughal paintings. It was founded in 1814 at the cradle of the Asiatic Society of Bengal. Indian Museum is the earliest and the largest multipurpose Museum not only in the Indian subcontinent but also in the Asia-Pacific region of the world.

Hence, the correct option is (B).

30. Sum of first 222 whole numbers

$0 + 1 + 2 \ldots \ldots \ldots 221$

$$\frac{n(n+2)}{2}$$

$$= \frac{221(221+1)}{2}$$

$$= 221 \times 111$$

Unit digit = 1

Hence, the correct option is (C).

31. Given,

k is an odd number

Let $k = 1$

$$\left(8^{2k} + 5^{2k}\right)$$

$$= (8^{2 \times 1} + 5^{2 \times 1})$$

$$= 8^2 + 5^2$$

$$= 64 + 25$$

$$= 89$$

Hence, the correct option is (A).

32. 37 min 45 sec $= \dfrac{151}{4}$ min

1 days $= 24$ hrs $= 24 \times 60$ min

$$\Rightarrow \frac{151}{4 \times 24 \times 60} \times 100 = 2.62\%$$

Hence, the correct option is (A).

33. The concentration of new solution is

$$\frac{40 \times \frac{60}{100} + 35 \times \frac{80}{100}}{75} \times 100$$

$$= \frac{24 + 28}{3} \times 4$$

$$= 69\frac{1}{3}\%$$

Hence, the correct option is (C).

34. Ever and anon means occasionally.

Occasionally: something occurring now and then.

For example, Ever and anon their grandchildren visit them.

Hence, the correct option is (B).

35. Backbite means to slander someone, in his/her absence.

Slander someone in his/her absence: to talk maliciously about someone who is not present.

For example, Anuj was tired of all the backbiting and gossip in the office.

Hence, the correct option is (D).

36. World Environment Day is observed globally on 5th June every year.

This day is observed to raise awareness about protecting the environment and to remind people not to take nature for granted.

Hence, the correct option is (C).

37. The United Nations General Assembly had decided to observe international Democracy day on every 15 September.

This year's theme was "Democracy and the 2030 Agenda for sustainable development.

Hence, the correct option is (C).

38. Dubious means hesitating or doubting.

Trustworthy means able to be relied on as honest or truthful.

Shady means of doubtful honesty or legality.

Suspicious means having or showing a cautious distrust of someone or something.

Doubtful means feeling uncertain about something.

The option that is opposite in meaning to the underlined word 'dubious' is 'trustworthy'.

Hence, the correct option is (C).

39. Unmindful means not conscious or aware.

Vigilant means keeping careful watch for possible danger or difficulties.

Careless means not concerned or worried about.

Stupid means having or showing a great lack of intelligence or common sense.

Fatuous means silly and pointless.

The option that is opposite in meaning to the underlined word 'unmindful' is vigilant'.

Hence, the correct option is (A).

40. Given,

Curved surface area of X = 196% of Curved surface area of Y

$\because$ Curved surface area of sphere $\propto$ (radius)^2

(Radius of X)^2 = 1.96 × (Radius of Y)^2

Taking square root on both sides,

Radius of X = 1.4 × Radius of Y   ---(1)

Similarly,

Curved surface area of Z = 144% of Curved surface area of Y

(Radius of Z)^2 = 1.44 × (Radius of Y)^2

Taking square root on both sides,

Radius of Z = 1.2 × Radius of Y   ---(2)

Dividing (1) by (2), we get,

$$\frac{\text{Radius of X}}{\text{Radius of Z}} = \frac{7}{6} \quad ---(3)$$

Now, Volume of sphere $\propto$ (Radius)^3

$$\frac{\text{Volume of sphere X}}{\text{Volume of sphere Z}} = \left(\frac{\text{Radius of X}}{\text{Radius of Z}}\right)^3$$

$$= \left(\frac{7}{6}\right)^3 = \frac{343}{216}$$

$\therefore$ Ratio of volumes of sphere X and sphere Z = 343 : 216

Hence, the correct option is (C).

41. SWAMITVA Scheme:

- Union Budget 2021: SWAMITVA Scheme to be extended to all States/UTs, 1.80 lakh property-owners in 1,241 villages have already been provided cards

- SVAMITVA Scheme is a Central Sector scheme launched by Hon'ble Prime Minister of India on National Panchayat Day i.e 24th April 2020.

- The Ministry of Panchayati Raj (MoPR) is the Nodal Ministry for the implementation of the scheme. So, statement 1 is incorrect.

- In the States, the Revenue Department / Land Records Department will be the Nodal Department and shall carry out the scheme with the support of the State Panchayati Raj Department. Survey of India shall work as the technology partner for implementation.

- The scheme will help in streamlining planning and revenue collection in rural areas and ensuring clarity on property rights. Hence, statement 2 is correct.

- It is a scheme for mapping the land parcels in rural inhabited areas using drone technology and a Continuously Operating Reference Station (CORS).

- The scheme will enable the creation of better-quality Gram Panchayat Development Plans (GPDPs), using the maps created under this program. So, statement 3 is correct.

Hence, the correct option is (B).

42. Following are the important points associated with Limited Liability Partnership (LLP):

- Budget 2021 proposed Decriminalisation of the Limited Liability Partnership (LLP) Act, 2008.

- It is a partnership in which some or all partners (depending on the jurisdiction) have limited liabilities. In an LLP, each partner is not responsible or liable for another partner's misconduct or negligence. So, statement 1 is correct.

- The LLP can continue its existence irrespective of changes in partners. It is capable of entering into contracts and holding property in its own name.

- The LLP is a separate legal entity, is liable to the full extent of its assets but the liability of the partners is limited to their agreed contribution in the LLP.

- The internal governance structure of a company is regulated by statute (i.e. Companies Act, 2013) whereas for an LLP it would be by a contractual agreement between partners. So, statement 2 is incorrect.

Hence, the correct option is (A).

43. The Earth is divided into four main layers: the solid crust on the outside, the mantle, the outer core, and the inner core.

Crust:

- The **uppermost layer** over the earth's surface is called the crust.

- It is the **thinnest** of all the layers.

- On the continental masses, It is about 35 km and on the ocean floors, only 5 km.

- The crust is the thinnest layer of the Earth and it amounts to less than 1% of our planet's volume.

- The earth is made up of several concentric layers with one inside another, just like an onion.

- The crust is the outermost layer of Earth and is made up of igneous, metamorphic, and sedimentary rocks.

- The Earth's crust is unstable because of the exogenic forces.

Mantle:

- The Mantle extends up to a depth of 2900 km below the crust.

- It is the widest section of the Earth.

- The uppermost part of the mantle is known as **the asthenosphere.**

Core:

- The innermost layer is the core with a radius of about 3500 km.

- The central core has a very high temperature and pressure.

- The inner core (1200 km) is in the solid-state whereas the outer core (2300 km) is in the liquid state.

- The innermost layer is the core with a radius of about 3500 km and divided into Inner and Outer cores.

So it is clear that the crust is the thinner most layer of the earth.

Hence, the correct option is (A).

44. Exogenetic forces:

- Erosion and deposition both are the product of the exogenetic forces.

- It means the forces responsible have an external origin.

- The agents involved in the exogenetic processes are river, wind, sea wave, groundwater, glacier, etc.

- They complete a process through erosion, transportation, and deposition.

- The landforms formed due to the detachment, removal, transportation, and deposition of rock debris are known as erosion.

Hence, the correct option is (B).

45. The **movement of air** from high-pressure areas to low-pressure areas is called wind. There are three kinds of winds including permanent, seasonal, and local winds.

Type	Wind
Permanent Winds	• These are the winds that blow continuously for the entire year in a specific direction. • Permanent winds blow extensively over continents and oceans. • Some important examples of Permanent wind are Westerlies, Easterlies, and Trade winds. • Westerlies winds: Flow from the west to east. • Easterlies winds: Flow from the east to west. • Trade winds: Flow from the east to west.
Seasonal Winds	• These are movements of air repetitively and predictably driven by changes in patterns. • Seasonal winds occur in many locations throughout the world. • For example, a monsoon is a type of seasonal wind in low-latitude climates.
Local Winds	• Local winds are winds that cover smaller vicinity than global winds and usually possess some sort of peculiarity. • For example, land and sea breeze, Loo, Blizzard, Sirocco, Harmattan, etc

Hence, the correct option is (B).

46. The preposition 'for' is used for saying a length of time or a distance.

Complete Sentence: I have known her for a long time.

Hence, the correct option is (B).

47. The preposition 'on' means concerning a particular subject.

Complete Sentence: I accepted the offer on certain conditions.

Hence, the correct option is (A).

48. The preposition 'of' is used for saying who or what has a particular feature, aspect, or quality.

Complete Sentence: She is a woman of humble origin.

Hence, the correct option is (B).

49. Given,

$$\text{LCM} = 56(x^4 + x)$$

$$\text{HCF} = 4(x^2 - x + 1)$$

$$P(x) = 28(x^3 + 1)$$

$$\text{LCM} = 28 \times 2 \times x(x^3 + 1)$$

$\therefore$ Q(x) HCF $\times$ factors which are not in P (x)

$$= 4(x^2 - x + 1) \times 2x$$

$$= 8x(x^2 - x + 1)$$

Hence, the correct option is (A).

50.

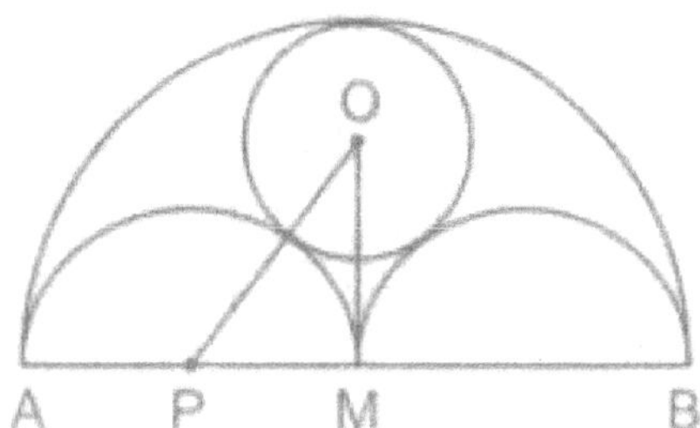

$$\text{AM} = \frac{4a}{2} = 2a$$

M is mid - point of AB

Length of OM = 2a - r

Let mid - point of AM be P.

PM = a

OP = a + r

OPM is a right - angled triangle.

$$OP^2 = OM^2 + PM^2$$

$$\Rightarrow (a + r)^2 = (2a - r)^2 + a^2$$

$$\Rightarrow r = \frac{2a}{3}$$

Hence, the correct option is (B).

51. Given,

A circular wire of radius 49 cm is bent in the form of a rectangle whose sides are in the ratio of 9 : 5.

Perimeter of the circular wire $= 2\pi r$

$$= 2 \times \left(\frac{22}{7}\right) \times 49$$

$$= 308 \text{ cm}$$

Now, Perimeter of circular wire = Perimeter of rectangular wire = 308 cm.........(1)

Sides of rectangular wire are in the ratio 9 : 5.

$$9x + 5x + 9x + 5x = 308$$

$$\Rightarrow 2(9x + 5x) = 308$$

$$\Rightarrow 14x = \frac{308}{2} = 154$$

$$\therefore x = \frac{154}{14} = 11$$

$\therefore$ Smaller side $= 5x$

$$= 5 \times 11$$

$$= 55 \text{ cm}$$

Hence, the correct option is (A).

52. The given sentence is of present perfect tense and it is in Active voice. The structures for Active/Passive voices are:

Active: Subject + has/have + verb (IIIrd form) + object

Passive: Object + has/have + been + verb (IIIrd form) + by + subject

So, the passive voice of the given sentence would be:

The word has been misspelt by you.

Hence, the correct option is (C).

53. The given sentence is in Active voice of past continuous interrogative tense. The structures for Active/Passive voices are:

Active: Wh-question word + was/were + subject + verb (ing form) + object?

Passive: Wh-question word + was/were + being + verb (IIIrd from) + by + subject?

So, with the help of the above structures, we can convert the given sentence into Passive voice:

What was being drawn on the blackboard by you?

Hence, the correct option is (B).

54. Given:

$$4b^2 + \frac{1}{b^2} = 2$$

$$\Rightarrow (2b)^2 + \left(\frac{1}{b}\right)^2 + 4 - 4 = 2$$

$$\Rightarrow \left(2b + \frac{1}{b}\right)^2 - 4 = 2$$

$$\Rightarrow \left(2b + \frac{1}{b}\right)^2 = 6$$

$$\Rightarrow 2b + \frac{1}{b} = \sqrt{6}$$

Take cube both sides

$$\Rightarrow \left(2b + \frac{1}{b}\right)^3 = \left(\sqrt{6}\right)^3$$

$$\Rightarrow 8b^3 + \frac{1}{b^3} + 3 \times 2b \times \frac{1}{b}\left(2b + \frac{1}{b}\right) = 6\sqrt{6}$$

$$\Rightarrow 8b^3 + \frac{1}{b^3} + 6\sqrt{6} = 6\sqrt{6}$$

$$\Rightarrow 8b^3 + \frac{1}{b^3} = 6\sqrt{6} - 6\sqrt{6}$$

$$\Rightarrow 8b^3 + \frac{1}{b^3} = 0$$

Hence, the correct option is (A).

55. Buenos Aires is the capital of Argentina.

Following a long period of unrest and a power struggle, Buenos Aires emerged even stronger and was named the federal capital of Argentina in 1880.

Hence, the correct option is (C).

56. Balban is the king of Delhi Sultanate and he established the "divine theory of kingship".

Balban's kingship ideology was basically based on Iranian theory that the king was 'semi-divine and was only answerable to God.

He established the theory that the sultan was the shadow of the almighty Zil-i-Allah, and emphasized it by insisting people to perform Sijada and Pabos, which according to theologians were reserved alone for God.

Hence, the correct option is (C).

57. Famous Indian mountaineer Santosh Yadav achieved the feat to be the first woman in the world to climb Mount Everest twice.

She was born in 1969 and hails from the small village of Adygreg in Haryana.Her first time to scale Mt Everest was in May 1992 followed by another one in May 1993 she even saved the life of another mountaineer by sharing her oxygen.

Hence, the correct option is (D).

58. Rig Veda is included in the UNESCO's Memory of World Register.

Rig Veda is the oldest among the four Vedas and is the fountain source of the Aryan culture. It is also known as the scriptures of the Hindu community. In 2007 this Documentary heritage was submitted by India and recommended for inclusion in the Memory of the World Register.

Hence, the correct option is (A).

59. KUSUM scheme is related to Solar pumps.

Ministry of New and Renewable Energy (MNRE) has launched the Pradhan Mantri Kisan Urja Suraksha Evem Utthan Mahabhiyan (PM KUSUM) Scheme for farmers for installation of solar pumps and grid-connected solar and other renewable power plants in the country. The scheme aims to add solar and another renewable capacity of 25,750 MW by 2022 with the total central financial support of Rs. 34,422 Crore including service charges to the implementing agencies

Hence, the correct option is (A).

60. Klinberg introduced the concept of 'imaginary reference group'.

Imaginary reference group by Kleinberg: Any person or group (actual or imaginary) that serves as a point of comparison for an individual in the formation of either general or specific values, attitudes, or behavior.

Hence, the correct option is (C).

61. According to Weber, the three types of leadership are legal, traditional and charismatic

The sociologist and philosopher Max Weber distinguishes three types of authority—charismatic, traditional and legal—each of which corresponds to a brand of leadership that is operative in contemporary society. This leader is someone who depends on established tradition or order.

Hence, the correct option is (B).

62. Plaque is a sticky, colorless film that forms on your enamel. It's made up of bacteria from your saliva. When it interacts with the sugars and starches left on your teeth from food, it creates an acid that can erode enamel, making teeth prone to decay. Tartar is plaque that has hardened.
Hence, the correct option is (B).

63. Blood sugar levels can be decreased by intravenous injection of insulin.

Intravenous injection of insulin is the injection of insulin directly into the blood. It is used to control blood sugar in people, where the body does not make insulin and therefore cannot control the amount of sugar in the blood. Insulin cannot be taken orally because the oral dose of insulin degenerates in the stomach by digestive enzymes.

Hence, the correct option is (C).

64. Five men who were camping in the Cascade Mountains of Washington saw a group of huge apelike creatures coming out of the woods. They hurried back to their cabin and locked themselves inside.
Hence, the correct option is (B).

65. After the incident when five men saw the big foots they returned to the town and told the people of their adventure. However, only a few people accepted their story.
Hence, the correct option is (A).

66. Then in 1967, Roger Patterson, a man who was interested in finding Bigfoot went into the northern California jungles with a friend. While riding, they were suddenly thrown off from their horses. Patterson saw a tall apelike animal standing not far away. Therefore the first people to have seen these apelike creatures before the five campers was Roger Patterson and his friend.
Hence, the correct option is (C).

67. Neighbouring means: a person or place which is adjacent with the given person of place. Therefore nearby will be correct option which can replace the word 'neighbouring'
Hence, the correct option is (B).

68. Local Native Americans were certain that a race of apelike animals had been living in the neighboring mountain for

centuries. They called these creatures Sasquatch.
Hence, the correct option is (C).

69. Given

(0.1 × 0.004) + (0.02 × 0.3) – (0.04 × 0.03) = ?

⇒ 0.0004 + 0.006 – 0.0012 = ?

⇒ 0.0064 – 0.0012 = ?

∴ ? = 0.0052

Hence, the correct option is (D).

70. Some of the elements are hydrogen, nitrogen, oxygen, and silicon. As of 2007, a total of 118 elements have been discovered or found, out of which 14 elements are naturally present on the earth.

Hence, the correct option is (D).

71. Bismuth is a chemical element with the symbol Bi and atomic number 83. It is a pentavalent post-transition metal and one of the pnictogens with chemical properties resembling its lighter group 15 siblings arsenic and antimony.
Hence, the correct option is (C).

72. We know that,

$$\text{Profit} = SP - CP$$

$$\text{Profit \%} = \frac{\text{Profit}}{\text{CP}} \times 100$$

Let the cost price of one cold-drink be $'x'$

CP of 6 cold-drinks $= 6x$

CP of 8 cold-drinks $= 8x$

Selling price of 6 cold-drinks $= CP$ of 8 cold-drinks $= 8x$

Profit = SP of 6 cold-drinks - CP of 6 cold-drinks

$$8x - 6x = 2x$$

$$\text{Profit \%} = \frac{\text{Profit}}{\text{CP}} \times 100$$

$$\left(\frac{2x}{6x}\right) \times 100 = \frac{100}{3}$$

$$\therefore \text{Profit} = 33\frac{1}{3}\%$$

Hence, the correct option is (A).

73. Given:

He bought 54 watermelons for Rs. 2700

Calculation:

Price of one watermelons = Rs $\dfrac{2700}{54}$ = Rs. 50

Price of one watermelon when he is selling = $\dfrac{280}{4}$ = Rs. 70

Profit on one watermelon = 70 - 50 = Rs. 20

For Rs. 1200 profit he will sale watermelon = $\dfrac{1200}{20}$ = 60

∴ The required result will be 60.

Hence, the correct option is (B).

74. We know that,

If $a_1, a_2,....., a_n$ are n observations arranged in ascending order. Then median of the given observation is:

1. If n is odd then there will be only one middle term which will be the median for the given observation.

2. If n is even then there will be two middle terms, so the average of two middle terms will be the median for the given observation.

It is given that,

The median of the observations 22, 24, 33, 37, x + 1, x + 3, 46, 47, 57, 58 in ascending order is 42.

∵ there 10 observations ⇒ n = 10.

Hence, there are two middle terms which are (x + 1) and (x + 3).

So, the median for the given observation $= \dfrac{(x+1)+(x+3)}{2} = x + 2$

∵ It is given that the median is 42.

⇒ x + 2 = 42 ⇒ x = 40.

⇒ The 5th observation is (x + 1) = 41 and the 6th observation is (x + 3) = 43.

Hence, the correct option is (B).

75. We know that,

The standard deviation of N observations is given by: $\sigma = \sqrt{\dfrac{1}{N} \times \sum_{i=1}^{N}(x_i - \mu)^2}$ where μ is the arithmetic mean.

It is given that,

$$\mu = 60, \ N = 10 \text{ and } \sum_{i=1}^{10}(x_i - 50)^2 = 5000$$

As we know, $\mu = \dfrac{\sum_{i=1}^{10} x_i}{10} = 60 \Rightarrow \sum_{i=1}^{10} x_i = 600$

$$\Rightarrow \sum_{i=1}^{10}(x_i - 50)^2 = \sum_{i=1}^{10} x_i^2 - 100 \sum_{i=1}^{10} x_i + 25000 = 5000\$$$

--(1)

By substituting the value of $\sum_{i=1}^{10} x_i = 600$ in equation (1), we get

$$\Rightarrow \sum_{i=1}^{10} x_i^2 = 40000 \quad -----(2)$$

As we know that, the standard deviation of N observations is given by:

$$\sigma = \sqrt{\dfrac{1}{N} \times \sum_{i=1}^{N}(x_i - \mu)^2}$$ where μ is the arithmetic mean.

$$\Rightarrow \sigma^2 = \frac{1}{N} \times \sum_{i=1}^{N}(x_i - \mu)^2$$

$$\Rightarrow \sigma^2 = \frac{1}{N} \times$$
$$\left(\sum_{i=1}^{N} x_i^2 + \mu^2 \times \sum_{i=1}^{N} 1 - 2\mu \times \sum_{i=1}^{N} x_i\right) \quad ---- \quad (3)$$

By substituting the values of $\mu = 60$, $N = 10, \sum_{i=1}^{10} x_i^2$ and $\sum_{i=1}^{10} x_i$ in equation (3), we get

$$\Rightarrow \sigma^2 = 400$$

$$\Rightarrow \sigma = 20$$

Hence, the correct option is (A).

76. Statement 1 is correct. One of the major aims and purpose with which ILO was set up was the extension of social security worldwide which was clearly set out in the Preamble to the ILO Constitution (1919).

Statement 2 is correct. Post-2003, ILO has set up a dedicated department to cater to Social security-related initiatives: the Social Security Department which has explored, analyzed, and piloted various ways and means to extend the coverage of health care systems and basic universal cash benefits, notably to people in the informal economy. And, ILO launched a Global Campaign on "Social Security and Coverage for All".

Statement 3 is incorrect. In accordance with this Social security was declared as a basic human right under the Universal Declaration of Human Rights (UDHR), 1948.

Statement 4 is correct. ILO mandate of extension of social security measures was restated in 1944 in the Declaration of Philadelphia to provide a basic income to all in need of such protection and comprehensive medical care.

Hence, the correct option is (C).

77. The International Monetary Fund (IMF) is an organization of 189 countries, working to foster global monetary cooperation, secure financial stability, facilitate international trade, promote high employment and sustainable economic growth, and reduce poverty around the world.

- Created in 1945, the IMF is governed by and accountable to the 189 countries that make up its near-global membership.

- The IMF's primary purpose is to ensure the stability of the international monetary system – the system of exchange rates and international payments that enables countries (and their citizens) to transact with each other.

Hence, the correct option is (D).

78. This is the autobiography of legend and the renowned personality in cricket, Sachin Tendulkar. Sachin Tendulkar played for good 24 years and retired in 2013. In this book, Sachin talks about his journey from his first Test match at the age of 16 to his 100th international century and the final farewell.

Hence, the correct option is (B).

79. Dr. Zakir Hussain (February 8, 1897 – May 3, 1969) was a freedom fighter and the third President of India, and the first Muslim President, whose term was from 13 May 1967 to 3 May 1969.

Hence, the correct option is (A).

80. The error is in part (C) of the sentence. The use of verb "purchased" and the word "yesterday" makes it clear that the given sentence is in past tense. Therefore, it is grammatically incorrect to use present verb "have given" in part (C) of the sentence. Thus, replace 'have given' with 'gave'.

Hence, the correct option is (C).

81. Since the introductory part is already there, Q will be the 1st statement as it furthers the statement in S1.

The next statement will be R as it takes us to another aspect of body movement mentioned as 'breathing'.

Now the statement R must be followed by P as it talks about the idea of catalyst needed for an activity.

And the concluding statement will be S.

So the correct order will be: Q-R-P-S.

Hence, the correct option is (C).

82. Let their initial investments be $x, 4x,$ and $6x$ respectively.

We know:

When investments of all the partners are for the same time, the gain or loss is distributed among the partners in the ratio of their investments.

According to the question:

$$A : B : C = (x \times 6 + 2x \times 6) :$$
$$\Rightarrow \left(4x \times 6 + \left(\tfrac{4x}{2}\right) \times 6\right) : \left(6x \times 6 + \left(\tfrac{6x}{2}\right)6\right)$$

$$\Rightarrow (6x + 12x):(24x + 12x):(36x + 18x)$$

$$\Rightarrow 18x:36x:54x = 1:2:3$$

Hence, the correct option is (A).

83. Let the fraction be $x,$

So, according to the question,

$$\Rightarrow \frac{5}{7} + x = 1$$

$$\Rightarrow 1 - \frac{5}{7} = x$$

$$\therefore x = \frac{2}{7} = \frac{6}{21}$$

Hence, the correct option is (A).

84. Amitabh Vijayvargiya (born 13 November 1965) is an Indian cricketer. He played in 38 first-class matches for Madhya Pradesh from 1986-87 to 1993-94. He later became the secretary of the Indore Divisional Cricket Association.

Hence, the correct option is (C).

85. The 1987 Cricket World Cup (known as the Reliance Cup 1987 for sponsorship reasons) was the fourth Cricket World Cup. It was held from 8 October to 8 November 1987 in India and Pakistan–the first such tournament to be held outside England.

Hence, the correct option is (A).

86. Given,

Number of days taken by 3 men or 6 women to harvest a field = 40 days

As we know,

$$\text{Efficiency} = \frac{Total\ Work}{Time\ taken}$$

If M_1 persons can do a piece of work in D_1 days and M_2 persons can do the same work in D_2 days, then $M_1 \times D_1 = M_2 \times D_2$

Let Men and women be represented as 'm' and 'w'. respectively.

As we know,

$M_1 \times D_1 = M_2 \times D_2$

$\Rightarrow (3m \times 40) = (6w \times 40)$

$\Rightarrow (\dfrac{m}{2}) = w...(1)$

According to the question

$(3m \times 40) = (2m + 6w) \times D_2$

$\Rightarrow 120m = [2m + 3m] \times D_2$ [From equation (1)]

$\Rightarrow 120m = (5m) \times D_2$

$\Rightarrow 24\ days = D_2$

∴ Time taken by 2 men and 6 women to harvest a field is 24 days.

Hence, the correct option is (A).

87. Given,

Number of men = 50

Income earn = Rs. 45,000

Number of days = 5

As we know,

If 'M_1' persons work 'D_1' days and earn 'Income$_1$' and 'M_2' person works 'D_2' days and earn 'Income$_2$' then

$$\frac{(M_1 \times D_1)}{Income_1} = \frac{(M_2 \times D_2)}{Income_2}$$

$M_1 = 50$, $D_1 = 5$ and Income$_1$ = Rs. 45,000

$M_2 = 20$, $D_2 = 25$ and Income$_2$ = Rs. x

$$\frac{(50 \times 5)}{45000} = \frac{(30 \times 25)}{x}$$

$\Rightarrow x = \dfrac{(30 \times 25 \times 45000)}{(50 \times 5)}$

$\Rightarrow x = $ Rs. 1,35,000

∴ 30 men will earn Rs. 1,35,000 in 25 days.

Hence, the correct option is (A).

88. The political ideas that do not embody or articulate class or social interests is not a feature of ideology.

- Ideology, is a set of beliefs and values of a social movement, institutions, class or large group which explains how society should work and offers some political and cultural blueprint for a certain social order.
- Some of the political ideologies developed over the years are; anarchism, communitarianism, communism, conservatism, environmentalism, fascism, liberalism and etc.

Hence, the correct option is (D).

89. According to Article 75(1) of the Constitution of India the Prime Minister shall be appointed by the President of India. He is the head of the Council of States and the leader of majority party in the Lok Sabha.

Hence, the correct option is (C).

90. During learning, a child makes mistakes willingly-unwillingly or due to some alternative conceptions. It is the job of a teacher to help students to correct those mistakes after diagnosing them. The method so followed is known as remedial teaching.

The following are its characteristics:

- It can be used for improving language skills and concentrating the trouble spot by arranging intensive practice revision, drill, and reviewing.
- To rectify a particular problem area, it can be used. For example, a student is confused about the pronunciation of 'no' and 'know', he can be taught the concept of silent letters.
- It also helps teachers to know which areas are left during regular teaching.
- It is carried out after the identification of problems (malady) and challenges faced by students.
- A teacher should be well aware of students' strengths and weaknesses to apply this method.
- It is a systematic process as the teacher first diagnoses the problem of students and then applies appropriate remedial) methods.
- Thus, we conclude that in remedial teaching concentration on trouble spots is best done by arranging intensive practice.

Hence, the correct option is (A).

91. A collection of historical documents or records providing information about a place, institution, or group of people is known as archives.

For Example - The film archive ensures that old movies are preserved for future generations.

Hence, the correct option is (D).

92. A person who abstains from all kinds of alcoholic drinks is known as a teetotaller.

For Example - He was a non-smoker and a teetotaller.

Hence, the correct option is (B).

93. Prime factorising 392, we get,

392 = 2 × 2 × 2 × 7 × 7

We know, a perfect cube has multiples of 3 as powers of prime factors.

Here, a number of 2's is 3, and a number of 7's is 2.

So we need to multiply another 7 to the factorization to make 392 a perfect cube.

Therefore, the smallest number by which 392 must be multiplied to obtain a perfect cube is 7.

Hence, the correct option is (A).

94. Given,

Number of students = 7

Number of subjects = 6

Average marks obtained in Physics by all the seven students

$$= \frac{1}{7} \times [(90\% \text{ of } 120) + (80\% \text{ of } 120) + (70\% \text{ of } 120) + (80\% \text{ of } 120) + (85\% \text{ of } 120) + (65\% \text{ of } 120) + (50\% \text{ of } 120)]$$

$$= \frac{1}{7} \times [(90 + 80 + 70 + 80 + 85 + 65 + 50)\% \text{ of } 120]$$

$$= \frac{1}{7} \times [520\% \text{ of } 120]$$

$$= \frac{624}{7}$$

$$= 89.14$$

∴ Average marks obtained in Physics by all the seven students is 89.14.

Hence, the correct option is (B).

95. Given,

Number of students = 7

Number of subjects = 6

Aggregate marks obtained by Sajal

$$= (90\% \text{ of } 150) + (60\% \text{ of } 130) + (70\% \text{ of } 120) + (70\% \text{ of } 100) + (90\% \text{ of } 60) + (70\% \text{ of } 40)]$$

$$= [135 + 78 + 84 + 70 + 54 + 28]$$

$$= 449$$

∴ Aggregate marks obtained by Sajal is 449.

Hence, the correct option is (D).

96. We shall find the overall percentage (for all seven students) with respect to each subject.

The overall percentage for any subject is equal to the average of percentages obtained by all seven students since the maximum marks for any subject are the same for all the students.

Therefore, the overall percentage for:

(i) Maths

$$= \left[\frac{1}{7} \times (90 + 100 + 90 + 80 + 80 + 70 + 65)\right]\%$$

$$= \left[\frac{1}{7} \times (575)\right]\%$$

$$= 82.14\%$$

(ii) Chemistry

$$= \left[\frac{1}{7} \times (50 + 80 + 60 + 65 + 65 + 75 + 35)\right]\%$$

$$= \left[\frac{1}{7} \times (430)\right]\%$$

$$= 61.43\%$$

(iii) Physics

$$= \left[\frac{1}{7} \times (90 + 80 + 70 + 80 + 85 + 65 + 50)\right]\%$$

$$= \left[\frac{1}{7} \times (520)\right]\%$$

$$= 74.29$$

(iv) Geography

$$= \left[\frac{1}{7} \times (60 + 40 + 70 + 80 + 95 + 85 + 77)\right]\%$$

$$= \left[\frac{1}{7} \times (507)\right]\%$$

$$= 72.43\%$$

(v) History

$$= \frac{1}{7} \times (70 + 80 + 90 + 60 + 50 + 40 + 80)\%$$

$$= \left[\frac{1}{7} \times (470)\right]\%$$

$$= 67.14\%$$

(vi) Comp. Science

$$= \left[\frac{1}{7} \times (80 + 70 + 70 + 60 + 90 + 60 + 80)\right]\%$$

$$= \left[\frac{1}{7} \times (510)\right]\%$$

$$= 72.86\%$$

Clearly, this percentage is highest for Maths.

Hence, the correct option is (A).

97. Given,

The difference between a number and 37.5% of the number is 45.

Let the number be x

$x - 37.5\%$ of $x = 45$

$\Rightarrow x - \left(\frac{3}{8}\right)x = 45$

$\Rightarrow \frac{8x-3x}{8} = 45$

$\Rightarrow \frac{5x}{8} = 45$

$\Rightarrow x = \frac{45 \times 8}{5}$

$\Rightarrow x = 72$

$\therefore$ The number is 72 .

Hence, the correct option is (C).

98. Given,

$$9\frac{3}{4} \div \left[2\frac{1}{6} \div \left\{4\frac{1}{3} - \left(2\frac{1}{2} + \frac{3}{4}\right)\right\}\right]$$

Follow BODMAS rule to solve,

$$= \frac{39}{4} \div \left[\frac{13}{6} \div \left\{\frac{13}{3} - \left(\frac{5}{2} + \frac{3}{4}\right)\right\}\right]$$

$$= \frac{39}{4} \div \left[\frac{13}{6} \div \left\{\frac{13}{3} - \frac{13}{4}\right\}\right]$$

$$= \frac{39}{4} \div \left[\frac{13}{6} \div \frac{13}{12}\right]$$

$$= \frac{39}{4} \div \left[\frac{13}{6} \times \frac{12}{13}\right]$$

$$= \frac{39}{4} \div 2$$

$$= \frac{39}{8}$$

Hence, the correct option is (B).

99. Given,

A, B, C subscribe Rs. 50000 for a business

A subscribes Rs. 4000 more than B

B subscribes Rs. 5000 more than C

Total profit = Rs. 35000

Let C subscribes in business $= x$

Then, B subscribes in business $= x + 5000$

and A subscribes in business $= x + 5000 + 4000$

$$= x + 9000$$

So, according to question,

$$x + x + 5000 + x + 9000 = 50000$$

$$\Rightarrow 3x + 14000 = 50000$$

$$\Rightarrow 3x = 50000 - 14000$$

$$\Rightarrow 3x = 36000$$

$$\Rightarrow x = \frac{36000}{3}$$

$$\Rightarrow x = 12000$$

Therefore,

A subscribes in business $= 12000 + 5000 + 4000$

$$= 21000$$

B subscribes in business $= 12000 + 5000$

$$= 17000$$

C subscribes in business $= 12000$

$A : B : C = 21000 : 17000 : 12000$

$$= 21 : 17 : 12$$

$\therefore$ A's share $=$ Rs. $\left(35000 \times \frac{21}{50}\right)$

$=$ Rs. 14,700

Hence, the correct option is (D).

100. Given,

Principle $(P) =$ Rs. 24,000

Rate $(R) = 8\frac{1}{2}\%$

Time $(T) = 8$ months $= \frac{8}{12}$

Simple interest $(SI) = \frac{P \times R \times T}{100}$

$$\Rightarrow SI = \frac{24000 \times \frac{17}{2} \times \frac{8}{12}}{100}$$

$$\Rightarrow SI = \frac{24000 \times 17 \times 8}{100 \times 2 \times 12}$$

$$\Rightarrow SI = 1360$$

$\therefore$ Simple interest is Rs. 1360.

Hence, the correct option is (D).

Q.1 In which of the following national parks the eight African cheetahs is shifted?

[Delhi Forest Guard, 2020]

A. Kuno Palpur National Park
B. Jim Corbett National Park
C. Ranthambore National Park
D. Kaziranga National Park

Q.2 Which country has signed a $ 2.25 billion deal with a Russian state-run nuclear energy company 'ASE' in August 2022?

[RBI Assistant, 2020], [UPSSSC Rajasva Lekhpal, 2015]

A. India
C. Japan
B. China
D. South Korea

Q.3 The World Bank has sanctioned USD 350 million to which state to implement the Systems Reform Endeavours for Transformed Health Achievement?

A. Gujarat
C. Rajasthan
B. Maharashtra
D. Uttar Pradesh

Q.4 Which bank has signed an MoU with the Central Board of Direct Taxes (CBDT) and Central Board of Indirect Taxes and Customs (CBIC) for tax collection?

A. Kotak Mahindra Bank
B. Dhanlaxmi Bank
C. Federal Bank
D. DCB Bank

Q.5 Who was the first chairman of ISRO?

A. Udupi Ramachandra Rao
B. Satish Dhawan
C. Vikram Sarabhai
D. M.G.K. Menon

Q.6 The marked price of an item is Rs. 800. On purchase of 1 item discount is 15% on purchase of 4 items discount is 38%. Rajshri buys 5 items, what is the effective discount?

A. 33.4%   **B.** 16%   **C.** 9%   **D.** 17.5%

Q.7 Consider the following statements regarding the Hague Convention on the Civil Aspects of International Child Abduction:

1. The convention seeks to return children abducted or retained overseas by a parent to their country of habitual residence.

2. The convention applies to the child, up to the age of 18 years.

3. All the members of the United Nations are the party to the Hague Convention.

Which of the statements given above is/are correct?

A. 1 and 2 only
C. 1 only
B. 1, 2 and 3
D. 2 and 3 only

Q.8 Consider the following statements regarding the World Trade Organization.

1. The World Trade Organization is an international body that deals with the rules of trade between nations.

2. The World Trade Organization (WTO) has chosen Italian's former finance minister Ngozi Okonjo-Iweala as its first female leader.

Which of the statements given above is/are correct?

A. 1 only
C. Both 1 and 2
B. 2 only
D. Neither 1 nor 2

Ques (9-10):Direction: In the following question, a sentence has been given in Active/Passive Voice. Out of the four alternatives suggested, select the one which best expresses the same sentence in Passive/Active Voice.

Q.9 Mohini has written a letter to her father.
A. A letter was written to her father by Mohini.
B. A letter has been written to her father by Mohini.
C. A letter was been being written by Mohini to her father.
D. A letter was written by Mohini to her father.

Q.10 The enemies have destroyed the 'Ajooba' town.
A. The 'Ajooba' town was destroyed by the enemies.
B. The 'Ajooba' town had been destroyed by the enemies.
C. The 'Ajooba' town have been destroyed by the enemies.
D. The 'Ajooba' town has been destroyed by the enemies.

Q.11 Which of the following is used in gene cloning?
A. Nucleoid
C. Mesosomes
B. Lomsomes
D. Plasmid

Q.12 Ecology is related to-
A. Cell fate
B. Body structure and environment
C. Fiber
D. Birds

Q.13 If A, B and C are subsets of a given set, then which one of the following relations is not correct?

[UPSC NDA, 2019]

A. $A \cup (A \cap B) = A \cup B$
B. $A \cap (A \cup B) = A$
C. $(A \cap B) \cup C = (A \cup C) \cap (B \cup C)$
D. $(A \cup B) \cap C = (A \cap C) \cup (B \cap C)$

Q.14 If the sum of first n terms of a series is (n + 12), then what is its third term?

[UPSC NDA, 2019]

A. 1   **B.** 2   **C.** 3   **D.** 4

Q.15 Out of the following, who was also popularly known as the 'Fuhrer'?

[NCHM JEE (Hotel Mgmt & Catering), 2019]

A. Adolf Hitler
B. Napoleon Bonaparte
C. William Shakespeare
D. Mahatma Gandhi

Q.16 The famous Physicist "Stephen William Hawking" was born in which country?

[NCHM JEE (Hotel Mgmt & Catering), 2019]

A. England   **B.** Japan   **C.** America   **D.** Russia

Ques (17-18):Direction: Fill in the blank with the appropriate option given below.

Q.17 Democracy in any country demands discipline and .... to the rules.

A. follow   **B.** adherence
C. agreement   **D.** obligation

Q.18 Columbus ___________America.

[NCHM JEE (Hotel Mgmt & Catering), 2019]

A. invented   **B.** discovered
C. created   **D.** found

Q.19 If $\dfrac{9^n \times 3^5 \times (27)^3}{3} \times (81)^4 = 27$, then the value of n is:

A. 0   **B.** 2   **C.** 3   **D.** 4

Q.20 A rectangular block 6 cm × 12 cm × 15 cm is cut into exact number of equal cubes. The possible number of cubes will be:

A. 11   **B.** 40   **C.** 6   **D.** 33

Q.21 The volume of a hemisphere is 18π cm². The total area of hemisphere is:

A. 21π cm²   **B.** 18π cm²   **C.** 27π cm²   **D.** 24π cm²

Q.22 The radii on the ends of bucket 16 cm height are 20 cm and 8 cm. Find the outer curved surface area of the bucket.

A. 880 cm²   **B.** 3120 cm²
C. 1760 cm²   **D.** 2400 cm²

Q.23 The value of $\sqrt{\dfrac{(0.1)^2+(0.01)^2+(0.009)^2}{(0.01)^2+(0.001)^2+(0.0009)^2}}$ is:

A. 10^2 **B.** 10   **C.** 0.1   **D.** 0.001

Q.24 Direction: Rearrange the following sentences (P), (Q), and (R) to make a meaningful paragraph and answer the questions that follow.

He spent a third

P. was of any consequence

Q. made sure that none of them

R. of the time describing his tax proposals, but

A. QRP   **B.** QPR   **C.** PRQ   **D.** RQP

Q.25 What do you understand by Kalaripayattu?
A. An ancient Bhakti cult of Shaivism
B. An ancient form of dance or drama
C. An ancient martial art
D. An ancient coin made up of bronze and copper

Q.26 The area of the rhombus is 240 cm ^{2} and, if the length of one diagonal is 24 cm then find the area of square that side is $\left(\dfrac{1}{\sqrt{61}}\right)$ times to the side of rhombus.

A. 4 cm ^{2} **B.** 6 cm ^{2} **C.** 8 cm ^{2} **D.** 10 cm ^{2}

Q.27 The area of an equilateral triangular park is equal to $5\sqrt{3}$ times the area of a triangular field with sides 18 m, 80 m, and 82 m. What is the side of the triangular park?

A. 125 m   **B.** 120 m   **C.** 140 m   **D.** 100 m

Q.28 Which one is correct option:

$$(3x + 2)^3 - (2x^2 + 3)$$

A. $27x^3 + 52x^2 + 36x + 5$
B. $27x^3 - 52x^2 + 36x - 5$
C. $2x^3 - 52x^2 + 63x - 5$
D. $7x^3 + 28x^2 - 36x - 5$

Q.29 Who among the following has recently authored the book named, 'The Ministry of Utmost Happiness'?

[KVS Trained Graduate Teacher, 2017]

A. C. M. Pokhriyal   **B.** Arundhati Roy
C. David Grossman   **D.** Michael Clarke

Q.30 Which of the following day was observed as the 'World Nature Conservation Day' this year?

[KVS Trained Graduate Teacher, 2017]

A. 15 August   **B.** 28 July
C. 27 June   **D.** 25 March

Q.31 Which of the following day was observed as International Literacy Day in 2017?

[KVS Trained Graduate Teacher, 2017]

A. August, 15   **B.** January, 26
C. September, 8   **D.** April, 2

Q.32 Smallest cricket stadium in the world by boundary?
A. Carisbrook Stadium
B. Feroz Shah Kotla
C. Melbourne Cricket Ground
D. Sydney Cricket Stadium

Q.33 Consider the following statements about the Cripps Mission proposals, 1941:

1. It outrightly rejected the demand for a separate Pakistan put forward by Muslim League.

2. It proposed that a constitution-making body after the second world war would be set up.

Which of the statements given above is/are correct?

A. 1 only   **B.** 2 only
C. Both 1 and 2   **D.** Neither 1 nor 2

Q.34 Identify the aircraft carrier from which of the following naval ships?

A. I. N. S. Virat   **B.** I. N. S. Talvar
C. I. N. S. Rajput   **D.** I. N. S. Masoor

Q.35 Who invented the aircraft?

A. Orville wright and wilbur wright
B. Sir Frank Hritley
C. Michael Faraday
D. Christian Haugenes

Q.36 Direction: In the following question, some part of the sentence may have errors. Find out which part of the sentence has an error and select the appropriate option. If the sentence is free from error, select 'No error'.

The teacher taught (A)/ to the students (B)/ like his own children. (C)/ No error (D)

A. A   **B.** B   **C.** C   **D.** D

Q.37 Match List-I (Temples) with List-II (Districts) and select the correct answer using the codes given below the lists:

List I	List II
A. Bhartrihari	1. Pushkar
B. Karni Mata	2. Tonk
C. Atmateshwar	3. Bikaner
D. Bisaldeo	4. Alwar

A. A-2, B-3, C-1, D-4   **B.** A-4, B-3, C-1, D-2
C. A-3, B-1, C-4, D-2   **D.** A-1, B-2, C-3, D-4

Ques (38-42):Direction: Kindly read the passage carefully and answer the question that follows.

India has a major child malnutrition problem. The Rapid Survey on Children (2012-13) found that about 4 in 10 children are stunted. On average, children who are stunted do less well in school, earn less, and die sooner than children who are not. There are many causes of child stunting. Addressing poverty and improving education would help, but development is not the only factor. Research shows that poor sanitation spreads diseases that sap children's energy and stunts their growth. Also, the health of a child's mother matters critically for whether or not the child is stunted.

The first two years of life are the most important time for a child's physical and cognitive growth. During this time, she depends heavily on her mother for nutrition. As a growing foetus, she gets all her food from her mother's bloodstream, and after birth, is ideally breastfed for at least six months. Unfortunately, research shows that many Indian women start pregnancy underweight and gain little weight during pregnancy. This leads to low birth weight babies, high rates of neonatal mortality, and less successful breastfeeding. Women's undernourishment contributes substantially to India's unacceptably high rates of child stunting.

Why are Indian women so malnourished? Here, too, poverty and sanitation play a role. But a recent survey that I conducted with a team of economics and sociology researchers suggests that widespread discrimination against women in their own homes likely plays an important role too. Social Attitudes Research for India (SARI) is a new phone survey that seeks to interview representative samples of 18-65-year-olds. Recently, we interviewed 1,270 adults in Delhi and 1,470 adults in Uttar Pradesh. One of the things SARI measures is discrimination against women.

In India, girls are less likely to survive infancy than boys, and if they do, parents invest less in their education. Women are far

less likely to work outside the home and have their own bank accounts than men. Many report little decision-making power over their own lives. One aspect of discrimination against women that matters for health is whether women eat less or worse quality food than men. In order to measure discrimination in women's food intake, SARI used a question that was previously tested and used by the India Human Development Survey (2011): "When your family eats lunch or dinner, do the women usually eat with the men? Or do the women usually eat first? Or do the men usually eat first?" Answers to these questions have implications for nutrition because in households with a limited food budget, or where there is no refrigerator to store leftover food, the person who eats last very often gets less or lower quality food than people who eat before her.

The IHDS 2011 survey interviewed married women aged 15-49 and found that one in five women in Delhi and half of the women in Uttar Pradesh said they ate after men did. When we decided to include the same question in the SARI survey five years later, we found even higher numbers. One in three adults in Delhi, and six in ten adults in U.P. said they lived in households where men eat first. Why are these numbers even higher than what the IHDS found in 2011?

Part of the reason is that SARI and the IHDS asked different people. The IHDS asked only women, while SARI asked both women and men. In U.P. (but not in Delhi) men were significantly more likely to say that they eat first. We do not know why men in U.P. reported more often than women that women eat last. Studies of discrimination in other contexts suggest that where discrimination is severe, it is often easier to get people to admit to engaging in acts of discrimination than to experiencing it.

Nor do we know for sure why even among women, the SARI figures are higher than the IHDS figures. It may have to do with how respondents react to a phone survey versus a face-to-face survey. The women surveyors who conducted IHDS interviews may have been seen by respondents as progressive women having jobs and moving around without their family members. For a respondent in a conservative household, it may be easier to admit discrimination to a stranger on the phone than to a progressive woman sitting in front of her.

No matter what the exact figures, it is clear that the practice of making women eat last is widespread in Delhi and U.P., and that it has important implications for a child's health. What is unclear is how to address the problem.

Q.38 Which one of these words is similar to the word 'cognitive' in the given passage?
A. Impudent   **B.** Mental
C. Overall   **D.** Raid

Q.39 Which of the following words is the antonym of the word 'stunted' in the passage?
A. Impeded   **B.** Encouraged
C. Improvised   **D.** Deluded

Q.40 Which one of these words is similar to the word 'implication' in the given passage?

A. Intangibility
B. Influence
C. Inference
D. Reason

Q.41 Which of the following assumptions is implicit in the context of the passage?

I. Survey results regarding an issue may or may not depict a clear picture of the problem.

II. Sampling is crucial while conducting a research.

III. Results of two different researches on the same topic will always vary.

A. Only I
B. Only II
C. I and III
D. I and II

Q.42 Which of the following can be inferred from the passage?

A. Child malnutrition problem in India is more intense issue to be tackled than women empowerment.
B. A mother's undernourishment leads to child's malnutrition.
C. Male population in South India is more caring towards their women than that of North India.
D. All of the above

Q.43 Messaging application named 'Secure Application for Internet' (SAI) developed by which Indian armed force?

A. Indian Navy
B. Indian Coast Guard
C. Indian Air Force
D. Indian Army

Q.44 Quantum theory was proposed by whom for the first time in the year 1900?

A. Albert Einstein
B. Max Planck
C. C V Raman
D. Louis de Broglie

Q.45 Which of the following is not a perfect square?

[RRB/RRC Group D, 2018]

A. 1250
B. 16641
C. 2025
D. 9801

Q.46 How many of the factors of 512 are perfect squares?

[RRB/RRC Group D, 2018]

A. 3
B. 5
C. 6
D. 4

Q.47 Laterite soil is rich in:

A. Phosphorus
B. Calcium carbonate
C. Potassium
D. Iron oxide

Q.48 Topographical map are those:

A. Prepared based on the actual survey of an area.
B. Large scale map than cadastral maps.
C. Used by the fisher mans mostly.
D. Shows the disaster and hazardous events.

Q.49 Consider the following statements with respect to Ring of Fire :

1. It is located along the Atlantic ocean.

2. It is characterized by active volcanoes and frequent earthquakes.

Which of the statements given above is/are **not** correct?

A. 1 only
B. 2 only
C. Both 1 and 2
D. Neither 1 nor 2

Q.50 The value of c for which the 4-digit number $51c3$ is divisible by 9 is

A. 2 or 3
B. 0 or 9
C. 0 or 3
D. 3 or 9

Ques (51-52):Direction: In the following question, four alternatives are given for the idiom/phrase. Choose the alternative which best expresses the meaning of the idiom/phrase.

Q.51 Die-hard
A. Unwilling to change
B. Ready to change
C. Egoist
D. Arrogant

Q.52 To pull one's socks up
A. To Postpone
B. To get ready
C. To try hard
D. To depart

Q.53 If the ratio of two numbers is in the ratio 4 : 9 and their LCM is 720, then find the sum of both the numbers?

A. 260
B. 240
C. 180
D. 390

Q.54 Select the most appropriate synonym of the given word
Accorded

A. Solitary
B. Aloof
C. Give
D. Crowded

Q.55 Select the most appropriate synonym of the given word:
Assertions

A. Grow
B. Reproduce
C. Breed
D. Declaration

Q.56 In which year, hindi names 'Rajya Sabha' and 'Lok Sabha' were adopted for the Council of States and the House of People respectively?

A. 1950
B. 1947
C. 1954
D. 1962

Q.57 Who appoints the chairman of the Estimates Committee?

A. President
B. Prime Minister
C. Speaker of Lok Sabha
D. Chairman of Lok Sabha

Q.58 The density of silver is 10.8×10^3 kgm $^{-3}$ and the density of water is 10^3 kgm $^{-3}$. What is the relative density of Ag?

[RRB/RRC Group D, 2018]

A. 0.108
B. 1.08
C. 0.0108
D. 10.8

Q.59 The chemical formula of Ammonium phosphate is ....

[RRB/RRC Group D, 2018]

A. $(NH_4)_3PO_4$
B. $(NH_4)_2PO_4$
C. $(NH_4)_2PO_2$
D. NH_4PO_4

Q.60 How many natural numbers less than 500, when divided by 35 and 49, will leave a remainder of 30 in each case?

[RRB/RRC Group D, 2018]

A. 4
B. 3
C. 1
D. 2

Q.61 X attempts 100 questions and gets 340 marks. If for every correct answer is 4 marks and the wrong answer is negative one mark, then the number of questions wrongly answered by Mr. X is:

[RRB/RRC Group D, 2018]

A. 14   **B.** 15   **C.** 12   **D.** 13

Q.62 The total cost of a chair and table is Rs. 600 and the ratio of cost of one chair and table is $7:5$. Find the cost of chair.

A. Rs. 400   **B.** Rs. 350   **C.** Rs. 250   **D.** Rs. 450

Q.63 In a rally of 256 students, boys and girls are in the ratio $9:7$. Find the number of girls.

A. 120   **B.** 114   **C.** 112   **D.** 115

Q.64 A person invests Rs. 30000 as a fixed deposit at a bank of 10% p.a. S.I. But due to some problem, he has to withdraw the entire money after 3 yrs for which the bank allowed him a lower rate of interest. If he gets Rs. 7800 less than what he would have got at the end of 5 yrs; Find R.O.I allowed by the bank?

A. 2%   **B.** 5%   **C.** 4%   **D.** 8%

Q.65 A sum of Rs. 1000 is increased by 100% of its original after 7 years at compound interest. What will be the time period when the amount will be increased by 700% of the principal at the same rate of interest compound interest?

A. 14 years   **B.** 21 years   **C.** 28 Years   **D.** 35 years

Q.66 By selling 90 chocolate Rs. 160, a chocolate trader loses 20%. How many chocolates should he sell for Rs. 96 to make a profit of 20%?

A. 45   **B.** 36   **C.** 54   **D.** 28

Q.67 If the cost price of 15 oranges is equal to the selling price of 20 oranges, the loss percent is:

A. 25%   **B.** 30%   **C.** 75%   **D.** 40%

Q.68 'Rajatarangini' was composed by:

[DSSSB TGT Social Science, 2014]

A. Kalhana
B. Mahendravarman I
C. Parameshwaravarman
D. Bilhana

Q.69 Under which of the following schemes, Rajasthan Government provides financial incentives to SC / ST candidates passing the all India Civil Services examination and State Civil Services examination?

A. Palanhar yojana
B. Swayam siddha yojana
C. Vishwas yojana
D. Anupriti yojana

Q.70 What is the sum of the measures of the angles ∠A, ∠B, ∠C, ∠D, ∠E, and ∠F in the given figure?

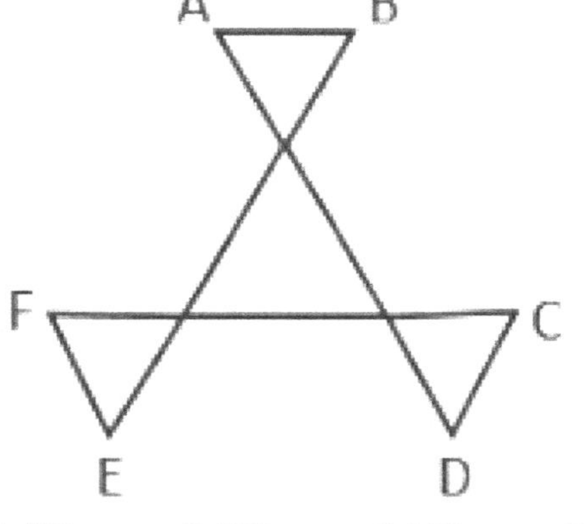

A. 180°   **B.** 360°   **C.** 540°   **D.** 720°

Q.71 P and Q invested in a business. The profit earned was divided in the ratio 2 : 3. If P invested Rs 40000, the amount invested by Q is:

A. Rs. 40000   **B.** Rs. 50000
C. Rs. 60000   **D.** Rs. 70000

Q.72 Find the standard deviation of 8, 12, 13, 15, 22.

A. 3.54   **B.** 3.7   **C.** 4.21   **D.** 4.6

Q.73 A set of 5 values 3, 5, 7, 9, 11 has standard deviation σ. What is the standard deviation of 5 values 5, 7, 9, 11, 13?

A. σ   **B.** σ + 2   **C.** σ - 2   **D.** 2σ

Q.74 Consider the following statements with reference to Vehicle Scrappage Policy:

1. Personal vehicles older than 20 years and commercial vehicles older than 15 years will have to undergo a fitness test at the government-registered 'Automated Fitness Centres'.

2. Vehicles that fail to pass the test will be declared as 'end-of-life vehicles'.

3. Vehicle owner will not get any type of benefit after obtaining a 'scrappage certificate'.

Which of the statements given above is/are correct?

A. 1 and 2 only   **B.** 2 and 3 only
C. 1 and 3 only   **D.** 1, 2 and 3

Q.75 What is/are the objectives of the recently announced National Hydrogen Energy Mission?

1. To generate hydrogen from green power resources.

2. To link India's growing renewable capacity with the hydrogen economy.

3. To reduce import dependency on fossil fuels.

Select correct code:

A. 1 only   **B.** 2 and 3
C. 1 and 3   **D.** 1, 2 and 3

Q.76 Three solid spheres of radii 3 cm, 4 cm and 5 cm respectively are melted and made a large solid sphere. Radius of this sphere is:

A. 12   **B.** 10   **C.** 6   **D.** 4

Ques (77-78):Direction: Rearrange the following six sentences, (A), (B), (C), (D), (E) and (F), in a proper sequence to form a meaningful paragraph, then answer the questions that follow.

(A) While these disadvantages of biofuels are serious, there are numerous advantages as they are the only alternative energy source of future and the sooner we find solutions to these problems, the faster we will be able to solve the problems we are now facing with gasoline.

(B) This fuel can also help to stimulate jobs locally since they are also much safer to handle than gasoline and can thus have the potential to turnaround a global economy.

(C) These include dependence on fossil fuels for the machinery required to produce biofuel which ends up polluting as much as the burning of fossil fuels on roads and the exorbitant cost of biofuels which makes it very difficult for the common man to switch to this option.

(D) This turnaround can potentially help to bring world peace and end the need to depend on foreign countries for energy requirements.

(E) Biofuels are made from plant sources and since these sources are available in abundance and can be reproduced on a massive scale, they form an energy source that is potentially unlimited.

(F) However, everything is not as green with the biofuels as it seems as there are numerous disadvantages involved which at times overshadow their positive impact.

Q.77 Which of the following sentence should be the SECOND after rearrangement?

A. (A) **B.** (B) **C.** (D) **D.** (F)

Q.78 Which of the following sentence should be the FIRST after rearrangement?

A. (A) **B.** (B) **C.** (C) **D.** (E)

Q.79 Who among the following badminton players is hearing - impaired?

A. Jwala Gutta **B.** Ami Ghia
C. Pullela Gopichand **D.** Rajeev Bagga

Q.80 With which sports Saikhom Mirabai Chanu is associated?

A. Swimming **B.** Boxing
C. Weight lifting **D.** Gymnastics

Q.81 Social norms refer to:

A. Right type of behavior
B. The most frequently observed behavior in a society
C. Those standards or rules which specify appropriate and inappropriate behavior
D. All types of behaviour

Q.82 The basis of slave system is:

A. Political **B.** Economic
C. Custom **D.** Social need

Q.83 Ganesh and Bhima can complete a work in 6 days. If Ganesh alone can finish it in 10days, in how many days Bhima can complete the work?

A. 18 **B.** 14 **C.** 12 **D.** 15

Q.84 A alone can complete a work in 12 days and B alone can complete the same work in 15 days. If they finish the work together and received Rs. 3600. Then find the share of A.

A. Rs. 1200 **B.** Rs. 3000 **C.** Rs. 1500 **D.** Rs. 2000

Q.85 What is the national currency of South Korea?

A. Rial **B.** Pound **C.** Krona **D.** Won

Q.86 Sabarimala Temple is located:

A. Kerala **B.** Karnataka
C. Tamil Nadu **D.** Odisha

Q.87 Which state is associated with the "Chaitra Jatra Festival" held annually?

A. Chhattisgarh **B.** Andra Pradesh
C. Karnataka **D.** Odisha

Q.88 Which strategy can be used to train students for good speech?

A. Demonstration of correct pronunciation
B. Group practice to ensure the correct position of the tongue and lips
C. Both (A) and (B)
D. Proper training for eye movement

Q.89 A town has 40% men and 35% women in its population. Of all the children in the town, 40% are girls. If the total number of girls is 1200 what is the total population?

A. 15500 **B.** 14000 **C.** 12000 **D.** 11500

Q.90 When the price of an article was reduced by 20% its sale increased by 80%. What was the net effect on the sale?

A. 44% increase **B.** 44% decrease
C. 66% increase **D.** 75% increase

Q.91 If the roots of the quadratic equation $x^2 + kx + 18 = 0$ are equal, then find the value of 'k'.

A. $-7\sqrt{2}$ **B.** -18 **C.** 18 **D.** $6\sqrt{2}$

Q.92 The selling price of an article is Rs. 144. If the profit percentage is equal to the cost price of the article, what is the cost price of the article?

A. 80 **B.** 60 **C.** 90 **D.** 120

Q.93 Length and breadth of the rectangular field are in the ratio 5 : 2. If the perimeter of the field is 238 m. Find the length of the field.

A. 83 m **B.** 82 m **C.** 84 m **D.** 85 m

Q.94 Direction: Select the most appropriate option to fill in the blank.

He slept like a horse ______ of all the commotion in the room.

A. although **B.** because **C.** in spite **D.** in case

Ques (95-96):Direction: In the questions, out of the four alternatives, choose the one which can be substituted for the given words/sentences.

Q.95 A person who believes that only selfishness motivates human actions

A. agnostic **B.** cynic
C. sceptic **D.** misogynist

Q.96 One who can not be corrected

A. incorrigible   **B.** hardened

C. invulnerable   **D.** incurable

Q.97 What will come in the place of question mark (?).

$$\sqrt[3]{\sqrt{0.000064}} = ?$$

A. 0.02   **B.** 0.2   **C.** 2   **D.** 0.002

Ques (98-100):Direction: The circle-graph given here shows the spendings of a country on various sports during a particular year. Study the graph carefully and answer the questions given below it.

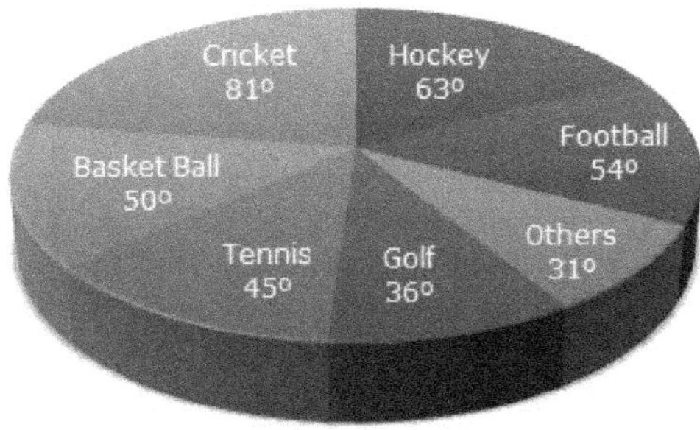

Q.98 How much percent more is spent on Hockey than that on Golf?

A. 27%   **B.** 35%   **C.** 37.5%   **D.** 75%

Q.99 How much percent less is spent on Football than that on Cricket?

A. $22\frac{2}{9}\%$ **B.** 27%   **C.** $33\frac{1}{3}\%$ **D.** $37\frac{1}{7}\%$

Q.100

If the total amount spent on sports during the year was Rs. 2 crores, the amount spent on Cricket and Hockey together was:

A. Rs. 8,00,000   **B.** Rs. 80,00,000

C. Rs. 1,20,00,000   **D.** Rs. 1,60,00,000

// Smart Answer Sheet //

Correct — Percentage of students who answered correctly. **Skipped** — Percentage of students who skipped.

Q.	Ans.	Correct	Skipped
1	A	85.09 %	0.0 %
2	D	88.1 %	0.0 %
3	A	42.47 %	1.81 %
4	B	55.09 %	1.21 %
5	C	60.36 %	1.24 %
6	A	29.08 %	4.99 %
7	C	40.55 %	1.94 %
8	A	58.51 %	1.94 %
9	B	80.24 %	0.0 %
10	D	77.48 %	0.0 %
11	D	58.15 %	1.7 %
12	B	69.06 %	1.51 %
13	A	57.39 %	1.12 %
14	A	53.85 %	1.63 %
15	A	56.75 %	1.72 %
16	A	25.61 %	4.9 %
17	B	64.3 %	1.35 %
18	B	76.67 %	0.0 %
19	C	63.91 %	1.84 %
20	B	87.29 %	0.0 %
21	C	62.88 %	1.59 %
22	C	59.75 %	1.67 %
23	B	51.87 %	1.63 %
24	D	52.98 %	1.28 %
25	C	63.31 %	1.11 %
26	A	56.28 %	1.73 %
27	B	32.57 %	4.41 %
28	A	58.55 %	1.4 %
29	B	29.15 %	3.56 %
30	B	42.68 %	1.84 %
31	C	61.08 %	1.91 %
32	B	41.51 %	1.06 %
33	B	53.56 %	1.62 %
34	A	89.94 %	0.0 %
35	A	81.46 %	0.0 %
36	B	60.66 %	1.32 %
37	B	30.87 %	3.94 %
38	B	69.84 %	1.11 %
39	B	11.87 %	3.17 %
40	C	10.41 %	4.44 %
41	D	23.59 %	3.87 %
42	B	31.04 %	3.47 %
43	D	50.09 %	1.94 %
44	B	52.35 %	1.04 %
45	A	81.91 %	0.0 %
46	B	76.92 %	0.0 %
47	D	76.95 %	0.0 %
48	A	88.17 %	0.0 %
49	A	48.68 %	1.16 %
50	B	51.37 %	1.24 %
51	A	89.63 %	0.0 %
52	C	56.73 %	1.8 %
53	A	87.81 %	0.0 %
54	C	84.56 %	0.0 %
55	D	85.44 %	0.0 %
56	C	85.05 %	0.0 %
57	C	81.85 %	0.0 %
58	D	69.12 %	1.01 %
59	A	78.33 %	0.0 %
60	C	78.34 %	0.0 %
61	C	87.62 %	0.0 %
62	B	42.83 %	1.77 %
63	C	86.88 %	0.0 %
64	D	43.82 %	1.43 %
65	B	56.62 %	1.25 %
66	B	66.44 %	1.19 %
67	A	60.57 %	1.5 %
68	A	45.37 %	1.4 %
69	D	44.34 %	1.64 %
70	B	29.01 %	4.15 %
71	C	50.17 %	1.57 %
72	D	58.89 %	1.49 %
73	A	65.38 %	1.59 %
74	A	66.76 %	1.21 %
75	D	53.6 %	1.47 %
76	C	55.8 %	1.35 %
77	D	25.88 %	3.77 %
78	D	69.68 %	1.41 %
79	D	59.03 %	1.83 %
80	C	19.5 %	4.06 %
81	B	80.41 %	0.0 %
82	B	81.25 %	0.0 %
83	D	80.63 %	0.0 %
84	D	69.64 %	1.09 %
85	D	51.78 %	1.53 %
86	A	40.24 %	1.04 %
87	D	50.32 %	1.73 %
88	C	87.13 %	0.0 %
89	A	49.92 %	1.87 %
90	A	43.52 %	1.56 %
91	D	47.34 %	1.82 %
92	A	78.62 %	0.0 %
93	D	51.29 %	1.55 %
94	C	86.11 %	0.0 %
95	B	50.57 %	1.64 %
96	A	65.89 %	1.73 %
97	B	60.9 %	1.52 %
98	D	25.32 %	3.4 %
99	C	23.86 %	3.92 %
100	B	80.73 %	0.0 %

//Hints and Solutions//

1. Eight African cheetahs from Namibia in South Africa have been relocated to Kuno Palpur National Park in Madhya Pradesh.

After the Cheetahs arrive in the National Park, they will stay in smaller enclosures during the quarantine phase before being shifted to the bigger ones. From 1952 onwards, cheetahs gradually started becoming extinct in India, then in 2009 the 'African Cheetah Introduction Project in India' was started.

Hence, the correct option is (A).

2. South Korea has signed a $ 2.25 billion deal with a Russian state-run nuclear energy company 'ASE'in August 2022.

- It has been signed to provide components for Egypt's first nuclear power plant.
- ASE is a subsidiary of Rosatom, a state-owned Russian nuclear conglomerate.
- South Korea has also signed a $ 20 billion contract to build nuclear power reactors in the UAE.

Hence, the correct option is (D).

3. The World Bank has sanctioned USD 350 million to Gujarat to implement the Systems Reform Endeavours for Transformed Health Achievement in Gujarat (SHRESTHA-G). Under the SHRESTHA-Gujarat project, the government will undertake the initiative to improve the quality of the health system of the state by expanding the health services to the rural and urban people.

- The project also focuses to increase the quality of non-communicable and psychiatric services in the state as well as the quality of mother and child nutrition services.
- The five-year total cost of the project will be around USD 500 million which is approximately Rs 3,750 crore.
- Of this, USD 350 billion which is approximately Rs 2,625 crore, will be provided by the World Bank.
- While Gujarat will spend Rs 1125 crore in five years.

Hence, the correct option is (A).

4. Dhanlaxmi Bank has signed a pact with the Central Board of Direct Taxes (CBDT) and Central Board of Indirect Taxes and Customs (CBIC) for tax collection on April 2022. This MoU will help customers to pay their direct taxes and GST payments and other indirect taxes through the branch network and digital platforms of the bank. The bank has been authorized by the Reserve Bank of India (RBI) based on a recommendation from the Controller General of Accounts for the collection of various taxes.

Hence, the correct option is (B).

5. Vikram Sarabhai was the first chairman of ISRO.

ISRO was formed by Vikram Sarabhai in the year 1969. Vikram Ambalal Sarabhai was an Indian physicist and astronomer who initiated space research and helped develop nuclear power in India. He was honored with Padma Bhushan in 1966 and the Padma Vibhushan in 1972.

He is internationally regarded as the Father of the Indian Space Program.

Hence, the correct option is (C).

6. Given,

Marked price$= 800$

Discount $= 15\%$ and 38%

Let the effective discount be x.

Amount saved on buying 1 item $= \dfrac{15}{100} \times 800 =$ Rs. 120

Marked price of 4 items $= 4 \times 800 =$ Rs. 3200

Amount saved on buying 4 items $= \dfrac{38}{100} \times 3200 =$ Rs. 1216

Thus, on buying 5 items, the total amount saved $= 120 + 1216 =$ Rs. 1336

Total marked price of 5 items $= 5 \times 800 =$ Rs. 4000

$\therefore$ Effective discount $= \dfrac{1336}{4000} \times 100$

$= \dfrac{334}{10} = 33.4\%$

Hence, the correct option is (A).

7. Hague Convention on the Civil Aspects of International Child Abduction is a multilateral treaty that came into existence on 1st December 1983.

The convention seeks to protect children from the harmful effects of abduction and retention across international boundaries by providing a procedure to bring about their prompt return.

The convention is intended to enhance the international recognition of rights of custody and access arising in place of habitual residence and to ensure the prompt return of the child who is wrongfully removed or retained from the place of habitual residence.

It seeks to return children abducted or retained overseas by a parent to their country of habitual residence for the courts of that country to decide on matters of residence and contact.

So, Statement 1 is correct.

The convention shall apply to any child, up to the age of 16 years who is a habitual resident of any of the contracting states.

So, Statement 2 is not correct.

Over 90 countries are party to the Convention. Despite pressure from the US and European countries, India (a UN member) is yet to ratify it.

So, Statement 3 is not correct.

Hence, the correct option is (C).

8. The WTO's 164 members unanimously selected the 66-year-old development economist to serve a four-year term as director-general.

The appointment came after new United States President Joe Biden endorsed her candidacy, which had been blocked by former President Donald Trump.

Okonjo-Iweala, formerly Nigeria's finance minister, had a 25-year career at the World Bank, where she rose to the number-two position of managing director. She holds both US and Nigerian citizenship.

The World Trade Organization is an international body that deals with the rules of trade between nations. So statement 1 is correct.

At its heart are the WTO agreements, negotiated among the bulk of the world's nations and ratified in their legislatures.

Hence, the correct option is (A).

9. The given sentence is of present perfect tense and it is the active form. The structures for active/passive voices are:

Active: Subject + has/have + verb (IIIrd form) + object.

Passive: Object + has/have + been + verb (IIIrd form) + by + subject.

So, the passive voice of the given sentence would be:

A letter has been written to her father by Mohini.

Hence, the correct option is (B).

10. The given sentence is of present perfect tense and it is the active form. The structures for active/passive voices are:

Active: Subject + has/have + verb (IIIrd form) + object.

Passive: Object + has/have + been + verb (IIIrd form) + by + subject.

So, the passive voice of the given sentence would be:

The 'Ajooba' town has been destroyed by the enemies.

Hence, the correct option is (D).

11. Gene cloning is a set of experimental methods in molecular biology that are used to assemble recombinant DNA molecules and to direct their replication within host organisms. Plasmids are used as vectors in this process.

Hence, the correct option is (D).

12. Ecology is the scientific analysis and study of interactions among organisms and their environment. Environmental science focuses on the interactions between the physical, chemical, and biological components of the environment, including their effects on all types of organisms.

Hence, the correct option is (B).

13. We know that

If A, B and C are subsets of a set X. Then

I. $A \cup (B \cap C) = (A \cup B) \cap (A \cup C)$

II. $A \cup A = A$, $A \cap (A \cup B) = A$, $A \cup (A \cap B) = A$ and $A \cap A = A$

III. $(A \cap B) \cup C = (A \cap C) \cup (B \cap C)$

IV. $(A \cup B) \cap C = (A \cap C) \cup (B \cap C)$

From the options,

$\Rightarrow A \cup (A \cap B) = (A \cup A) \cap (A \cup B) = A \cap (A \cup B) = A$ ---
(Using property I and II)

So, option (A) is not correct.

$\Rightarrow A \cap (A \cup B) = (A \cap A) \cup (A \cap B) = A \cup (A \cap B) = A$ ---
(Using property I and II)

So, option (B) is correct.

$\Rightarrow (A \cap B) \cup C = (A \cup C) \cap (B \cup C)$ --- (Using property III)

So, option (C) is correct.

$\Rightarrow (A \cup B) \cap C = (A \cap C) \cup (B \cap C)$ --- (Using property IV)

So, option (D) is correct.

Hence, the correct option is (A).

14. S_n denotes the sum of the first n terms of the sequence.

It is given that,

$S_n = n + 12$

By substituting n = 2 in the given equation, we get

$\Rightarrow S_2 = 2 + 12 = 14$

Similarly by substituting n = 3 in the given equation, we get

$\Rightarrow S_3 = 3 + 12 = 15$

$\Rightarrow a_3 = S_3 - S_2 = 15 - 14 = 1$

Hence, the correct option is (A).

15. Führer, also spelled Fuehrer, German Führer, ("Leader"), a title used by Adolf Hitler to define his role of absolute authority in Germany's Third Reich (1933–45).

Adolf Hitler was a German politician of Austrian origin who became the leader of Nazi Germany.

Hitter also led the Nazi Party, the democratically elected party which ruled Germany and called himself the Fuhrer which means leader of the German Empire.

Hence, the correct option is (A).

16. Stephen Hawking, in full Stephen William Hawking, (born January 8, 1942, Oxford, Oxfordshire, England—died March 14, 2018, Cambridge, Cambridgeshire), English theoretical physicist whose theory of exploding black holes drew upon both relativity theory and quantum mechanics.

Hence, the correct option is (A).

17. Adherence means "sticking to" or "being faithful to,".

The correct answer is: Democracy in any country demands discipline and **adherence** to the rules.

Hence, the correct option is (B).

18. Invented means to find or learn something that nobody had found or knew before.

The correct answer is: Columbus **discovered** America.

Hence, the correct option is (B).

19. $\dfrac{\{9^n \times 3^5 \times (27)^3\}}{3} \times (81)^4$

$= 27 \Rightarrow \dfrac{\{(3^2)^n \times 3^5 \times (3^3)^3\}}{3 \times (3^4)^4}$

$= 3^3 \Rightarrow \dfrac{(3^{2n} \times 3^5 \times 3^{(3 \times 3)})}{3 \times 3^{(4 \times 4)}} = 3^3$

$\Rightarrow \dfrac{3^{2n+5+9}}{3 \times 3^{16}}$

$= 3^3 \Rightarrow \dfrac{3^{2n+14}}{3^{17}}$

$= 3^3 \Rightarrow 3^{(2n+14-17)} = 3^3$

$\Rightarrow 3^{2n-3} = 3^3$

From the equation powers:

$\Rightarrow 2n - 3 = 3$

$\Rightarrow 2n = 6$

$\Rightarrow n = 3.$

Hence, the correct option is (C).

20. Given:

A cuboid block of 6 cm × 12 cm × 15 cm is cut up into an exact number of equal cube

The given 6 cm × 12 cm × 15 cm

HCF = 3

Then cube = a = 3 cm

Then the possible number of cubes = $\dfrac{6 \times 12 \times 15}{3 \times 3 \times 3}$

The number of cubes = 2 × 4 × 5 = 40

Hence, the number of cubes = 40

Hence, the correct option is (B).

21. Given-

The volume of a hemisphere - 18π cm³

The total area of the hemisphere- 3πr²

We know the volume of the hemisphere is given as $\dfrac{2}{3}\pi r^3$

$\therefore 18\pi = \dfrac{2}{3}\pi r^3$

$\Rightarrow r^3 = \dfrac{18 \times 3 \times \pi}{2 \times \pi}$

$\Rightarrow r^3 = 27$

$\Rightarrow r = 3$ cm

Radius is 3 cm

Total area of the hemisphere is given as $= 3\pi r^2$

Inserting value of r, we get -

$\therefore$ Area of the hemisphere $= 3 \times \pi \times (3)^2$

$\Rightarrow$ Area of the hemisphere $= 27\pi$ cm²

Hence, Total area of the hemisphere is 27π cm².

Hence, the correct option is (C).

22. Given:

r = 8 cm

R = 20 cm

h = 16 cm

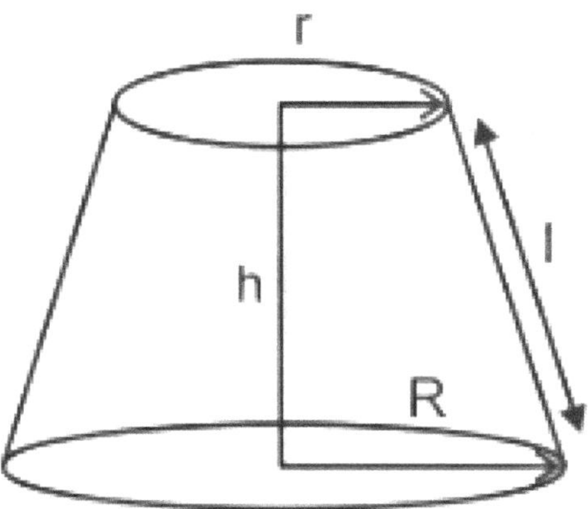

The bucket is in the form of a frustum.

The outer curved surface area of the frustum $= \pi(r + R) \times l$

We know that,

$l = \sqrt{h^2 + (R - r)^2}$

$\Rightarrow l = \sqrt{16^2 + (20 - 8)^2}$

$\Rightarrow l = \sqrt{256 + 144}$

$\Rightarrow l = \sqrt{400}$

$\Rightarrow l = 20$ cm

Now, we know that the outer curved surface area of the frustum

$= \pi(r + R) \times l$

$\Rightarrow \dfrac{22}{7}(20 + 8) \times 20$

$\Rightarrow 1760$ cm²

Hence, the outer curved surface area of the bucket is 1760 cm².

Hence, the correct option is (C).

23. $\sqrt{\dfrac{(0.1)^2+(0.01)^2+(0.009)^2}{(0.01)^2+(0.001)^2+(0.0009)^2}}$

$\Rightarrow \sqrt{\dfrac{0.01+0.0001+0.000081}{0.0001+0.000001+0.00000081}}$

$\Rightarrow \sqrt{\dfrac{0.010181}{0.00010181}}$

$\Rightarrow \sqrt{100}$

$\Rightarrow 10$

Hence, the correct option is (B).

24. Part R tells us what the 'third' is of so, it will come first. Part Q will come next as part P is the ending part and does not suits to join with 'but' with which part R is ending. Thus, the correct sequence is given by RQP.

Hence, the correct option is (D).

25. Ancient martial art is known as Kalaripayattu.

Kalaripayattu is also known as Kalari is the oldest martial art that originated in Kerala in South India. It includes strikes, kicks, grappling, weaponry, and healing methods.

Hence, the correct option is (C).

26. Given,

Area of rhombus $= 240$ cm^2

Length of one diagonal $= 24$ cm

Side of square $= \left(\dfrac{1}{\sqrt{61}}\right) \times$ side of rhombus

Area of rhombus $= \left(\dfrac{1}{2}\right) \times d_1 \times d_2$

$\Rightarrow \left(\dfrac{1}{2}\right) \times 24 \times d_2 = 240$

$\Rightarrow d_2 = 20$ cm

$(d_1)^2 + (d_2)^2 = 4 \times (\text{ Side })^2$

$\Rightarrow (24)^2 + (20)^2 = 4 \times (\text{ Side })^2$

$\Rightarrow 4 \times (\text{ Side })^2 = 576 + 400$

$\Rightarrow (\text{ Side })^2 = 244$

$\Rightarrow \text{Side} = \sqrt{244}$

$\Rightarrow \text{Side} = 2\sqrt{61}$

Side of squareside of rhombus $= \left(\dfrac{1}{\sqrt{61}}\right) \times$

$= \left(\dfrac{1}{\sqrt{61}}\right) \times 2\sqrt{61}$

$= 2$ cm

Area of square $= (\text{ Side })^2$

$= 2^2 = 4$ cm^2

$\therefore$ Area of square is 4 cm^2.

Hence, the correct option is (A).

27. Given,

Sides of triangular field = 18 m, 80 m and 82 m

Area of a triangular park $= 5\sqrt{3} \times$ The area of a triangular field

Area of an equilateral triangle $= \left(\dfrac{\sqrt{3}}{4}\right) a^2$

Area of triangle with sides a, b, and c $=$

$\sqrt{[s(s-a)(s-b)(s-c)]}$

Where, $s = \dfrac{(a+b+c)}{2}$

$\Rightarrow s = \dfrac{(18+80+82)}{2}$

$\Rightarrow s = 90$

The area of a triangular field $=$

$\sqrt{[90(90-18)(90-80)(90-82)]}$

$= \sqrt{[90 \times 72 \times 10 \times 8]}$

$= 720$ m^2

According to the question,

$\left(\dfrac{\sqrt{3}}{4}\right) a^2 = 5\sqrt{3} \times 720$

$a = 120$

$\therefore$ Side of the triangular park = 120 m

Hence, the correct option is (B).

28. Given:

$(3x + 2)^3 - (2x^2 + 3)$

Using formula,

$(a + b)^3 = (a^3 + b^3 + 3a^2b + 3ab^2)$

$(3x + 2)3 = [(3x)^3 + (2)^3 + 3(3x)^2(2) + 3(3x)(2)^2]$

$\Rightarrow (3x + 2)^3 = [27x^3 + 8 + 54x^2 + 36x]$

According to question:

$(27x^3 + 8 + 54x^2 + 36x) - (2x^2 + 3)$

$\Rightarrow 27x^3 + 5 + 52x^2 + 36x$

$\Rightarrow (27x^3 + 8 + 54x^2 + 36x) - (2x^2 + 3)$

$= 27x^3 + 5 + 52x^2 + 36x$

$$= 27x^3 + 52x^2 + 36x + 5$$

Hence, the correct option is (A).

29. The Ministry of Utmost Happiness is the second novel by Indian writer Arundhati Roy, published in 2017, twenty years after her debut, The God of Small Things. The novel weaves together the stories of people navigating some of the darkest and most violent episodes of modern Indian history, from land reform that dispossessed poor farmers to the 2002 Godhra train burning and Kashmir insurgency. Roy's characters run the gamut of Indian society and include an intersex woman (hijra), a rebellious architect, and her landlord who is a supervisor in the intelligence service. The narrative spans across decades and locations, but primarily takes place in Delhi and Kashmir.

Hence, the correct option is (B).

30. World Nature Conservation Day is celebrated every year on 28 July. In the present scenario, many species of fauna and flora are becoming extinct. Its purpose is to take a pledge on the World Nature Conservation Day to protect the extinct fauna and flora. Conservation of nature is closely related to the life of all living beings and all the natural environment of this earth. The whole earth is getting polluted due to pollution and the end of human civilization is visible in the near future. Keeping this situation in mind, in 1992, 'Earth Conference' of 174 countries of the world was organized in Brazil. After this, in 2002, the Earth Conference was organized in Johannesburg and many measures were suggested to all the countries of the world to pay attention to environmental protection. In fact, life on earth can be preserved only by the conservation of nature.

Hence, the correct option is (B).

31. On 17 November 1965, UNESCO declared 8 September as International Literacy Day. It was first celebrated in 1966. Its aim is to highlight the importance of literacy in individual, community and social settings. This festival is celebrated all over the world.

About 775 million youth are affected by the lack of literacy; That is, one in five youth is not yet literate and two third of these are women. 67 million children do not reach schools and many children lack regularity or drop out.

Hence, the correct option is (C).

32. Smallest cricket stadium in the world by boundary Feroz Shah Kotla.

The Feroz Shah Kotla Ground is a cricket ground built in 1883 in New Delhi is the second oldest international cricket stadium still functional in India, after the Eden Gardens in Kolkata. It also holds the record of the smallest cricket stadium in the world by boundary.

The Feroz Shah Kotla Stadium in New Delhi was renamed Arun Jaitley Stadium last year.

Hence, the correct option is (B).

33. The Declaration promised India Dominion Status and a constitution-making body after the second world war whose members would be elected by the provincial assemblies and nominated by the rulers in case of the princely states.

The Pakistan demand was accommodated by the provision indirectly that any province which was not prepared to accept the new constitution would have the right to sign a separate agreement with Britain regarding its future status. For the present, the British would continue to exercise sole control over the defence of the country.

Hence, the correct option is (B).

34. Indian Navy Virat (INS Virat) is a military class aircraft carrier in the Indian Navy. After Indian Navy Vikrant was discharged in 1997, it filled the vacant position of Vikrant. It is currently one of the two aircraft carriers in the Indian Ocean.

Hence, the correct option is (A).

35. The modern aircraft were first built by the Wright brothers. There was a difference of only four years between Wilver and Orville. When he thought of making airplanes, Wilver was only 11 years old and Orville was 7 years old.

Hence, the correct option is (A).

36.

- The error lies in the second part of the sentence as the verb "taught" will not take any preposition in the given context.

- A preposition is a word or group of words used before a noun, pronoun, or noun phrase to show direction, time, place, location, spatial relationships, or to introduce an object.

- Some examples of prepositions are words like "in," "at," "on," "of," and "to."

Hence, the correct option is (B).

37. The correct match is A-4, B-3, C-1, D-2.

Bhartrihari Temple:

- Bhartrihari Temple is located in Alwar, the nearest city to the Sariska National Tiger Reserve.

Karni Mata Temple:

- The Karni Mata Mandir in Bikaner is popular not for its location or architecture, but for being home to over 25,000 rats that inhabit and freely meander around the temple complex.

Atmateshwar Temple:

- Atmateshwar Temple is located in Pushkar.

- This beautiful 12th-century temple is dedicated to Lord Shiva and has an underground component.

Bisaldeo Temple:

- Bisaldeo Temple is located in Bisalpur, located around 60-80 kilometers from Tonk.

Hence, the correct option is (B).

38. The word similar to 'cognitive' is mental.

Cognitive: Connected with thinking or conscious mental processes.

Mental: Connected with or happening in the mind.

Impudent: very rude.

Overall: Including everything.

Raid: a short sudden attack, usually by a small group of people.

Hence, the correct option is (B).

39. The antonym of 'stunted' is encouraged.

Stunted: To stop somebody/something growing or developing properly.

Encouraged: To give hope, support or confidence to somebody.

Impeded: To make it difficult for somebody/something to move or go forward.

Improvised: To make, do, or manage something without preparation, using what you have.

Deluded: To make somebody believe something that is not true.

Hence, the correct option is (B).

40. The word similar to 'implication' is inference.

Implication: The effect that something will have on something else in the future.

Inference: A guess that you make or an opinion that you form based on the information that you have.

Intangibility: Incapable of being perceived by the sense of touch, as incorporeal or immaterial things.

Influence: The power to affect, change or control somebody/something.

Reason: A cause or an explanation for something that has happened or for something that somebody has done.

Hence, the correct option is (C).

41. I and II are implicit assumptions.

Statement I can be derived from the line 'Nor do we know for sure why even among women, the SARI figures are higher than the IHDS figures'.

Statement II can be derived from the line 'Part of the reason is that SARI and the IHDS asked different people. The IHDS asked only women, while SARI asked both women and men'.

However, Statement III is not implied in the passage.

Hence, the correct option is (D).

42. A mother's undernourishment leads to child's malnutrition can be inferred from the passage.

This can be concluded from the line 'Women's undernourishment contributes substantially to India's unacceptably high rates of child stunting'.

Hence, the correct option is (B).

43. The Indian Army has developed and launced an in-house messaging application called the 'Secure Application for Internet (SAI)'.

This messaging application supports an end-to-end secure voice, text and video calling services for android platform over Internet

SAI was first developed by Colonel Sai Shankar, the commanding officer of a signals unit in Rajasthan, and then upgraded to military-grade standards.

India's first Chief of Defence Staff: General Bipin Rawat.

Hence, the correct option is (D).

44. Max Planck was a German theoretical physicist who discovered the quantum of action, now known as Planck's constant, h, in 1900. This work laid the foundation for quantum theory, which won him the Nobel Prize for Physics in 1918.

Hence, the correct option is (B).

45. (A) $\sqrt{1250} = 35.35$

(B) $\sqrt{16641} = \sqrt{(129 \times 129)} = 129$

(C) $\sqrt{2025} = \sqrt{(45 \times 45)} = 45$

(D) $\sqrt{9801} = \sqrt{(99 \times 99)} = 99$

Now, we can say 1250 is not a perfect square.

Hence, the correct option is (A).

46. Factors of 512 are 1, 2, 4, 8, 16, 32, 64, 128, 256 and 512.

∴ We can say 1, 4, 16, 64 and 256 are the perfect square of numbers 1, 2, 4, 8, 16 respectively.

Hence, the correct option is (B).

47. Laterite, soil layer that is rich in iron oxide and derived from a wide variety of rocks weathering under strongly oxidizing and leaching conditions.

Hence, the correct option is (D).

48.

- Topographic maps refer to maps at large and medium scales that incorporate a massive variety of information.
- The maps are prepared to base on the actual ground survey.
- These are also known as toposheet by the Survey of India.
- Features are depicted using conventional symbols.
- Always follow the grid method for the location and extent.
- Topographic maps refer to maps at large and medium scales that incorporate a massive variety of information.
- All the components of topographic maps carry equal importance.
- It is a two-dimensional representation of a three-dimensional surface, so distortion also found.

- A topographic map is a detailed and accurate illustration of man-made and natural features on the ground such as roads, railways, power transmission lines, contours, elevations, rivers, lakes, and geographical names.

Hence, the correct option is (A).

49. Ring of Fire:

- The Ring of Fire is also referred to as the Circum-Pacific Belt.

- It is a path along the Pacific Ocean. So, statement 1 is incorrect.

- It is characterized by active volcanoes and frequent earthquakes. So, statement 2 is correct.

- Its length is approximately 40,000 kilometers (24,900 miles).

- It traces boundaries between several tectonic plates— including the Pacific, Juan de Fuca, Cocos, Indian-Australian, Nazca, North American, and Philippine Plates.

- The belt follows chains of island arcs such as Tonga and New Hebrides, the Indonesian archipelago, the Philippines, Japan, the Kuril Islands, and the Aleutians, as well as other arc-shaped geomorphic features, such as the western coast of North America and the Andes Mountains.

- Volcanoes are associated with the belt throughout its length; for this reason, it is called the "Ring of Fire."

Hence, the correct option is (A).

50. Given, four-digit number is $51c3$.

Sum of each digits $= 5 + 1 + c + 3 = 9 + c$

Therefore, the given number $51c3$ will be divisible by 9 if its sum of each digit is divisible by 9.

So, $9 + c$ is divisible by 9, which is only possible, when we take $c = 0$ or 9

Hence, the correct option is (B).

51. The idiom "die-hard" means strongly opposing change and new ideas; unwilling to change.

Hence, the correct option is (A).

52. The idiom "To pull one's socks up" means to make an effort to improve one's work or behavior because it is not good enough. Thus, option C conveys the best meaning of the idiom.

Hence, the correct option is (C).

53. Given:

Ratio of numbers = 4 : 9

LCM of the numbers = 720

Let the numbers be $4a$ and $9a$.

$\therefore$ Prime factors of $4a = a \times 2 \times 2$

Prime factors of $9a = a \times 3 \times 3$

$\therefore$ LCM of $4a$ and $9a = a \times 2 \times 2 \times 3 \times 3$

$= 36 \times a$

LCM of 4 and $9a = 720$ ..... (Given)

$\therefore 36 \times a = 720$

$\Rightarrow a = \dfrac{720}{36}$

$\Rightarrow a = 20$

$\therefore$ Numbers are $4a = 4 \times 20 = 80$

$9a = 9 \times 20 = 180$

$\therefore$ Sum of numbers $= 180 + 80$

$= 260$

Hence, the correct option is (A).

54. The most appropriate synonym of the given word 'Accorded' is 'Give'.

Let's look at the meaning and examples of the given options:

Therefore, as per the points mentioned above, we find that the correct answer is Option C.

Hence, the correct option is (C).

55. The most appropriate synonym of the given word 'Assertions' is 'Declaration'.

Let's look at the meaning and examples of the given options:

Hence, the correct option is (D).

56. In 1954, the Hindi names 'Rajya Sabha' and 'Lok Sabha' were adopted for the Council of States and the House of People. The Rajya Sabha represented the states and the union territories, and the Lok Sabha represented the people of India in collective.

Hence, the correct option is (C).

57. The chairman of the Estimates Committee is appointed by the Speaker of the Lok Sabha from amongst its members and he is invariably from the ruling party. The committee examines the estimates included in the budget and suggest 'economies' in public expenditure.

Hence, the correct option is (C).

58. Given:

The density of silver is 10.8×10^3 kgm $^{-3}$ and the density of water is 10^3 kgm $^{-3}$

We know that,

$\text{Relative density} = \dfrac{\text{Density of silver}}{\text{Density of water}}$

$\text{Relative density} = \dfrac{10.8 \times 10^3}{10^3} = 10.8$

Hence, the correct option is (D).

59. The chemical formula of Ammonium phosphate is $(NH_4)_3PO_4$.

- It is the salt of Ammonia and Phosphoric acid.
- Other names of this salt are Triammonium phosphate, Diazanium hydrogen phosphate.

Hence, the correct option is (A).

60. LCM of 35 and 49 is 245.

The numbers which are divided by 35 and 49 and leave a remainder 30 in each case are

⇒ 245×1+30 = 245+30 = 275

⇒ 245×2+30 = 490+30 = 520

520 is more than 500 so, there is only 1 number that is 275.

Hence, the correct option is (C).

61. Let the number of the correct answers be x, then the number of wrong answers is (100-x).

According to the question,

⇒ 4x-(100-x) = 340

⇒ 4x+x = 440

⇒ x = 88

Therefore the number of questions wrongly answered by Mr. X = (100-88) =12

Hence, the correct option is (C).

62. Given, cost of a chair and table is Rs. 600 and the ratio of cost of one chair and table is $7:5$.

Let the cost of one chair be a and one table be b.

$$\therefore \frac{a}{b} = \frac{7}{5}$$

$$\Rightarrow a = \frac{7b}{5}$$

Now, $a + b = 600$

$$\Rightarrow \left(\frac{7b}{5} + b\right) = 600$$

$$\Rightarrow 12b = 3000$$

$$\Rightarrow b = \text{Rs. } 250$$

$$\therefore a = \text{Rs. } 350$$

Hence, the correct option is (B).

63. Given,

In a rally of 256 students, boys and girls are in the ratio $9:7$.

$$\therefore \text{Number of girls} = \left(\frac{7}{16}\right) \times 256.$$

$$= 112$$

Hence, the correct option is (C).

64. Given:

Principal $=$ Rs. 30000

Rate $= 10\%$

Time $= 5$ years

Let the $R.O.I$ allowed by bank be r%

According to question

$$7800 = \left(\frac{30000 \times 10 \times 5}{100}\right) - \left(\frac{30000 \times r \times 3}{100}\right)$$

$$7800 = 15000 - 900r$$

$$r = 8\%$$

$\therefore$ R.O.I allowed by bank is 8%.

Hence, the correct option is (D).

65. Given:
A sum of Rs. 1000 is increased 100% of its original after 7 years at compound interest.

Let the amount be A and principal be P.

Amount = principal $\times \left(1 + \frac{rate}{100}\right)^n$

After 7 years,

$$A = P \times \left(1 + \frac{rate}{100}\right)^7 = 2P \quad (\because P \text{ is increased by } 100\%)$$

$$\Rightarrow \left(1 + \frac{rate}{100}\right)^7 = 2$$

Amount will be increased by 700%

$\Rightarrow$ A will be $8P$

$$\Rightarrow A = 2^3 \times P = \left(\left\{\left(1 + \frac{rate}{100}\right)^7\right\}^3\right) \times P$$

$$= \left(1 + \frac{rate}{100}\right)^{21} \times P$$

$\Rightarrow$ time $= 21$ years

$\therefore$ After 21 years the amount will be increased by 700% of its initial value / Principal.
Hence, the correct option is (B).

66. Let, the cost price of chocolate be Rs. x.

Selling price of a chocolate = Rs. $\frac{160}{90}$ = Rs. $\frac{16}{9}$

According to the question,

$$x - x \times \frac{20}{100} = \frac{16}{9}$$

$$\Rightarrow 0.8x = \frac{16}{9}$$

$$\Rightarrow x = \frac{16}{9} \times \frac{10}{8}$$

$$\Rightarrow x = \frac{20}{9}$$

Selling price of a chocolate at 20% profit = Rs. $\left(\dfrac{20}{9} + \dfrac{20}{9} \times \dfrac{20}{100}\right) = Rs. \dfrac{24}{9}$

Let, Number of chocolates he should sell for Rs. 96 be k.

$\Rightarrow \dfrac{24k}{9} = 96$

$\Rightarrow k = 96 \times \dfrac{9}{24} = 36$

∴ He should sell 36 chocolates for Rs. 96

Hence, the correct option is (B).

67. Let, the cost price of orange be Rs. x.

The selling price of orange be Rs y.

According to the question,

$15x = 20y$

$\Rightarrow y = \dfrac{15x}{20}$

$\Rightarrow y = 0.75x$

∴ Loss percentage = $\dfrac{(x - 0.75x)}{x} \times 100\% = \dfrac{0.25x}{x} \times 100\% = 25\%$

Hence, the correct option is (A).

68. The Rajatarangini', 'The River of Kings' was composed by Kalhan from Kashmiri to Sanskrit in the 12th Century. The Rajataringini provides the earliest source on Kashmir that can be labeled as a "historical" text on this region. This book provides an invaluable source of information about early Kashmir and its neighbors in the north western parts of the Indian subcontinent, and has been widely referenced by later historians and ethnographers.

Hence, the correct option is (A).

69. Rajasthan Government provides financial incentives to SC / ST candidates passing the all India Civil Services examination and State Civil Services examination under Rajasthani Anuprati Yojana.

Following are the points of Rajasthan Anuprati Yojana :

- The Rajasthan Government has launched the Rajasthan Anuprati Yojana for the meritorious students of minority families.
- It covers the residents of Rajasthan State who belong to SC / ST / Special Backward Class and general category BPL families.
- The approval scheme was launched by the state government in January 2005.

Hence, the correct option is (D).

70. Given:

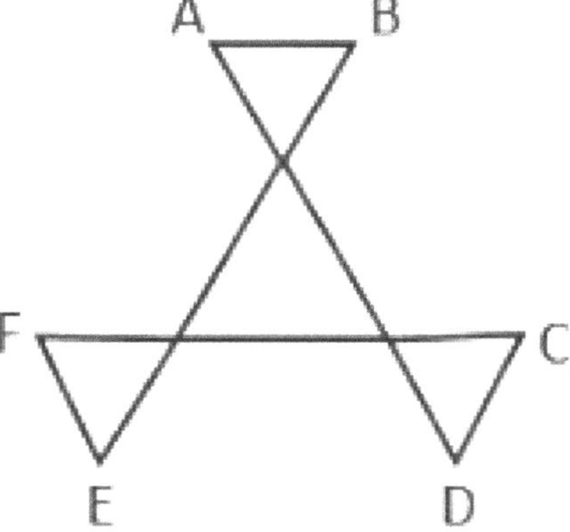

Calculation:

As, the given figure is

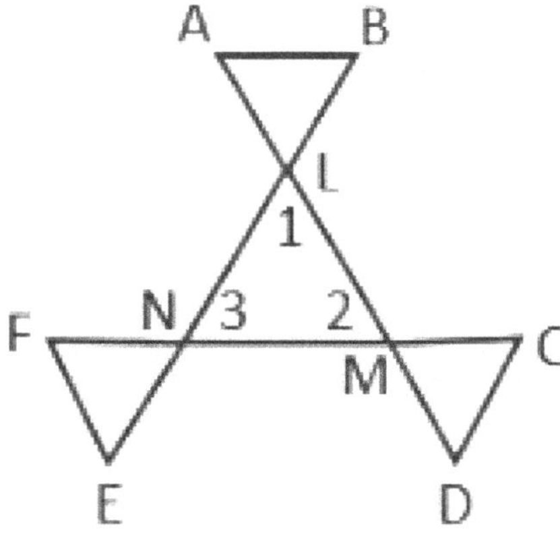

Here, in Δ LMN, ∠1 + ∠2 + ∠3 = 180°   ----(i) (Sum of interior angles of a triangle = 180°)

As, ∠BLM is the exterior angle for Δ ABL,

So, ∠A + ∠B = (∠BLM Sum of two interior angle is equal to the exterior angle)

$\Rightarrow$ ∠A + ∠B = 180° - ∠1   ----(ii)

Similarly, ∠CML and ∠FNL are the exterior angles of Δ CDM and Δ FEN,

So, ∠C + ∠D = 180° - ∠2   ----(iii)

And, ∠E + ∠F = 180° - ∠3   ----(iv)

Adding equations (ii), (iii) and (iv) we get

∠A + ∠B + ∠C + ∠D + ∠E + ∠F = 180° × 3 - (∠1 + ∠2 + ∠3)   ----(v)

From (i) and (v), we get

∠A + ∠B + ∠C + ∠D + ∠E + ∠F = 180° × 3 - 180°

$\Rightarrow$ ∠A + ∠B + ∠C + ∠D + ∠E + ∠F = 360°

∴ The sum of the measures of the angles ∠A, ∠B, ∠C, ∠D, ∠E, and ∠F in the given figure is 360°.

Hence, the correct option is (B).

71. P and Q invested in a business. The profit earned was divided in the ratio $2:3$. If P invested Rs. 40000.

Concept used:

Amount invested P to $Q =$ ratio of their profit

Calculation:

The amount of P invested Rs. 40000 and amount invested by Q is y.

Amount invested P to $Q =$ ratio of their profit

$\Rightarrow \dfrac{40000}{y} = \dfrac{2}{3}$

$\Rightarrow y = 40000 \times \dfrac{3}{2}$

$\Rightarrow y = Rs.\, 60000$

$\therefore$ The amount invested by Q is Rs. 60000.

Hence, the correct option is (C).

72. Standard deviation $= \sqrt{\dfrac{\sum(x-\overline{x})^2}{N}}$

Where $\overline{x}$ is the mean of data

N is the number of terms

$\overline{x} = \dfrac{\sum x}{N} = \dfrac{8+12+13+15+22}{5}$

$= \dfrac{70}{5} = 14$

$$\begin{array}{ccccccc} x = & & 8 & 12 & 13 & 15 & 22 \\ (x-\overline{x})^2 = & & 36 & 4 & 1 & 1 & 64 \end{array}$$

$\sum(x - x)^2 = 36 + 4 + 1 + 1 + 64 = 106$

Standard deviation $= \sqrt{\dfrac{106}{5}} = 4.6$

Hence, the correct option is (D).

73. Given,

A set of 5 values 3, 5, 7, 9, 11 has standard deviation σ.

Consider, the data 5, 7, 9, 11, 13

Here, each observation is increased by a constant 2,

we know that, if each observation is increased by a constant k, then the standard deviation is unchanged.

So, the standard deviation of 5 values 5, 7, 9, 11, 13 is σ

Hence, the correct option is (A).

74. Vehicle Scrappage Policy:

The Union Road and Transport Minister announced the Vehicle Scrapping Policy in the Lok Sabha. It was first announced in the Union Budget for 2021-22.

Aim: Reducing the population of old and defective vehicles, bringing down vehicular air pollutants, improving road and vehicular safety.

Fitness Test:

- Old vehicles will have to pass a fitness test before re-registration and as per the policy government commercial vehicles more than 15 years old and private vehicles which are over 20 years old. So, statement 1 is correct.

- Vehicles that fail to pass the test will be declared as 'end-of-life vehicles' and will be scrapped. So, statement 2 is correct.

- Old vehicles will be tested at the Automated Fitness Center and the fitness test of the vehicles will be conducted according to international standards.

- After you scrap your vehicle with the government registered agency, you will be provided with the 'scrapping certificate.'

Hence, the correct option is (A).

75. National Hydrogen Energy Mission (NHM):

The Union Budget for 2021-22 has announced a National Hydrogen Energy Mission (NHM) that will draw up a road map for using hydrogen as an energy source. The initiative has the potential of transforming transportation.

NHM initiative will capitalize on one of the most abundant elements on earth (Hydrogen) for a cleaner alternative fuel option.

Objectives:

- Focus on the generation of hydrogen from green power resources. So, statement 1 is correct.

- To link India's growing renewable capacity with the hydrogen economy. So, statement 2 is correct.

- To reduce import dependency on fossil fuels. So, statement 3 is correct.

Hence, the correct option is (D).

76. Given:

Three solid spheres of radii 3 cm, 4 cm, and 5 cm.

Volume of sphere $= \dfrac{4}{3}\pi r^3$

Let radius of the larger sphere is 'R'.

Volume of large solid sphere is:

$= \dfrac{4}{3} \times \pi \times (3^3 + 4^3 + 5^3)$

$= \dfrac{4}{3} \times \pi(27 + 64 + 125)$

$= \dfrac{4\pi}{3} \times 216 \text{ cm}^3$

Now,

$\dfrac{4\pi}{3} \times R^3 = \dfrac{4\pi}{3} \times 216$

$$\Rightarrow R^3 = 216$$

$$\Rightarrow R = (216)^{\frac{1}{3}}$$

$$\Rightarrow R = 6$$

∴ The radius of the larger sphere is 6 cm.

Hence, the correct option is (C).

77. While arranging sentences in a sequence, it is important to understand the theme of the passage so that the introductory and the following statements can be chosen accordingly. The passage central theme revolves around biofuels and their advantages -disadvantages. The first statement should be E as it introduces the topic 'biofuels' and mentions that they form an energy source that is potentially unlimited. Next should be statement F. It states a contradiction to the fact mentioned about biofuels in E that everything is good about the biofuels. It states that the biofuels have disadvantages too. Next should be statement C as it talks about the disadvantages of biofuels which have been introduced in the prior statement. Next should be statement A. It states that despite having disadvantages, biofuels have numerous advantages as well. It should be followed by statement B which talks about some other advantages as well. B mentions 'turnaround' which has also been mentioned in statement D making BD, a mandatory pair.

So, the correct logical order is EFCABD.

Hence, the correct option is (D).

78. While arranging sentences in a sequence, it is important to understand the theme of the passage so that the introductory and the following statements can be chosen accordingly. The passage central theme revolves around biofuels and their advantages -disadvantages. The first statement should be E as it introduces the topic 'biofuels' and mentions that they form an energy source that is potentially unlimited. Next should be statement F. It states a contradiction to the fact mentioned about biofuels in E that everything is good about the biofuels. It states that biofuels have disadvantages too. Next should be statement C as it talks about the disadvantages of biofuels which have been introduced in the prior statement. Next should be statement A. It states that despite having disadvantages, biofuels have numerous advantages as well. It should be followed by statement B which talks about some other advantages as well. B mentions 'turnaround' which has also been mentioned in statement D making BD, a mandatory pair.

So, the correct logical order is EFCABD.

Hence, the correct option is (D).

79. Rajeev Bagga, a deaf badminton player born in India, represents Britain. He was the Indian national champion and, the only deaf person to do so, reached the main stage of the 1990 All England Open Badminton Championships.

From 1989 to 2001, he won 12 golds and was singles champion at the Deaflympics, and was voted 'Deaflympian of the Century' in 2001 by the Comité International des Sports des Sourds (International Deaf Sports Committee).

He received India's highest sporting honour, the Arjuna medal, in 1991. He narrowly missed his sixth gold at the 2009 Deaflympics.

He won the gold medal in the men's singles at the World Deaf Badminton Championships in 2003 and 2007.

Hence, the correct option is (D).

80. Mirabai chanu won India's first gold medal in the Commonwealth Games.

The 23-year-old won her first medal in the 2014 Commonwealth Games, the silver in the women's 48-kg weight class.

She got the Rajiv Gandhi Khel Ratna award in 2018.

She clinched a gold medal at the EGAT Cup in Thailand, making a strong comeback from the lower back injury that kept her out of action for more than half of 2018.

Hence, the correct option is (C).

81. Social norms refer to the most frequently observed behavior in a society.

Social norms are shared standards of acceptable behavior by groups. Social norms can both be informal understandings that govern the behavior of members of a society, as well as be codified into rules and laws. Social normative influences or social norms, are deemed to be powerful drivers of human behavioral changes and well organized and incorporated by major theories which explaining human behavior.

Hence, the correct option is (B).

82. The basis of slave system is Economic.

Slavery is a system of stratification in which one person owns another, as he or she would own property, and exploits the slave's labor for economic gain. Slaves are one of the lowest categories in any stratification system, as they possess virtually no power or wealth of their own.

Hence, the correct option is (B).

83. As we know,

If a person completes a piece of work in 'n' days, then work of 1 day is $\dfrac{1}{n}$ part of work.

Time taken by Ganesh and Bhima complete a work $= 6$ days

The part of the work that is completed by Ganesh and Bhima in 1 day $= \dfrac{1}{6}$

Time taken by Ganesh to complete a work $= 10$ days

The part of work that is completed by Ganesh in 1 day $= \dfrac{1}{10}$

Now, we first find the part of work completed by Bhima in 1 day

$$= \dfrac{1}{6} - \dfrac{1}{10}$$

$$= \dfrac{(10-6)}{60}$$

$$= \dfrac{4}{60}$$

$= \dfrac{1}{15}$

∴ Bhima completes the whole work in 15 days.

Hence, the correct option is (D).

84. Given,

A alone can complete a work in = 12 days

B alone can complete the same work in = 15 days

As we know,

Wages are distributed into efficiency ratio.

Efficiency is inversely proportional to time.

Time ratio of A and B = 12 : 15 = 4 : 5

Efficiency ratio of A and B = 5 : 4

According to the question,

5 + 4 = 9 units

⇒ 9 units = 3600

⇒ 1 unit = 400

⇒ 5 units = 5 × 400 = Rs. 2000

∴ Share of A is Rs. 2000.

Hence, the correct option is (D).

85. The Korean won (KRW) is the national currency of South Korea. Its users denote the won by using the symbol "₩," as in "₩1,000." It became the currency of South Korea in 1962, replacing the hwan. It was pegged to the U.S. dollar at various rates until 1997 when it became a floating currency.
Hence, the correct option is (D).

86. Sabarimala is a famous Hindu temple located in the Periyar Tiger Sanctuary in Kerala. It has the largest annual pilgrimage in the world, which attracts about 2 crore devotees every year.

Sabarimala is a wonderful link between Shaivites and Vaishnavites. In Malayalam, 'Shabarimala' means mountain.

There is a temple of Lord Ayyappan in Sabarimala.
Hence, the correct option is (A).

87. The Chaitra Jatra festival is held every year at the "Tara Tarini hill temple" on the Tuesday of the Hindu month of Chaitra. Tara Tarini Pahari Temple is located in Kumari Pahari on the banks of river Rushikulya. It is a major center of Shakti Puja in Odisha. Tara Tarini hill temple is one of the four major ancient Tantra Peeths and Shakti Peethas in India.

Hence, the correct option is (D).

88. Good speech training leads to better learning in language A teacher must introduce speech training right from the beginning. Encourage learners to take interest in their own progress. It is probably the best, in the beginning, to allow children to use such expressions as good morning, good aftenoon, thank you, please excuse me, may I come in, etc. These will help build up their confidence. Similar expressions from the language taught by you may be taken up.

Speech training lessons should begin with the following exercises:

- Correct use of speech organs for pronouncing different sounds.
- Demonstration of correct pronunciation by you.
- Group practice to ensure the correct position of the tongue and lips.
- Diagnosis of the errors at an individual level and individual practice to correct the pronunciation.
- Providing an opportunity to each child to speak two or three sentences coherently for about one minute to enable you to diagnose the error.
- During the speech, training does not be discouraged if you do not see improvement in the spoken language of your pupils.
- A well-directed sounds drill will definitely bring improvement among your learners.

Thus, we conclude that all the above strategies can be used to train students for good speech.

Hence, the correct option is (C).

89. Given,

Men = 40%

Women = 35%

Childrens = 100 - 75 = 25%

Of all the children in the town, 40% are girls

Total number of girls = 1200

Let the total population be x

40% of 25% of x = 1200

$\Rightarrow \left[\dfrac{1000}{(100 \times 100)}\right] \times x = 1200$

$\Rightarrow x = \dfrac{(1200 \times 100 \times 100)}{1000}$

$\Rightarrow x = 12000$

∴ The total population is 12000.

Hence, the correct option is (A).

90. Let the initial selling price be S.P and the initial sale be of Y units.

Thus,

Total sale amount initial

A = S.P × Y

The selling price got reduced by 20%.

New selling price

$= S.P - \dfrac{20}{100} \times S.P$

$= 0.8\, S.P$

Also, the sale got increased by 80%. Therefore, new sale units

$$= Y + \frac{80}{100} \times Y$$

$$= 1.8\,Y$$

Total sales amount finally

$$A' = 0.8(S.P) \times 1.8Y$$

$$A' = 1.44(S.P \times Y)$$

Thus there is an increase in total sale amount.

Percentage increase

$$= \frac{A'-A}{A} \times 100$$

$$= \frac{1.44(\,S.P \times Y) - S.P \times Y}{S.P \times Y} \times 100$$

$$= 44\%$$

∴ There is a rise of 44% in the total sales amount.

Hence, the correct option is (A).

91. Given,

The roots of the quadratic equation $x^2 + kx + 18 = 0$ are equal.

If the roots of the quadratic equation $ax^2 + bx + c = 0$ are equal, then $b^2 - 4ac = 0$

$$x^2 + kx + 18 = 0$$

$$\Rightarrow a = 1, b = k, c = 18$$

For equal roots,

$$b^2 - 4ac = 0$$

$$\Rightarrow k^2 - 4(1)(18) = 0$$

$$\Rightarrow k = \sqrt{72}$$

$$\Rightarrow k = 6\sqrt{2}$$

∴ The value of k is $6\sqrt{2}$.

Hence, the correct option is (D).

92. Let Rs. x is the cost price of the article.

$$\text{Profit } \% = \frac{\text{S.P - C.P}}{\text{C.P}} \times 100$$

$$x = \frac{(144 - x)}{x} \times 100$$

$$\Rightarrow x^2 = 14400 - 100x$$

$$\Rightarrow x^2 + 100x - 14400 = 0$$

$$\Rightarrow x^2 + 180x - 80x - 14400 = 0$$

$$\Rightarrow (x + 180)(x - 80) = 0$$

$$\Rightarrow x = 80$$

∴ Cost price of the article $=$ Rs. 80

Hence, the correct option is (A).

93. Given,

The ratio of length and breadth of the rectangular field = 5 : 2.

The perimeter of the rectangular field = 238 m.

Perimeter of the rectangle = 2(l + b)

Ratio of length and breadth of the rectangular field = $5x : 2x$

According to the question,

$$2 \times (5x + 2x) = 238$$

$$\Rightarrow 2 \times 7x = 238$$

$$\Rightarrow x = \frac{238}{14}$$

$$\Rightarrow x = 17 \text{ m}$$

Length of the field

= 5 × 17 = 85 m.

∴ Length of the field is 85 m.

Hence, the correct option is (D).

94. The correct answer is 'in spite'.

He slept like a horse **in spite** of all the commotion in the room.

The prepositional expression 'In spite of' is used to express something that surprisingly does not prevent something else from being true.

Example:

They enjoyed the rides in spite of the long queues.

Hence, the correct option is (C).

95. A person who believes that only selfishness motivates human actions is a **cynic**.

'Cynic' means a person who believes that people are motivated purely by self-interest.

Hence, the correct option is (B).

96. One who can not be corrected is **incorrigible.**

Incorrigible: (of a person or their behaviour) not able to be changed or reformed.

Hence, the correct option is (A).

97. Given,

$$\sqrt[3]{\sqrt{0.000064}} = ?$$

Then,

$$\sqrt{0.000064}$$

$$= \sqrt{\frac{64}{10^6}}$$

$$= \frac{8}{10^3}$$

$$= \frac{8}{1000}$$

$$= 0.008$$

$$\therefore \sqrt[3]{\sqrt{0.000064}}$$

$$= \sqrt[3]{0.008}$$

$$= \sqrt[3]{\frac{8}{1000}}$$

$$= \frac{2}{10}$$

$$= 0.2$$

Hence, the correct option is (B).

98. Let the total spendings on sports be Rs. x.

Then,

Amount spent on Golf $= $ Rs. $\left(\frac{36}{360} \times x\right)$

$= $ Rs. $\frac{x}{10}$

Amount spent on Hockey Rs. $= \left(\frac{63}{360} \times x\right)$

$= $ Rs. $\frac{7x}{40}$

Difference $= $ Rs. $\left(\frac{7x}{40} - \frac{x}{10}\right)$

$= $ Rs $\frac{3x}{40}$

Required percentage $= $ Rs. $\left[\left(\frac{\frac{3x}{40}}{\frac{x}{10}}\right) \times 100\right]\%$

$$= 75\%$$

$\therefore$ Required percentage is 75%.

Hence, the correct option is (D).

99. Let the total spendings on sports be Rs. x

Then,

Amount spent on Cricket $= $ Rs. $\left(\frac{81}{360} \times x\right)$

$= $ Rs. $\frac{9x}{40}$

Amount spent on Football $= Rs \left(\frac{54}{360} \times x\right)$

$= $ Rs. $\frac{3x}{20}$

Difference $= $ Rs. $\left(\frac{9x}{40} - \frac{3x}{20}\right)$

$= $ Rs $\frac{3x}{40}$

Required percentage $= $ Rs. $\left[\left(\frac{\frac{3x}{40}}{\frac{9x}{40}}\right) \times 100\right]\%$

$$= 33\frac{1}{3}\%$$

$\therefore$ Required percentage is $33\frac{1}{3}\%$.

Hence, the correct option is (C).

100. Given,

Total amount spent during year = Rs. 2 crore

Amount spent on Cricket and Hockey together

$= $ Rs. $\left[\frac{(81+63)}{360} \times 2\right]$ crores

$= $ Rs. 0.8 crores

$= $ Rs. $80,00,000$

Hence, the correct option is (B).

Q.1 What was the theme of International Girls in ICT Day 2022 which is observed annually on the fourth Thursday in April?

A. Access and safety

B. Inspiring the Next Generation

C. Case For Change, Connected Women, IoT and Tech4Girls

D. Powering Change: Women in Innovation and Creativity

Q.2 Tamil Nadu Assembly Election 2021 was won by which political party?

[UPSSSC Preliminary Eligibility Test, 2021]

A. DMK

B. BJP

C. AIADMK

D. PMK

Q.3 Who assassinated W.C. Rand, the Plague Commissioner of Pune in 1897?

A. Ganesh Savarkar

B. Chapekar Brothers

C. Vasudev Balwant Phadke

D. Chiplunkar Brothers

Q.4 At present, who is the Secretary-General of UNO?

[Haryana Police Constable Commando Wing, 2021]

A. Antonio Guterres

B. Paul R. Milgrom

C. Robert B. Wilson

D. None of these

Q.5 Who is the first Indian woman President of the UN General Assembly?

A. Kiran Bedi

B. Indira Gandhi

C. Vijaya Lakshmi Pandit

D. Leila Seth

Q.6 Direction: In the following question, some part of the sentence may have errors. Find out which part of the sentence has an error and select the appropriate option. If the sentence is free from error, select 'No error'.

The reason we were late for (A)/ the meeting is that there (B)/ was an accident on the highway. (C)/ No error (D)

A. (A)

B. (B)

C. (C)

D. (D)

Ques (7-8):Direction: In the following question, a sentence has been given in Active/Passive Voice. Out of the four alternatives suggested, select the one which best expresses the same sentence in Passive/Active Voice.

Q.7 The call to donate blood was not responded to by anyone.

A. No one responded to the call for donation.

B. No one responded to the call to donate blood.

C. No one responds for call to donate blood.

D. The call to donate blood would not be responded to by anyone.

Q.8 They have decided to increase the school fees this year.

A. It has been decided to increase the school fees this year.

B. It had been decided to increase the school fees this year.

C. It was decided to increase the school fees this year.

D. It will be decided to increase the school fees this year.

Q.9 The author of "Life of Pi" is:

A. Eleanor Catton

B. Aravind Adiga

C. Yann Martel

D. Kiran Desai

Ques (10-11):Direction: In the following question, out of the four alternatives, select the alternative which best expresses the meaning of the Idiom/Phrase.

Q.10 To sleep with the fishes

A. Always be in a dream world

B. To make absurd excuses

C. To sleep peacefully

D. To be dead

Q.11 Name is mud

A. In trouble

B. Liked

C. Respected

D. Wanted and desired

Q.12 Remedial teaching in English will help the language teacher in identification of:

A. The topic which the learner hasn't learnt

B. Malady on language test and its causes

C. Accurate class size

D. Intelligent learners of the class

Q.13 The purpose of remedial teaching is to:

A. Introduce new language items

B. Test recently taught items

C. Teach again the language items not properly learnt

D. Teach again the language items already learnt

Q.14 QUANTAS is a popular airline of:

[NCHM JEE (Hotel Mgmt & Catering), 2019]

A. Australia

B. Netherlands

C. Korea

D. Japan

Q.15 Regulatory body 'TRAI' associated with which of the following?

[NCHM JEE (Hotel Mgmt & Catering), 2019]

A. Telecom

B. Technical Education

C. Tourism

D. Transport

Q.16 Simplify:

$$\sqrt{\left[4 + \sqrt{\left(44 + \sqrt{10000}\right)}\right]}$$

A. 8

B. 4

C. 6

D. 16

Q.17 What is the value of $\dfrac{11.2 \times 0.36 + 0.42 \times 3.2}{0.8 \times 4.2}$?

A. 2

B. 1.6

C. 3

D. $\dfrac{3}{2}$

Q.18 A shopkeeper sold an article at cost price but use the weight of 960 gm in place of 1 kg weight. Find his profits %?

A. $2\frac{1}{3}\%$ **B.** $3\frac{1}{6}\%$ **C.** $4\frac{1}{6}\%$ **D.** $3\frac{1}{5}\%$

Q.19 A person bought 15 pens at Rs. 10 each and sold 5 of them at Rs. 8 and the other 7 at Rs. 12 and the remaining at Rs. 16. What is the profit/loss percentage?

A. 13.66%   **B.** 12.33%   **C.** 14.66%   **D.** 12.66%

Q.20 The marked price of an item is Rs. 200. On purchase of 1 item discount is 22%, on purchase of 4 items discount is 33%. Rabia buys 5 items, what is the effective discount?

A. 35 percent   **B.** 30.8 percent
C. 34 percent   **D.** 20.4 percent

Q.21 Manganiyars is a well-known community famous for:
A. South India classical vocal music
B. North-West India musical tradition
C. North-East India martial arts
D. None of the above

Q.22 Consider the following matches:
1.Kena Upanishad: Sama Veda
2.Katha Upanishad: Krishna Yajurveda
3.Prashna Upanishad: Samaveda
4.Mandukya Upanishad: Atharvaveda
Which among the above is/are correct?
A. 1, 2, 3 only   **B.** 1, 2, 4 only
C. 2, 3, 4 only   **D.** All are correct

Q.23 In blocked water-
A. There is no energy
B. There is static energy
C. There is kinetic energy
D. To reduce the pressure generated by the car

Q.24 Within an environment, what is horizontal heat transfer called as?
A. Conduction   **B.** Radiation
C. Absorption   **D.** Advection

Q.25 In Gymnosperms seeds are________?
A. Always naked
B. Always covered
C. Naked in some and covered in others
D. Absent

Q.26 Light respiration occurs, only:
A. All over the plant
B. In green parts of plants
C. In the stem
D. In roots and branches

Q.27 If x, y, z are three consecutive positive integers, then $\log (1 + xz)$ is:

A. $\log y$ **B.** $\log \frac{y}{2}$ **C.** $\log (2y)$ **D.** $2 \log (y)$

Q.28 The critical point and nature for the function $f(x, y) = x^2 - 2x + 2y^2 + 4y - 2$ is:
A. (1,1) Maximum   **B.** (1,-1), Maximum
C. (1,1) Minimum   **D.** (1,-1) Minimum

Q.29 In the following question what will come in place of (?).
9999 × 19 + 1111 × 111 + 777 × 7 = ?

[UP Police Sub Inspector, 2017]

A. 390031   **B.** 291301   **C.** 191131   **D.** 318741

Q.30 In the following question what will come in place of (?).
$$90 \times 11 \div 15 \times 45 - 980 + 42 \times 48 = ?$$

[UP Police Sub Inspector, 2017]

A. 4019   **B.** 4016   **C.** 4006   **D.** 4009

Q.31 A sum of $Rs.\,800$ amounts to $Rs.\,920$ in 3 years at simple interest. If the interest rate is increased by 3%, then what would be the amount?
A. $Rs.\,652$ **B.** $Rs.\,752$ **C.** $Rs.\,992$ **D.** $Rs.\,562$

Q.32 At what rate percent per annum will a sum of money double in 16 years?
A. $6\frac{1}{4}\%$ **B.** $9\frac{1}{4}\%$ **C.** $16\frac{1}{5}\%$ **D.** $6\frac{2}{3}\%$

Ques (33-37):Direction: Read the passage carefully to answer the given question.

The next ingredient is a very remarkable one: Good Temper. "Love is not easily provoked." Nothing could be more striking than to find this here. We are inclined to look upon bad temper as a very harmless weakness. We speak of it as a mere infirmity of nature, a family failing, a matter of temperament, not a thing to take into very serious account in estimating a man's character. And yet here, right in the heart of this analysis of love, it finds a place; and the Bible again and again returns to condemn it as one of the most destructive elements in human nature. The peculiarity of ill temper is that it is the vice of the virtuous. It is often the one blot on an otherwise noble character. You know men who are all but perfect, and women who would be entirely perfect, but for an easily ruffled quick-tempered or "touchy" disposition. This compatibility of ill temper with high moral character is one of the strangest and saddest problems of ethics. The truth is there are two great classes of sins - sins of the Body, and sins of Disposition. The Prodigal son may be taken as a type of the first, the Elder Brother of the second. Now society has no doubt whatever as to which of these is the worse. Its brand falls, without a challenge, upon the Prodigal. But are we right? We have no balance to weigh one another's sins, and coarser and finer are but human words; but faults in the higher nature may be less venial than those in the lower, and to the eye of Him who is Love, a sin against Love may seem a hundred times more base. No form of vice, not worldliness, not agreed of gold, not drunkenness itself does more to un-christianise society than evil temper. For embittering life, for breaking up communities, for destroying the most sacred relationships, for devastating homes, for taking the bloom off childhood; in short for sheer

gratuitous misery-producing power, this influence stands alone. Jealousy, anger, pride, uncharity, cruelty, touchiness, doggedness, sullenness - in varying proportions these are the ingredients of all ill temper. Judge if such sins of the disposition are not worse to live in, and for others to live with than sins of the body. There is really no place in Heaven for a disposition like this. A man with such a mood could only make Heaven miserable for all the people in it.

Q.33 According to the comprehension, what is true regarding "bad temper"?
A. It is a remarkable ingredient
B. It is a harmless weakness
C. It is condemned in the Bible
D. It is a noble characteristic

Q.34 Bad temper is spoken of as which of the following?
A. Matter of temperament
B. Family failing
C. Infirmity of nature
D. All of the above

Q.35 Elder brother may be taken as what type of sins?
A. Sins of body
B. Sins of soul
C. Sins of disposition
D. None of the above

Q.36 Which among the following is not a constituent of ill/bad temper?
A. Self-righteousness
B. Cheerfulness
C. Sullenness
D. Pride

Q.37 Which of the following statements regarding "sins of disposition" is correct?
Statement I: Prodigal son may be considered as its type.
Statement II: Sins of body are worse than sins of disposition.
A. Statement I is correct
B. Statement II is correct
C. Both statement I and II are correct
D. Neither statement I nor statement II is correct

Q.38 Kongthong village has been nominated as UNWTO 'Best Tourism Village'. It is located in which state?
A. Arunachal Pradesh
B. Meghalaya
C. Manipur
D. Mizoram

Q.39 When is World Biodiversity Day celebrated?
A. 22 March
B. 22 April
C. 22 May
D. 22 June

Q.40 When is World Sparrow Day celebrated?
A. 18 March
B. 19 March
C. 20 March
D. 22 March

Q.41 In whose reign did the United Army fight at Tunga against the Marathas?
A. Jai Singh I
B. Pratap Singh
C. Man Singh
D. None of these

Q.42 Two pipes, when working one at a time can fill a cistern in 2 hours and 3 hours, respectively while a third pipe can drain the cistern empty in 6 hours. All three pipes were opened together when the cistern was $\frac{1}{6}$ full. How long will it take for the cistern to be completely full?
A. 1 hour
B. 1 hour 20 minutes
C. 1 hour 30 minutes
D. 1 hour 15 minutes

Q.43 Person B is 50% more efficient than person A and the time taken by person A alone to do work are 6 days more than that taken by B alone, then in how much time the work will be finished if both A and B together started working?
A. 7.2 days
B. 8 days
C. 9.6 days
D. 10.8 days

Q.44 Find the value of $\sqrt{\dfrac{1.96 \times 0.64}{1.6 \times 4.9}}$:
A. 4
B. 0.4
C. 0.2
D. 2

Q.45 On simplification $\sqrt{(0.65)^2 - (0.16)^2}$ reduces to:
A. 0.63
B. 0.65
C. 0.54
D. None of these

Q.46 In a trapezium ABCD, AB ‖ CD and diagonals AC, BD cut at O. If area of $\triangle$AOB and $\triangle$COD is 19.2 cm^2 and 30 cm^2 then find the area of trapezium.
A. 92.4 cm^2
B. 86.4 cm^2
C. 97.2 cm^2
D. 96.6 cm^2

Q.47 Difference between lengths of two parallel sides of trapezium is 10 cm and perpendicular length between the parallel sides is 6 cm. If area of trapezium is 72 cm^2, then find the length of longest parallel side.
A. 17 cm
B. 18 cm
C. 19 cm
D. 20 cm

Q.48 Select the statements regarding the Development Financial Institution (DFI) proposed in the budget 2021-22:
1. It will provide medium to long-term finance for infrastructure in the country.
2. Central government's share of expenditure in the National Infrastructure Pipeline (NIP) will be completely funded by this institution.
Select the correct answer using the code given below
A. 1 only
B. 2 only
C. Both 1 and 2
D. Neither 1 nor 2

Q.49 Which of the following correctly describes the term 'homemade leverage'?
A. It refers to overnight borrowing a substantial amount of cash for intraday stock trading.
B. It refers to the practice of printing currency in order to insulate the economy from black swan events.
C. It refers to the unfair trade advantage reaped by an economy by devaluating its own currency.
D. It is the use of personal borrowing by investors to change the amount of financial leverage of the firm.

Q.50 Minister of Railway Piyush Goyal has been elected to Rajya Sabha from which of the following states?
A. Tamil Nadu
B. Rajasthan
C. Maharashtra
D. Uttar Pradesh

Q.51 Who has been appointed as the 14th Comptroller Auditor General of India?

A. Rajiv Mehrishi
B. Manoj Sinha
C. Girish Chandra Murmu
D. Pradeep Kumar Joshi

Q.52 A box has 300 coins of denominations one-rupee and fifty paise only. The ratio of their respective values is $13:11$. The number of one-rupee coin is:

A. 150   **B.** 152   **C.** 154   **D.** 111

Q.53 In what proportion must a man mix tea at Rs. 121 per kg and Rs. 141 per kg, so as to make a mixture worth Rs. 129 per kg?

A. 4 : 3   **B.** 4 : 2   **C.** 2 : 5   **D.** 3 : 2

Q.54 The perimeter of a rectangular field is 84 m. If the length of the field is 3 m more than twice the breadth, then what is the length of the filed?

A. 23 m   **B.** 25 m
C. 27 m   **D.** None of these

Q.55 A sphere of radius 3 cm is dropped into a cylindrical vessel partly filled with water. The radius of the vessel is 6 cm. If the sphere is submerged completely. Then the surface of the water is raised by:

A. 1 cm   **B.** 2 cm   **C.** 3 cm   **D.** 4 cm

Q.56 A wire of 8800 m length is in the form of a square. It is cut and made a circle. Then, the ratio of the area of square to that of the circle is:

A. 14: 11   **B.** 11: 14   **C.** 11: 13   **D.** 11: 15

Q.57 What is the objective of National Ayush Mission in Rajasthan?

[Rajasthan Police Sub Inspector, 2016]

A. Promotion of medical facilities in Western districts
B. To provide the medical insurance facility to the BPL families in the State
C. Development of Ayurveda, Homeo, Unani, Yoga and Naturopathy in the State
D. To provide free medical facilities to SC/ST and OBC families of the State

Q.58 Direction: The sentence given with the blank is to be filled with an appropriate word. Four alternatives are suggested for each question. Choose the correct alternative.

Speak softly lest the baby _______ wake up.

A. would   **B.** might   **C.** may   **D.** should

Q.59 Direction: Fill in the blank with the correct option.

The new vaccine Covaxin will help in ______ the body against the covid-19 virus.

A. prevent   **B.** preventing
C. will prevent   **D.** to prevent

Q.60 Direction: Fill in the blank with correct option.

Having _______ in both government and private schools, Palak is the most suitable person to take over as the principal of the school.

A. works   **B.** working
C. worked   **D.** was working

Q.61 Direction: In the following sentence, choose the word nearest in meaning to the word printed in bold in the sentence. Loose-fitting sleepwear is the most comfortable since it does not bind or **constrain**.

A. Stress   **B.** Contradict
C. Restrict   **D.** Skipped

Q.62 Select the most appropriate antonym of the given word.
SYMPATHY

A. Dawdle   **B.** Indifference
C. Convene   **D.** Muster

Q.63 A teacher goes through the student's notebooks and gives remarks. This is called as"

A. Notebook checking   **B.** Daily Remarks
C. Evaluation   **D.** Assessment

Q.64 The purpose of formative evaluation is to:

A. Monitor progress and plan remedial instruction
B. Know the understanding of students
C. Know that teacher's objectives are fulfilled
D. Assign grades

Q.65 What is the Currency of Malaysia?

[RBI Office Attendant, 2017]

A. Ringgit   **B.** Koruna   **C.** Litas   **D.** Rufiy

Q.66 What will come in the place of question mark (?).

$$(25)^{7.5} \times (5)^{2.5} \div (125)^{1.5} = 5^?$$

A. 8.5   **B.** 13   **C.** 16   **D.** 17.5

Q.67 What will come in the place of the question mark $'?'$ in the following question?

$$15\% \text{ of } 150\% \text{ of } ? = 45\% \text{ of } 45$$

A. 45   **B.** 90   **C.** 105   **D.** 135

Q.68 If X is 25% more than Y then by what percentage is Y less than X?

A. 25%   **B.** 20%   **C.** 12.5%   **D.** 16%

Q.69 Who appoints the judges of the Supreme Court?

A. Chief Justice of India
B. President
C. Prime Minister
D. Council of Ministers

Q.70 Which of the following comes under the territory of India?

A. States
B. Union Territories
C. Any other area for the time being included in the territory of India
D. All of the above

Q.71 The HCF of two numbers is 23 and the other two factors of their LCM are 13 and 14. The larger of the two numbers is:

A. 276 **B.** 299 **C.** 322 **D.** 345

Q.72 Direction: Given below are four sentences in jumbled order. Pick the option that gives their correct order.

A. "Well, then I know just the place for you," he said.

B. "Yes," he replied. "Do you want one in the city"?

C. "Can you suggest a good hotel?" I asked the taxi driver.

D. "No, I would prefer a quiet place".

A. CBDA **B.** CADB **C.** ACBD **D.** BDAC

Q.73 With respect to Guru Nanak, consider the following statements.

I. Established a centre at Kartarpur named Dera Baba Nanak on the river Ravi.

II. The sacred space thus created by Guru Nanak was known as dharmsal.

III. Before his death Guru appointed Lehna as his successor.

Choose the correct statements.

A. I and II

B. II and III

C. I and III

D. All the statements are correct

Q.74 Match the List 1 with List 2 and select the correct answer from the given options.

List- I	List- II
a. Parijatapaharanam	1. Nandi Thimmana
b. Panduranga Mahathyam	2. Gangadevi
c. Kalahasti Mahatyam	3. Tenali Ramalinga
d. Madura Vijayam	4. Dhurajati

A. a-1, b-3, c-4, d-2 **B.** a-2, b-4, c-3, d-1

C. a-2, b-4, c-3, d-1 **D.** a-2, b-1, c-3, d-4

Q.75 The Lami's theorem is applicable only for:

A. Coplanar forces

B. Concurrent forces

C. Coplanar and concurrent forces

D. Any type of forces

Q.76 The set of forces, whose resultant is zero, are known as:

A. Equilibrium forces **B.** Collinear forces

C. Coplanar forces **D.** Concurrent forces

Q.77 In the given figure rays P || Q || R || S and the ray l || m. find θ_1 and θ_2 respectively.

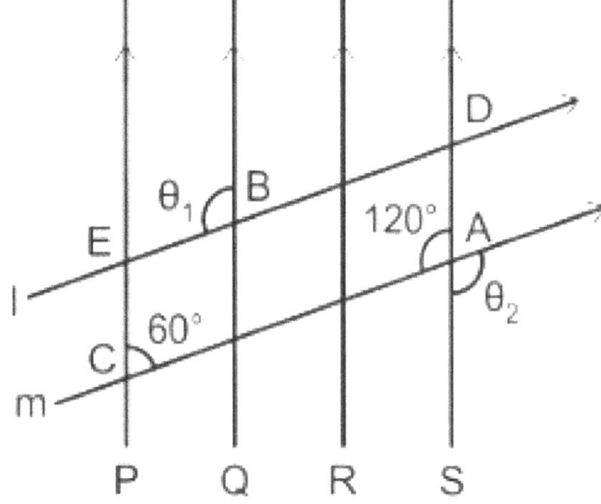

A. 120°, 140° **B.** 120°, 120°

C. 160°, 150° **D.** 60°, 120°

Q.78 Which of the following clubs was declared the winner of the second-tier Women's Championship by England's Football Association (FA) in June 2020?

A. Aston Villa **B.** Birmingham City

C. Liverpool **D.** West Ham

Q.79 Ms. Sonia Lather is associated with which of the following sports?

[Haryana Primary Teacher (PRT), 2020]

A. Wrestling **B.** Kabaddi

C. Atheletics **D.** Boxing

Q.80

A and B invest in a business in the ratio 3 : 2. If 5% of the total profit goes to charity and A's share is Rs. 855, the total profit is:

A. Rs. 1425 **B.** Rs. 1500

C. Rs. 1537.50 **D.** Rs. 1576

Q.81 Coromandel Coast in India is located:

A. Along the Western Ghats

B. Along the Eastern Ghats

C. Along the Subarnarekha river

D. None of the Above

Q.82 The unstratified rock is:

A. Igneous rock **B.** Sedimentary rock

C. Metamorphic rock **D.** None of the above

Q.83 To reduce the language barrier, which is suitable to use in map?

A. Representative fraction scale

B. Statement scale

C. Labelling

D. Title

Q.84 A sphere of radius 5 cm is melted and recast into spheres of radius 2 cm each. How many such spheres can be made?(approx)

A. 15 **B.** 16 **C.** 17 **D.** 18

Q.85 With reference to Champaran Satyagraha, consider the following statements:

1. The movement was led by Mahatma Gandhi along with Rajendra Prasad, Narhari Parikh, and J.B Kripalani.

2. The satyagraha ended when planters agreed to refund all of the money they had taken illegally from the peasants.

Which of the statements given above is/are correct?

A. 1 only   **B.** 2 only

C. Both 1 and 2   **D.** Neither 1 nor 2

Ques (86-87):Direction: Read the following group of sentences. The 1st and the last sentences are numbered 1 and 6, the rest are numbered P,Q,R,S. Arrange these four sentences in proper order to form a meaningful paragraph/sentence.

Q.86 1. Youths are the assets and hope of a nation

P. in making India a great

Q. Steeped in old cultural values

R. They can play a vital role

S. democratic, progressive and prosperous country.

6. But equipped with modern scientific knowledge.

A. SPRQ   **B.** PRSQ   **C.** RPSQ   **D.** QPRS

Q.87 1. Optimism is not a deep complicated philosophy

P. In some persons it is an inborn trait.

Q. In fact, it is always taking a positive and bright view of life.

R. It is more of a general attitude of life.

S. They are tuned that way by nature and temperament.

6. However, in most cases it is an acquired and nurtured habit.

A. RQPS   **B.** QRPS   **C.** PSRQ   **D.** PSQR

Q.88 The value of $\omega^{15} + \omega^{20} + \omega^{25}$ is:

A. 1   **B.** 0   **C.** 2   **D.** 3

Q.89 Evangelista Torricelli is the inventor of which of the following devices?

A. Barometer   **B.** Ammeter

C. Telescope   **D.** Anemometer

Q.90 Edward Jenner discovered _______.

A. Smallpox Vaccine   **B.** Anthrax Vaccine

C. Insulin   **D.** Rubella Vaccine

Q.91 Who among the following is associated with authority?

A. Locke   **B.** Hobbes

C. M. Weber   **D.** Rousseau

Q.92 The three-tier system of Panchayati Raj was recommended by:

A. Simon Commission

B. Jai Prakash Narain Committee

C. Kaka Kalekar Committee

D. Balwant Rai Mehta Committee

Q.93 Which of the following does not increase when we move from left to right along a period in the periodic table?

A. Oxidising Power of elements

B. Electronegativity

C. Non-metallic Character

D. Reducing power

Q.94 The energy required to remove an electron from the outermost shell of an atom in its isolated gaseous state is called?

A. Electron Affinity   **B.** Reducing Potential

C. Ionization Potential   **D.** Ionization Potential

Ques (95-99):Direction: Study the bar – graph and table and find a solution to the given question.

Bar graph given below shows the number of mobile sold (in thousands) in different months and the table shows the ratio between two types of mobile sold in these months.

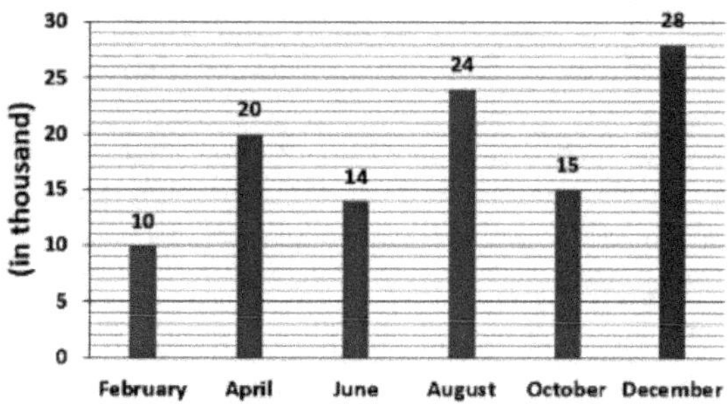

	Samsung	:	Iphone
February	1	:	4
April	2	:	3
June	4	:	3
August	3	:	5
October	2	:	1
December	2	:	5

Only two types of Mobile (Samsung and Iphone) are selling in these given months.

Q.95 Find the ratio between the Samsung mobile sold in June and December together to Iphone mobile sold in February and August together?

A. 23 : 16   **B.** 16 : 23   **C.** 15 : 23   **D.** 23 : 15

Q.96 Number of Iphone mobile sold in December is how much percentage more or less than the number of Samsung mobile sold in April and June together?

A. 10%   **B.** 20%   **C.** 30%   **D.** 25%

Q.97 If in the month of September, sale of Samsung mobile increased by $33\frac{1}{3}$ and sale of Iphone mobile also increase by $33\frac{1}{3}$ as compared to the previous month, then find the number of mobile sold in September?

A. 24000   **B.** 32000   **C.** 30000   **D.** 28000

Q.98 If for some reason, 10% of Samsung mobile and 20% of Iphone mobile are not sold in the month of February then what is the total number of mobile sold in February?

A. 4600   **B.** 1400   **C.** 1580   **D.** 8200

Q.99 How much percentage increase in sales of mobile from August to December?

A. $16\frac{1}{3}\%$ **B.** $16\frac{2}{3}\%$ **C.** $14\frac{1}{3}\%$ **D.** $14\frac{2}{3}\%$

Q.100 What is the meaning of logos in the term sociology?

A. Science/Study

B. Society

C. Social

D. Companion

// Smart Answer Sheet //

Correct — Percentage of students who answered correctly. **Skipped** — Percentage of students who skipped.

Q.	Ans.	Correct / Skipped	Q.	Ans.	Correct / Skipped	Q.	Ans.	Correct / Skipped	Q.	Ans.	Correct / Skipped	Q.	Ans.	Correct / Skipped	Q.	Ans.	Correct / Skipped
1	A	81.34 % / 0.0 %	18	C	23.32 % / 4.94 %	35	C	52.67 % / 1.71 %	52	D	49.28 % / 1.63 %	69	B	83.52 % / 0.0 %	86	C	69.71 % / 1.62 %
2	A	24.89 % / 4.63 %	19	C	68.17 % / 1.84 %	36	B	77.64 % / 0.0 %	53	D	54.21 % / 1.22 %	70	D	62.62 % / 1.13 %	87	A	54.84 % / 1.49 %
3	B	57.37 % / 1.47 %	20	B	44.06 % / 1.95 %	37	A	82.8 % / 0.0 %	54	D	45.44 % / 1.09 %	71	C	54.07 % / 1.15 %	88	B	44.43 % / 1.78 %
4	A	47.87 % / 2.0 %	21	B	81.44 % / 0.0 %	38	B	46.91 % / 1.38 %	55	A	44.89 % / 1.84 %	72	A	40.42 % / 1.56 %	89	A	40.53 % / 1.59 %
5	C	32.24 % / 3.51 %	22	B	62.03 % / 1.99 %	39	C	58.02 % / 1.7 %	56	B	40.5 % / 1.46 %	73	D	12.44 % / 4.83 %	90	A	16.94 % / 3.97 %
6	B	48.43 % / 1.7 %	23	B	61.9 % / 1.55 %	40	C	57.85 % / 1.06 %	57	C	42.55 % / 1.89 %	74	A	20.64 % / 4.59 %	91	C	48.64 % / 1.3 %
7	B	44.97 % / 1.97 %	24	D	42.14 % / 1.61 %	41	B	63.82 % / 1.64 %	58	D	62.05 % / 1.07 %	75	C	60.98 % / 1.78 %	92	D	87.77 % / 0.0 %
8	A	54.63 % / 1.41 %	25	A	69.04 % / 2.0 %	42	D	28.68 % / 3.26 %	59	B	84.79 % / 0.0 %	76	A	64.7 % / 1.85 %	93	D	68.84 % / 1.18 %
9	C	44.46 % / 1.43 %	26	B	47.87 % / 1.76 %	43	A	69.67 % / 1.51 %	60	C	89.83 % / 0.0 %	77	B	65.88 % / 1.81 %	94	C	85.95 % / 0.0 %
10	D	55.86 % / 1.05 %	27	D	53.82 % / 1.76 %	44	B	86.4 % / 0.0 %	61	C	31.9 % / 3.91 %	78	A	30.76 % / 4.27 %	95	B	60.81 % / 1.95 %
11	A	56.46 % / 1.54 %	28	D	65.87 % / 1.67 %	45	A	47.57 % / 1.24 %	62	B	85.49 % / 0.0 %	79	D	49.41 % / 1.32 %	96	D	10.37 % / 4.97 %
12	B	44.05 % / 1.5 %	29	D	40.74 % / 1.41 %	46	C	23.99 % / 4.41 %	63	D	87.65 % / 0.0 %	80	B	51.45 % / 1.98 %	97	B	44.66 % / 1.43 %
13	C	46.27 % / 1.84 %	30	C	61.38 % / 1.09 %	47	A	64.15 % / 1.8 %	64	A	66.37 % / 1.61 %	81	B	56.21 % / 1.04 %	98	D	45.31 % / 1.22 %
14	A	85.24 % / 0.0 %	31	C	41.94 % / 1.55 %	48	A	27.12 % / 4.42 %	65	A	51.86 % / 1.49 %	82	A	43.34 % / 1.57 %	99	B	81.02 % / 0.0 %
15	A	47.44 % / 1.57 %	32	A	56.56 % / 1.18 %	49	D	63.83 % / 1.65 %	66	B	62.68 % / 1.83 %	83	A	85.81 % / 0.0 %	100	A	86.14 % / 0.0 %
16	B	88.75 % / 0.0 %	33	C	80.09 % / 0.0 %	50	C	55.85 % / 1.27 %	67	B	81.35 % / 0.0 %	84	A	76.99 % / 0.0 %			
17	B	41.0 % / 1.12 %	34	D	57.53 % / 1.69 %	51	C	57.2 % / 1.81 %	68	B	57.82 % / 1.06 %	85	A	54.69 % / 1.03 %			

//Hints and Solutions//

1. The theme of International Girls in ICT Day 2022 was Access and Safety. It is celebrated every year on the fourth Thursday in April. International Girls in ICT Day aims to inspire a global movement to increase the representation of girls and women in technology.

Hence, the correct option is (A).

2. Tamil Nadu Assembly Election 2021 was won by DMK political party.

- The Dravida Munnetra Kazhagam (DMK) won the election, ending the decade-long reign of the All India Anna Dravida Munnetra Kazhagam (AIADMK).

- The DMK's leader M. K. Stalin became the eighth Chief Minister of Tamil Nadu and the 12th Chief Minister since the 1956 reorganization.

- He replaced Edappadi K. Palaniswami of the AIADMK.

- The poll was Tamil Nadu's first assembly election after the demises of the two most prominent Chief Ministers in the state's modern history, J. Jayalalithaa—general secretary of the AIADMK, and M. Karunanidhi—president of the DMK, who died in 2016 and 2018 respectively.

Hence, the correct option is (A).

3. Chapekar Brothers assassinated W.C. Rand, the Plague Commissioner of Pune in 1897.

On 22 June 1897, brothers Damodar Hari Chapekar and Balkrishna Hari Chapekar assassinated British officer W.C. Rand and his military escort, Lieutenant Ayerst, in Pune, Maharashtra. This was the first case of militant nationalism in India after the revolt of 1857.

Hence, the correct option is (B).

4. Antonio Guterres, the ninth Secretary-General of the United Nations, took office on 1st January 2017.

Antonio Manuel de Oliveira Guterres is a Portuguese politician and diplomat. Since 2017, he has served as Secretary-General of the United Nations, the ninth person to hold this title. A member of the Portuguese Socialist Party, Guterres served as Prime Minister of Portugal from 1995 to 2002. Guterres served as secretary-general of the Socialist Party from 1992 to 2002. He was elected Prime Minister in 1995 and resigned in 2002, after his party was defeated in the 2001 Portuguese local elections.

Hence, the correct option is (A).

5. Vijaya Lakshmi Pandit was the first Indian woman President of the UN General Assembly.

Vijaya Lakshmi Pandit (18 August 1900 – 1 December 1990) was an Indian diplomat and politician who was the first female elected to 6th Governor of Maharashtra and 8th President of the United Nations General Assembly.

Hence, the correct option is (C).

6. The error is in part (B) of the sentence. We do not use "because" for a reason as it is redundant. So, replace "because" with "that" in the given sentence.

So, the correct sentence is- The reason we were late for the meeting is that there was an accident on the highway.

Hence, the correct option is (B).

7. The given sentence is in the passive form of simple past tense. The structures for active/passive voices are:

Active: Subject + verb (IInd form) + object

Passive: Object + was/were + verb (IIIrd form) + by + subject

So, with the help of the above structures, we can convert the given sentence into active voice:

No one responded to the call to donate blood.

Hence, the correct option is (B).

8. This is a sentence of the present perfect tense. The active and passive voice structures of such sentences are:

Active: Subject + has/have verb (IIIrd form) + object.

Passive: Object + has/have + been + verb (IIIrd form) + by + subject.

As we can see that in the given sentence, there is no object mentioned. So, we can use "it" as an object. The passive voice of the given sentence would be:

It has been decided to increase the school fees this year (by them).

Please note that "by + subject" is optional to use.

Hence, the correct option is (A).

9. The author of "Life of Pi" is Yann Martel.

Life of Pi is a Canadian adventure novel by Yann Martel published in 2001. The protagonist is Piscine Molitor "Pi" Patel, an Indian boy from Pondicherry who explores issues of spirituality and practicality from an early age. He survives 227 days after a shipwreck while stranded on a lifeboat in the Pacific Ocean with a Bengal tiger named Richard Parker.

Hence, the correct option is (C).

10. The best expresses the meaning of the Idiom/Phrase **to sleep with the fishes is to be dead**.

The idiom **"sleep with the fishes"** means to be killed or to be murdered and have one's body disposed of in a river, lake, or ocean.

Example: Rocco tried to siphon money off from the Mob for himself. Now he **sleeps with the fishes**.

Hence, the correct option is (D).

11. The best expresses the meaning of the Idiom/Phrase **name is mud** is **in trouble**.

The idiom **"name is mud"** is used when people get angry with you because of something you have said or done or you are **in trouble** because people are angry with you.

Example: If he doesn't turn up tonight, his name will be mud.

Hence, the correct option is (A).

12. Remedial language teaching refers to the teaching which is intended to improve the ability of slow learners to learn something. It is an integral part of the teaching-learning program, also known as compensatory or corrective teaching.

The objective of remedial teaching is to give additional help to learners who have fallen behind the rest of the class in any topic or subject.

The teacher must understand the learner's strength and weaknesses to provide them with the necessary help and guidance to overcome their problems.

Hence, the correct option is (B).

13. Remedial Teaching is an integral part of the teaching-learning program, also known as compensatory or corrective teaching.

The objective of remedial teaching is to give additional help to learners who have fallen behind the rest of the class in any topic or subject.

It is the process of identifying slow learners and providing them with the necessary help and guidance to overcome their problems.

Purpose of Remedial Teaching:

- To eliminate ineffective habits
- To make learners learn better by giving additional help
- To teach again the language items not properly learned
- To arise learners' interest in learning with stimulating approaches
- To transmit practical experiences to learners according to their diverse needs

Hence, it becomes clear that the purpose of remedial teaching is to teach again the language items not properly learnt.

Hence, the correct option is (C).

14. Qantas Airlines is the flag-carrier airline of Australia.

It operates out of its hubs at Sydney Airport, Melbourne Airport and Brisbane Airport. Qantas Airlines is the third oldest airline in the world.

Hence, the correct option is (A).

15. Regulatory body 'TRAI' associated with Telecom.

The Telecom Regulatory Authority of India (TRAI) is a regulatory body set up by the Government of India under section 3 of the Telecom Regulatory Authority of India Act, 1997. It is the regulator of the telecommunications sector in India.

Hence, the correct option is (A).

16. Given

$$\sqrt{\left[4 + \sqrt{(44 + \sqrt{10000})}\right]}$$

$$= \sqrt{\left[4 + \sqrt{(44 + 100)}\right]}$$

$$= \sqrt{\left[4 + \sqrt{144}\right]}$$

$$= \sqrt{[4 + 12]}$$

$$= \sqrt{[16]}$$

$$= 4$$

Hence, the correct option is (B).

17. Given,

$$\frac{11.2 \times 0.36 + 0.42 \times 3.2}{0.8 \times 4.2}$$

$$\Rightarrow \frac{4.032 + 1.344}{3.36}$$

$$\Rightarrow \frac{5.376}{3.36}$$

$$\Rightarrow 1.6$$

Hence, the correct option is (B).

18. Given:

True weight $= 1\,\text{kg} = 1000\,\text{gm}$

Flase weight $= 960\,\text{gm}$

We know that,

$$\text{Profit }\% = \frac{\text{True weight - False weight}}{\text{False weight}} \times 100$$

$$= \frac{1000 - 960}{960} \times 100$$

$$= \frac{40}{960} \times 10$$

$$= \frac{25}{6} = 4\frac{1}{6}\%$$

Hence, the correct option is (C).

19. Total cost price $= 15 \times 10 = 150$

Total selling price $= 5 \times 8 + 12 \times 7 + 3 \times 16$

$$= 40 + 84 + 48 = 172$$

Profit percent $= \frac{172 - 150}{150 \times 100}$

$$= 14.66\%$$

Hence, the correct option is (C).

20. Given,

Marked price of item is Rs 200 and discount 22% and 33%.

Let the effective discount be $x\%$

By mixture allegation method,

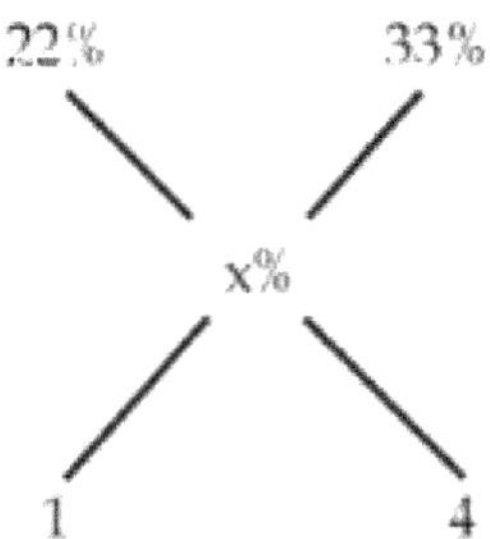

$\therefore \dfrac{33-x}{x-22} = \dfrac{1}{4}$

$x = 30.8\%$

Hence, the correct option is (B).

21. Manganiyars is a well-known community famous for North-West India musical tradition.

The Manganiyars are professional Muslim folk musicians belonging to Jaisalmer, Barmer, parts of Jalor, Bikaner and Jodhpur districts in Western Rajasthan.

Hence, the correct option is (B).

22. The Kena Upanishad is a Vedic Sanskrit text classified as one of the primary or Mukhya Upanishads that is embedded inside the last section of the Talavakara Brahmanam of the Samaveda. The Katha Upanishad is one of the mukhya (primary) Upanishads, embedded in the last short eight sections of the Katha school of the Krishna Yajurveda. The Prashna Upanishad is an ancient Sanskrit text, embedded inside Atharva Veda. The Mandukya Upanishad is the shortest of all the Upanishads and is assigned to Atharvaveda.

Hence, the correct option is (B).

23. Static electricity is the imbalance of electric charge on a surface of a material. Static means fixed or stationary, therefore it is used in contrast to dynamic (moving) electricity which are in the form of electric currents. Typically atoms are neutral, which means they have the same number of electrons and protons. Thus, Static energy is in blocked water.

Hence, the correct option is (B).

24. Advection is defined as the transfer of heat or matter by the flow of a fluid, especially horizontally in the atmosphere.

Hence, the correct option is (D).

25. Gymnosperms are called so because they have naked ovules/seeds. In terms of plant evolution, they are the first seed-bearing plants. They are inferior to Angiosperms because in Angiosperms, the ovules are covered.

Hence, the correct option is (A).

26. Respiration occurs in both plants and animals, while photosynthesis only occurs within plants, algae, and some bacteria. The light reactions of photosynthesis only occur during the day, but the dark reactions can occur either day or night. Respiration has no restriction to the time of day.

Hence, the correct option is (B).

27. Let x, y, z are three consecutive positive integers.

$y = x + 1$ and $z = y + 1$

$z = x + 2$

Consider, $\log(1 + xz)$

$= \log[1 + x(x + 2)]$

$= \log[1 + x^2 + 2x]$

$= \log(1 + x)^2$

$= 2\log(1 + x)$

$= 2\log y$

Hence, the correct option is (D).

28. Given:

$$f(x, y) = x^2 - 2x + 2y^2 + 4y - 2$$

Partial derivatives:

$f'(x) = 2x - 2$ and $f'(y) = 4y + 4$

Now, for critical points, $f(x) = 0$

$2x - 2 = 0$

$x = 1,$

Also, $f'(y) = 0$

$4y + 4 = 0$

$y = -1,$

So, critical points (1,-1)

$f''(x) = 2 > 0$ and $f'(y) = 4 > 0$

So, at (1,-1) minimum.

Hence, the correct option is (D).

29. The given equation is,

$\Rightarrow 9999 \times 19 + 1111 \times 111 + 777 \times 7 = ?$

$\Rightarrow (10000 - 1) \times 19 + (1100 + 11) \times 111 + (700 + 77) \times 7 = ?$

$\Rightarrow 190000 - 19 + 122100 + 1221 + 4900 + 539 = ?$

$\therefore ? = 318741$

Hence, the correct option is (D).

30. The given equation is:

$\Rightarrow 90 \times 11 \div 15 \times 45 - 980 + 42 \times 48 = ?$

$$\Rightarrow 90 \times \frac{11}{15} \times 45 - 980 + 42 \times 48 =?$$

$$\Rightarrow 2970 - 980 + 2016 =?$$

$$\Rightarrow 4986 - 980 =?$$

$$\therefore ? = 4006$$

Hence, the correct option is (C).

31. Given-

Principal $P = Rs.\,800$

Amount $A = Rs.\,920$

Simple Interest $SI = A - P$

$$SI = Rs.\,(920 - 800)$$

$$SI = Rs.\,120$$

Rate $R = \frac{100 \times SI}{P \times T}$

$$R = \frac{100 \times 120}{800 \times 3}$$

$$R = 5\%$$

New rate $r = (5 + 3)\%$

$$r = 8\%$$

New simple interest $I = \frac{800 \times 8 \times 3}{100}$

$$I = Rs.\,192$$

New amount $A' = Rs.\,(800 + 192)$

$$A' = Rs.\,992$$

Hence, the correct option is (C).

32. Let the principal be P.

The sum of money doubles itself in 16 years.

Amount $A = 2P$

Time $T = 16 \; years$

Simple Interest $SI = A - P$

$$SI = 2P - P$$

$$SI = P$$

According to the formula-

$$R = \frac{100 \times SI}{P \times T} \quad \text{where } R \text{ is rate of interest}$$

$$\Rightarrow R = \frac{100 \times P}{P \times 16}$$

$$\Rightarrow R = \frac{25}{4}\%$$

$$\Rightarrow R = 6\frac{1}{4}\%$$

Hence, the correct option is (A).

33. According to the passage, the Bible condemns bad temper as one of the most destructive elements in human nature.

Hence, the correct option is (C).

34. The writer of passage has said that "we speak of it (bad temper) as a mere infirmity of nature, a family failing, a matter of temperament, not a thing to take into very serious account in estimating a man's character".

Hence, the correct option is (D).

35. According to the passage, Prodigal son may be taken as a type of sins of body, the Elder Brother is a type of sins of disposition.

Hence, the correct option is (C).

36. According to the passage, all the other options are given as the ingredients of ill-temper in varying proportions.

Hence, the correct option is (B).

37. According to the passage, it has been said that sins of disposition are far worse than sins of the body, which makes Statement II incorrect. Statement I hold true to the passage.

Hence, the correct option is (A).

38. Kongthong village has been nominated as UNWTO 'Best Tourism Village'. It is located in Meghalaya.

Meghalaya's Whistling village, Kongthong, has been nominated by the Ministry of Tourism for the UNWTO (World Tourism Organisation) 'Best Tourism Villages' award. Two other villages had also been nominated for UNWTO 'Best Tourism Villages' award- Ladhpura Khas in Madhya Pradesh and Pochampally in Telangana.

Hence, the correct option is (B).

39. International Biodiversity Day is celebrated on 22 May. Its purpose is to protect biodiversity.

Hence, the correct option is (C).

40. World Goureya Day is observed on March 20. This day began to be celebrated due to the dwindling number of Gauraiya and Sparrow Day was celebrated for the first time in the year 2010. According to the reports, the sparrow number has come down by about 60%. The purpose of this day is to preserve the sparrow's bird.

Hence, the correct option is (C).

41. The battle of Tunga was fought between Maratha General Mahadji Scindia and Rajputs of Jaipur and Jodhpur, led by Sawai Pratap Singh.

The battle was fought on July 28, 1787.

This battle is also called the Battle of Madhogarh.

Hence, the correct option is (B).

42. Two pipes can fill a cistern in 2 hours and 3 hours, while a third pipe can drain the cistern empty in 6 hours,

When three pipes opened then their 1 hour's work = $\dfrac{1}{2} + \dfrac{1}{3} - \dfrac{1}{6} = \dfrac{2}{3}$

Total cistern full = $\dfrac{1}{6}$

$\Rightarrow$ Remaining part to filled = 1 - $\dfrac{1}{6} = \dfrac{5}{6}$

$\Rightarrow$ time taken by three to fill $\dfrac{5}{6}$th of the cistern is = $\dfrac{\left(\frac{5}{6}\right)}{\left(\frac{2}{3}\right)}$

= 1.25

$\therefore$ It will take 1 hour and 15 minutes to fill the cistern.

Hence, the correct option is (D).

43. Since B is 50% more efficient than A.

Ratio of efficiency of A to B = 100 : 150 = 2 : 3

The ratio of time taken by A to B to finish the work = $\left(\dfrac{1}{2}\right) : \left(\dfrac{1}{3}\right)$

= 3 : 2

Let the time taken by A and B alone to do work be 3x and 2x respectively.

According to the question:

3x - 2x = 6

x = 6

Time taken by A and B alone to do work is 18 days and 12 days respectively.

The efficiency of A and B when they work together = $\dfrac{1}{8} + \dfrac{1}{12}$

= $\dfrac{5}{36}$

The required time is taken when both A and B together started working = $\dfrac{36}{5}$ = 7.2 days

Hence, the correct option is (A).

44. Given:

$\sqrt{\dfrac{1.96 \times 0.64}{1.6 \times 4.9}}$

$= \sqrt{\dfrac{1.2544}{7.84}}$

$= \sqrt{0.16}$

$= 0.4$

$\therefore 0.4$

Hence, the correct option is (B).

45. $\sqrt{(0.65)^2 - (0.16)^2}$

Since,

$a^2 - b^2 = (a - b)(a + b)$

$\Rightarrow \sqrt{(0.65 + 0.16)(0.65 - 0.16)}$

$\Rightarrow \sqrt{(0.81)(0.49)}$

$\Rightarrow \sqrt{(0.9)(0.9) \times (0.7)(0.7)}$

$\Rightarrow 0.9 \times 0.7$

$= 0.63$

Hence, the correct option is (A).

46. Given,

Area of $\triangle AOB$ = 19.2 cm^2

Area of $\triangle COD$ = 30 cm^2

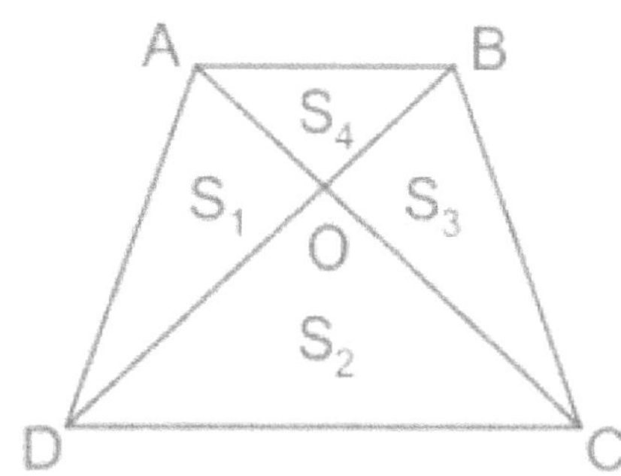

$S_4 = 19.2$ cm^2

$S_2 = 30$ cm^2

We know that,

$S_1 = \sqrt{S_2 S_4}$

$= \sqrt{19.2 \times 30}$

$= \sqrt{576}$

$S_1 = 24$ cm^2

We also know that,

$S_1 = S_3$

Area of trapezium $= S_1 + S_2 + S_3 + S_4$

$= 24 + 19.2 + 24 + 30$

$= 97.2$ cm^2

Hence, the correct option is (C).

47. Difference between the length of two parallel sides of trapezium = 10 cm

Perpendicular length between the parallel sides = 6 cm

Area of trapezium = 72 cm²

Let sides of parallel sides are 'a' and 'b' respectively. (a > b)

Area of trapezium $= \frac{1}{2} \times (a + b) \times h = 72$

$\Rightarrow (a + b) \times 6 = 144$

$\Rightarrow (a + b) = 24$....(1)

According to the question,

$(a - b) = 10$.......(2)

From equation (1) and (2), we get

$a = 17$ and $b = 7$

So,

Length of longest parallel side = 17 cm

Hence, the correct option is (A).

48. Development Financial Institutions are organizations that are involved in medium to long-term financing at a low cost for development. Profit is not their prime motive rather they are guided by the developmental needs of the economy. So, statement 1 is correct.

Expenditure of National Infrastructure Pipeline will be shared between the centre, states and private sector in the ratio of 39, 40 and 21 respectively. DFI proposed in the budget helps in raising finance for the centre, states, and the private sector in meeting the expenditure towards National Infrastructure Pipeline. It has no commitment to completely fund the central government's share of expenditure in the National Infrastructure Pipeline. So, statement 2 is not correct.

Hence, the correct option is (A).

49. Homemade leverage is used by an individual investor to artificially adjust the leverage of a company. An individual investing in a company with no leverage can recreate the effect of leverage using homemade leverage, which includes taking out personal loans on the investment. However, differences in the tax rate between the corporation and the individual will likely disrupt the ability of the investor to construct the leveraging scenario accurately.

Hence, the correct option is (D).

50. Piyush Goyal has been elected to Rajya Sabha from Maharashtra state. He is the current Minister of Railways and Minister of Coal. Another council member, who represents Maharashtra in Rajya Sabha, is Shri. Ramdas Athawale. He is currently working as the 'Minister of State for Social Justice and Empowerment'.

Hence, the correct option is (C).

51. In August 2020, Former Jammu & Kashmir Governor Girish Chandra Murmu (1985 batch IAS officer of Gujarat cadre) has been appointed as the Comptroller Auditor General (CAG). CAG audits all receipts and expenditure of the Government of India and the state governments. GC Murmu succeeded Rajiv Mehrishi.

Hence, the correct option is (C).

52. Respective ratio of the number of coins;

$= 13 : 11 \times 2$

$= 13 : 22$

Therefore, number of 1 rupee coins;

$= \frac{13 \times 300}{13 + 22}$

$= \frac{3900}{35}$

$= 111$

The number of one-rupee coin is 111.

Hence, the correct option is (D).

53. According to the question, a man mixed tea at Rs. 121 per kg and Rs. 141 per kg, so as to make a mixture worth Rs. 129 per kg

The proportion of tea and water $= x : y$

$121\, x + 141y = 129\, (x + y)$

$141y - 129y = 121x - 129x$

$-12y = -8x$

$3y = 2x$

$x : y = 3 : 2$

So, the proportion of tea and water is $3 : 2$ to make a mixture worth Rs. 129 per kg.

Hence, the correct option is (D).

54. Let the length and breadth of the field be 'l' m and 'b' m respectively.

According to the question, the length of the field is 3 m more than twice the breadth

$\Rightarrow$ l = (2b + 3) m

We know that,

Perimeter of a rectangular field = 2(l + b)

$\Rightarrow$ 84 = 2(2b + 3 + b)

$\Rightarrow \frac{84}{2}$ = 3b + 3

$\Rightarrow$ b = $\frac{39}{3}$ = 13 m

$\therefore$ b = 13 m

l = 2b + 3 = 2 × 13 + 3 = 29 m

$\therefore$ l = 29 m

Hence, the correct option is (D).

55. Volume of cylinder = πr²H

Volume of sphere = $\left(\dfrac{4}{3}\right)\pi R^3$

Where,

r → Radius of the cylinder

H → Height of the cylinder

R → Radius of the sphere

When the sphere is submerged then,

The volume of sphere = Volume of cylinder

$\Rightarrow \left(\dfrac{4}{3}\right) \times \pi \times (3)^3 = \pi \times (6)^2 \times H$

$\Rightarrow H = \left(\dfrac{36}{36}\right)$

$\Rightarrow H = 1$ cm

∴ The surface of the water is raised by 1cm

Hence, the correct option is (A).

56. It is given that, Perimeter of the square = 8800 m

$\Rightarrow 4 \times$ side = 8800

$\Rightarrow$ Side = $\dfrac{8800}{4}$

$\Rightarrow$ Side = 2200 m

The same wire is converted into the form of a circle.

Therefore, Circumference of the circle = Perimeter of the square

$\Rightarrow 2\pi r = 8800$

$\Rightarrow 2 \times \pi \times r = 8800$

$\Rightarrow r = \dfrac{4400}{\pi}$

We know that area of the square: Area of the circle = (side)^2 : πr^2

$\Rightarrow$ Area of square: area of circle = (2200)^2 : $\pi \left(\dfrac{4400}{\pi}\right)^2$

$\Rightarrow$ Area of square: area of circle = 11: 14

Hence, the correct option is (B).

57. Development of Ayurveda, Homeo, Unani, Yoga, and Naturopathy in the State is the objective of the National Ayush Mission in Rajasthan.

National Ayush Mission in Rajasthan:

The basic objective of NAM is to promote AYUSH medical system through cost-effective services, strengthening the educational system, facilitate the enforcement of quality control Ayurveda, Siddha, Unani & Homoeopathy (ASU&H) Drugs, and sustainable availability of ASU&H raw-material.

Hence, the correct option is (C).

58. Complete sentence: Speak softly lest the baby <u>should</u> wake up.

Modals are used as helping verbs in sentences to express certainty, possibility, willingness, obligation, necessity or ability.

The modal 'should' denotes suggestion or duty.

- For example: You should chew your food properly.

The correlative pair 'lest...should' conveys a negative meaning.

- For example: Work hard lest you should fail. (Work hard; otherwise, you will fail.)

Modals are always followed by the base form of the verb.

Thus, 'should' is the correct word for the given blank.

Hence, the correct option is (D).

59. Generally, the '-ing' form is used after a preposition like in, under, etc except for 'to - preposition'.

We know that preposition always takes the objective case after it. In the sentence 'the body' is the object and 'preventing' is the present participle that is qualifying the noun 'the body'.

Thus, the complete sentence is- The new vaccine Covaxin will help in preventing the body against the covid-19 virus.

Hence, the correct option is (B).

60. In the past tense, we use the second form of the verb (V2).

In the above sentence, palak has already worked in different schools, after that decision is made.

Thus, we will use past these to complete the sentence.

The complete sentence is- Having worked in both government and private schools, Palak is the most suitable person to take over as the principal of the school.

Hence, the correct option is (C).

61. Let's first learn the meanings of the given words:

Constrain means to control and limit something.

Restrict means put a limit on; keep under control.

Stress means pressure or tension exerted on a material object.

Contradict means assert the opposite of a statement made by (someone).

Skipped means fail to attend or deal with as appropriate; miss

Hence, the correct option is (C).

62. Let's understand the meaning of the words:

Sympathy means feelings of pity and sorrow for someone else's misfortune.

Indifference means a lack of interest, concern, or sympathy.

Dawdle means to waste time.

Convene means to come or bring together for a meeting or activity.

Muster means to assemble (troops), especially for inspection or in preparation for battle.

Hence, the correct option is (B).

63. Assessment is a process of evaluating, measuring, grading or documenting the academic progress of the students.

It provides feedback on the performance of the student and helps in determining the areas of improvement. It is process-oriented which diagnose the areas of improvement for the student. When a teacher goes through a student's notebooks and gives remarks this is called assessment.

Hence, the correct option is (D).

64. Evaluation is a systematic way to assess learner's abilities, analyze performance, provide appropriate feedback to each learner and help them to progress. The formative evaluation assesses the performance of students, tests comprising various types of questions are constructed and administered during the period of instruction.

Purpose of Formative Evaluation:

- Its main objective is to provide continuous feedback to both teacher and student concerning learning successes and failures while instruction is in process.

- It is used to monitor the learning progress of students during the period of instruction.

- Feedback to students reinforces successful learning and identifies the specific learning errors that need correction.

- Feedback to the teacher provides information for max living instruction and for prescribing group and individual remedial work.

- The formative evaluation depends on tests, quizzes homework, classwork, oral questions prepared for each segment of instruction.

Hence, from the above explanation, it can be concluded that the purpose of formative evaluation is to monitor progress and plan remedial instruction.

Hence, the correct option is (A).

65. The Malaysian ringgit is the currency of Malaysia.

The currency abbreviation for the currency is RM, and the currency code is MYR. This is the code seen when requesting a currency quote, such as USD/MYR which shows the rate of exchange between the U.S. dollar (USD) and the Malaysian ringgit.

Hence, the correct option is (A).

66. Let,

$$(25)^{7.5} \times (5)^{2.5} \div (125)^{1.5} = 5^x$$

Then,

$$\frac{\left(5^2\right)^{7.5} \times (5)^{2.5}}{(5^3)^{1.5}} = 5^x$$

$$\Rightarrow \frac{5^{(2 \times 7.5)} \times 5^{2.5}}{5^{(3 \times 1.5)}} = 5^x$$

$$\Rightarrow \frac{5^{15} \times 5^{2.5}}{5^{4.5}} = 5^x$$

$$\Rightarrow 5^x = 5^{(15+2.5-4.5)}$$

$$\Rightarrow 5^x = 5^{13}$$

$$\therefore x = 13$$

Hence, the correct option is (B).

67. Given:

$$15\% \text{ of } 150\% \text{ of } ? = 45\% \text{ of } 45$$

Let us solve step by step

$$\Rightarrow 15\% \text{ of } 150\% \text{ of } ? = 45\% \text{ of } 45$$

$$\Rightarrow ? = \frac{(45\% \ of \ 45)}{(15\% \ of \ 150\%)}$$

$$\Rightarrow ? = \frac{\{\left(\frac{45}{100}\right) of \ 45\}}{\{\left(\frac{15}{100}\right) of \left(\frac{150}{100}\right)\}}$$

$$\Rightarrow ? = \frac{(45 \times 45 \times 100)}{(15 \times 150)}$$

$$\Rightarrow ? = 90$$

$$\therefore 90 \text{ will come in the place of '?'}$$

Hence, the correct option is (B).

68. Given:

We have to find 15% of Rs. 34

As X is 25% more than Y

$\therefore$ If Y = 100 then X = 125

Thus Y is less than X by 25 where X is 125.

$$\Rightarrow \text{Percentage by which Y is less than X} = \left(\frac{25}{125}\right) \times 100 = 20\%$$

Hence, the correct option is (B).

69. The President appoints the judges of the Supreme Court of India. The chief justice of India is appointed by the president in consultation with such judges of the Supreme Court and high courts as he deems necessary.

Hence, the correct option is (B).

70. The Parliament is empowered to make laws for the whole or any part of the territory of India. The territory of India refers to the states, the union territories, and any other area for the time being included in the territory of India.

Hence, the correct option is (D).

71. The HCF of a group of numbers will be always a factor of their LCM.

HCF is the product of all common prime factors using the least power of each common prime factor.

LCM is the product of the highest powers of all prime factors.

Clearly, the numbers are (23 × 13) and (23 × 14)

$\therefore$ Larger number = (23 × 14) = 322

Hence, the correct option is (C).

72. Sentence C is independent of any other sentence as it is introducing a conversation between a man and a taxi driver.

In sentence is C, a question is asked by the man, and its answer is given in sentence B by the taxi driver. So, 'B' follows 'C'.

The question asked by the taxi driver in sentence B is answered by the man in sentence D. So, 'D' follows 'B'.

Sentence A ends the conversation. Thus, A is the last sentence.

Hence, the correct option is (A).

73. Established a centre at Kartarpur named Dera Baba Nanak on the river Ravi.

The sacred space thus created by Guru Nanak was known as dharmsal. It is now known as Gurdwar.

Before his death Guru appointed Lehna also known as Guru Angad as his successor.
Hence, the correct option is (D).

74. The correct match is a-1, b-3, c-4, d-2.

Parijatapaharanam is a Telugu poem composed by Nandi Thimmana.

Panduranga Mahathyam is a magnum opus of 16th century poet Tenali Ramalinga.

Dhurajati was a Telugu poet in the court of the king Krishnadevaraya . He wrote Kalahasti Mahatyam.

Madura Vijayam, meaning "The Conquest of Madurai", is a 14th-century C.E Sanskrit poem written by the poet Gangadevi.

Hence, the correct option is (A).

75. Lami's theorem:

If three coplanar and concurrent forces acting on a particle, keep it in equilibrium, then each force is proportional to the sine of the angle between the other two and the constant of proportionality is the same.

Consider three forces F_1, F_2, F_3 acting on a particle or rigid body making angles α, β, and γ with each other.

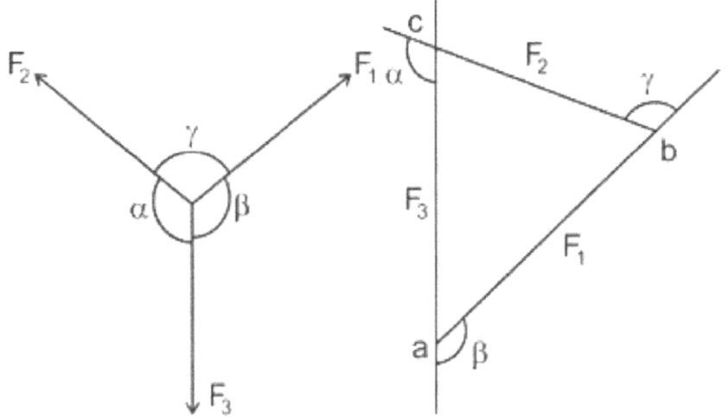

Mathematically,

$$\frac{F_1}{\sin\alpha} = \frac{F_2}{\sin\beta} = \frac{F_3}{\sin\gamma}$$

Hence, the correct option is (C).

76. If the resultant of forces acting on a particle is zero, the particle will be in equilibrium. Such a set of forces, whose resultant is zero, are called equilibrium forces. The force, which brings the set of forces in equilibrium, is called an equilibrant.

When two or more forces act on a body, they are called to form a system of forces.

1. Concurrent forces: The forces, which meet at one point, are known as concurrent forces. The concurrent forces may or may not be collinear. When a number of non-parallel forces hold a rigid body in equilibrium, they must be concurrent forces.

2. Coplanar forces: The forces, whose lines of action lie on the same plane, are known as coplanar forces.

3. Collinear forces: The forces, whose lines of action lie on the same line, are known as collinear forces.

4. Coplanar concurrent forces: The forces, which meet at one point and their lines of action also lie on the same plane, are known as coplanar concurrent forces.

5. Coplanar non-concurrent forces: The forces, which do not meet at one point, but their lines of action lie on the same plane, are known as coplanar non-concurrent forces.

6. Non-coplanar concurrent forces: The forces, which meet at one point, but their lines of action do not lie on the same plane, are known as non-coplanar concurrent forces.

7. Non-coplanar non-concurrent forces: The forces, which do not meet at one point and their lines of action do not lie on the same plane, are called non-coplanar non-concurrent forces.

Hence, the correct option is (A).

77. Given:

Rays P ‖ Q ‖ R ‖ S and the ray l ‖ m.

Calculation:

We are given that, $\angle ECA = 60°$

So, $\angle IBQ = 60°$ (Opposite angles in a parallelogram are equal)

Now, $\angle IBQ + \theta_1 = 180°$ (Linear pairs)

$\Rightarrow \theta_1 = 180° - 60°$

$\Rightarrow \theta_1 = 120°$

Now, we know that vertically opposite angles are equal

$\therefore \angle CAD = \theta_2 = 120°$

$\therefore \theta_1 = 120°$ and $\theta_2 = 120°$

Hence, the correct option is (B).

78. Chelsea has been awarded the Women's Super League title.

Aston Villa was declared the winner of the second-tier Women's Championship by England's Football Association (FA) on 5 June 2020.

Bottom-placed Liverpool, whose men's team are two wins away from securing a first top-flight crown in 30 years, will be relegated to the second-tier for the 2020-21 season.

Hence, the correct option is (A).

79. Sonia Lather is an Indian boxer.

She was a silver medallist at the 2016 AIBA Women's World Boxing Championships and a twice silver medallist at the Asian Amateur Boxing Championships.

Hence, the correct option is (D).

80. Let the total profit be Rs. 100

After paying to charity, A's share = $\left(95 \times \frac{3}{5}\right)$

= Rs. 57

If A's share is Rs. 57, total profit = Rs. 100

If A's share Rs. 855, total profit = $\left(\frac{100}{57} \times 855\right)$

= Rs. 1500

Hence, the correct option is (B).

81. Eastern coast extends from the Subarnarekha river along the West Bengal-Odisha border to Kanyakumari.

- This plain is known as the Northern Circars between the Mahanadi and the Krishna rivers and Carnatic/Coromandel between the Krishna and the Cauvery rivers.
- As compared to the western coastal plain, the eastern coastal plain is broader and is an example of an emergent coast.
- There are well-developed deltas here, formed by the rivers flowing eastward into the Bay of Bengal.
- These include the deltas of the Mahanadi, the Godavari, the Krishna and the Kaveri.
- Because of its emergent nature, it has less number of ports and harbours.

Hence, the correct option is (B).

82. A rock is any naturally occurring solid mass or aggregate of minerals. It is categorized by the minerals included its chemical composition and the way in which it is formed.

Stratified rock: These rocks consist of different layers in their structure and these layers are separated by planes of stratification.

- These planes are also called cleavage planes or bedding planes.
- These rocks can easily split up along these bedding planes.
- Most of the sedimentary rocks such as sandstone, limestone, shale, etc. are the best examples of stratified rocks.
- The structure of unstratified rocks is crystalline or compact granular.

- They possess a similar kind of structure throughout their whole body.
- Most of the igneous rocks and some sedimentary rocks come under unstratified rocks.
- Granite, marble, trap are few examples of Unstratified rocks.

Hence, the correct option is (A).

83. A map is a representation or a drawing of the earth's surface or a part of it drawn on a flat surface according to a scale. There are three Components of Maps – distance, direction, and symbol.

Distance:

- Maps are drawn to reduced scales.
- But this reduction is done very carefully so that the distance between the places is real.
- Therefore, a scale is chosen for this purpose which is the ratio between the actual distance on the ground and the distance shown on the map.
- When a large distance is shown in the map it is called a small scale map and vise versa.

Hence, the correct option is (A).

84. Let the number of small spheres be n.

We know that,

Volume of sphere = $\frac{4}{3} \times \pi \times R^3$

According to the question,

$\frac{4}{3} \times \pi \times R^3 = n \times \frac{4}{3} \times \pi \times r^3$

$\Rightarrow R^3 = n \times r^3$

$\Rightarrow 5^3 = n \times 2^3$

$\Rightarrow n = \frac{125}{8} = 15$ (Approx)

Thus, 15 such spheres can be made.

Hence, the correct option is (A).

85. Champaran Satyagraha took place in 1917 under the leadership of Mahatma Gandhi. It was the first civil disobedience action in the history of the Indian National Movement.

Gandhiji and his colleagues, who now included Brij Kishore, Rajendra Prasad and other members of the Bihar intelligentsia, Mahadev Desai and Narhari Parikh, two young men from Gujarat who had thrown in their lot with Gandhiji, and J.B. Kripalani, toured the villages and from dawn to dusk recorded the statements of peasants, interrogating them to make sure that they were giving correct information.

The Government appointed a Commission of Inquiry to go into the whole issue and nominated Gandhiji as one of its members. As a compromise with the planters, he agreed that they refund only twenty-five percent (not a hundred percent) of the money they had taken illegally from the peasants. Answering critics who asked why he did not ask for a full refund, Gandhiji explained that

even this refund had done enough damage to the planters' prestige and position. As was often the case, Gandhiji's assessment was correct and, within a decade, the planters left the district altogether.
Hence, the correct option is (A).

86. The given sentence is complete. So the next sentence is either a new sentence or starts with a conjunction. Here we see R is the starting of a new sentence, hence, follows 1. But they can play a vital role in what? In making India a great, democratic, progressive and prosperous country. Hence P comes next in the sequence followed by S. The youths of our country should not only have cultural values but also modern scientific knowledge. Hence, Q comes last in the sequence.

Hence, the correct option is (C).

87. The second sentence should have a direct reference to the 1st sentence and most certainly it should start with a pronoun referring to optimism. Hence, R follows 1. The author continues to define optimism. Hence Q is next. If we now read the two sentences that are left, we see that S starts with 'they' hence it can't come next. So the next sentence is P followed by S.

Hence, the correct option is (A).

88. $\omega^{15} + \omega^{20} + \omega^{25}$

$= \omega^{15}(1 + \omega^5 + \omega^{10})$

$= \omega^{15} \times (1 + \omega^3 \cdot \omega^2 + \omega^9 \cdot \omega)$

$= (\omega^3)^5 \times (1 + \omega^2 + \omega)$

$= 1 \times (1 + \omega + \omega^2)$

$= 1 \times 0$

$= 0$

Hence, the correct option is (B).

89. Evangelista Torricelli, (born Oct. 15, 1608, Faenza, Romagna— died Oct. 25, 1647, Florence), Italian physicist and mathematician who invented the barometer and whose work in geometry aided in the eventual development of integral calculus.

Hence, the correct option is (A).

90. Edward Jenner was a well-known physician. His name is also famous in the world because he invented the 'smallpox' vaccine. With this invention of Edward Jenner, crores of people are recovering from deadly diseases like smallpox.

Hence, the correct option is (A).

91. M. Weber is associated with authority.

Weber said, Legitimate authority (sometimes just called authority), is power whose use is considered just and appropriate by those over whom the power is exercised. In short, if a society approves of the exercise of power in a particular way, then that power is also legitimate authority.

Hence, the correct option is (C).

92. The three-tier system of Panchayati Raj was recommended by Balwant Rai Mehta Committee.

The Balwant Rai Mehta Committee was a committee appointed by the Government of India in January 1957 to examine the working of the Community Development Programme (1952). The Act aims to provide a 3-tier system of Panchayati Raj for all States having a population of over 2 million, to hold Panchayat elections regularly.

Hence, the correct option is (D).

93. The oxidizing power of elements increases on moving left to right along a period in the periodic table. This is because electronegativity and the non-metallic character increases from left to right.
Hence, the correct option is (D).

94. Ionization potential is the energy required to remove an electron from the outermost shell of an atom in its isolated gaseous state. As we move down the group, ionization potential decreases. As we move across the period, ionization potential increases Electron affinity is the energy released on adding an electron to the outermost shell of an atom in its isolated gaseous state.
Hence, the correct option is (C).

95. Samsung mobile sold in June and December together

$$= \frac{4}{7} \times 14000 + \frac{2}{7} \times 28000$$

$$= 8000 + 8000 = 16000$$

Iphone mobile sold in February and August together

$$= \frac{4}{5} \times 10000 + \frac{5}{8} \times 24000 = 8000 + 15000 =$$
23000 Desired ratio $= \frac{16000}{23000} = \frac{16}{23} = 16:23$

Hence, the correct option is (B).

96. Iphone mobile sold in December $= \frac{5}{7} \times 28000 = 20000$

Samsung mobile sold in April and June

अप्रैल और जून को मिलाकर बेचे गए सैमसंग मोबाइल

$$= \frac{2}{5} \times 20000 + \frac{4}{7} \times 14000$$

$=8000+8000=16000$

We know that:

Desired $\% = \frac{x_2 - x_1}{x_1}$

Where, $x_1 = $ Samsung mobile sold in April and June

$x_2 = $ Iphone mobile sold in December

Desired $\% = \frac{20000 - 16000}{16000} \times 100 = 25\%$

Hence, the correct option is (D).

97. Given:

Month	Total number of mobiles sold (in thousand)	Number of Samsung mobiles sold (in thousand)	Number of Iphone mobiles sold (in thousand)
February	10	2	8
April	20	8	16
June	14	8	6
August	24	9	15
October	15	10	5
December	28	8	20

Samsung mobile sold in September

$$= \frac{3}{8} \times 24000 \times \frac{4}{3} = 12000$$

Iphone mobile sold in September $= \frac{5}{8} \times 24000 \times \frac{4}{3} =$ 20000

Total mobile sold in September $= 12000 + 20000 =$ 32000

$\therefore$ Total mobile sold in September is 32000

Hence, the correct option is (B).

98. Samsung mobile sold in February $= \frac{1}{5} \times 10000 \times$ $\frac{90}{100} = 1800$ Iphone mobile sold in February $=$ $\frac{4}{5} \times 10000 \times \frac{80}{100} = 6400$

Total mobile sold in February $= 1800 + 6400 = 8200$

Hence, the correct option is (D).

99. We know that:

Desired $\% = \frac{x_2 - x_1}{x_1}$

Where, $x_1 =$ Sales of mobile in August $x_2 =$ Sales of mobile in December Desired $\% = \frac{28000 - 24000}{24000} \times 100$

$$= \frac{4}{24} \times 100$$

$$= \frac{100}{6} \%$$

$$= \frac{50}{3} \%$$

$$= 16 \frac{2}{3} \%$$

Hence, the correct option is (B).

100. Science/Study is the meaning of logos in the term sociology.

The word "sociology" is derived from the Latin word socius (companion) and the Greek word logos (study of), meaning "the study of companionship." While this is a starting point for the discipline, sociology is actually much more complex.

Hence, the correct option is (A).

Q.1 Which medal did Devendra Jhajharia win in World Para Athletics Grand Prix 2022?

A. Gold **B.** Silver
C. Bronze **D.** None of the above

Q.2 The Indian Railways has placed a purchase order for 39,000 wheels for LHB coaches from the manufacturer of which of the following country in July 2022?

A. Ukraine **B.** China
C. Russia **D.** Germany

Q.3 GE Aerospace and Tata Advanced Systems Ltd have extended their long term contract worth USD _______ for production and supply of several commercial aircraft engine components.

A. 1 billion **B.** 1.5 billion
C. 2 billion **D.** 2.5 billion

Q.4 Jharkhand CM Hemant Soren has launched Jharkhand ___ Policy 2022 in Ranchi on 13th September 2022?

A. Farmer's **B.** Sports
C. Unskilled Labour **D.** All of the above

Q.5 Raj got a new chair for 35% discount. Had Raj got no discount, Raj would have had to pay Rs. 224 more. How much did Raj pay for the chair?

A. Rs. 416 **B.** Rs. 640 **C.** Rs. 208 **D.** Rs. 224

Q.6 How many inter-state water tribunals have been set up so far?

A. Seven **B.** Eight **C.** Nine **D.** Twelve

Q.7 Who appoints the presiding officer of Gram Nyayalaya?

A. State Government **B.** Governor
C. Chief Minister **D.** Prime Minister

Ques (8-10):Direction: Fill in the blanks with the most suitable option.

Q.8 _________ infants start their first few days of life, they are able to imitate facial expressions.

A. As far as **B.** As soon as
C. Through **D.** As well as

Q.9 ______ part of a short-lived and laughable health kick, I had invested in a Fitbit in spring 2016.

A. At **B.** If **C.** As **D.** To

Q.10 The stadium was ______ which was good news for the organizers.

A. Packed **B.** Packed in
C. Packed out **D.** Packed up

Q.11 A device for finding out what pupils understand and can do with the purpose of adapting future teaching to the needs of the individual or the class is known as:

[Rajasthan Teachers Eligibility Test - Level 1 Primary Level (RTET), 2017]

A. Summative Assessment
B. Information Assessment
C. Diagnostic Assessment
D. Testing

Q.12 What type of efforts are needed to be made in the learning of Mathematics in early primary years i.e. up to class IV?

[KVS PRT, 2018]

A. Diagnosing learning difficulties
B. Providing enrichment programmes
C. Completing the course/competencies
D. Ensuring regularity in attending the class/school

Q.13 The chairmanship/presidency of the UN Security Council rotates among the Council Members-

A. Every 6 months **B.** Every 3 months
C. Every year **D.** Every month

Q.14 Which one of the following is not related to disarmament?

A. SALT **B.** NPT **C.** CTBT **D.** NATO

Q.15 Which of the following metal is used for galvanization?

A. Zinc **B.** Copper **C.** Iron **D.** Silver

Q.16 The Element of an electric heater is made of___.

A. Nichrome **B.** Copper
C. Aluminum **D.** Silver

Ques (17-18):Direction: In the following question, out of the four alternatives, select the alternative which best expresses the meaning of the Idiom/Phrase.

Q.17 In black and white

A. Useless **B.** In writing
C. In short **D.** In full swing

Q.18 Stick one's neck out

A. Interfere **B.** Look outside
C. Move **D.** Invite trouble

Q.19 Equinox is a state in which the duration of day and night is equal. It falls on:

A. 22th March and 31st September
B. 10th March and 13th September
C. 21st March and 23rd September
D. 21th June and 22nd December

Q.20 GPS is an instrument used to capture the:

A. Cross sectional measurement of an area
B. Location of an area
C. Relative relief of an area
D. Graphical measurement and inclination

Q.21 The difference in the duration of day and night increases as one moves from:

A. West to east
B. East and west of the prime meridian
C. Poles to equator
D. Equator to poles

Q.22 The meaning of SATH-E is Sustainable Action for _____ Human capital in Education.

A. Traversing
B. Transferring
C. Transforming
D. Transgressing

Q.23 In the following question, the 1st and the last part of the passage are numbered 1 and 6. The rest of the passage is split into four parts and named P, Q, R, and S. These four parts are not given in their proper order. Read the passage and find out which of the four combinations is correct.

1. A man wearing dark sunglasses walked into the bank.

P. Then he shouted, "Give me all your money, all the money in this bank right now."

Q. Everyone in the lobby screamed and started running.

R. He went up to the teller and held up a hand grenade for all to see.

S. Nervously the young female teller handed the man three big bags loaded with cash.

6. Holding the grenade in one hand and the bags in the other, he walked out of the building.

A. PSRQ
B. QSPR
C. RPQS
D. SRQP

Q.24 Which of the following statements is/are incorrect about Rig Veda?

1. The Upaveda of Rig Veda is Gandharv Veda.

2. It is recited by Hota or Hotri priest.

3. Gayatri Mantra is taken from third Mandal of Rigveda.

A. Only 1
B. Only 2
C. 1 and 3
D. 2 and 3

Q.25 The length of a rectangular garden is 4 m. larger than the width and its half perimeter is 36 m. The length of garden is

[Joint Entrance Examination (Polytechnic), 2017]

A. 20 m
B. 16 m
C. 10 m
D. 15 m

Q.26 A rectangular park is to be constructed whose width is less by 3m from its length. It's area is 4 sq.m. more than the isosceles triangular park already constructed whose base is equal to the width of the rectangular park and height is 12 m. The length of this rectangular park will be

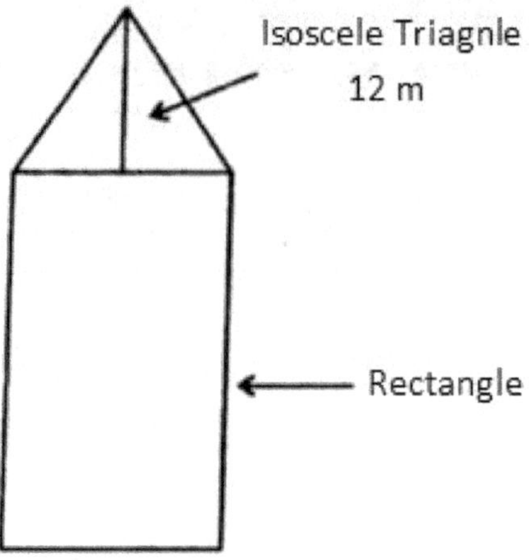

[Joint Entrance Examination (Polytechnic), 2017]

A. 7 m
B. 4 m
C. -1 m
D. 6 m

Q.27 A ladder is rested along the wall in such a way that its bottom is 2.5 m away from the wall and the top end of it rested on the window at a height of 6 m from the ground. The length of the ladder is:

[Joint Entrance Examination (Polytechnic), 2017]

A. 7.0 m
B. 7.5 m
C. 6.0 m
D. 6.5 m

Q.28 Find the least number which will leaves remainder 5 when divided by 8, 12, 16 and 20.

A. 240
B. 245
C. 265
D. 235

Q.29 Find the remainder when 2^{256} is divided by 17.

A. 1
B. 16
C. 14
D. None of the above

Q.30 Practice of welcoming guests, by spitting on their body is practiced by:

A. Onges
B. Masai
C. Azande
D. Sherdukpens

Q.31 Who among the following authors initially used the term 'social physics' for Sociology?

A. Weber
B. Comte
C. Tonnies
D. Spencer

Q.32 The popular TV serial 'Neem ka Ped' was written by:

A. Rahi Masoom Raza
B. Sharad Joshi
C. Ashapurna Devi
D. Harivansh Rai Bachachan

Q.33 Consider the following statements about 1937 elections:

1. Only provincial elections were held and no elections were held at the federal level.

2. Congress Ministries were formed in all the provinces except Bengal and Punjab.

Which of the statements given above is/are correct?

A. 1 only
B. 2 only
C. Both 1 and 2
D. Neither 1 nor 2

Q.34 If $x = 2015, y = 2014$ and $z = 2013$, then value of $x^2 + y^2 + z^2 - xy - yz - zx$ is:
A. 3   B. 4   C. 6   D. 2

Q.35 Name the first woman who became a doctor in India?
A. Kadambini Ganguli   B. Cornelia Sorabji
C. Ujwala Rai   D. Anita Bose

Q.36 $(1000)^{12} \div (10)^{30} = ?$
A. $(1000)^2$ B. 10   C. 100   D. $(100)^{12}$

Q.37 What is the capital of Bulgaria?
A. Beirut   B. Bucharest
C. Sofia   D. Tashkent

Q.38 Blood groups were discovered by:
A. Landsteiner   B. William Harvey
C. Weismann   D. Morgan

Q.39 Insulin was discovered by:
A. Frederick Banting   B. Edward Jenner
C. Ronald Ross   D. S.A. Wakesman

Q.40 A starts business with Rs. 3500 and after 5 months, B joins with A as his partner. After a year, the profit is divided in the ratio 2 : 3. What is B's contribution in the capital?
A. Rs. 7500   B. Rs. 8000   C. Rs. 8500   D. Rs. 9000

Ques (41-42):Direction: In the following question, a sentence has been given in Active/Passive Voice. Out of the four alternatives suggested, select the one which best expresses the same sentence in Passive/Active Voice.

Q.41 They were playing hockey in the garden.
A. Hockey is being played by them in the garden.
B. Hockey was played by them in the garden.
C. Hockey were being played by them in the garden.
D. Hockey was being played by them in the garden.

Q.42 Mohan has not eaten anything.
A. Nothing has not been eaten by Mohan.
B. Mohan does not eat anything.
C. Nothing has been eaten by Mohan.
D. Anything had not been eaten by Mohan.

Q.43 With reference to the newly announced strategic disinvestment policy in the budget 2021, consider the following statements:
1. Under this policy disinvestment proceeds will be credited into the National Investment and Infrastructure Fund.
2. Strategic disinvestment in India includes the transfer of management control from the government to the private sector.
Which of the statements given above is/are correct?
A. 1 only   B. 2 only
C. Both 1 and 2   D. Neither 1 nor 2

Q.44 Which of the following is/are the indicators of a robust credit flow for enterprises?
1. Rise in commercial paper issuances.
2. Easing of corporate bond yields.
3. Declining rate of corporate loan default.
Select the correct answer using the code given below.
A. 1 and 2 only   B. 2 only
C. 1 and 3 only   D. 1, 2 and 3

Q.45 The least perfect square, which is divisible by each of 21, 36, and 66 is:

[DSSSB TGT Social Science, 2014]

A. 214444   B. 213444   C. 215444   D. 216444

Q.46 An amount of Rs. 3900 is received on a principal amount of Rs. 1500 when kept at simple interest for 5 years. What will be the amount received if rate of interest decreases by 2%?
A. Rs. 3550   B. Rs. 3750   C. Rs. 3250   D. Rs. 3450

Q.47 An amount of Rs. 15400 is divided among uday and lavi. Uday invests his sum of money at 5% simple interest for 3 years and lavi invests his sum of money received at 10% simple interest for four years. If the interest received by uday is same as that of lavi then calculate uday's share.
A. Rs. 12,800   B. Rs. 11,200
C. Rs. 12,400   D. Rs. 13,200

Q.48 In a class, each of the students contributed as many paise as the numbers of students are there in the class. If the total collection was $Rs. 64$, what is the number of students in the class?
A. 90   B. 82
C. 80   D. None of these

Q.49 Regarding the mansabdari system, it cannot be said that:
A. It was a hereditary policy
B. It was of Central Asian origin
C. Mansabdars were generally assigned jagirs in lieu of cash pay
D. Mansabdars constituted the imperial bureaucracy

Q.50 Given below are three sentences which are jumbled. Pick the option that gives the correct order.
His exact date of birth is not known
P: but it is believed that he was born in
Q: late May and later on he decided to celebrate May 29 as his birthday,
R: as this was the date he climbed Everest
A. RQP   B. QRP   C. PQR   D. RPQ

Q.51 Who among the following had discovered the Smallpox vaccine?
A. Jonas E. Salk   B. Paul Muller
C. Edward Jenner   D. Robert Frost

Q.52 Which of the following disease is non-communicable in nature?
A. Cholera   B. Chicken-pox
C. Tuberculosis   D. Cancer

Ques (53-54):Direction: Each item in this section consists of a sentence with an underlined word followed by four options.

Select the option that is nearest in meaning to the underlined word.

Q.53 Ravi loves <u>seclusion</u>. Therefore, he lives in the mountains.

[UPSC NDA, 2019]

A. nature

B. scripture

C. seafaring

D. solitariness

Q.54 Hitler was a <u>despot</u>.

[UPSC NDA, 2019]

A. conservative

B. dictator

C. passionate

D. monstrous

Q.55 Directions: Each of the following items in this section has a sentence with three parts labelled as (a), (b) and (c). Read each sentence to find out whether there is any error in the given parts and indicate your response corresponding letter i.e., (a) or (b) or (c). if you find no error, your response should be indicated as (d).

a) This building

b) comprises of six houses

c) three parking lots and one basement

d) No error

[UPSC NDA, 2020]

A. (a)　　**B.** (b)　　**C.** (c)　　**D.** (d)

Q.56 Cashew nuts are worth Rs. 145/kg & Rs. 116/kg is mixed with a third variety in ratio 1: 1: 2. If the mixture is worth Rs. 153 per kg, then the price of the third variety per kg will be?

A. Rs. 175.5

B. Rs. 165.5

C. Rs. 172.5

D. Rs. 192.5

Q.57 If $(a + b):(b + c):(c + a) = 7:6:5$ and $a + b + c = 27$, then what will be the value of $\dfrac{1}{a}:\dfrac{1}{b}:\dfrac{1}{c}$?

A. 4: 3: 6　　**B.** 3: 2: 4　　**C.** 3: 4: 2　　**D.** 3: 6: 4

Ques (58-62):Direction: Read the passage carefully and answer the question given beside.

Air India's disinvestment, first attempted by the Atal Bihari Vajpayee government, is being revived. The sale bid the last time was a flop, shelved prematurely after all the bidders were either disqualified or dropped out. The many factors that were and may still be at work against the sale are not widely understood. Unless overcome, they may again endanger the sale.

In May 2000, bids were invited for a 40% stake in Air India, with a cap of 26% on foreign investment. The airline had reported losses for six **straight** years, had $70 million debt on its books and was fast losing traffic. More than 18,000 workers were on its rolls for a fleet of just about two dozen planes. Its employee-aircraft ratio, 750, was among the worst. Singapore Airlines, in contrast, had 91 employees per aircraft. Inefficiency, typical in a government-controlled set up, was bleeding Air India. Yet, the quantum of stake on offer made it clear that the government intended to retain a crucial stake, appoint its own directors and continue to have a say in running the business. Put off by the substantial degree of control the government wanted to retain

in the airline after the disinvestment, several potential bidders stayed away from the sale, including, possibly the worthiest contender. Plus, in a sale carried out through competitive bidding, reduced interest can impact the valuation.

The sale's stated purpose was to bring on board a strategic partner who would turn around Air India. But the sale's rules were loaded against candidates with a proven track record — foreign airlines. Lufthansa, Swissair, Emirates, British Airways and Air France-Delta in combination were among those to have expressed interest formally in buying the stake. However, a bidding rule that required foreign airlines to team up with a local partner forced them to opt out. Singapore Airlines, which had also expressed interest formally, roped in the Tatas to proceed with its bid.

Those who remained in the fray had their expressions of interest evaluated; those ineligible were disqualified. In the end, the contest was down to two bidders — the Hinduja group and the Singapore Airlines-Tata joint venture. Both were invited to inspect Air India's books. The Hindujas' bid was already under fire from the Opposition over allegations related to the Bofors arms scandal. After studying Air India's financial records, the group presented to the government a whole set of conditions on management control, threatening to withdraw if these were not met. The government barred the Hindujas from pursuing its bid, leaving a sole bidder: the Singapore Airlines-Tatas combine.

Private airline owners who had so far **orchestrated** resistance to the sale from the background, now openly pointed out that the majority stakeholder in Singapore Airlines was a foreign government. The unmasked attack made Singapore Airlines pull out. The airline said in a statement that the intensity of opposition to the privatisation from political groups and the trade unions had surprised it and that in such an adverse climate, it was not confident it could play a useful role.

The then Disinvestment Minister, Arun Shourie, clarified that the Tata group, Air India's **erstwhile** owner before its nationalisation in 1953, could proceed with its bid without a partner. But the Tatas too withdrew, forcing the government to abort the disinvestment.

Q.58 Which of the following facts discouraged the deserving bidders to go for the sale?

I. Sizeable control by the government.

II. Their several demands about maintenance issues went unheeded.

III. The government's will to have its own directors.

A. I and II

B. I and III

C. Only II

D. All of these

Q.59 Which of the following is/are true in the context of the passage?

I. The government still wanted to be a majority share holder and decision maker in Air India.

II. Earlier attempts for disinvestment were stopped by the government itself.

III. Inefficiency is a common scene in major government departments.

A. Only I
C. Only III
B. I, II and III
D. None of these

Q.60 What made Singapore Airlines withdraw from the sale?
A. Allegations of corruption.
B. Some political groups vehemently opposed the privatization.
C. They later got to know that it was not a worthwhile investment and might bring them losses.
D. They were unhappy with the management control.

Q.61 Why does the author seem to be apprehensive about the success of Air India's current disinvestment plan?
I. Author is aware of the corrpution that exists in government machinery.
II. Excessive participation of foreign investors.
III. Author believes that Disinvestment is not an apprpriate plan.
A. Only I and II
B. Only II
C. Only I
D. None of these

Q.62 In what aspect Singapore Airlines is better than Air India?
A. Efficiency of work staff
B. Upgraded technology
C. Employee-aircraft ratio
D. Maintenance issues

Q.63 A solid cylinder of 14 cm radius and 25 cm height is melted into a number of solid sphere of radius 3.5 cm. How many such complete sphere can be made?
A. 72
B. 85
C. 73
D. 70

Q.64 The world-famous 'Khajuraho' sculptures are located in:
A. Gujarat
B. Madhya Pradesh
C. Orissa
D. Maharashtra

Q.65 Anuvrata concept was given by:
A. Jainism
B. Hinayana Budhism
C. Mahayana Buddhism
D. None of the above

Q.66 Which of the following practice belongs to the method of Diagnostic Evaluation?
A. The teacher conducts evaluation in the beginning of teaching-learning process
B. The teacher conducts evaluation at the end of the teaching-learning process
C. An end-semester examination
D. An internal assessment test

Q.67 A teacher while offering feedback in a classroom transaction utters 'No, you are incorrect'. This will be called which type of feedback?

[UGC NET Sociology, 2019]

A. Positive
B. Negative
C. Confirmatory
D. Corrective

Q.68 Panna Lal Ghosh is related to which musical instrument?
A. Flute
B. The clarinet
C. Sarod
D. Tabla

Q.69 Who started the painting with the film's posters?
A. Satish gujral
B. Manjeet Baba
C. M.F. Hussain
D. Amrita Shergill

Q.70 What is the theme of National Youth Day (Yuva Diwas) 2019?
A. Sankalp Se Siddhi
B. Transforming Education
C. Youth for Digital India
D. Indian Youth for Development, Skills and Harmony

Q.71 On which day is International Yoga Day celebrated?

[UPTET Social Studies, 2022]

A. 21st June
B. 20th June
C. 25th June
D. 28th June

Q.72 If one diagonal of a rhombus is 62 cm more than other diagonal and length of side of rhombus is 41 cm, then find the area of rhombus.
A. 774 cm^2
B. 720 cm^2
C. 666 cm^2
D. 992 cm^2

Q.73 In a given figure ΔABC is a right-angle triangle in which AB = 6 cm and BC = 8 cm and ∠ABC = 90° and PQRB is a largest square in it, and ΔXYZ is an equilateral triangle, then find area of ΔXYZ.

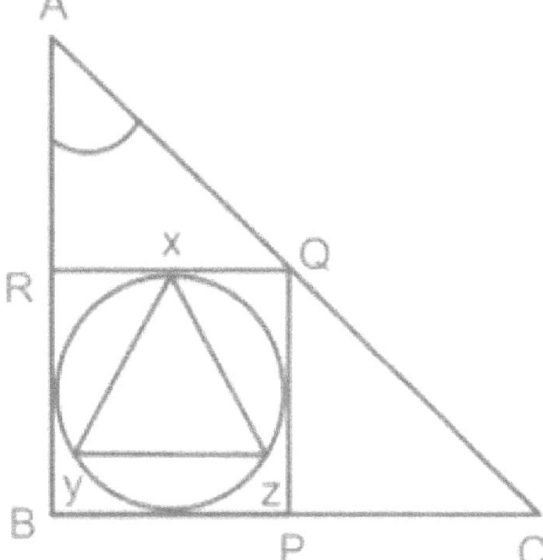

A. $\left(\frac{108\sqrt{3}}{49}\right)$ cm ^{2}
B. $\left(\frac{54\sqrt{2}}{7}\right)$ cm ^{2}
C. $\left(\frac{108\sqrt{2}}{49}\right)$ cm ^{2}
D. $\left(\frac{54\sqrt{3}}{7}\right)$ cm ^{2}

Q.74 When 75 is added to 75% of a number, the result obtained is the number itself. Find the number.
A. 50
B. 60
C. 300
D. 400

Q.75 The sum of two numbers is 2490. 6.5% of the first number is equal to 8.5% of the second number. Find the greater number.
A. 1876
B. 1600
C. 1411
D. 1380

Q.76 One of the two inlet pipes works twice as efficiently as the other. The two can fill the empty cistern in 12 hours. A drain pipe can empty a cistern all by itself in 12 hours. How many hours will the more efficient inlet pipe take to fill the empty cistern by itself?

[RRB/RRC Group D, 2018]

A. 9 **B.** 15 **C.** 12 **D.** 18

Q.77 Garima and her sister together can paint the walls of their house in 45 days. If Garima alone did the job, it would have taken her 81 days. If the duo started painting together but Garima's sister had to leave 9 days before the completion of the work, how many days in all would it take the sisters to paint their house?

[RRB/RRC Group D, 2018]

A. 49 **B.** 48 **C.** 52 **D.** 50

Q.78 The value of $\dfrac{3.157 \times 4126 \times 3.198}{63.972 \times 2835.121}$ is closest to:

A. 0.002 **B.** 0.02 **C.** 0.2 **D.** 2

Q.79 The distribution of weights (in kg) of 44 students in a class is as follows:

Weight	No. of Students
35 - 38	3
38 - 41	13
41 - 44	13
44 - 47	10
47 - 50	5

What is the average weight of the class?

A. 40.26 **B.** 41.88 **C.** 42.56 **D.** 43.25

Q.80 Which one of the following measures is determined only after the construction of cumulative frequency distribution?

A. Arithmetic mean **B.** Mode
C. Median **D.** Geometric mean

Q.81 If the rice is sold at Rs. 48 per kg, then there would be a 20% loss. To earn a profit of 20% what should be the price of rice (per kg)

[SSC MTS, 2017]

A. 72 **B.** 76 **C.** 78 **D.** 84

Q.82 The marked price of an article is 50% more than its cost price. If a discount of 10% is given, then what is the profit percentage?

[SSC MTS, 2017]

A. 25 **B.** 30 **C.** 35 **D.** 20

Q.83 Who was the hero of the 1st Garhwal Rifles during the First World War (1914-18)?

A. Gabar Singh Negi
B. Darwan Singh Negi
C. Major Somnath Sharma
D. Shoorveer Singh Panwar

Q.84 Select the wrong pair from the following?

A. Deep Joshi – Ramon Magsaysay
B. Sundar Lal Bahuguna – Ramon Magsaysay

C. Govind Vallabh Pant – Bharat Ratna
D. Hansa Manral – Dronacharya Award

Q.85 Solve : 345678 x 999999?

A. 345677653422 **B.** 354677654322
C. 345677654322 **D.** 346577564322

Q.86 Who among the following is NOT a recipient of Rajiv Gandhi Khel Ratna 2020?

A. Vinesh Phogat
B. Rohit Sharma
C. Mariyappan Thangavelu
D. Mirabai Chanu

Q.87 In which city is the summer Olympic Games 2024 to be held?

[Bihar Police SI, 2019]

A. Los Angeles **B.** London
C. Beijing **D.** Paris

Q.88 If A = { x : x ∈ N, 0 < x < 6} and B = {x : x is a prime natural number, 0 < x < 10} Find A - B ?

A. {2, 3, 5} **B.** {1, 4} **C.** {2, 3} **D.** {2, 3, 4}

Q.89 Find the value of $^{n}C_r + 2 \times (^{n}C_{r-1}) + ^{n}C_{r-2}$?

A. $(n+2)C_r$ **B.** $(n+1)C_r$
C. $(n-2)C_r$ **D.** $(n-1)C_r$

Q.90 Three numbers are in ratio 1 : 2 : 3 and HCF is 12. The numbers are:

A. 12, 24, 36 **B.** 11, 22, 33
C. 12, 24, 32 **D.** 5, 10, 15

Q.91 In the given figure, AB ∥ CD, ∠APQ = 50° and ∠PRD = 127°, find the value of y – x?

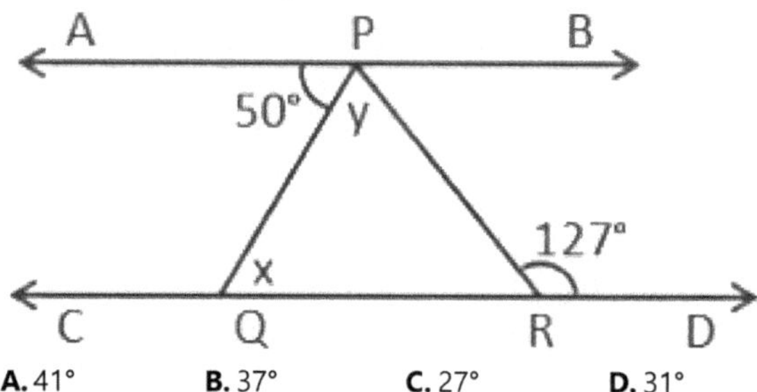

A. 41° **B.** 37° **C.** 27° **D.** 31°

Q.92 Direction: Given below are four sentences in jumbled order. Pick the option that gives their correct order.

A. But Mr Oliver did not feel nervous at all.

B. The pine trees made sad eerie sounds in the forest.

C. When the light fell on the figure of a boy, sitting on a rock, Mr Oliver stopped.

D. He kept along the forest path guided by flickering torchlight.

A. BADC **B.** CABD **C.** DABC **D.** BDCA

Q.93 Which of the following chemical is used in the preservation of fruit juice?

A. Citric acid **B.** Sodium Chloride
C. Sodium Benzoate **D.** None of these

Q.94 To which of the following groups do noble gases belong?

A. Group 15   **B.** Group 18

C. Group 17   **D.** Group 16

Q.95 Remedial method is used for:

A. Normal Children

B. Problematic Children

C. Normal and Problematic Children

D. Gifted Children

Ques (96-100):Direction: The following line graph gives the percentage of qualified candidates out of the total number of candidates who appeared for the examination over a period of seven years from the year 1994 to 2000.

Percentage of candidates qualified to appear in an examination in different years.

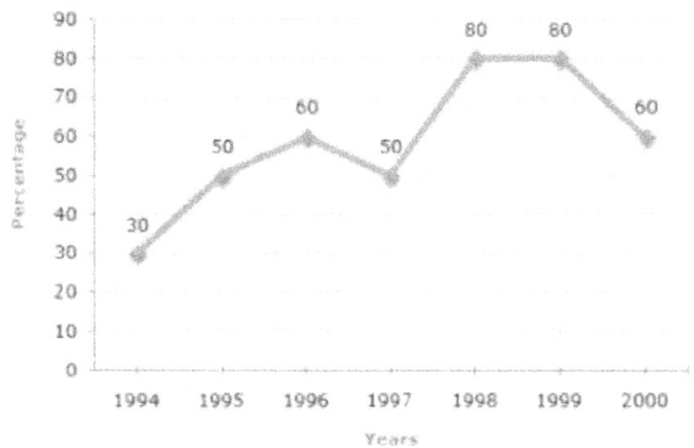

Q.96 The difference between the percentage of candidates qualified to appeared was maximum in which of the following pairs of years?

A. 1994 and 1995   **B.** 1995 and 1996

C. 1998 and 1999   **D.** 1997 and 1998

Q.97 In which pair of years was the number of candidates qualified, the same?

A. 1994 and 1995   **B.** 1995 and 1997

C. 1998 and 1999   **D.** Data inadequate

Q.98 If the number of candidates qualified in 1998 was 21200, what was the number of candidates who appeared in 1998?

A. 32000   **B.** 28500   **C.** 26500   **D.** 25000

Q.99 If the total number of candidates who appeared in 1996 and 1997 together was 47400, then the total number of candidates qualified in these two years together was?

A. 34700   **B.** 32100

C. 31500   **D.** Data inadequate

Q.100 The total number of candidates qualified in 1999 and 2000 together was 33500 and the number of candidates appeared in 1999 was 26500. What was the number of candidates in 2000?

A. 24500   **B.** 22000   **C.** 20500   **D.** 19000

// Smart Answer Sheet //

Correct Percentage of students who answered correctly. **Skipped** Percentage of students who skipped.

Q.	Ans.	Correct	Skipped	Q.	Ans.	Correct	Skipped	Q.	Ans.	Correct	Skipped	Q.	Ans.	Correct	Skipped	Q.	Ans.	Correct	Skipped	Q.	Ans.	Correct	Skipped
1	B	80.59 %	0.0 %	18	D	60.14 %	1.84 %	35	A	51.33 %	1.81 %	52	D	82.09 %	0.0 %	69	C	57.13 %	1.86 %	86	D	79.24 %	0.0 %
2	B	60.88 %	1.43 %	19	C	60.01 %	1.44 %	36	A	46.28 %	1.93 %	53	D	46.75 %	1.84 %	70	B	87.42 %	0.0 %	87	D	41.16 %	1.07 %
3	A	57.77 %	1.38 %	20	B	85.54 %	0.0 %	37	C	25.76 %	3.47 %	54	B	63.54 %	1.02 %	71	A	52.87 %	1.73 %	88	B	53.31 %	1.86 %
4	B	50.25 %	1.27 %	21	D	18.03 %	4.61 %	38	A	51.31 %	1.13 %	55	B	63.36 %	1.53 %	72	B	56.12 %	1.27 %	89	A	61.47 %	1.51 %
5	A	53.63 %	1.64 %	22	C	60.08 %	1.33 %	39	A	55.09 %	1.91 %	56	A	58.51 %	1.05 %	73	A	12.74 %	3.92 %	90	A	79.32 %	0.0 %
6	C	89.26 %	0.0 %	23	C	45.88 %	1.95 %	40	D	51.4 %	1.11 %	57	A	68.94 %	1.95 %	74	C	82.53 %	0.0 %	91	C	50.32 %	1.92 %
7	A	78.12 %	0.0 %	24	C	51.64 %	1.05 %	41	D	61.13 %	1.94 %	58	B	65.1 %	1.39 %	75	C	68.73 %	1.27 %	92	A	32.6 %	4.94 %
8	B	84.34 %	0.0 %	25	A	57.48 %	1.5 %	42	C	59.28 %	1.49 %	59	D	64.05 %	1.08 %	76	D	62.09 %	1.27 %	93	C	45.06 %	1.3 %
9	C	81.93 %	0.0 %	26	A	53.65 %	1.61 %	43	B	52.47 %	1.71 %	60	B	77.9 %	0.0 %	77	A	13.4 %	3.21 %	94	B	84.07 %	0.0 %
10	C	52.78 %	1.58 %	27	D	57.05 %	1.59 %	44	A	65.35 %	1.62 %	61	D	57.16 %	1.96 %	78	C	46.32 %	1.84 %	95	B	48.01 %	1.58 %
11	C	61.34 %	1.51 %	28	B	58.53 %	1.82 %	45	B	57.8 %	1.2 %	62	C	89.43 %	0.0 %	79	C	66.38 %	1.0 %	96	D	58.89 %	1.68 %
12	A	48.17 %	1.36 %	29	A	61.85 %	1.81 %	46	B	30.28 %	4.54 %	63	B	47.61 %	1.67 %	80	C	45.29 %	1.5 %	97	D	63.22 %	1.44 %
13	D	67.52 %	1.32 %	30	B	51.47 %	1.31 %	47	B	49.79 %	1.72 %	64	B	83.04 %	0.0 %	81	A	46.94 %	1.76 %	98	C	89.63 %	0.0 %
14	D	45.84 %	1.17 %	31	B	47.08 %	1.69 %	48	C	45.13 %	1.91 %	65	A	66.32 %	1.64 %	82	C	48.2 %	1.61 %	99	D	24.25 %	3.43 %
15	A	26.15 %	3.18 %	32	A	10.75 %	3.98 %	49	A	88.66 %	0.0 %	66	A	42.41 %	1.15 %	83	B	62.69 %	1.83 %	100	C	10.75 %	3.46 %
16	A	28.82 %	3.67 %	33	A	41.6 %	1.38 %	50	C	53.58 %	1.03 %	67	B	46.06 %	1.33 %	84	D	56.97 %	1.15 %				
17	B	76.64 %	0.0 %	34	A	24.28 %	4.2 %	51	C	87.31 %	0.0 %	68	A	64.07 %	1.33 %	85	C	56.36 %	1.75 %				

//Hints and Solutions//

1. Indian javelin thrower, Devendra Jhajharia has clinched a silver medal in the World Para Athletics Grand Prix 2022 in Morocco.

Paralympics gold medalist Devendra Jhajharia threw the javelin to a distance of 60.97 meters to capture the silver. He is a three-time Paralympics medalist.

Hence, the correct option is (B).

2. The Indian Railways has placed a purchase order for 39,000 wheels for LHB Coaches from the Chinese manufacturer Taiyuan against a global tender." Due to the ongoing war between Russia and Ukraine, the supplies against the ongoing contracts with the firms from Russia and Ukraine have been affected. The contract rate is 1.68% higher than the rate per wheel given in a Ukrainian firm's earlier Letter of Acceptance (LoA).

Hence, the correct option is (B).

3. GE Aerospace and Tata Advanced Systems Ltd have extended their long term contract worth USD 1 billion for production and supply of several commercial aircraft engine components.

The engine parts will be manufactured at the Tata Centre of Excellence for Aero Engines (Tata-TCoE). Under the extended agreement, TASL will continue to produce and supply several commercial aircraft engine components to GE's global engine manufacturing factories.

Hence, the correct option is (A).

4. Jharkhand CM Hemant Soren has launched Jharkhand Sports Policy 2022 in Ranchi on 13th September 2022.

- This policy is aimed at reducing bottlenecks in the path of sportspersons in excelling at national and international events.
- The sports policy made for five years is the second such policy framework in Jharkhand.
- The last such policy was made in 2007.

Hence, the correct option is (B).

5. Given:

Raj got 35% discount

If there was no discount, Raj would pay Rs. 224

This means giving 35% discount $=$ Rs. 224 off

$\therefore 35\%$ of Marked Price $=$ Rs. 224

$\therefore \dfrac{35}{100} \times$ Marked price $= 224$

$\therefore$ Marked Price $=$ Rs. 640

$\therefore$ Raj paid $= 640 - 224 =$ Rs. 416

Hence, the correct option is (A).

6. So far the Central government has set up nine inter-state water dispute tribunals. The first inter-state water tribunal was constituted in the year 1969 called the Krishna Water Disputes Tribunal-I.

Hence, the correct option is (C).

7. The Gram Nyayalaya is a court of Judicial Magistrate of the first class. Its presiding officer or the Nyayadhikari shall be appointed by the State Government in consultation with the High Court.

Hence, the correct option is (A).

8. 'As soon as' is the most suitable option here. It is used here to express the meaning that the earliest that infants become capable of imitating facial expressions is their first few days of life.

Hence, the correct option is (B).

9. The context of the sentence suggests that the blank should contain a preposition.

Given the context, the only word that can fill the blank is 'as'.

Hence, the correct option is (C).

10. The correct option here is 'packed up'. It is a phrasal verb which means a venue is filled up.

Hence, the correct option is (C).

11. Techniques, strategies, or methods used as an assessment to know the problems faced by the students and their weak points are called diagnostic assessments.

Diagnostic assessments find out the ability, skill, speed, and amount of learning of a student. It helps in future-learning and outcomes according to the objective.

Hence, the correct option is (C).

12. A diagnostic evaluation helps in revealing an individual's weaknesses and strengths in mathematics. It helps the teachers to know the gaps in learner's understanding and then providing them with the necessary help and guidance to overcome.

It is concerned with the persistent or recurring learning difficulties that are left unsolved.

The main aim of the diagnostic evaluation is to determine the causes of learning problems and to formulate a plan for remedial action.

It will pinpoint the types of errors that were made along with their causes and plays a significant role in improving learning outcomes for all students.

Hence, the correct option is (A).

13. The chairmanship/presidency of the UN Security Council rotates every month among the Council Members.

The presidency of the United Nations Security Council rotates on a monthly basis alphabetically among all of the members based on their English name.

Hence, the correct option is (D).

14. NATO stands for The North Atlantic Treaty Organisation. It was established in the year 1949. It's headquarter is located in Brussels, Belgium. Unlike NPT, SALT, and CTBT, NATO is not related to disarmament. Its main purpose is to safeguard the freedom and securities of its member countries.

Hence, the correct option is (D).

15.

- <u>Galvanization</u> is a process of applying a protective layer of <u>zinc</u> to iron or steel to prevent rusting.

- Rusting is defined as the process of slow eating away due to the attack of oxygen and moisture on its surface.

- Rusting can be avoided by Paint, Oiling, and Galvanization.

Hence, the correct option is (A).

16.

- The Element of an electric heater is made up of <u>Nichrome</u>.

- This is because Nichrome has A very high melting point when compared to other elements.

- Nichrome converts Electrical energy into Heat energy.

Hence, the correct option is (A).

17. The idiom "in black and white" means in writing or in print.

The phrase plays on the binary opposition of the two colors and shows the inherent contrast which govern them.

Hence, the correct option is (B).

18. The idiom "stick your neck out" means risk incurring criticism or anger by acting or speaking boldly, to take a risk or invite trouble by your actions.

Hence, the correct option is (D).

19. An equinox is an event in which a planet's subsolar point passes through its Equator. The equinoxes are the only time when both the Northern and Southern Hemispheres experience roughly equal amounts of daytime and nighttime.

- There are two equinoxes every year: one around March 21 and another around September 23.

- Sometimes, the equinoxes are nicknamed the "vernal equinox" (spring equinox) and the "autumnal equinox" (fall equinox).

- During the equinoxes, solar declination is 0°. Solar declination describes the latitude of the Earth where the sun is directly overhead at noon.

- The subsolar point is an area where the sun's rays shine perpendicular to the Earth's surface at a right angle.

- Only during equinox is the Earth's 23.5° axis not tilting toward or away from the sun: the perceived center of the Sun's disk is in the same plane as the Equator.

Hence, the correct option is (C).

20. The global positioning system (GPS) is a network of satellites and receiving devices used to determine the location of something on Earth. Some GPS receivers are so accurate they can

establish their location within 1 centimeter (0.4 inches). GPS receivers provide location in latitude, longitude, and altitude.

Hence, the correct option is (B).

21. The Earth orbits the sun once every 365 days and rotates about its axis once every 24 hours. Day and night are due to the Earth rotating on its axis, not its orbit around the sun.

- Due to the rotation of the earth in its axis, the phenomena of day and night happens.

- To complete a complete rotation the earth takes 23 hours and 56 minutes.

- During the rotation in its axis (23.5° inclined) when a part of the come in front of the Sun, it considered as day time at that place, and night remains on the opposite side of that place.

- The inclination also causes variation in the energy received on the surface of the earth.

- The sun rays almost perpendicular to the equatorial region all over the year, but it becomes oblique towards the pole.

- The duration of the day and night is almost the same at the equator.

- So the difference in the duration of day and night increases as one moves from the Equator to poles.

- For most of us here on the planet Earth, sunrise, sunset, and the cycle of day and night (the diurnal cycle) are just simple facts of life.

- As a result of seasonal changes that happen with every passing year, the length of day and night can vary and be either longer or shorter by just a few hours.

Hence, the correct option is (D).

22. Sustainable Action for Transforming Human Capital in Education (SATH-E) Project of NITI Aayog, is being undertaken in partnership with three participating States of Jharkhand, Madhya Pradesh, and Odisha.

SATH-E project aims at promoting vocational education, skill development, teacher training, and introducing technology in classrooms.

Hence, the correct option is (C).

23. The correct sequence is RPQS.

A man wearing dark sunglasses walked into the bank. He went up to the teller and held up a hand grenade for all to see. Then he shouted, "Give me all your money, all the money in this bank right now." Everyone in the lobby screamed and started running. Nervously the young female teller handed the man three big bags loaded with cash. Holding the grenade in one hand and the bags in the other, he walked out of the building.

Hence, the correct option is (C).

24. The correct answer is 1 and 3.

- Rig Veda is the oldest Veda dating back to 1500 to 1000 BC.

- It is divided into 10 mandals.

- 2-7 mandals are the oldest and are family books describe to a particular family of Rishis.

- 8th Mandal is related to the Kanva family.

- 9th Mandal contains the compilation of Soma Hymns.

- 1st and 10th mandals are the latest and contain Purushsukta which defines the four varnas.

- It is recited by Hota or Hotri Priest. Hence statement 2 is correct.

- The Upveda of rigveda is Ayurveda. Hence statement 1 is not correct.

- Gayatri Mantra is taken from the third Mandal of Rig Veda and was composed by Vishva Mitra to convert non-Aryans to Aryans. It is devoted to Savitra. Hence statement 3 is not correct.

- It consists of 1028 hymns.

- Indra is mentioned 250 times in Rigveda.

Hence, the correct option is (C).

25. Let the width of the garden $= x$ meter

Then length $= (x + 4)$ meter

Half perimeter $= 36$ m

So perimeter of garden $= (2 \times 36) = 72$ meters

According to the question,

$$\Rightarrow 2(l + b) = 72$$

$$\Rightarrow 2(x + x + 4) = 72$$

$$\Rightarrow 2x + 2x + 4 = 74$$

$$\Rightarrow 4x = 64$$

$$\Rightarrow x = 16 \text{ meters}$$

So, the width of the garden $= 16$ meters

The length of the garden $= (16 + 4) = 20$ meters

Hence, the correct option is (A).

26. Length of Rectangular Park $= l$

Breadth of Rectangular Park $= l - 3$

Altitude of Triangular Park $= 12$

Breadth of Triangular Park $= l - 3$

Now,

Area of Rectangle $= l(l - 3)$

Area of Triangle $= \frac{1}{2} \times 12(l - 3)$

Area of Rectangle - Area of Triangle = 4

$$\Rightarrow l(l - 3) - \frac{1}{2} \times 12(l - 3) = 4$$

$$\Rightarrow l^2 - 91 + 14 = 0$$

$$\Rightarrow (l - 2)(l - 7) = 0$$

$$\Rightarrow l = 2, 7$$

Since, breadth is $l - 3, l \neq 2$

$$\therefore l = 7 \text{ m}$$

Hence, the correct option is (A).

27. It is given that, a ladder is rested along the wall in such a way that its bottom is 2.5 m away from the wall and the top end of it rested on the window at a height of 6 m from the ground.

Therefore,

Here, distance from wall = BC $= 2.5 \, m$

Height of window = AC $= 6 \, m$

Since the wall will be perpendicular to ground.

$$\therefore \angle ACB = 90°$$

So, using Pythagoras theorem,

$$(\text{Hypotenuse})^2 = (\text{Height})^2 + (\text{Base})^2$$

$$\Rightarrow (AB)^2 = (AC)^2 + (BC)^2$$

$$\Rightarrow AB^2 = (6)^2 + (2.5)^2$$

$$\Rightarrow AB^2 = (6 \times 6) + (2.5 \times 2.5)$$

$$\Rightarrow AB^2 = 36 + 6.25$$

$$\Rightarrow AB^2 = 42.25$$

$$\Rightarrow AB = \sqrt{42.25}$$

$$\Rightarrow AB = 6.5 \, m$$

Hence, the correct option is (D).

28. We have to find the Least number, therefore we find out the LCM of 8, 12, 16 and 20.

$8 = 2 \times 2 \times 2$;

$12 = 2 \times 2 \times 3$;

$16 = 2 \times 2 \times 2 \times 2$;

$20 = 2 \times 2 \times 5$;

$LCM = 2 \times 2 \times 2 \times 2 \times 3 \times 5 = 240$;

This is the least number which is exactly divisible by 8, 12, 16 and 20

Thus,

Required number which leaves remainder 5 is,

$240 + 5 = 245$

Hence, the correct option is (B).

29. Given,

$$\frac{2^{256}}{17}$$

We can write it as: $(2^4)^{64}$

$$\frac{16^{64}}{17}$$

Individually, when 16 is divided by 17,

Gives a negative reminder of - 1.

Required Remainder

$$(-1)^{64} = 1$$

Alternatively,

$\dfrac{16^{64}}{17}$, can be written as,

$$\frac{(16 \times 16 \times 16 \times 16 \times 16 \ldots \ldots 64\text{ times})}{17}$$

Now, we take the negative remainder of each,

16 divided by 17 gives negative remainder - 1.

So, the Remainder will be

$$(-1 \times -1 \times -1 \times -1 \times -1 \ldots \ldots .64 \text{ times })$$

$= 1$

Hence, the correct option is (A).

30. Practice of welcoming guests, by spitting on their body is practiced by Masai.

While spitting is often considered an uncivilized and unhealthy gesture around the world, Kenyan and Tanzanian people of the Maasai tribe have incorporated it into their greeting ritual. The Maasai spits into their palms before a handshake.

Hence, the correct option is (B).

31. Comte used the term 'social physics' for Sociology.

Auguste Comte, the founder of modern sociology, coined the phrase "social physics" back in the 19th century. Comte and others in that era aspired to explain social reality by developing a set of universal laws—the sociological equivalent of physicists' quest to create a theory of everything.

Hence, the correct option is (B).

32. Neem Ka Ped is an Indian television drama series that was edited and directed by Gurbir Singh Grewal and produced by Nouman Malik. It was written by Dr. Rahi Masoom Raza.

Hence, the correct option is (A).

33. Provincial elections were held in British India in the winter of 1936-37 as mandated by the Government of India Act 1935. Elections were held in eleven provinces - Madras, Central Provinces, Bihar, Orissa, United Provinces, Bombay Presidency, Assam, NWFP, Bengal, Punjab and Sindh. As the federal part did not come into existence after the Government of India Act, 1935 due to reservations of princely states, no elections were held at the Federal Level.

After a few months' tussles with the Government, the Congress Working Committee decided to accept office under the Act of 1935. During July, it formed Ministries in six provinces: Madras, Bombay, Central Provinces, Orissa, Bihar and U.P. Later, Congress Ministries were also formed in the North-West Frontier Province and Assam. The Non-Congress Ministries were formed in Bengal (Krishi Praja Party with the support of Muslim League and Independent Muslims), Punjab (Unionist Party) & Sindh (United Sindh Party).

Hence, the correct option is (A).

34. $x - y = 2015 - 2014 = 1$

$y - z = 2014 - 2013 = 1$

$z - x = 2013 - 2015 = -2$

$\therefore x^2 + y^2 + z^2 - xy - yz - zx$

Numerator and denominator multiplied by 2

$$= \frac{1}{2}(2x^2 + 2y^2 + 2z^2 - 2xy - 2yz - 2zx)$$

$$= \frac{1}{2}(x^2 + y^2 - 2xy + y^2 + z^2 - 2yz + z^2 + x^2 - 2zx)$$

$$= \frac{1}{2}[(x - y)^2 + (y - z)^2 + (z - x)^2]$$

$$= \frac{1}{2}[1 + 1 + 4]$$

$$= \frac{1}{2} \times 6$$

$$= 3$$

Hence, the correct option is (A).

35. Kadambini Ganguli, the first woman became a doctor in India.

Kadambini Ganguly was one of the first Indian female doctors who practiced with a degree in modern medicine. She was the first Indian woman to practice medicine in India.

Hence, the correct option is (A).

36. $\dfrac{(1000)^{12}}{(10)^{30}}$

$= \dfrac{(10^3)^{12}}{(10)^{30}}$

$= \dfrac{(10)^{(3\times12)}}{(10)^{30}}$

$= \dfrac{(10)^{36}}{(10)^{30}}$

$= (10)^{(36-30)}$

$= 10^6$

$= (10^3)^2$

$= (1000)^2$

Hence, the correct option is (A).

37. Sofia is the capital of Bulgaria and it is the 15th largest city in the European Union with a population of around 13 million people. It has been ranked by the Globalization and World Cities Research Network as a Beta city. Many of the major universities, cultural institutions, and commercial companies of Bulgaria are concentrated in Sofia.

Hence, the correct option is (C).

38. Blood groups were discovered by Landsteiner.

The ABO blood group system is widely credited to have been discovered by the Austrian scientist Karl Landsteiner, who identified the O, A, and B blood types in 1900. He was awarded the Nobel Prize in Physiology or Medicine in 1930 for his work.

Hence, the correct option is (A).

39. Frederick Banting was a Canadian medical scientist, doctor and Nobel laureate noted as one of the main discoverers of insulin. In 1923 Banting and John James Rickard Macleod received the Nobel Prize in Medicine, becoming the youngest recipient of the Nobel Prize in Physiology/Medicine.

Hence, the correct option is (A).

40. Let B's capital be Rs. x

$\therefore$ A's share in 12 months $= 3500 \times 12$

And, B's share in 7 months $= 7x$

Then, $\dfrac{3500\times12}{7x} = \dfrac{2}{3}$

$\Rightarrow 14x = 126000$

$\Rightarrow x = 9000$

Hence, the correct option is (D).

41. The given sentence is in the active voice. Its tense is past continuous. The structures for active/passive voices are:
Active: Subject + was/were + verb (ing) + object.

Passive: Object + was/were + being + verb (IIIrd from) + by + subject.

So, with the help of the above structures, we can convert the given sentence into passive voice:

Hockey was being played by them in the garden.

Hence, the correct option is (D).

42. The given sentence is of present perfect tense and it is in the active form. The structures for active/passive voices are:
Active: Subject + has/have + verb (IIIrd form) + object.

Passive: Object + has/have + been + verb (IIIrd form) + by + subject.

So, the passive voice of the given sentence would be:

Anything has not been eaten by Mohan.

OR

Nothing has been eaten by Mohan.

Hence, the correct option is (C).

43. Disinvestment means the sale or liquidation of assets by the government, usually Central and state public sector enterprises, projects, or other fixed assets.

To address various problems associated with central public enterprises, the government has brought out this policy to completely overhaul the government's presence in various sectors and minimize the number of PSUs to an absolute minimum. This Policy covers existing CPSEs, Public Sector Banks, and Public Sector Insurance Companies.

Hence, the correct option is (B).

44. Bond yield is the return that an investor gets on that bond or on particular government security. A fall/rise in interest rates in an economy pushes up/pulls down bond prices. When prices of bonds rise then it means a fall/easing in the Bond yields. So easing of bond yield implies the fall in the rate of interest, which further tends to enhance the credit attractiveness for the enterprises.

A sharp rise in commercial paper issuances, easing yields, and sturdy credit growth to MSMEs portend revamped credit flows for enterprises to survive and grow. So, statements 1 and 2 are correct.

Hence, the correct option is (A).

45. As given,

L.C.M. of 21, 36, 66 = 2772

Now, 2772 = 2 × 2 × 3 × 3 × 7 × 11

To make it a perfect square, it must be multiplied by 7 × 11.

So, the required number

$= 2^2 \times 3^2 \times 7^2 \times 11^2$

= 213444

Hence, the correct option is (B).

46. Given:

$A =$ Rs. 3900

$N = 5$ years

$P =$ Rs. 1500

$I = \dfrac{PRN}{100}$

Where $P =$ Principal amount, $R =$ Rate of interest in %, $N =$ Number of years, $I =$ Interest earned

$A = P + 1$

Where $A =$ Amount received

$I = 3900 - 1500$

$\Rightarrow I =$ Rs. 2400

Accordingly,

$2400 = \dfrac{(1500 \times R \times 5)}{100}$

$\Rightarrow \dfrac{2400 \times 100}{(1500 \times 5)} = R$

$\Rightarrow R = 32\%$

Now, rate of interest is reduced by 2%

$\Rightarrow$ New rate of interest is $(32 - 2) = 30\%$

$I = \dfrac{(1500 \times 30 \times 5)}{100}$

$\Rightarrow I = 2250$

$\Rightarrow A = 1500 + 2250$

$\therefore$ The received amount will be Rs. 3750.

Hence, the correct option is (B).

47. Given:

$A =$ Rs. 15400

Uday: $R = 5\%$, $N = 3$ years

Lavi: $R = 10\%$, $N = 4$ years

Interest obtained by lavi = Interest obtained by uday

$I = \dfrac{PRN}{100}$

Where $P =$ Principal amount, $R =$ Rate of interest in %, $N =$ Number of years, $I =$ Interest earned

$A = P + 1$

Where $A =$ Amount received

Let uday's share be X then lavi's share $= 15400 - X$

Accordingly,

$\dfrac{(X \times 5 \times 3)}{100} = (15400 - X) \times 10 \times \dfrac{4}{100}$

$\Rightarrow 15X = (15400 - X) \times 40$

$\Rightarrow 3X = 123200 - 8X$ [Dividing both sides by 5]

$\Rightarrow 11X = 123200$

$\Rightarrow X = 11200$

$\therefore$ Uday's share is Rs. $11,200$.

Hence, the correct option is (B).

48. Let the number of students in the class be x.

Now, each of the students has contributed to x paise.

So, the total collection will be x^2 paise.

Given, collection $Rs.\,64 = 6400$ paise

According, to the question $x^2 = 6400$

$x = 80$

Thus, the number of students in the class is 80.

Hence, the correct option is (C).

49. Regarding the mansabdari system, it cannot be said that it was a hereditary policy.

Mansabdari System:

Akbar introduced the Mansabdari system in his administration.

The mansab rank was not hereditary.

All appointments and promotions, as well as dismissals, were directly made by the emperor.

Mansabdars were paid either in cash or in the form of assignments of areas of land.

Who received pay in cash were known as naqdi.

Those paid through assignments of jagirs were called jagirdars.

The lowest rank was 10 and the highest was 5000 for the nobles.

Hence, the correct option is (A).

50. For Parajumbles, the best approach is to find connecting links between statements.

After close inspection of the given options, we see statement P is the 1st sentence.

Further, 2nd sentence should contain a time related word as P ends with 'born in'.Statement Q fulfills the required purpose.

Hence the correct arrangement would be- PRQ.

Hence, the correct option is (C).

51. Edward Jenner had discovered the Smallpox vaccination. It was the first successful vaccine developed. Smallpox vaccine is no longer available to the public. In 1972, routine smallpox vaccination in the United States ended. In 1980, the World Health Organization (WHO) declared smallpox was eliminated.

Hence, the correct option is (C).

52. Cancer disease is non-communicable in nature, rest all the diseases are communicable. A non-communicable disease is a disease that is not transmissible directly from one person to another.

Hence, the correct option is (D).

53. Seclusion means the state of being private and away from other people.

Solitariness means a person who lives alone or in solitude.

The option that is nearest in meaning to the underlined word 'seclusion' is solitariness'.

Hence, the correct option is (D).

54. Despot means a ruler or other person who holds absolute power, typically one who exercises it in a cruel or oppressive way.

Dictator means a ruler with total power over a country, typically one who has obtained control by force.

The option that is nearest in meaning to the underlined word 'despot' is 'dictator'.

Hence, the correct option is (B).

55. 'comprises six houses' should be there in place of 'comprises of six houses'.

'comprises' is not followed by 'of' preposition.

Correct sentence: This building comprises six houses three parking lots and one basement.

Hence, the correct option is (B).

56. Since first and second varieties are mixed in equal proportions,

So their average price $=$ Rs. $\dfrac{(116+145)}{2} =$ Rs. 130.50

So, now the mixture is formed by mixing two varieties,

One at Rs. 130.50 per kg and the other at say Rs. ' x' per kg in the ratio $2:2$,

i.e., $1:1$

We have to find ' x'

$\Rightarrow \dfrac{130.5+x}{2} = 153$

$\Rightarrow 130.5 + x = 306$

$\Rightarrow x = 306 - 130.5 =$ Rs. 175.5

Hence, the correct option is (A).

57. Given,

$(a+b):(b+c):(c+a) = 7k:6k:5k$

$\Rightarrow (a+b+c) \times 2 = 18k$

$\Rightarrow (a+b+c) = 9k$

$\Rightarrow 9k = 27$

$\Rightarrow k = 3$

$\Rightarrow a+b = 21$......(i)

$\Rightarrow b+c = 18$....(ii)

$\Rightarrow c+a = 15$......(iii)

Adding equation (i) and (iii),

$a+b+c+a = 21 + 15$

$\Rightarrow 2a+b+c = 36$

Putting the value of $b+c$ from equation (ii),

$\Rightarrow 2a + 18 = 36$

$\Rightarrow 2a = 36 - 18$

$\Rightarrow 2a = 18$

$\Rightarrow a = 9$

Putting the value of a in equation (i),

$\Rightarrow 9 + b = 21$

$\Rightarrow b = 21 - 9$

$\Rightarrow b = 12$

Putting the value of b in equation (ii),

$\Rightarrow 12 + c = 18$

$\Rightarrow c = 18 - 12$

$\Rightarrow c = 6$

$\therefore a = 9, b = 12, c = 6$

$\Rightarrow \dfrac{1}{a}:\dfrac{1}{b}:\dfrac{1}{c} = \dfrac{1}{9}:\dfrac{1}{12}:\dfrac{1}{6}$

$\Rightarrow \dfrac{1}{a}:\dfrac{1}{b}:\dfrac{1}{c} = 4:3:6$

Hence, the correct option is (A).

58. According to the passage, from 2nd paragraph, yet, the quantum of stake on offer made it clear that the government intended to retain a crucial stake, **appoint its own directors and continue to have a say in running the business**. Put off by the substantial degree of control the government wanted to retain in the airline after the disinvestment, several potential bidders stayed away from the sale, including, possibly the worthiest contender.

Statement II is a specific point and we can't say anything about it as it is not mentioned in the passage.

Hence, the correct option is (B).

59. According to the 2nd paragraph of the passage, yet, the quantum of stake on offer made it clear that the government intended to retain a crucial stake, appoint its own directors and continue to have a say in running the business.

So, the statement I is correct.

Statement II is nowhere suggested in the passage that the government itself tried to cancel the idea of disinvestment.

According to the 2nd paragraph of the passage, inefficiency, typical in a government-controlled setup, was bleeding Air India.

So, statement III suggests that it is usual to have inefficient officers in the government and there was nothing new in it.

It clearly validates that only statements I and III are correct.

Hence, the correct option is (D).

60. According to the 5th paragraph of the passage, **the airline said in a statement that the intensity of opposition to the privatization from political groups and the trade unions had surprised it and that in such an adverse climate, it was not confident it could play a useful role.**

The allegation of corruption was related to the Hinduja group.

Further, the passage has not mentioned any specific demands made by Singapore Airlines.

Thus, except option (B), all other statements are absurd and illogical.

Hence, the correct option is (B).

61. According to the 1st paragraph of the passage, air India's disinvestment, first attempted by the Atal Bihari Vajpayee government, is being revived. The **sale bid the last time was a flop,** shelved prematurely after all the bidders were either disqualified or dropped out. **The many factors that were and may still be at work against the sale are not widely understood. Unless overcome, they may again endanger the sale.**

The highlighted part above implies that none of the given statements is appropriate.

Hence, the correct option is (D).

62. According to the 2nd paragraph of the passage, in May 2000, bids were invited for a 40% stake in Air India, with a cap of 26% on foreign investment. The airline had reported losses for six straight years, had $70 million debt on its books and was fast losing traffic. More than 18,000 workers were on its rolls for a fleet of just about two dozen planes. Its employee-aircraft ratio, 750, was among the worst. **Singapore Airlines, in contrast, had 91 employees per aircraft.** Inefficiency, typical in a government-controlled setup, was bleeding Air India. Yet, the quantum of stake on offer made it clear that the government intended to retain a crucial stake, appoint its own directors and continue to have a say in running the business. Put off by the substantial degree of control the government wanted to retain in the airline after the disinvestment, several potential bidders stayed away from the sale, including, possibly the worthiest contender. Plus, in a sale carried out through competitive bidding, reduced interest can impact the valuation.

The highlighted sentence in the paragraph above clearly validates the fact what has been mentioned in option (C).

Hence, the correct option is (C).

63. Given:

Radius of cylinder (R) = 14 cm

Height of cylinder (h) = 25 cm

Radius of sphere (r) = 3.5 cm

Volume of the metal remains same before and after melting process.

Volume of the cylinder $= \pi R^2 h$

$= \dfrac{22}{7} \times 14 \times 14 \times 25$ = 15,400 cm³

Volume of sphere $= \dfrac{4}{3}\pi r^3$

$= \dfrac{4}{3} \times \dfrac{22}{7} \times 3.5 \times 3.5 \times 3.5$ = 179.67 cm³

$\therefore$ Number of sphere $= \dfrac{\text{Volume of cylinder}}{\text{volume of sphere}}$

$= \dfrac{15400}{179.67} = 85.71 \approx 85$

Thus, 85 such complete sphere can be made.

Hence, the correct option is (B).

64. The world-famous 'Khajuraho' sculptures are located in Madhya Pradesh.

The Khajuraho Group of Monuments are a group of Hindu and Jain temples in Chhatarpur district, Madhya Pradesh, India, about 175 kilometres southeast of Jhansi. They are a UNESCO World Heritage Site. The temples are famous for their nagara-style architectural symbolism and their erotic sculptures. Most Khajuraho temples were built between 885 AD and 1050 AD by the Chandela dynasty.

Hence, the correct option is (B).

65. Anuvrata concept was given by Jainism.

Anuvrata is the philosophy of change given by Jainism. Its sole purpose is to enable man to introspect, understand his own nature and to make efforts to transform it.

Hence, the correct option is (A).

66. The teaching-learning process takes place in three phases. Evaluation is integral to the teaching-learning process as it helps in facilitating student learning and improving instruction. It is a systematic way of collecting information to make a judgment about student learning. It is conducted during different stages of a teaching-learning process, i.e. at the beginning, during, and at the end. Diagnostic evaluation is one of the techniques of evaluation the teacher uses in the teaching-learning process.

Hence, the correct option is (A).

67. Assessment of the child's abilities can only be done through feedback. It helps us to know whether the child has learned what you have taught and whether your teaching is effective. Giving and receiving feedback is a difficult undertaking as it requires the ability to deal with the feelings that arise.

In the case of negative feedback, there is always some resistance and some degree of unwillingness in its acceptance.

It is not almost always accepted. Students might show resistance because they want to hear always only good news and resist bad and unpleasant news.

It creates fear, a sense of humiliation, and frustration.

For example, "No, you are incorrect" is negative feedback as it provides a negative response to the activity being done.

Hence, the correct option is (B).

68. The flute is considered to be the most popular musical instrument, as it is made from natural bamboo, hence people also

call it 'bamboo flute'. The flute-making process is not very difficult. Firstly the knots inside the flute are removed. Then a total of seven holes are dug on his body. The first hole is left to blow through the mouth, the remaining holes give the job of making different sounds.

Hence, the correct option is (A).

69. M.F. Hussain started the painting with the film's posters. M.F. Hussain is a famous painter from Maharashtra whose entire life was devoted to painting and who are considered to be progressive painters. Maqbool Fida Hussain was awarded the Padma Vibhushan, India's second highest civilian award, in 1991 by the Government of India in the field of art.

Hence, the correct option is (C).

70. The theme for National Youth Day (Yuva Diwas) 2019 is "Transforming Education".

National Youth Day (Yuva Diwas) is celebrated in India on 12th January on the birthday of a social reformer, philosopher and thinker Swami Vivekananda (156th).

Hence, the correct option is (B).

71. International Yoga Day is celebrated every 21st June. Its inception in 2015. It is an international day for yoga was declared unanimously by the United Nations General Assembly. Yoga is a physical, mental and spiritual practice that originated in India.

Hence, the correct option is (A).

72. Given,

One diagonal of a rhombus is 62 cm more than another diagonal.

Length of side of rhombus = 41 cm

Let length of diagonals of rhombus is '2a' and '2a + 62' respectively.

Now,

Side^2 = Half of first diagonal^2 + Half of second diagonal^2

$$41^2 = \left(\frac{2a}{2}\right)^2 + \left(\frac{2a+62}{2}\right)^2$$

$$\Rightarrow 1681 = a^2 + (a+31)^2$$

$$\Rightarrow a = 9$$

So,

$$\text{Area of rhombus} = \frac{1}{2} \times d_1 \times d_2$$

$$= \frac{1}{2} \times 2a \times (2a + 62)$$

$$= \frac{1}{2} \times 18 \times 80$$

$$= 720 \text{ cm}^2$$

Hence, the correct option is (B).

73. Given,

ΔABC is a right-angle triangle.

AB = 6 cm

BC = 8 cm

∠ABC = 90°

PQRB is a largest square in right-angle triangle.

ΔXYZ is an equilateral triangle.

$$\text{Side of largest square in right-angle triangle} = \frac{(P \times B)}{(P+B)}$$

$$= \frac{(6 \times 8)}{(6+8)}$$

$$= \frac{48}{14}$$

$$= \left(\frac{24}{7}\right) \text{ cm}$$

Radius of a circle which is inscribed in a square = (Side of square)/2

$$= \frac{\left(\frac{24}{7}\right)}{2}$$

$$= \left(\frac{12}{7}\right) \text{ cm}$$

Radius of outer circle in equilateral triangle = (Side of equilateral triangle)/ $\sqrt{3}$

$$\frac{12}{7} = (\text{Side of triangle}/ \sqrt{3})$$

$$\text{Side of triangle} = \frac{12\sqrt{3}}{7}$$

$$\text{Area of equilateral triangle} = \left(\frac{\sqrt{3}}{4}\right) \times (\text{side})^2$$

$$= \left(\frac{\sqrt{3}}{4}\right) \times \left(\frac{12\sqrt{3}}{7}\right)^2$$

$$= \left(\frac{\sqrt{3}}{4}\right) \times \frac{(144 \times 3)}{49}$$

$$= \left(\frac{108\sqrt{3}}{49}\right) \text{ cm}^2$$

$$\therefore \text{Area of equilateral triangle} = \left(\frac{108\sqrt{3}}{49}\right) \text{ cm}^2$$

Hence, the correct option is (A).

74. Given-

75 is added to 75% of a number and the result obtained is the number itself.

Let the number be a.

$$\Rightarrow 75 + (75\% \times a) = a$$

$$\Rightarrow 75 + \left(\frac{75}{100} \times a\right) = a$$

$$\Rightarrow 75 + \frac{3a}{4} = a$$

$\Rightarrow 75 = a - \dfrac{3a}{4}$

$\Rightarrow 75 = \dfrac{a}{4}$

$\Rightarrow 75 \times 4 = a$

$\Rightarrow a = 300$

Hence, the correct option is (C).

75. Given-

The sum of two numbers is 2490.

Let the two numbers are A, B.

$\Rightarrow A + B = 2490$

6.5% of the first number is equal to 8.5% of the second number.

$\Rightarrow 6.5\% \times A = 8.5\% \times B$

$\Rightarrow \dfrac{65}{1000} \times A = \dfrac{85}{1000} \times B$

$\Rightarrow 13 \times A = 17 \times B$

$\Rightarrow \dfrac{A}{B} = \dfrac{17}{13}$

Let $A = 17k, B = 13k$.

$\Rightarrow A + B = 2490$

$\Rightarrow 17k + 13k = 2490$

$\Rightarrow 30k = 2490$

$\Rightarrow k = 83$

First number $= 17k$

$= 17 \times 83$

$= 1411$

Second number $= 13k$

$= 13 \times 83$

$= 1079$

Greater number $= 1411$

Hence, the correct option is (C).

76. Let the two inlet pipes be A and B.

Let the total work be 36 units and the efficiency of A and B be $2x$ and x.

∵ The two can fill the empty cistern in 12 hours,

∴ $\dfrac{36}{(2x+x)} = 12$

$\Rightarrow x = 1$

$\Rightarrow$ Time taken by more efficient pipe $A = \dfrac{36}{2x} = \dfrac{36}{2} = 18$ hours

Hence, the correct option is (D).

77. As we know,

Efficiency is inversely proportional to time

Efficiency ratio of Garima and (Garima's sister + Garima) = 45 : 81 = 5 : 9

Efficiency of Garima's sister + Garima = 9

Efficiency of Garima's sister = 9 – 5 = 4

Total work = 45 × 9 = 405

Let the work be completed in x days

According to the question

$\Rightarrow$ 5x + 4(x – 9) = 405

$\Rightarrow$ 9x – 36 = 405

$\Rightarrow$ x = 49 days

Hence, the correct option is (A).

78. $= \dfrac{3.157 \times 4126 \times 3.198}{63.972 \times 2835.121}$

$\approx \dfrac{3.2 \times 4126 \times 3.2}{64 \times 2835}$

$= \dfrac{32 \times 4126 \times 32}{64 \times 2835} \times \dfrac{1}{100}$

$= \dfrac{66016}{2835} \times \dfrac{1}{100}$

$= \dfrac{23.28}{100}$

$= 0.23$

≈ 0.2

Hence, the correct option is (C).

79. Mean of the given data

$\Rightarrow \dfrac{35+38}{2} = 36.5$

$\Rightarrow \dfrac{38+41}{2} = 39.5$

$\Rightarrow \dfrac{41+44}{2} = 42.5$

$\Rightarrow \dfrac{44+47}{2} = 45.5$

$\Rightarrow \dfrac{47+50}{2} = 48.5$

Average weight of all class

$\Rightarrow \dfrac{36.5 \times 3 + 39.5 \times 13 + 42.5 \times 13 + 45.5 \times 10 + 48.5 \times 5}{44}$

$\Rightarrow \dfrac{1873}{44}$

∴ 42.56 is the average of the class.

Hence, the correct option is (C).

80. Median for the distribution is given by $L + \dfrac{\frac{N}{2} - c.f.}{f} \times h$

Where L is the lower limit of the median class

$c.f.$ is the cumulative frequency of the class preceding the median class.

f is the frequency of median class

h is the length of the class interval

So, the median requires the construction of the cumulative frequency distribution.

Hence, the correct option is (C).

81. Selling price $=$ Rs. 48

Loss $\% = 20\%$

Discount $= MP - SP$

$CP = \dfrac{SP}{100 - \text{Percentage loss}} \times 100$

$\Rightarrow$ Cost price $= \dfrac{48}{(100 - 20)} \times 100$

$= \dfrac{480}{8} =$ Rs. 60

Now, to earn 20% profit,

$\Rightarrow$ Selling price $= 60 + \left(\dfrac{20}{100} \times 60\right)$

$= 60 + 12 =$ Rs. 72

Hence, the correct option is (A).

82. Let the cost price of the article $=$ Rs. 100

Marked price $= 100 + \left(\dfrac{50}{100} \times 100\right)$

$= 100 + 50 =$ Rs. 150

Discount $\% = 10\%$

Selling price $= 150 - \left(\dfrac{10}{100} \times 150\right)$

$= 150 - 15 =$ Rs. 135

So, Profit $\% = \dfrac{(135 - 100)}{100} \times 100 = 35\%$

Hence, the correct option is (C).

83. Darwan Singh Negi was the hero of the 1st Garhwal Rifles during the First World War (1914-18).

Darwan Singh Negi VC (November 1881 – 24 June 1950) was the second Indian soldier ever to receive the Victoria cross from the hands of H.M. The King Emperor on the field of battle and was among the earliest Indian recipients of the Victoria Cross (VC), the highest and most prestigious award for gallantry in the face of the enemy that can be awarded to British and Commonwealth forces.

Hence, the correct option is (B).

84. Hansa Manral – Dronacharya Award

Dronacharya Award by the President of India, His Excellency KR Narayan on 29 September 2001. Smt. Hansa Manral Sharma believes that innumerable talents are hidden in Uttaranchal.

Hence, the correct option is (D).

85. 345678 x 999999

Here, we can write 999999 as = 1000000 - 1

Now, solving by taking above representation

345678 × (1000000 - 1)

= 345678000000 - 345678

= 345677654322

Hence, the correct option is (C).

86. Among the options, only Mirabai Chanu is NOT a recipient of Rajiv Gandhi Khel Ratna 2020.

Mirabai Chanu is an Indian weightlifter.

- She was honored with the Rajiv Gandhi Khel Ratna in 2018.

Rajiv Gandhi Khel Ratna 2020 winners:

- Rohit Sharma (Cricket)
- Mariyappan Thangavelu (Paralympian)
- Manika Batra (Table Tennis)
- Vinesh Phogat (Wrestler)
- Rani Rampal (Hockey)

Hence, the correct option is (D).

87. The summer Olympic Games 2024 to be held in Paris.

- Paris will become the second city to host the Olympics three times, after London (1908, 1948, and 2012).
- It was previously the host in the year 1900 and 1924. The year 2024 will mark the centenary of the Paris Games of 1924.
- These will be the sixth Olympic Games hosted by France (three summers and three winters).
- Paris was elected as the host city on September 13, 2017, at the 131st IOC Session in Lima, Peru.
- Paris is the capital of France.
- Currencies: Euro, CFP franc.

Hence, the correct option is (D).

88. Given:

A = { x : x ∈ N, 0 < x < 6}

B = {x : x is a prime natural number, 0 < x < 10}

A = { x : x ∈ N, 0 < x < 6}

A = {1, 2, 3, 4, 5}

B = {x : x is a prime natural number, 0 < x < 10}

B = {2, 3, 5, 7}

A - B = {1, 2, 3, 4, 5} - {2, 3, 5, 7}

= {1, 4}

∴ The value A - B is {1, 4}.

Hence, the correct option is (B).

89. Given:

$$^{n}C_r + 2 \times (^{n}C_{r-1}) + {}^{n}C_{r-2}$$
$$= {}^{n}C_r + (^{n}C_{r-1}) + (^{n}C_{r-1}) + {}^{n}C_{r-2}$$
$$= {}^{(n+1)}C_r + {}^{(n+1)}C_{r-1} \quad (\because {}^{n}C_r + {}^{n}C_{r-1} = {}^{(n+1)}C_r)$$
$$= (n+2)C_r$$

Hence, the correct option is (A).

90. Since the numbers are given in the form of a ratio that means their common factors have been canceled.

Each one's common factor is HCF.

And here HCF = 12,

So, the numbers are 12, 24, and 36.
Hence, the correct option is (A).

91. Given:

AB ∥ CD

∠APQ = 50°

∠PRD = 127°

Calculation:

∠APQ = ∠x   ---- (Alternate angles are equal)

⇒∠x = 50° ------ (1)

∠APR = ∠PRD = 127°   ---- (Alternate angles are equal)

Since, ∠APR = ∠APQ + ∠y

⇒∠APQ + ∠y = 127°

⇒ 50° + ∠y = 127°

⇒ ∠y = 127° - 50°

⇒ ∠y = 77° ------(2)

So, from (1) & (2) we get,

∠y - ∠x = 77° - 50° = 27°

∴ The value of y − x is 27°.

Hence, the correct option is (C).

92. The sentence 'B' is independent of any other sentences as it is giving general information about "sad eerie sounds". So, 'B' is the first sentence.

The phrase "feel nervous" mentioned in the sentence 'A' is linked with the "sad eerie sounds" which is mentioned in the sentence 'B'. So, 'A' follows 'B'.

The pronoun "He" mentioned in the sentence 'D' refers back to the noun "Mr. Oliver" mentioned in the sentence 'A'. So, 'D' follows 'A'.

The sentence 'C' is concluding the paragraph. So, 'C' makes the last sentence.

Hence, the correct option is (A).

93. Sodium Benzoate is used extensively in the preservation of various foods and beverages like fruit juices. It has anti-fungal properties i.e., it doesn't let the fungus grow.

Citric acid is a natural preservative and is also used to add an acidic (sour) taste to foods and soft drinks.

Sodium chloride In its edible form of table salt, it is commonly used as a condiment and food preservative.

Hence, the correct option is (C).

94. A noble gas, any of the seven chemical elements that make up Group 18 (VIII-A) of the periodic table. The elements are helium (He), neon (Ne), argon (Ar), krypton (Kr), xenon (Xe), radon (Rn), and oganesson (Og).

Hence, the correct option is (B).

95. Remedial method refers to the method of teaching that helps the teacher to provide learners with the necessary help and guidance to overcome the problems which are determined through diagnosing them.

Remedial method is used for 'Problematic Children' as the objective of the remedial method is to give additional help to learners who have fallen behind the rest of the class in any topic or subject. It is the process of identifying slow learners and improving their ability to learn something. It transmits practical experiences to learners according to their diverse needs

Problematic Children' are provided with remedial actions to correct the difficulties. These remediation actions are done individually and specific to the problem.

Hence, the correct option is (B).

96. The difference between the percentage of candidates qualified to appear in different year pairs are:

For 1994 and 1995 = 50% - 30% = 20%

For 1995 and 1996 = 60% - 50% = 10%

For 1998 and 1999 = 80% - 80% = 0

For 1999 and 2000 = 80% - 60% = 20%

For 1997 and 1998 = 80% - 50% = 30%

Thus, the maximum difference is between the years 1997 and 1998.

Hence, the correct option is (D).

97. The given graph gives the data for the percentage of candidates qualified to appear and unless the absolute values of number of candidates qualified or candidates appeared is known we cannot compare the absolute values for any two years.

So, the data is inadequate to solve this question.

Hence, the correct option is (D).

98. Given,

The number of candidates qualified in 1998 = 21200

Let the number of candidates appeared in 1998 be x.

According to the question,

80% of x = 21200

$$\Rightarrow x = \frac{21200 \times 100}{80}$$

$$\Rightarrow x = 26500$$

Hence, the correct option is (C).

99. The total number of candidates qualified in 1996 and 1997 together, cannot be determined until we know at least, the number of candidates appeared in any one of the two years 1996 or 1997 or the percentage of candidates qualified to appear in 1996 and 1997 together.

So, the data is inadequate.

Hence, the correct option is (D).

100. Given,

The total number of candidates qualified in 1999 and 2000 together = 33500

The number of candidates appeared in 1999 = 26500

According to question,

The number of candidates qualified in 1999 = (80% of 26500) = 21200

Therefore the number of candidates qualified in the year 2000 = (33500 - 21200) = 12300

Let the number of candidates appeared in the year 2000 be x.

Then,

$$60\% \text{ of } x = 12300$$

$$\Rightarrow x = \left(\frac{12300 \times 100}{60}\right)$$

$$\Rightarrow x = 20500$$

Hence, the correct option is (C).

Q.1 Which company has signed an MoU with the Gujarat govt to set up an IT-enabled Services (ITeS) Park in Vadodara in August 2022?

A. Aditya Birla Group
B. Reliance Industries Ltd
C. Larsen & Toubro (L&T) Ltd
D. Adani Group

Q.2 Which organisation has partnered with NITI Aayog to use AI, IoT, Blockchain and Drones to support small and marginal farmers?

A. World Bank
B. WEF
C. IMF
D. ADB

Q.3 In 2022, India has nominated which dance form to be inscribed on UNESCO's intangible cultural heritage list?

A. Loor
B. Garba
C. Khor
D. Ghoomar

Q.4 Pradeep Kumar Rawat assumed charge as India's new ambassador to_____ in March 2022.

A. China
B. Malaysia
C. Poland
D. USA

Q.5 Which of the following describe correctly the Group of Seven Countries (G-7)?

A. They are developing countries
B. They are industrialized countries
C. They are holding Atomic Bomb technology
D. They are the countries that can launch their own satellites

Q.6 Which of the following country is not a member of the SAARC?

A. Myanmar
B. Bhutan
C. Nepal
D. Maldives

Q.7 The HCF of two numbers a and b is c. What is the LCM of those two numbers?

A. $\frac{ab}{c}$
B. $\frac{ac}{b}$
C. $\frac{b}{ca}$
D. abc

Q.8 The sum of radii of two spheres is 10 cm and the sum of their volume is 880 cm³. What will be the product of their radii?

A. $\frac{79}{3}$
B. $\frac{64}{3}$
C. $\frac{75}{7}$
D. $\frac{87}{3}$

Q.9 If $^nP_r = 720\,{}^nC_r$, then the value of r is:

A. 4
B. 5
C. 6
D. 7

Q.10 Find the value of x where $^xP_3 = {}^{(2x-1)}P_2, x \geq 3, x \in N$.

A. 3
B. 1
C. 5
D. 7

Q.11 If the mean of a set of 10 observations $x_1, x_2, ..., x_{10}$ is 30 then the mean of $x_1 + 5, x_2 + 10, ..., x_{10} + 50$ is:

A. 27.5
B. 57.5
C. 53.5
D. 59.5

Q.12 For two variables x and y, the two regression coefficients are $b_{yx} = -\frac{3}{2}$ and $b_{xy} = -\frac{1}{6}$. The correlation coefficient between x and y is:

A. $-\frac{1}{4}$
B. $\frac{1}{4}$
C. $-\frac{1}{2}$
D. $\frac{1}{2}$

Q.13 $\dfrac{(469+174)^2-(469-174)^2}{(469\times174)} = ?$

[HSSC Canal Patwari, 2019]

A. 1
B. 4
C. 295
D. 643

Q.14 The credit for discovering the Valley of Flowers goes to:

A. William Smith
B. Margaret Laigi
C. Richard Holdsworth
D. Frank Smythe

Q.15 Who has been awarded the Padma Shri from Uttarakhand in 2021?

A. Prem Chand Sharma
B. Narendra Singh Negi
C. Anil Baluni
D. Pritam Bhartwan

Q.16 One of two equal sides and perimeter of an isosceles triangular table is 100 cm and 360 cm respectively. The area of the triangular table is:

A. 2400 cm²
B. 4500 cm²
C. 6000 cm²
D. 4800 cm²

Q.17 In the figure given below, if the area of triangle BCD is 28% of the area of parallelogram ACDE, then find the ratio of the lengths of the parallel sides of the trapezium ABDE.

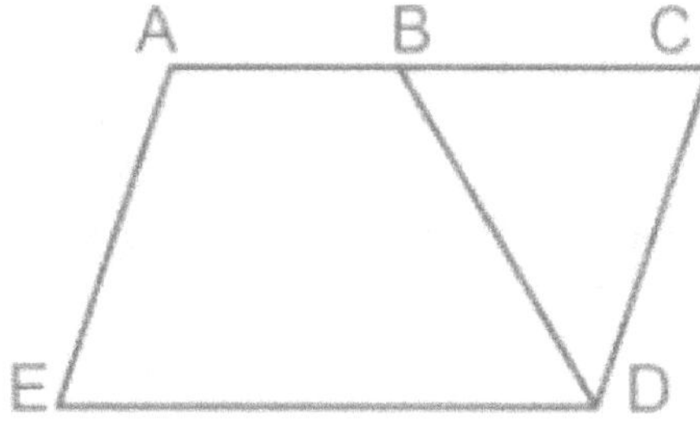

A. 11 : 25
B. 17 : 25
C. 21 : 50
D. 29 : 50

Q.18 At what rate% per annum will Rs. 2304 amounts to Rs. 2500 in two years compounded annually?

A. $4\frac{1}{6}\%$
B. $6\frac{1}{4}\%$
C. $5\frac{1}{6}\%$
D. $4\frac{1}{5}\%$

Q.19 If a certain sum of money becomes 9 times itself in 2 years. Find the rate of compound interest.

A. 50%
B. 100%
C. 200%
D. 80%

Q.20

Name	Chemical formula
1. Baking Powder	$NaHCO_3$

2. Vinegar	$C_2H_4O_3$
3. Bleaching powder	$Ca(ClO)_2$
4. Chalk	$CaCl_2$

Which of the above matching is correct? Choose the correct option.

A. 1, 2 and 4 only
B. 1 and 3 only
C. 1, 3 and 4 only
D. 1, 2 and 3 only

Q.21 The chief source of naphthalene is ________.

A. Coal-tar
B. Diesel
C. Charcoal
D. Camphor

Q.22 The difference between two complementary angles is 15°. Find the ratio of greater and smaller angles.

A. 7 : 5
B. 6 : 5
C. 7 : 6
D. 5 : 4

Q.23 National Education Day is celebrated on ______ every year.

[UP Police Constable, 2018]

A. 27th October
B. 4th March
C. 17th September
D. 11th November

Q.24 When is National Hindi Day observed in India?

[UP Police Constable, 2018]

A. 14th September
B. 14th November
C. 14th December
D. 14th June

Q.25 Mukul, Atul and Rahul started a business. Mukul invested $\frac{2}{7}$th of the total investment and the total investment of Mukul and Atul is equals to the investment of Rahul. If they distributed profit in the capital ratio and Atul received Rs 1530, find the total profit.

A. Rs. 6550
B. Rs. 6920
C. Rs. 7140
D. Rs. 7350

Ques (26-27):Direction: In the following question, out of the four alternatives, select the alternative which best expresses the meaning of the Idiom/Phrase.

Q.26 Fold like a cheap suitcase

A. To attain good health
B. Of strong determination
C. To submit or give up easily
D. To do a cheap business

Q.27 To take to task

A. To forgive
B. To slap
C. To give extra work
D. To reprimand

Ques (28-30):Direction: In the following question, the sentence is given with blank to be filled in with an appropriate word. Select the correct alternative out of the four and indicate it by selecting the appropriate option.

Q.28 He knew that an apple ________ not be plucked while it is green.

A. Should
B. Is
C. Shall
D. Can

Q.29 You haven't many teeth left, but ______ few you have are sharp enough to make me shudder.

A. A
B. An
C. Very
D. The

Q.30 I can always tell when my friend is ______ because she bites her lip.

A. Lying
B. Lain
C. Lye
D. Lay

Ques (31-32):Direction: In the following question, a sentence has been given in Active/Passive Voice. Out of the four alternatives suggested, select the one which best expresses the same sentence in Passive/Active Voice.

Q.31 Stamp collection interested the boy.

A. The boy were interested in stamp collection
B. The boy interested in stamp collection
C. The boy was interested for stamp collection
D. The boy was interested in stamp collection

Q.32 It is your duty to make tea at eleven O'clock.

A. You are asked to make tea at eleven O'clock
B. You are required to make tea at eleven O'clock
C. You are supposed to make tea at eleven O'clock
D. Tea is to be made by you at eleven O'clock

Q.33 A number when divided by 6 leaves a remainder 3. When the square of the number is divided by 6, the remainder is __________.

[NCHM JEE (Hotel Mgmt & Catering), 2016]

A. 0
B. 1
C. 2
D. 3

Q.34 Find the sum of all even natural numbers less than 75.

[NCHM JEE (Hotel Mgmt & Catering), 2016]

A. 1410
B. 1406
C. 1408
D. 1412

Ques (35-39):Direction: Study the following bar graph carefully to answer the given questions.

The following bar graph shows the income and expenditures (in crore) of five companies A, B, C, D, E in the year 2017.

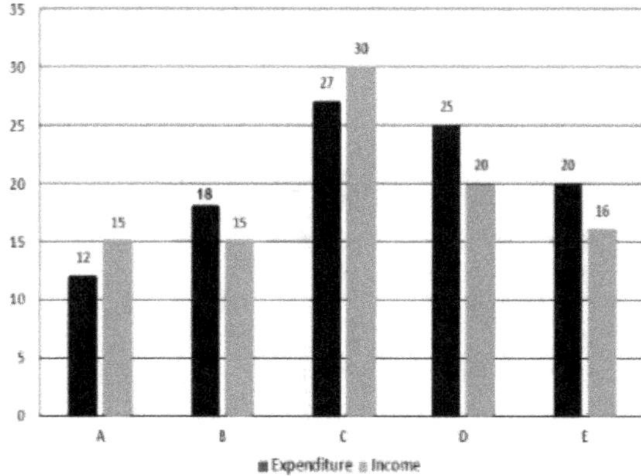

Q.35 Company C had a percentage of profit/loss of (If it is calculated on expenditure):

A. 10% loss
B. 10% profit
C. 11.11% loss
D. 11.11% profit

Q.36 What was the approximate percentage of profit/loss of all the five companies together? (If it is calculated on expenditure)

A. 5.9% loss
B. 5.9% profit
C. 6.3% loss
D. 6.3% profit

Q.37 Which company earned the maximum profit percentage?

A. A **B.** B **C.** C **D.** D

Q.38 If the income of company A in the year 2017 was 10% less than its income in the year 2016 and the company had earned a profit of 10% in the year 2016, then find its expenditure in the year 2016 (in crores).

A. 22 **B.** 25 **C.** 25.2 **D.** 30

Q.39 If the income of company A in the year 2017 was 10% less than its income in the year 2016 and the company had earned a profit of 10% in the year 2016, then find its expenditure in the year 2016 (in crores).

A. 13 **B.** 15 **C.** 16 **D.** 18

Q.40 Sri Lanka gets more radiation than Srinagar because:

A. It located in temperate region
B. It located in torrid zone
C. Most of the areas are desert
D. It has continental location

Q.41 Which of the following is not true about about the Equator:

A. It divides the Earth in to two equal halves
B. The shortest distance between any two points lies over Great circle
C. Most of the sunrays receives directly received here
D. The equator lies between 23.5°N to 66.5°N

Q.42 Which of the following statements can be taken as evidence to show that the Earth is spherical?

A. The rotation of the earth from east to west
B. Earth's various parts have night or day
C. The horizon of the earth is seen to be curved when seeing from satellite
D. The revolution of the earth around the sun

Q.43 Direction: Rearrange the following sentences (P), (Q), and (R) to make a meaningful paragraph and answer the questions that follow.

It is a good sign
P. that the ratio remains the same despite
Q. the revenue base coming down because
R. of increased devolution to States

A. QRP **B.** RPQ **C.** PRQ **D.** PQR

Q.44 Moscow is situated on the banks of ____________.

A. Moskva river **B.** Spree river
C. Volga river **D.** Tagus river

Q.45 The famous Gayatri mantra was created by whom?

A. Manu **B.** Kaushtikya
C. Vishvamitra **D.** Udgatri

Q.46 Direction: In the following question, some part of the sentence may have errors. Find out which part of the sentence has an error and select the appropriate option. If a sentence is free from error, select 'No Error' option.

Ten new members (A)/have been enrolled (B)/and seven have resigned. (C)/No error (D).

A. (A) **B.** (B) **C.** (C) **D.** (D)

Q.47 If $x + \left(\dfrac{1}{x}\right) = 3$, then the value of $\dfrac{(3x^2-4x+3)}{(x^2-x+1)}$ is:

A. $\dfrac{4}{3}$ **B.** $\dfrac{3}{2}$ **C.** $\dfrac{5}{2}$ **D.** $\dfrac{5}{3}$

Q.48 How much work is done in moving a charge of 4 C across two points having a potential difference of 12 V?

[RRB/RRC Group D, 2018]

A. 48 J **B.** 3 J **C.** 40 J **D.** 12 J

Q.49 Find the energy possessed by an object of mass 10 kg when it is at a height of 8 m above the ground. Given $g = 9.8$ ms $^{-2}$

[RRB/RRC Group D, 2018]

A. 784 J **B.** 588 J **C.** 520 J **D.** 528 J

Q.50 $\dfrac{3.8}{1.25}$, written as a pure decimal, will be:

[RRB/RRC Group D, 2018]

A. 3.14 **B.** 3.04 **C.** 3.06 **D.** 3.08

Q.51 Find the value of- $\left(\dfrac{\sqrt{180}\times\sqrt{18}\times\sqrt{5}\times\sqrt{3}}{\sqrt{96\times5}}\right)^{-2} + \sqrt[3]{4\dfrac{12}{125}}$

A. $\dfrac{256}{135}$ **B.** $\dfrac{405}{668}$ **C.** $\dfrac{668}{405}$ **D.** $\dfrac{568}{405}$

Q.52 The 'Kathasaritsagara' is written by:

[SSC Sub Inspector (CPO), 2020]

A. Kalidasa **B.** Bhasa
C. Jayadeva **D.** Somadeva

Q.53 How much assistance will be given under the Indira Gandhi Matritva Poshan Yojana of the Rajasthan government?

A. Rs. 2,000 **B.** Rs. 6,000
C. Rs. 4,000 **D.** Rs. 8,000

Ques (54-58):Direction: Read the following passage carefully and answer the question given below it.

Two principles are involved in the controversy about the presence of foreign-controlled media in the country; the free flow of ideas and images across national borders and the need to safeguard the national interest and preserve cultural autonomy. Both are valid but both are at loggerheads because each has been used to promote less lofty goals. The first principle conforms to a moral imperative: the freedom to expression cannot rhyme with restrictions imposed by any government. But the free flow rhetoric also clouds the fact that the powerful Western, and especially American media, can and often do present, subtly or brazenly, news in a manner that promotes Western political, ideological and strategic interests. Besides, Western entertainment programmes present lifestyles and values that run counter to the lifestyles and values cherished by traditional societies. All this explains why so many Indian newspapers, magazines and news agencies have sought protection from the courts to prevent foreign publications and news agencies from operating in the country. Their arguments are weak on two counts. As the bitter debate on a new world information and communication order demonstrated in the late seventies and early eighties, many of those who resent Western 'invasion' in the fields of information and culture are no great friends of democracy. Secondly, the threat of such an 'invasion' has been aired by those media groups in the developing countries that fear that their business interests will be harmed if Western groups, equipped with large financial and technological resources and superior management skills, are allowed to operate in the country without let.The fear is valid but it goes against the grain of the economic reform programme. The presence of foreign newspapers and television channels will increase competition, which, in the course of time, can only lead to the upgradation of dynamic Indian newspapers and television channels, even while they drive the rest out of the market. One way to strike a balance between the two antagonistic principles would be to allow foreign media entry into the country, provided the India state treats them at par with the domestic media on all fronts. On the import of technology, for instance, foreign media cannot be allowed duty concessions denied to their Indian counterparts. Foreign media will also have to face legal consequences should they run foul of Indian laws. Why, for example, should the BBC, or Time magazine or The Economist get away by showing a map of Kashmir, which is at variance with the official Indian map? Why should they go scot-free when they allow secessionists and terrorists to air their views without giving the government the right to reply, or when they depict sexually explicit scenes, which would otherwise not be cleared by the Censor Board? Since the government can do precious little in the matter, especially about satellite broadcasts, what if it should consider attaching the properties of the offending parties? Demands of this kind are bound to be voiced unless New Delhi makes it clear to the foreign media that they will have to respect Indian susceptibilities, especially where it concerns the country's integrity and its culture. It may be able to derive some inspiration from France's successful attempts in the recent GATT to protect its cinematography industry.

Q.54 Choose the word or group of words that is most similar in meaning to the word given in the passage.

RHETORIC

A. Rhyming words

B. Persuasive speaking

C. Dull monologue

D. Tongue-in-cheek

Q.55 Choose the word or group of words that is most similar in meaning to the word given in the passage.

SUSCEPTIBILITIES

A. Norms

B. Weaknesses

C. Influences

D. Sensitivities

Q.56 Choose the word that is most opposite in meaning to the word given in the passage.

ANTAGONISTIC

A. Counteract

B. Coincidental

C. Equal

D. Corresponding

Q.57 Which of the following is the meaning of the phrase "at loggerheads", as used in the passage?

A. In league with

B. Unimportant

C. Out of place

D. Opposite to each other

Q.58 Which of the following seems to be the most likely purpose of writing this passage?

A. To criticize foreign media

B. To highlight the exploitation by developed nations

C. To highlight the steps and caution to be taken about the entry of foreign media

D. To make the public aware of the technological and managerial superiority of western media

Q.59 'Lakh Baksh' was a title of:

[DSSSB TGT Social Science, 2014]

A. Qutubuddin Aibak

B. Iltutmish

C. Alauddin Khilji

D. Firoz Shah

Q.60 Consider the following statements with respect to the Foreign Trade of India:

1. Financial services account for the majority of export services.

2. India is suffering from a capital account deficit in recent years.

3. Crude Petroleum is the highest imported commodity.

Which of the statements given above is/are incorrect?

A. 1 and 2 only

B. 3 only

C. 1 and 3 only

D. 1, 2 and 3

Q.61 Which of the following is/are the initiatives taken by the government to enhance the domestic production of steel in India?

1. Inclusion of specialty steel under Production Linked Incentive scheme.

2. Offering steel to MSMEs at export parity price.

3. Preference to domestically produced iron and steel in government procurement.

Select the correct answer using the code given below.

A. 1 and 2 only

B. 2 and 3 only

C. 3 only

D. 1, 2 and 3

Q.62 Direction: In this question, each item consists of six sentences of passage. The first and sixth sentences are given in the beginning as SI and S6. The middle four-sentence in each have been jumbled up and labelled as P, Q, R and S. You are required to find the proper sequence of the four sentences.

S1: The Indian Civil Service gradually developed into one of the most efficient and powerful civil services in the world.

S6: though these qualities obviously served British, and not Indian interests.

P: and often participated in the making of policy

Q: independence, integrity and hard work

R: They developed certain traditions of

S: Its members exercised vast power

The proper sequence should be

A. P Q R S   B. Q R S P   C. R S Q P   D. S P R Q

Q.63 Which country has no cinema theaters?
A. Saudi Arabia
B. Iraq
C. Pennsylvania
D. None of the above

Q.64 In which year was the Arjuna Award given to Sachin Tendulkar?

[Madhya Pradesh Public Service Commission (MPPSC), 2017]

A. 1990   B. 1994   C. 1997   D. 1999

Q.65 The commonwealth games were organised first time in:
[Madhya Pradesh Public Service Commission (MPPSC), 2017]

A. 1922   B. 1925   C. 1927   D. 1930

Q.66 The salaries of X, Y and Z are in the ratio of 10:12:15. They are awarded increments of 40%, 50% and 60% respectively. What is the new ratio of their salaries?

[Delhi Forest Guard, 2021]

A. 7 : 9 : 14
B. 7 : 9 : 12
C. 7 : 10 : 12
D. 8 : 9 : 12

Q.67 In a bag, there are coins of 25 paise, 50 paise and Rs 1 in the ratio of 8 : 4 : 1. In there is 30 in total, how many 50 paise coins are there?

[Delhi Forest Guard, 2021]

A. 48   B. 6   C. 12   D. 24

Q.68 The question below consists of a set of labeled sentences. Out of the four options given, select the most logical order of the sentences to form a coherent paragraph.

P. have a great influence
Q. and they often shape our personality
R. on our adult lives
S. events in our childhood

A. SPRQ   B. SQRP   C. SRQP   D. PQRS

Ques (69-70):Direction: Each item in this section consists of a sentence with an underlined word/words followed by four words. Select the option that is nearest in meaning to the underlined word and mark your response accordingly.

Q.69 The harder we kick, the better the ball bounces back.

[UPSC NDA, 2020]

A. Relapse   B. Deflates   C. Inflates   D. Ascends

Q.70 I plan and execute.

[UPSC NDA, 2020]

A. desire
B. debate
C. accomplish
D. discard

Q.71 Which of the numbers given below is the square root of 16384?

A. 132   B. 128   C. 118   D. 122

Q.72 Who had composed Brahmavadini the hymns of Vedas?
A. Gargi
B. Savitri
C. Brahmini
D. Ghosha

Q.73 Who among the following founded the Mahila Samajik Sammelan (Bharat Mahila Parishad) under the parent National Social Conference in 1904?
A. Ramabai Ranade
B. Pandita Ramabai Saraswati
C. Cornilia Sorabji
D. Tarabai Premchand

Q.74 A rectangular field 242 m long has got an area of 4840 sq.m. The cost of fencing that field on all the four sides, if 1 m of fencing costs 10 rupees, in rupees is

[Punjab Patwari, 2016]

A. 524   B. 262   C. 2620   D. 5240

Q.75 A sphere and hemisphere have the radius in the ratio 2 : 1. The ratio of their respective total surface area is?
A. 2 : 1   B. 16 : 3   C. 3 : 16   D. 1 : 2

Q.76 Spherical Marbles of diameter 1.4 cm are dropped into a cylindrical beaker containing some water and the diameter of the beaker is 7 cm. How many marbles have been dropped in it if the water rises by 5.6 cm?
A. 50   B. 150   C. 250   D. 350

Q.77 In an election, there were two candidates Arvind and Manoj. If 20% of votes were declared invalid and Arvind got 20% more votes than Manoj. Then find the total number of people who voted if Arvind won by 480 votes.
A. 3000   B. 30000   C. 2400   D. 9600

Q.78 If a number is subtracted from three-seventh of itself, the value so obtained is -48. Then, Find 75% of the number.
A. 84   B. 63   C. 36   D. 27

Q.79 Mark out the primary group among the following:
[UPPSC Staff Nurse, 2022]

A. Members of a trade union
B. Family
C. Students of history
D. The social workers

Q.80 Which among the following is not a secondary group?
A. Labour union
B. A city
C. Political party
D. Students in a class room

Q.81 The first woman who received a Sena Medal in India?
A. Dicky Dolma
B. Santosh Yadav
C. Bimla Devi
D. Kiran Devi

Q.82 Where is the blood filtered in the kidney?
A. Renal Artery
B. Ureter
C. Bowman's Capsule
D. Pituitary Gland

Q.83 Which among the following is a viral disease in plants?
A. Wilt of potato
B. The black arm of cotton
C. The mosaic disease of tobacco
D. None of the above

Q.84 The value

of $\sqrt{10 + \sqrt{25 + \sqrt{108 + \sqrt{154 + \sqrt{225}}}}}$ is:

A. 4   **B.** 6   **C.** 8   **D.** 10

Q.85 _______ was the first person to isolate methane gas. He discovered that methane mixed with air could be exploded using an electric spark.

A. William Thomson   **B.** William Crookes
C. Louis Pasteur   **D.** Alessandro Volta

Q.86 Who first discovered that the earth revolves around the sun?

A. Newton   **B.** Dalton
C. Copernicus   **D.** Einstein

Q.87 Which of the following can be used as assessment strategy to encourage interdisciplinary in Mathematics?

A. Projects
B. Field trips
C. Anecdotal records
D. Olympiad

[CTET Paper-II (Science & Mathematics), 2019]

A. A & B   **B.** A & C   **C.** B & C   **D.** C & D

Q.88 What is meant by reading a watch face to tell the time?

A. Learn to recognize the written form and meaning of words
B. Re-applying mathematical concepts of telling time
C. Learn to recognize words and match the words that rhyme
D. Read sentences aloud using proper tension and rhythm

Q.89 The market price of a car was Rs. 9,40,000. Mr. Suman bought the same for Rs. 8,46,000. What was the discount?

A. Rs. 12,000   **B.** Rs. 13,000
C. Rs. 94,000   **D.** Rs. 84,000

Q.90 A trader sells products at 25% less on cost price but weighs 600 gram instead of 1000 gram. What is his profit or loss percent?

A. 12%   **B.** 24%   **C.** 25%   **D.** 40%

Q.91 A shopkeeper increases the markup price of an article by 50% and then allows a discount of Rs. 50. If he received a profit of 25% then find the selling price of the article.

A. Rs. 150   **B.** Rs. 200   **C.** Rs. 250   **D.** Rs. 300

Q.92 Which of the following articles states about "the All India services"?

A. Article 310   **B.** Article 311
C. Article 312   **D.** Article 313

Q.93 Article 21 (A) of the Indian Constitution is:

A. Right to Freedom of Speech and Expression
B. Right to Education
C. Protection against Arrest and Detention
D. Right to Constitutional Remedies

Q.94 Out of the following which tool is not seems to be appropriate for formative assessment?

A. Quizzes
B. Criterion Referenced Test
C. Group discussion
D. Conversation

Q.95 Which one of the following Mathematical processes is an important aspect of algebra in Class VI?

A. Generalisation   **B.** Memorisation
C. Estimation   **D.** Visulisation

Q.96 In which style are the temples of Bhubaneswar and Puri built?

A. Nagar   **B.** Dravid
C. Besar   **D.** None of these

Q.97 Consider the following historical sites:

1. Ajanta Caves
2. Lepakshi Temple
3. Sanchi Stupa

Which of the above sites/murals are also known for painting?

A. Only 1   **B.** Only 1 and 2
C. 1, 2 and 3   **D.** No one

Q.98 Mr. X and Y can complete a piece of work in 45 days and 30 days respectively. If both work together, then find the time taken by them to complete the work together.

A. 15 days   **B.** 19 days   **C.** 24 days   **D.** 18 days

Q.99 Pipe A can fill a tank in 5 hours and pipe Q can empty a tank in 12 hours. If both the pipes are opened. How much time it will take to fill the tank?

A. $8\frac{4}{7}$ hours   **B.** $7\frac{1}{7}$ hours
C. $6\frac{1}{7}$ hours   **D.** $5\frac{1}{7}$ hours

Q.100 Which of the following resources/TLM can be used by the teacher to show that two rectangles of different dimensions can have same area? without using formula?

A. Scale
B. Graph paper
C. Thread
D. Tiles

[CTET Paper - I, 2019]

A. Only B   **B.** B & D   **C.** Only C   **D.** A & D

// Smart Answer Sheet //

Correct	Percentage of students who answered correctly.	Skipped	Percentage of students who skipped.

Q.	Ans.	Correct / Skipped	Q.	Ans.	Correct / Skipped	Q.	Ans.	Correct / Skipped	Q.	Ans.	Correct / Skipped	Q.	Ans.	Correct / Skipped	Q.	Ans.	Correct / Skipped
1	C	68.92 % / 1.0 %	18	A	54.77 % / 1.77 %	35	D	61.0 % / 1.37 %	52	D	58.44 % / 1.08 %	69	A	56.02 % / 1.61 %	86	C	84.24 % / 0.0 %
2	B	62.17 % / 1.81 %	19	C	60.28 % / 1.52 %	36	A	60.77 % / 1.87 %	53	B	55.1 % / 1.2 %	70	C	61.76 % / 1.77 %	87	A	58.18 % / 1.67 %
3	B	54.87 % / 1.76 %	20	B	55.18 % / 1.65 %	37	A	60.2 % / 1.05 %	54	B	46.17 % / 1.76 %	71	B	80.01 % / 0.0 %	88	B	44.05 % / 1.23 %
4	A	41.86 % / 1.58 %	21	A	45.73 % / 1.23 %	38	C	66.05 % / 1.39 %	55	D	16.19 % / 4.93 %	72	D	40.57 % / 1.67 %	89	C	81.75 % / 0.0 %
5	B	53.32 % / 1.3 %	22	A	29.69 % / 4.34 %	39	B	59.58 % / 1.99 %	56	D	77.69 % / 0.0 %	73	A	57.77 % / 1.79 %	90	C	47.5 % / 1.83 %
6	A	69.16 % / 1.71 %	23	D	85.16 % / 0.0 %	40	B	87.65 % / 0.0 %	57	D	64.76 % / 1.9 %	74	D	55.77 % / 1.27 %	91	C	76.89 % / 0.0 %
7	A	82.09 % / 0.0 %	24	A	64.93 % / 1.96 %	41	D	53.82 % / 1.06 %	58	C	83.63 % / 0.0 %	75	B	54.05 % / 1.42 %	92	C	32.62 % / 4.17 %
8	A	32.29 % / 4.23 %	25	C	26.0 % / 3.45 %	42	C	22.13 % / 3.39 %	59	A	43.38 % / 1.22 %	76	B	44.3 % / 1.14 %	93	B	24.52 % / 3.44 %
9	C	45.5 % / 1.73 %	26	C	78.37 % / 0.0 %	43	D	64.03 % / 1.84 %	60	A	41.99 % / 1.55 %	77	A	19.54 % / 3.94 %	94	B	66.26 % / 1.95 %
10	B	26.9 % / 4.08 %	27	D	87.78 % / 0.0 %	44	A	41.22 % / 1.53 %	61	D	55.12 % / 1.16 %	78	B	88.26 % / 0.0 %	95	A	65.79 % / 1.65 %
11	B	40.54 % / 1.08 %	28	A	51.46 % / 1.38 %	45	C	44.96 % / 1.25 %	62	D	47.0 % / 1.67 %	79	B	87.92 % / 0.0 %	96	A	59.32 % / 1.34 %
12	C	54.4 % / 1.23 %	29	D	78.72 % / 0.0 %	46	D	56.74 % / 1.55 %	63	A	82.9 % / 0.0 %	80	D	68.54 % / 1.32 %	97	B	61.59 % / 1.63 %
13	B	69.44 % / 1.97 %	30	A	87.07 % / 0.0 %	47	C	57.95 % / 1.95 %	64	B	42.2 % / 1.09 %	81	C	49.38 % / 1.98 %	98	D	82.61 % / 0.0 %
14	D	65.32 % / 1.74 %	31	D	30.76 % / 4.17 %	48	A	65.62 % / 1.83 %	65	D	26.47 % / 4.6 %	82	C	49.01 % / 1.48 %	99	A	76.67 % / 0.0 %
15	A	63.88 % / 1.09 %	32	C	24.18 % / 3.54 %	49	A	48.29 % / 1.97 %	66	B	51.47 % / 1.43 %	83	C	42.34 % / 1.57 %	100	B	40.44 % / 1.75 %
16	D	44.23 % / 1.42 %	33	D	43.65 % / 1.19 %	50	B	57.49 % / 1.68 %	67	D	56.86 % / 1.84 %	84	A	20.9 % / 3.27 %			
17	A	28.93 % / 3.62 %	34	B	45.93 % / 1.12 %	51	C	32.03 % / 3.79 %	68	A	86.72 % / 0.0 %	85	D	56.97 % / 1.95 %			

//Hints and Solutions//

1. Larsen & Toubro (L&T) Ltd has signed an MoU with the Gujarat govt to set up an IT and IT-enabled Services (ITeS) Park in Vadodara in August 2022.

- The park is being set up under the recently announced IT/ITeS policy of the state government.
- This policy was launched in February 2022 with an aim to generate one lakh 'high-skilled jobs' in the IT sector in the next five years.

Hence, the correct option is (C).

2. The World Economic Forum (WEF) has partnered with Government's think-tank Niti Aayog to use emerging technologies such as artificial intelligence (AI), Internet of Things (IoT), blockchain and drones, to support small and marginal farmers.

WEF had established a 'Centre for the Fourth Industrial Revolution' (C4IR) in India, to implement various innovative projects across the country.

Hence, the correct option is (B).

3. India has nominated the dance form Garba to be inscribed on UNESCO's intangible cultural heritage list in 2022.

In 2021, 'Durga Puja' was included in the UNESCO intangible cultural heritage representative.

India was elected by UNESCO to serve on the distinguished Intergovernmental Committee of the 2003 Convention for the Safeguarding of the Intangible Cultural Heritage in July 2022.

Hence, the correct option is (B).

4. India's new ambassador to China Pradeep Kumar Rawat assumed charge on 14 March 2022.

He succeeds Vikram Misri, who was appointed as Deputy National Security Advisor. Mr. Rawat, a 1990 batch Indian Foreign Service (IFS) officer, was India's ambassador to the Netherlands. He also served as the ambassador of India to Indonesia and Timor-Leste from September 2017-December 2020.

Hence, the correct option is (A).

5. The Group of 7 is a group consisting of Canada, France, Germany, Italy, Japan, the United Kingdom and the United States. These countries, with the 7 largest advanced economies in the world, represent more than 62% of the global net wealth. They are industrialized economies.

Hence, the correct option is (B).

6. Myanmar is not a member of the SAARC.

Myanmar is not a member of the SAARC. All the members of the SAARC are; Afghanistan, Bangladesh, Bhutan, India, Nepal, the Maldives, Pakistan and Sri Lanka.

Hence, the correct option is (A).

7. Given-

The two numbers are a and b.

$$HCF = c$$

According to the formula-

$$HCF \times LCM = \text{Product of two numbers}$$

$$\Rightarrow c \times LCM = a \times b$$

$$\Rightarrow LCM = \frac{a \times b}{c}$$

$$\Rightarrow LCM = \frac{ab}{c}$$

Hence, the correct option is (A).

8. Given:

Sum of radii of two sphere = 10 cm

Sum of their volume = 880 cm³

Volume of a sphere $= \frac{4}{3} \times \pi \times r^3$

Let r_1 and r_2 be the radii of two different sphere.

From question,

$$\Rightarrow r_1 + r_2 = 10 \text{ ....(i)}$$

$$\Rightarrow \frac{4}{3} \times \frac{22}{7} \times (r_1^3 + r_2^3) = 880$$

$$\Rightarrow (r_1^3 + r_2^3) = \frac{(880 \times 3 \times 7)}{(22 \times 4)}$$

$$\Rightarrow (r_1^3 + r_2^3) = 210$$

Now,

$$\Rightarrow (r_1 + r_1)^3 = (10)^3$$

$$\Rightarrow (r_1 + r_1)^3 = 1000 \text{ ....(ii)}$$

$$\Rightarrow (r_1 + r_1)^3 = r_1^3 + r_2^3 + 3r_1 r_2(r_1 + r_2)$$

$$\Rightarrow 1000 = 210 + 3r_1 r_2(10)$$

$$\Rightarrow 1000 - 210 = 30r_1 r_2$$

$$\Rightarrow 790 = 30r_1 r_2$$

$$\Rightarrow r_1 r_2 = \frac{790}{30}$$

$$\Rightarrow r_1 r_2 = \frac{79}{3}$$

Product of their radii $= \frac{79}{3}$

Hence, the correct option is (A).

9. It is given that,

$$^nP_r = 720 \, ^nC_r$$

$$\Rightarrow \frac{^nP_r}{^nC_r} = 720$$

$$\Rightarrow \frac{\frac{n!}{(n-r)!}}{\frac{n!}{(n-r)!r!}} = 720$$

$$\Rightarrow r! = 720 = 6 \times 5 \times 4 \times 3 \times 2 \times 1$$

$$\Rightarrow r! = 6!$$

$$\Rightarrow r = 6$$

Hence, the correct option is (C).

10. The given equation is,

$$^x P_3 = ^{(2x-1)} P_2$$

$$\Rightarrow \frac{x!}{(x-3)!} = \frac{(2x-1)!}{(2x-1-2)!}$$

$$\Rightarrow \frac{x!}{(x-3)!} = \frac{(2x-1)!}{(2x-3)!}$$

$$\Rightarrow \frac{x(x-1)(x-2)(x-3)!}{(x-3)!} = \frac{(2x-1)(2x-2)(2x-3)!}{(2x-3)!}$$

$$\Rightarrow x(x-1)(x-2) = (2x-1)(2x-2)$$

$$\Rightarrow x^3 - 3x^2 + 2x = 4x^2 - 6x + 2$$

$$\Rightarrow x^3 - 7x^2 + 8x - 2 = 0$$

$$\Rightarrow (x-1)(x^2 + 6x + 2) = 0$$

Which gives $x = 1$ and:

$$x^2 + 6x + 2 = 0$$

Using the Quadratic Formula where,

$$a = 1, b = 6, \text{ and } c = 2$$

$$x = \frac{-b \pm \sqrt{b^2 - 4ac}}{2a}$$

$$x = \frac{-6 \pm \sqrt{6^2 - 4(1)(2)}}{2(1)}$$

$$x = \frac{-6 \pm \sqrt{36 - 8}}{2}$$

$$x = \frac{-6 \pm \sqrt{28}}{2}$$

$$x = \frac{-6 \pm 2\sqrt{7}}{2}$$

$$x = \frac{-6}{2} \pm \frac{2\sqrt{7}}{2}$$

$$x = -3 \pm \sqrt{7}$$

$$x = -0.354249$$

$$x = -5.64575$$

Other imaginary roots of x which are impossible because $x \geq 3$ and $x \in N$.

Hence, the correct option is (B).

11. Using the formula for calculating Mean:

$$\frac{x_1 + x_2 + \cdots + x_{10}}{10} = 30$$

$$\Rightarrow x_1 + x_2 + \cdots + x_{10} = 300$$

Now using the same formula again, the mean of $x_1 + 5, x_2 + 10, \ldots x_{10} + 50$ will be:

$$\text{Mean} = \frac{(x_1 + 5) + (x_2 + 10) + \cdots + (x_{10} + 50)}{10}$$

$$= \frac{(x_1 + x_2 + \cdots + x_{10}) + (5 + 10 + \cdots + 50)}{10}$$

$$= \frac{(x_1 + x_2 + \cdots + x_{10}) + 5(1 + 2 + \cdots + 10)}{10}$$

$$= \frac{300 + 5 \times \frac{10 \times 11}{2}}{10}$$

$$= \frac{300 + 275}{10} = 57.5$$

Hence, the correct option is (B).

12. It is given that $b_{yx} = -\frac{3}{2}$ and $b_{xy} = -\frac{1}{6}$

The correlation coefficient (r)

$$= \sqrt{b_{yx} \times b_{xy}} = \sqrt{-\frac{3}{2} \times -\frac{1}{6}} = \pm \frac{1}{2}$$

Since both b_{yx} and b_{xy} are negative, so the correlation coefficient will also be negative.

Hence r $= -\frac{1}{2}$

Hence, the correct option is (C).

13. Given,

$$\frac{(469 + 174)^2 - (469 - 174)^2}{(469 \times 174)} = ?$$

We know that,

$$4ab = (a + b)^2 - (a - b)^2$$

$$\therefore \frac{(469 + 174)^2 - (469 - 174)^2}{(469 \times 174)}$$

$$= \frac{4 \times 469 \times 174}{469 \times 174}$$

$$= 4$$

Hence, the correct option is (B).

14. The credit for the discovery of the Valley of Flowers goes to the British mountaineer Franks S. Smythe, R.L. Holdsworth, and Eric Shipton who incidentally reached this valley after a successful expedition of Mount Kamet in 1931. Smythe wrote the book "The Valley of Flowers" in 1938.

The Valley of Flowers is situated in Bhyundar Valley at an elevation of 3,658 meters above sea level. The Valley of Flowers National Park is the second core zone of the Nanda Devi Biosphere Reserve. The Valley of Flowers National Park is an

Indian national park, located in North Chamoli and Pithoragarh, in the state of Uttarakhand, and is known for its meadows of endemic alpine flowers and the variety of flora. The Valley of flowers was declared as the National Park of India in the year 1982 and it is now a UNESCO world heritage site.

Hence, the correct option is (D).

15. Prem Chand Sharma gets Padma Shri Award for innovation in Agriculture in 2021.

He has been focusing to diversify farming by growing high-quality fruits, vegetables, and grains organically. His farm is in the village Hiatal-Sainj in Uttarakhand. Sharma dropped out of school and pursued his interest in farming from a young age. In 2020, he developed a nursery to grow high-yielding pomegranates and distributed them among 350 farmers in his state.

Hence, the correct option is (A).

16. Given,

One of two equal sides of an isosceles triangular table = 100 cm

The perimeter of the triangular table = 360 cm

Let a = 100 cm

Perimeter of an isosceles triangle = 2a + b

$\Rightarrow$ 2a + b = 360

$\Rightarrow$ 2 × 100 + b = 360

$\Rightarrow$ 200 + b = 360

$\Rightarrow$ b = 360 – 200

$\Rightarrow$ b = 160 cm

Area of isosceles triangle $= \frac{b}{4} \times \sqrt{(4a^2 - b^2)}$

$= \frac{160}{4} \times \sqrt{(4 \times 100^2 - 160^2)}$

$= 40 \times \sqrt{(4 \times 10000 - 25600)}$

$= 40 \times \sqrt{(40000 - 25600)}$

$= 40 \times \sqrt{(14400)}$

$= 40 \times 120$

$= 4800$ cm^2

$\therefore$ Area of the triangular table is 4800 cm^2.

Hence, the correct option is (D).

17. Given,

Area of triangle BCD is 28% of the area of parallelogram ACDE.

Let the length of the parallel sides AB and DE be 'a' units and 'b' units respectively and the height of the parallelogram AF be 'h' units, as shown below

Let the area of parallelogram ACDE be x sq. units.

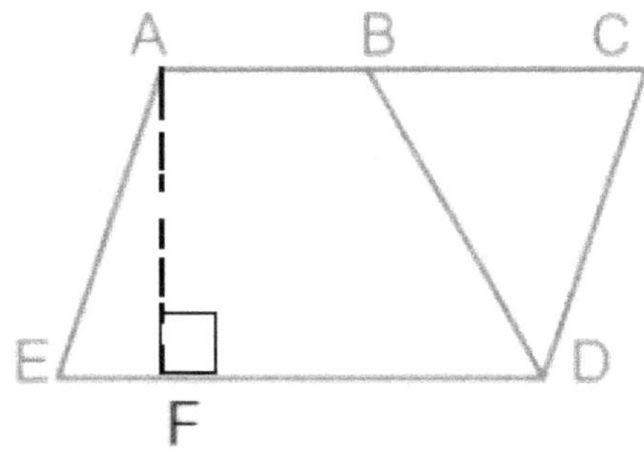

Area of parallelogram = Base × Height of parallelogram

$\Rightarrow$ Area of parallelogram ACDE = DE × AF = bh sq. units

Area of trapezium $= \frac{1}{2} \times$ sum of parallel sides $\times$ perpendicular distance between parallel sides

$\Rightarrow$ Area of trapezium ABDE $= \frac{1}{2} \times (a + b) \times h = \frac{(ah+bh)}{2}$ sq. units

Now,

Area of trapezium ABDE = Area of parallelogram ACDE – Area of triangle BCD

According to the question,

Area of triangle BCD = 28% of x

$\Rightarrow$ Area of triangle $BCD = \frac{7x}{25}$

$\Rightarrow$ Area of trapezium $ABDE = x - \frac{7x}{25}$

Area of trapezium $ABDE = \frac{18x}{25}$

$\Rightarrow \frac{(ah+bh)}{2} = \left(\frac{18}{25}\right) \times bh$

$\Rightarrow 25ah + 25bh = 36bh$

$\Rightarrow 25ah = 11bh$

$\Rightarrow 25a = 11b$

$\Rightarrow \frac{a}{b} = \frac{11}{25}$

$\therefore$ Ratio of lengths of parallel sides of trapezium ABDE = 11 : 25

Hence, the correct option is (A).

18. Given,

Principal $(P) =$ Rs. 2304

Amount $(A) =$ Rs. 2500

Time $(t) = 2$ years

As we know,

$$A = P\left(1 + \frac{r}{100}\right)^t$$

$$\Rightarrow 2500 = 2304 \left(1 + \frac{r}{100}\right)^2$$

$$\Rightarrow \frac{2500}{2304} = \left(1 + \frac{r}{100}\right)^2$$

$$\Rightarrow \sqrt{\left(\frac{2500}{2304}\right)} = 1 + \frac{r}{100}$$

$$\Rightarrow \frac{50}{48} = 1 + \frac{r}{100}$$

$$\Rightarrow \frac{25}{24} \times 100 = 100 + r$$

$$\Rightarrow \frac{625}{6} - 100 = r$$

$$\Rightarrow \frac{625-600}{6} = r$$

$$\Rightarrow \frac{25}{6} = r$$

$$\therefore r = 4\frac{1}{6}\%$$

Hence, the correct option is (A).

19. Given,

The sum becomes 9 times in 2 years.

Let P be the principal.

$$\therefore A = 9P$$

As we know,

$$A = P\left(1 + \frac{r}{100}\right)^t$$

$$\therefore 9P = P\left(1 + \frac{r}{100}\right)^2$$

$$\Rightarrow 9 = \left(1 + \frac{r}{100}\right)^2$$

$$\Rightarrow \sqrt{9} = 1 + \frac{r}{100}$$

$$\Rightarrow 3 = 1 + \frac{r}{100}$$

$$\Rightarrow 3 - 1 = \frac{r}{100}$$

$$\Rightarrow 2 = \frac{r}{100}$$

$$\Rightarrow r = 200\%$$

$\therefore$ The rate of interest is 200%.

Hence, the correct option is (C).

20.

Name	Chemical formula	Chemical Name
Baking soda	$NaHCO_3$	Sodium bicarbonate
Vinegar	CH_3COOH	Acetic acid
Bleaching powder	$Ca(OCl)_2$	Calcium hypochlorite
Chalk	$CaCO_3$	Calcium Carbonate

Hence, the correct option is (B).

21. Naphthalene is an organic compound with the formula $C_{10}H_8$. It is an aromatic hydrocarbon and thus consists of a fused pair of benzene rings. Naphthalene is the most abundant single component of coal tar. Typical coal tar is about 10% naphthalene by weight.

Hence, the correct option is (A).

22. Given:

The difference between two complementary angles is 15°

Calculation:

Let two complementary angles be $\angle x$ and $\angle y$ respectively.

$\angle x - \angle y = 15°$ ----(i) (given)

$\angle x + \angle y = 90°$ ----(ii) (Sum of complementary angles is 90°)

From (i), $\angle y = 15 + \angle x$ ----(iii)

From (ii), $\angle y = 90 - \angle x$ ----(iv)

On comparing the values of $\angle y$ from (iii) & (iv) we get,

$15 + \angle x = 90 - \angle x$

$\Rightarrow 2\angle x = 75$

$\Rightarrow \angle x = 37.5$

So, $\angle y = 90 - 37.5 = 52.5$

Since, $\angle x = 37.5$ and $\angle y = 52.5$

Therefore, Greater angle : Smaller angle = $\angle y : \angle x$

$\Rightarrow 52.5 : 37.5 = 7 : 5$

$\therefore$ Required ratio is 7 : 5

Hence, the correct option is (A).

23. National Education Day is celebrated in India on 11th November.

The day is celebrated as a mark of respect to Maulana Abdul Kalam Azad.

He was a freedom fighter and independent India's first Education Minister (served from 1947 to 1958). He was an eminent scholar of Urdu, Persian, and Arabic. He was awarded the Bharat Ratna in 1992.

Hence, the correct option is (D).

24. Hindi Diwas or Hindi Day is celebrated annually on September 14 in India as Hindi was declared as one of the official languages of India on 14th September, 1949.

The resolution which declares Hindi as one of the official languages was adopted under the Constitution of India in 1950.

Hence, the correct option is (A).

25. Let the total investment = Rs. x

Mukul's investment $= x \times \dfrac{2}{7}$

Rest investment $= x - x \times \dfrac{2}{7} = \dfrac{5x}{7}$

Let Atul's investment = Rs. a

Rahul's investment = Rs. b

Rahul's investment + Atul's investment $= \dfrac{5x}{7}$

$$a + b = \dfrac{5x}{7}$$

$$b = \dfrac{5x}{7} - a \,...\, 1$$

According to the question,

$$\dfrac{2x}{7} + a = b$$

$\Rightarrow \dfrac{5x}{7} - a = \dfrac{2x}{7} + a$ (value of b is taken out from equation 1)

$\Rightarrow \dfrac{5x}{7} - \dfrac{2x}{7} = a + a$

$\Rightarrow \dfrac{3x}{7} = 2a$

$\Rightarrow a = \dfrac{3x}{14}$ = Atul's investment

Rahul's investment $= x - \dfrac{3x}{14} - \dfrac{2x}{7}$

$= \dfrac{14x - 3x - 4x}{14}$

$= \dfrac{7x}{14} = \dfrac{x}{2}$

Investment Ratio,

Mukul : Atul : Rahul $= \dfrac{2x}{7} : \dfrac{3x}{14} : \dfrac{x}{2}$

$= 4 : 3 : 7$

As Atul's Profit = Rs. 1530

Total profit $= \dfrac{1530}{3} \times 14$

= Rs. 7140

Hence, the correct option is (C).

26. The best expresses the meaning of the Idiom/Phrase **fold like a cheap suitcase** is **to submit or give up easily**.

The idiom **fold like a cheap suit** means To offer little resistance; to submit easily.

For example, I think this team's defense will **fold like a cheap suitcase** if we just put a little more pressure on them.

Hence, the correct option is (C).

27. The best expresses meaning of the Idiom/Phrase **to take to task** is **to reprimand.**

The idiom **take to task** means to scold or criticize someone. The word "reprimand" also means to scold or to criticize someone.

For example, He's been **taken to task** for his habitual lack of punctuality.

Hence, the correct option is (D).

28. He knew that an apple <u>should</u> not be plucked while it is green.

The V2 verb in the first part of the sentence indicates that there should be a past form of the verb in the second part of the sentence too. Should is the only verb that is in the past form. So 'should' is the correct choice.

Hence, the correct option is (A).

29. You haven't many teeth left, but <u>the</u> few you have are sharp enough to make me shudder.

A few means some. It has a positive meaning. The few means not many, but all of those. Here we are talking about all the teeth that are left, so 'the' is the correct choice here.

Hence, the correct option is (D).

30. I can always tell when my friend is <u>lying</u> because she bites her lip.

Lie- be in or assume a horizontal or resting position on a supporting surface.

Forms- Lie, Lay, Lain

Lie- to say an intentionally false statement.

Forms- Lie, Lied, Lied

Lay- put (something) down gently or carefully.

Forms- Lay, Laid Laid

The lie is a verb that means 'to be in or put yourself into a flat position'. The lie can also mean 'say something which is not true'. Here lie is used in the second context and lying in the correct form to be put in this blank.

Hence, the correct option is (A).

31. The given sentence is in active form of simple past tense. The structures for active/passive voices are:

Active: Subject + verb (IInd form) + object.

Passive: Object + was/were + verb (IIIrd form) + by + subject.

For the given sentence, the verb "interest" will take the preposition "in" with it in the passive voice.

So, with the help of the above structures, we can convert the given sentence into passive voice:

The boy was interested in stamp collection.

Hence, the correct option is (D).

32. The passive voice of imperative sentences that suggest order, suggestion or request, etc can be made in two ways:

Active: Verb + object

Passive: 1. Let + object + be + past participle
2. You are requested/ordered/suggested/supposed + to + verb
(1st form) + object

So, going by the second type of passive voice, the given sentence would be written in the passive voice as:

You are supposed to make tea at eleven O'clock.

Hence, the correct option is (C).

33. As we know that,

If a number or square of a number is divided by the same number, a remainder is same in both the conditions.

Hence, square of a number is divided by 6, we get 3 as remainder.

Hence, the correct option is (D).

34. All natural numbers before 74 can be arranged to form an AP, Where

a=2

a_n=74

d=2

a_n=a+(n-1)d

74=2+(n-1)2

72=(n-1)2

36=n-1

n=37

S_n=($\dfrac{n}{2}$)[2a +(n -1)d]

= ($\dfrac{37}{2}$) [2 ×2+(37-1)2]

=($\dfrac{37}{2}$) ×(4+72)

=($\dfrac{37}{2}$) ×(76)

=37 ×38

Sn=1406

Hence, the correct option is (B).

35. Total income of company $C = 30$ crores

Total expenditure of Company $C = 27$ crores

As we know,

Profit $\% = \dfrac{\text{Income- Expenditure}}{\text{Expenditure}} \times 100$

$\therefore$ Profit $\% = \left(\dfrac{30-27}{27}\right) \times 100$

$= \dfrac{100}{9}$

$= 11.11\%$ profit

Hence, the correct option is (D).

36. Total expenditure of all the five companies =
$(12 + 18 + 27 + 25 + 20)$ crores $= 102$ crores

The total income of all the five companies = $(15 + 15 + 30 + 20 + 16)$ crores $= 96$ crores

Required percentage $= \dfrac{\text{Income-Expenditure}}{\text{Expenditure}} \times 100$

$= \dfrac{96-102}{102} \times 100$

$= -5.88\% \approx 5.9\%$ loss

Hence, the correct option is (A).

37. Profit percentage $= \dfrac{\text{Income-Expenditure}}{\text{Expenditure}} \times 100$

Profit percentage of $A = \dfrac{(15-12)}{12} \times 100$

$= 25\%$ profit

Profit percentage of $B = \dfrac{(15-18)}{18} \times 100$

$= -16.67\%$ loss

Profit percentage of $C = \dfrac{(30-27)}{27} \times 100$

$= 11.11\%$ profit

Profit percentage of $D = \dfrac{(20-25)}{25} \times 100$

$= -20\%$ loss

Profit percentage of $E = \dfrac{(16-20)}{20} \times 100 = -20\%$ loss

Therefore, A has the highest profit.

Hence, the correct option is (A).

38. Let the expenditure of company C in the year 2016 be x crores.

Then, the expenditure of company C in the year $2017 = \left(\dfrac{120}{100}\right) \times x$ crores

As the expenditure of company C in the year $2017 = 27$

$\therefore \dfrac{120x}{100} = 27$

$\Rightarrow x = \dfrac{27 \times 100}{120}$

$\Rightarrow x = 22.5$

Therefore, the expenditure of company C in the year 2016 $= 22.5$ crores

Let the income of company C in the year 2016 be y crores.

Given that Profit in the year $2016 = 12\%$

$$\therefore \frac{(y-22.5)}{22.5} \times 100 = 12$$

$$y - 22.5 = \frac{12 \times 22.5}{100}$$

$$y = 22.5 + 2.7$$

$$y = 25.2$$

Therefore, the income of company C in the year $2016 = 25.2$ crores

Hence, the correct option is (C).

39. Let, the income of company A in the year 2016 be x crores.

Then, the income of the company in the year $2016 = \frac{90x}{100}$

$$\Rightarrow \frac{90x}{100} = 15$$

$$\Rightarrow x = \frac{50}{3}$$

The income of company A in the year $2016 = \frac{50}{3}$ crores

As income $=$ Profit $+$ Expenditure

Profit $= 10\%$ of income in 2016 Expenditure will be 90% of income in $2016.$

$$\text{Expenditure} = \left(\frac{90}{100}\right) \times \left(\frac{50}{3}\right) = 15$$

$\therefore$ The expenditure of company A in the year $2016 = 15$ crores

Hence, the correct option is (B).

40. Based on the temperature characteristics the earth is divided into three zones:

1. **Torrid zone**: between tropic of Cancer and tropic of Capricorn.

2. **Temperate zone**: between arctic circle to the tropic of Cancer and tropic of Capricorn.

3. **Polar zone**: between arctic circle to the pole.

Hence, the correct option is (B).

41. A Great Circle is any circle that circumnavigates the Earth and passes through the center of the Earth. A great circle always divides the Earth in half, thus the Equator is a great circle (but no other latitudes) and all lines of longitude are great circles.

Features associated with the Great circle:

- The Equator is the only east-west line that is a great circle.

- A great circle always divides the Earth in half, the northern hemisphere and the southern hemisphere.

- The equator lies between 23.5°N to 23.5°S

- Thus the Equator is a great circle (but no other latitudes) and all lines of longitude are great circles.

- The shortest distance between any two points on the Earth lies along a great circle.

- The speed of the rotation of the earth is greatest along the great circle.

- Circumference of the Earth at 40-deg North = 30,600 kilometers.

- Time to complete one Rotation = 24 hours.

- Speed of Rotation at 40 North = Distance/Time = 30,600 km / 24 hr = 1280 km/hr.

- The equator is the circle that is equidistant from the North Pole and the South Pole.

Hence, the correct option is (D).

42. Technological advancement invented the use of geodesy, which is the science of measuring Earth's shape, gravity, and rotation. Geodesy provides accurate measurements that show Earth is round. With GPS and other satellites, scientists can measure Earth's size and shape to within a centimeter.

Pictures from space also show Earth is round like the moon. Even though our planet is a sphere, it is not a perfect sphere. Because of the force caused when Earth rotates, the North and South Poles are slightly flat. Earth's rotation, wobbly motion, and other forces are making the planet change shape very slowly, but it is still around. The spherical surface has a horizon that is closed when viewed from a lower altitude. The satellite view proves that the Earth's surface is locally convex.

If the degree of curvature is determined to be the same everywhere on Earth's surface, and that surface was determined to be large enough, the constant curvature would show that the Earth is spherical.

Hence, the correct option is (C).

43. The first part of the sentence ends with a complete sentence, which means that the next part must begin a new sentence. The new part must begin with or contain conjunction. 'That' is conjunction given by part P, which means P is the first part of the answer. P ends with the preposition 'despite', which means it must be followed by a noun or adjective (and its corresponding article). Only Q begins with an article. So, PQ is the correct sequence, as shown by option (D).

Hence, the correct option is (D).

44. Moscow is the capital city of Russia. It is the most populous city in Russia. Moscow has the status of a Russian federal city. It is the largest city on the entire European continent. Moscow is situated on the banks of Moskva River in the Central Federal District of Russia. This city is famous for its architecture, especially its historic buildings. Moscow is a major political, economic, cultural, and scientific center of Russia and Eastern Europe.

Hence, the correct option is (A).

45. The Gayatri mantra is a prayer for spiritual stimulation addressed to the Sun. It was created by Vishvmitra.

This mantra is taken from the third Mandala in Rig Veda. The Gayatri Mantra, also known as the Savitri Mantra, is a highly revered mantra from the Rig Veda (Mandala 3.62.10), dedicated to the Vedic deity Savitr.

Hence, the correct option is (C)

46. The given sentence is grammatically correct.

Hence, the correct option is (D).

47. Given,

$$x + \left(\frac{1}{x}\right) = 3$$

So, $\dfrac{(3x^2 - 4x + 3)}{(x^2 - x + 1)}$

$$\Rightarrow \frac{3x\{x - \left(\frac{4}{3}\right) + \left(\frac{1}{x}\right)\}}{x\{x - 1 + \left(\frac{1}{x}\right)\}}$$

$$= \frac{3[\{x + \left(\frac{1}{x}\right)\} - \left(\frac{4}{3}\right)]}{\{x + \left(\frac{1}{x}\right)\} - 1}$$

From equation (i),

$$= \frac{3\{3 - \left(\frac{4}{3}\right)\}}{3 - 1} = \frac{3\left(\frac{5}{3}\right)}{2}$$

$$= \frac{5}{2}$$

Hence, the correct option is (C).

48. We know that,

W = q×V

Where q is charge, W is the work done and V is the potential difference.

Given,

q = 4 Coulomb

V = 12 Volt

In the formula,

W = 4×12

W = 48 J

Hence, the correct option is (A).

49. The energy possessed by an object of mass at height will be Potential energy.

Given that, mass $(m) = 10$ kg, $g = 9.8$ ms $^{-2}$ and height $(h) = 8$ m

We know that,

The potential energy of an object $= mgh$

$$= 10 \times 8 \times 9.8 = 784 \text{ J}$$

Hence, the correct option is (A).

50. Given that,

$$\frac{3.8}{1.25}$$

Multiplying by $\dfrac{8}{8}$ to make 10 in the denominator,

$$\Rightarrow \frac{3.8}{1.25} \times \frac{8}{8}$$

$$\Rightarrow \frac{30.4}{10}$$

$$\Rightarrow 3.04$$

Hence, the correct option is (B).

51. Given-

$$\left(\frac{\sqrt{180} \times \sqrt{18} \times \sqrt{5} \times \sqrt{3}}{\sqrt{96} \times 5}\right)^{-2} + \sqrt[3]{4\frac{12}{125}}$$

$$\Rightarrow \left(\frac{6\sqrt{5} \times 3\sqrt{2} \times \sqrt{5} \times \sqrt{3}}{4\sqrt{6} \times 5}\right)^{-2} + \sqrt[3]{\frac{512}{125}}$$

$$\Rightarrow \left(\frac{9}{2}\right)^{-2} + \frac{8}{5}$$

$$\Rightarrow \frac{4}{81} + \frac{8}{5}$$

$$\Rightarrow \frac{20 + 648}{405}$$

$$\Rightarrow \frac{668}{405}$$

Hence, the correct option is (C).

52. The 'Kathasaritsagara' is written by Somadeva.

The Kathasaritsagara is also known as Ocean of the Streams of Stories is a famous 11th-century collection of Indian legends, fairy tales, and folk tales as retold in Sanskrit by Somadeva.

Hence, the correct option is (D).

53. The assistance of Rs. 6000 will be given under the Indira Gandhi Matritva Poshan Yojana of the Rajasthan government.

Indira Gandhi Matritva Poshan Yojana:

- The scheme was launched by Chief Minister Shri Ashok Gehlot.
- It was launched on November 19, 2020.
- The scheme comes under the aegis of the state's Department of Women and Child Development.
- The scheme was started in Udaipur, Pratapgarh, Banswara, and Dungarpur districts, based on the rankings of Mother & Child Nutrition indicators.

Hence, the correct option is (B).

54. Rhetoric-the art of effective or persuasive speaking or writing, especially the exploitation of figures of speech and other compositional techniques.

Hence, the correct option is (B).

55. Susceptibility-the state or fact of being likely or liable to be influenced or harmed by a particular thing.

Sensitivities - The quality or condition of being sensitive: sensitivity to the concerns of others.

Hence, the correct option is (D).

56. Antagonistic- showing or feeling active opposition or hostility towards someone or something. corresponding-analogous or equivalent in character, form, or function; comparable.

Hence the correct option is (D).

57. The meaning of the phrase "at loggerheads", as used in the passage opposite to each other.

Hence, the correct option is (D).

58. To highlight the steps and caution to be taken about the entry of foreign media.

Hence, the correct option is (C).

59. 'Lakh Baksh' was the title given to the Qutub-ud-din aibak.

Aibak was a slave of Muhammad Ghori, who made him the Governor of his Indian possessions. He set up his military headquarters near Delhi and captured the North India. Due to his liberal donations, Muslim writers called him Lakh Baksh.

Hence, the correct option is (A).

60. India has a significant presence in the services sector exports. It remained among the top ten trading countries in commercial services in 2019 accounting for 3.5 percent of world services exports. Notwithstanding the setback witnessed in the wake of the pandemic, India's services sector remained relatively resilient when compared to merchandise trade. The resilience of the services sector was primarily driven by software services, which accounted for 49 percent (largest component) of total services export. So, statement 1 is not correct.

According to Economics Survey 2020-21, net capital flows was modest in H1: FY 2020-21 at US$ 16.5 billion, as against US$ 40.0 billion in HI: FY 2019-20, mainly accounted for by net repayments of external commercial borrowings (ECBs) and decline in banking capital. During April-October, 2020, net FDI flows recorded an inflow of US$27.5billion, 14.8 percent higher as compared to the first seven months of 2019-20. According to RBI statistics, it can be said that India has been maintaining a capital account surplus in recent years. So, statement 2 is not correct.

Hence, the correct option is (A).

61. The GoI has taken various initiatives under the Atmanirbhar Abhiyan to enhance the domestic production of steel such as:

- Inclusion of 'Speciality Steel' incorporating four different product categories for incentives under the Production Linked Incentive (PLI) scheme; Hence, statement 1 is correct.

- Offering steel to MSMEs that are members of the Engineering Export Promotion Council at export parity price under the Duty Draw Back scheme of DGFT; Hence, statement 2 is correct.

- Measures to provide preference to domestically produced iron and steel in government procurement, where aggregates estimate of iron and steel products exceeds 25 crores; Hence, statement 3 is correct.

- Protecting the industry from unfair trade through appropriate remedial measures including the imposition of anti-dumping duty and countervailing duty on the products in which unfair trade practices were adopted by other countries.

Hence, the correct option is (D).

62. The passage begins with the sentence that introduces the topic at hand - it talks about the Indian Civil Service and how it has been developed into one of the world's finest civil services. This is followed by sentence S which talks about how the members of the Indian Civil Services hold vast power and this is followed by sentence P which talks about how these members with vast power often participated in policymaking. This is followed by sentence R which talks about how these members went onto to develop certain traditions that are specifically mentioned in sentence Q - independence, integrity and hard work. This is followed by the last sentence which talks about how these traditional qualities workes towards serving the British more than Indians.

Hence, the correct option is (D).

63. Saudi Arabia is the country in the world to have no cinema theaters.

With the exception of one IMAX theater in Khobar by Khalid, there were no cinemas in Saudi Arabia from 1983 to 2018, although there was occasionally talk of opening movie theaters, and in 2008 conference rooms were rented to show the comedy Mennahi.

Hence, the correct option is (A).

64. Sachin Tendulkar received the Arjuna Award in 1994 for his outstanding sporting achievement, the Khel Ratna award in 1997, India's highest sporting honor, and the Padma Shri and Padma Vibhushan awards in 1999 and 2008, respectively, India's fourth- and second-highest civilian awards.

Hence, the correct option is (B).

65. The first Commonwealth game organized in 1930 in Hamilton.

- Commonwealth games are a multinational game event that involves athletes from the Commonwealth Nations.

- The next commonwealth games will be organized in Bermingham, England in 2022.

Hence, the correct option is (D).

66. Given:

The ratio of the salaries of X, Y and $Z = 10 : 12 : 15$

Percentage = $\left(\dfrac{Actual}{Total} \right) \times 100$

Salaries after increments

$\Rightarrow Y = 12x + 50\%$ of $12x = 18x$

$\Rightarrow Z = 15x + 60\%$ of $15x = 24x$

The ratio of new salaries of X, Y and $Z = 14x : 18x : 24x$

$\Rightarrow 7 : 9 : 12$

Hence, the correct option is (B).

67. Given:

Total Money in bag = Rs. 30

Total value = no. of coins $\times$ value per coin

	25p	50p	Rs. 1
Value per coin	1 :	2 :	4
No. of coins	8 :	4 :	1
total Value	8 :	8 :	4

Total Value $= 30$

$\Rightarrow 20x = 30$

$\Rightarrow x = 1.5$

Value of $50p$ coins $= 8x = 8 \times 1.5 = Rs\,12$

No. of coins $= 12 \times 2 = 24$

$\therefore$ No. of 50 paise coins are 24.

Hence, the correct option is (D).

68. The correct sequence is- SPRQ

Thus the correct sentence is- Events in our childhood have a great influence on our adult lives and they often shape our personality.

Hence, the correct option is (A).

69. The word 'bounces back' means to regain a former or normal state.

The word 'relapse' means a deterioration in someone's state of health after a temporary improvement.

Hence, the correct option is (A).

70. The word 'execute' means to carry through (as a process) to completion.

The word 'accomplish' means to achieve or complete successfully.

Thus, we can say that 'accomplish' is nearest in meaning to the given word.

Hence, the correct option is (C).

71. The given number can be factored as shown below:

16384 = 2×2×2×2×2×2×2×2×2×2×2×2×2×2

The square root of 16384 = 2×2×2×2×2×2×2 =128.

Hence, the correct option is (B).

72. Ghosha composed Brahmavadini the hymns of Vedas.

Brahmavadini are the women who composed some hymns of the Vedas prominent among them were Lopamudra, Vishwawara, Sikta, Ghosha and Maitreyi.

Hence, the correct option is (D).

73. In 1904, Ramabai Ranade established the Mahila Samajik Sammelan (Bharat Mahila Parishad) under the parent National Social Conference in Bombay.

Hence, the correct option is (A).

74. Given:

Length of the field = 242 m

Area of the field = 4840 sq. m

Cost of fencing 1 m = Rs 10

Concept used:

Area of the field = length × breadth

Perimeter of the field = 2 × (length + breadth)

Calculation:

Let the breadth be B.

242 × B = 4840

$B = \dfrac{4840}{242} = 20$ m

Perimeter of the field = 2 × (242 + 20) = 524 m

Amount to fence the four sides of the field = 10 × 524 = Rs 5,240

$\therefore$ A total of Rs 5,240 is required to fence the field.

Hence, the correct option is (D).

75. Given:

Ratio of the radius of sphere and hemisphere = 2 : 1

Formula Used:

Total surface area of a Sphere = $4\pi r^2$

Total surface area of a hemisphere = $3\pi r^2$

Solution:

Let the radius of a hemisphere be x

$\Rightarrow$ Then the radius of a sphere is 2x.

$\Rightarrow$ Total surface area of a Sphere = $4\pi r^2$

$\Rightarrow$ Total surface area of a Sphere = $4\pi \times (2x)^2$

$\Rightarrow$ Total surface area of a hemisphere = $3\pi r^2$

$\Rightarrow$ Total surface area of a hemisphere = $3\pi \times (x)^2$

Now the ratio of their respective areas,

$\Rightarrow \dfrac{4\pi(2x)^2}{3\pi(x)^2}$

$$\Rightarrow \frac{4\left(4x^2\right)}{3\left(x^2\right)}$$

$$\Rightarrow \frac{16}{3}$$

∴ The ratio of their total surface area is 16 : 3.

Hence, the correct option is (B).

76. Given:

Diameter of beaker = 7 cm

Diameter of a marble = 1.4 cm

Water rise in the beaker = 5.6 cm

Concept:

Increase in volume of the beaker = n × Volume of a spherical marble

Formula used:

Volume of cylinder = $\pi r^2 h$

Volume of sphere = $\frac{4}{3}\pi r^3$

Calculation:

Radius of cylindrical beaker = $\frac{7}{2}$ cm

Since the water rise in the beaker is 5.6 cm, h = 5.6 cm.

Radius of a marble = $\frac{1.4}{2}$ = 0.7 cm

Suppose 'n' marbles are dropped in the beaker.

So,

$$\pi \times \left(\frac{7}{2}\right)^2 \times 5.6 = n \times \frac{4}{3} \times \pi \times (0.7)^3$$

$$\Rightarrow 100 \times 1.4 = n \times \frac{4}{3} \times 0.7$$

$$\Rightarrow n = \frac{420}{2.8}$$

$$\Rightarrow n = 150$$

So, 150 marble were dropped in the beaker.

Hence, the correct option is (B).

77. Given:

Invalid votes = 20% of the total votes

Arvind won by 480 votes.

And Arvind got 20% more votes than Manoj.

Let total votes be x.

Invalid votes = 20% of x = 0.2x

Valid votes = x – 0.2x = 0.8x

Arvind and Manoj gets 0.8x votes.

Arvind got 20% more votes than Manoj.

⇒ Arvind gets 60% of valid votes and Manoj gets 40% of valid votes.

⇒ Votes received by Arvind $= 0.8x \times \frac{60}{100}$ = 0.48x

⇒ Votes received by Manoj = 0.8x – 0.48x = 0.32x

Votes of Arvind – Votes of Manoj = 480

⇒ 0.48x – 0.32x = 480

⇒ 0.16x = 480

⇒ x = 3000

∴ Total number of people who voted are 3000.

Hence, the correct option is (A).

78. Given:

A number is subtracted from three-seventh of itself = -48

Let the number be x.

According to the question,

$$\left(\frac{3x}{7}\right) - x = -48$$

$$\Rightarrow \frac{(3x-7x)}{7} = -48$$

$$\Rightarrow (-4x) = (-48 \times 7)$$

$$\Rightarrow x = 12 \times 7$$

$$\Rightarrow x = 84$$

Now, 75% of number $= 84 \times \frac{75}{100}$

$$= \frac{(84 \times 3)}{4} = 63$$

∴ 75% of the number is 63.

Hence, the correct option is (B).

79. Family is an example of a primary group.

Primary group refers to those personal relations that are direct, face-to-face, relatively permanent, and intimate, such as the relations in a family, a group of close friends, and the like.

Hence, the correct option is (B).

80. Students in a class room is not a secondary group.

Secondary groups are large groups whose relationships are impersonal and goal oriented. People in a secondary group interact on a less personal level than in a primary group, and their relationships are generally temporary rather than long lasting.

Hence, the correct option is (D).

81. Bimla Devi, the first woman received a Sena Medal in India.

The Sena Medal is awarded to members of the Indian army, of all ranks, "for such individual acts of exceptional devotion to duty or courage as having special significance for the Army." Awards may be made posthumously and a bar is authorized for subsequent awards of the Sena Medal.

Hence, the correct option is (C).

82. The blood is filtered in the Bowman's Capsule in the kidney.

The Bowman's capsule is a cup-like structure situated in the nephrons in the kidney. Within it, is a coiled ball of capillaries known as a glomerulus. Renal arteries are those which carry blood to one or both kidneys. The pituitary gland is a tiny organ that is found at the base of the brain.

Hence, the correct option is (C).

83. Mosaic Disease is related to tobacco and it destroys the chlorophyll in the leaves. Wilt of potato is caused by Pseudomonas Solonacearum bacteria and in this, brown rings are formed around the xylem. The black arm of cotton is caused by Xanthomonas Bacteria and in this, a yellow-greenish spot is seen on both sides of the leaves.

Hence, the correct option is (C).

84. Given:

$$\sqrt{10 + \sqrt{25 + \sqrt{108 + \sqrt{154 + \sqrt{225}}}}}$$

$$= \sqrt{10 + \sqrt{25 + \sqrt{108 + \sqrt{154 + 15}}}}$$

$$= \sqrt{10 + \sqrt{25 + \sqrt{108 + \sqrt{169}}}}$$

$$= \sqrt{10 + \sqrt{25 + \sqrt{108 + 13}}}$$

$$= \sqrt{10 + \sqrt{25 + \sqrt{121}}}$$

$$= \sqrt{10 + \sqrt{25 + 11}}$$

$$= \sqrt{10 + \sqrt{36}}$$

$$= \sqrt{10 + 6}$$

$$= \sqrt{16} = 4$$

Hence, the correct option is (A).

85. Alessandro Volta was the first person to isolate methane gas. He discovered that methane mixed with air could be exploded using an electric spark. He is also known for inventing electric batteries and discovering contact electricity.

Hence, the correct option is (D).

86. Nicolaus Copernicus was an astronomer and mathematician who was the first to discover that the earth revolves around the sun giving birth to the heliocentric model in which the sun is at the center of the universe.

Hence, the correct option is (C).

87. Inter-disciplinary approach not just the combination of two or more disciplines, but one discipline, which is facilitated by one or more disciplines.

Since in question it is asked about assessment strategy which would help in encouragement, hence we have to choose those points which can be categorized under formative assessment because formative assessment helps to improve performance and encourage to achieve goals.

Hence, the correct option is (A).

88. Using a Watch: Before children are able to read time in a meaningful way they need to know a lot about the watch. There are different types of watches which children see around them. Mostly they first learn to use a clock that has a minute and an hour hand with numbers 1 to 12 marked on it circularly.

- Children take time to learn skills that are needed to read the time.
- Reading a watch face to tell the time is helpful in re-applying mathematical concepts of telling time.
- They should be initiated in this direction through talk. Like, it is nine o'clock, look at the clock, we shall now do mathematics.
- Example: The teacher was teaching the Class 4 children all the subjects, throughout the school hours, from 9 a.m. to 1 p.m., she had brought several cards with a time of a day written on it, like 10:00, 11:15, 11:40, 12:10, 12:30, and so on. There was a clock hanging on the wall. She told children to tell the time before starting the period.

Hence, we conclude that children read watch-face to re-apply mathematical concepts of telling time.

Hence, the correct option is (B).

89. Given:

Market price = Rs. 9,40,000

Selling price = Rs. 8,46,000

For formula, Discount = market price – selling price

Discount = Rs. 9,40,000 – Rs. 8,46,000

=Rs. 94,000

Hence, the correct option is (C).

90. Given:

Selling price = cost price – 25% of cost price

Let the cost price for 1000 gram = Rs. 1000

The selling price of 1000 gram = Rs. 750

But, due to false weighing,

The selling price of 600 gram = Rs. 750

Cost price of 600 gram = Rs. 600

So, there is a profit

Profit = Rs. 750 – Rs. 600

= Rs. 150

Profit% = $\left[\dfrac{Profit}{Cost\ price} \times 100\right]$ %

$= \left[\left(\dfrac{150}{600}\right) \times 100\right]$%

= 25%

Hence, the correct option is (C).

91. Given:

Discount = Rs. 50

Profit percentage = 25%

Calculation:

Let cost price be 100x.

So, marked price = 150% of 100x = 150x

Now, selling price = MP - Discount = 150x - 50   .....(i)

Also, if profit is 25%, then selling price = 125% of CP = 125x

From (i), we get,

150x - 50 = 125x

$\Rightarrow$ 25x = 50

$\Rightarrow$ x = 2

$\therefore$ Selling price = 125x = 125 × 2 = Rs. 250

Hence, the correct option is (C).

92. Article 312- States about the All India services. Article 310- States about the Tenure of office of persons serving the union or state. Article 311- States about the dismissal. removal or reduction on the rank of a person employed in civil capacities under the union or the state. Article 312 A- States about the Power of the parliament to vary or revoke a condition of service of the officers of certain services. Article 313- States about the Transitional provisions of public services.

Hence, the correct option is (C).

93. Earlier our constitution had 395 articles in 22 parts and 8 schedules at the time of commencement. Now the Constitution of India has 448 articles in 25 parts and 12 schedules.

Hence, the correct option is (B).

94. Formative assessment is a type of assessment which refers to monitor the child's progress throughout the learning and teaching process.

Quizzes, group discussion, conversation, portfolio, rating scale and anecdotal records, etc are the appropriate tools for formative assessment.

Hence, the correct option is (B).

95. During the Upper primary stage, slowly children must be given the opportunity to deal with abstract concepts. This is the stage at which algebra needs to be introduced. It should be introduced by connecting it to real-life situations and through its use in solving various life problems. In algebra, the emphasis has now been given to equations by broadening the base to include ideas such as mathematical sentences, replacement set and solution set.

Hence, the correct option is (A).

96. Jagannath Temple is located in Puri district of Odisha state. The famous Lingaraj Temple in Bhubaneswar and Sun Temple in Konark are located in this state. All these temples are built in the Nagara style.
Hence, the correct option is (A).

97. The evidence of mural painting in Ajanta caves and Lepakshi temple is quite clear but the evidence of mural painting in Sanchi Stupa is not clear. The pylons surrounding the stupa are filled with pictures of Buddha's life events and Jataka tales and are ornate from bottom to top. Toranas cannot be considered as part of stupas
Hence, the correct option is (B).

98. Given,

Mr. X complets a work in 45 days.

Mr. Y completes a work in 30 days.

Let the Mr. X and Y complete a work together in x days.

Work done by Mr. X and Y in 1 day $= \dfrac{1}{x}$

Work done in 1 day by Mr. X and Y $= \left(\dfrac{1}{45}\right) + \left(\dfrac{1}{30}\right)$

$\dfrac{1}{x} = \dfrac{2+3}{90}$

$\Rightarrow \dfrac{1}{x} = \dfrac{5}{90}$

$\Rightarrow \dfrac{1}{x} = \dfrac{1}{18}$

$\Rightarrow x = 18$ days

Hence, the correct option is (D).

99. Given,

Pipe A can fill a tank in 5 hours.

Pipe Q can empty a tank in 12 hours.

Total capacity of the tank $= 60$ (LCM of 5 and 12)

Tank filled in 1 hour $= \left(\dfrac{1}{5}\right) - \left(\dfrac{1}{12}\right)$

$= \dfrac{(12-5)}{60}$

$= \dfrac{7}{60}$

Time taken to fill the tank $= \dfrac{1}{\frac{7}{60}}$

$$= \frac{60}{7}$$

$$= 8\frac{4}{7} \text{ hours}$$

$\therefore$ Time taken by pipe A and Q to fill the tank is $8\frac{4}{7}$ hours.

Hence, the correct option is (A).

100. Teaching-learning materials (TLMs), also known as instructional aids, facilitate a teacher in achieving the learning objectives formulated by her/him before teaching learning activities start.

Hence, the correct option is (B).

Q.1 Financial Assistance to Non-School Going Disabled Children (less than 18 years) is the Financial Assistance Scheme of which Department of State Government of Haryana?

[Haryana Police Constable Commando Wing, 2021]

A. Finance
B. Women and Child Development
C. Social Justice and Empowerment
D. Health and Family Welfare

Q.2 Iconic French filmmaker ____________ passed away in September 2022.
A. Humbert Balsan
B. Jacques Bar
C. Christophe Barratier
D. Jean-Luc Godard

Q.3 Which of the following country has granted a patent to an 'artificial intelligence system' relating to a "food container based on fractal geometry" innovation?
A. Canada
B. South Africa
C. Australia
D. Russia

Q.4 Who among the following has been awarded for Ramon Magsaysay Award, 2018?

[Super TET Paper - I, 2019]

A. Bharat Vatwani
B. Bruce Rittmann
C. Robert Langlands
D. Richard H. Thaler

Q.5 ______ is generally considered to be an optimal blood pressure level.
A. 90/60 mmHg
B. 140/90 mmHg
C. 120/80 mmHg
D. 100/50 mmHg

Q.6 Which of the following disease is caused by bacteria?
A. Tuberculosis
B. Common-cold
C. AIDS
D. Dengue fever

Ques (7-8):Directions: Each item in this section consists of a sentence with an underlined word followed by four words. Select the option that is opposite in meaning to the underlined word and mark your response accordingly.

Q.7 For _important_ medical decisions, even finding a doctor you trust is not enough.

[UPSC NDA, 2020]

A. significant
B. trivial
C. basic
D. probable

Q.8 Planets _move_ in their orbits.

[UPSC NDA, 2020]

A. push
B. rotate
C. stall
D. flow

Ques (9-11):Directions: Each of the following items in this section consists of a sentence(s), the parts of which have been jumbled. These parts have been labelled as P, Q, R and S. You are required to rearrange the jumbled parts of the sentence and mark your response accordingly.

Q.9 P: several years ago
Q: a course on climate change at Texas A & M University
R: Professor Andrew Dessler created an introductory
S: for freshmen and sophomores

[UPSC NDA, 2020]

A. P R Q S
B. Q R P S
C. S Q R P
D. P Q R S

Q.10 P: I realize that solving the climate change problem
Q: than solving
R: will be much harder
S: the ozone depletion problem

[UPSC NDA, 2020]

A. P R Q S
B. Q R P S
C. S Q R P
D. P Q R S

Q.11 P: although the temperature of this layer of the
Q: when directly comparing the satellite
R: measurements of temperature
S: atmosphere should generally track the surface temperature, we must be careful

[UPSC NDA, 2020]

A. P R Q S
B. S Q R P
C. P R Q S
D. P S Q R

Q.12 The age of Guptas in Indian History is described as the Golden Age of Indian History. Which among the following options is not a valid reason behind this?

A. The age is known for extensive achievements in science, technology, engineering, art, dialectic, literature, logic, mathematics, astronomy, religion, and philosophy.
B. This age crystallized the common elements of Hindu Culture.
C. The age gave birth to eminent people like Kalidasa, Varahmihira, Vatsayana, AryaBhatta, Vishnu sharma, Gautama, Patanjali etc.
D. All are valid reasons

Q.13 Side of a triangle are in the ratio of 12 : 17 : 25 and its perimeter is 540 cm its area.
A. 8,000 cm^2
B. 7,000 cm^2
C. 2,000 cm^2
D. 9,000 cm^2

Q.14 An isosceles triangle has perimeter 30 cm and each of the equal side is 12 cm. Find the area of the triangle.

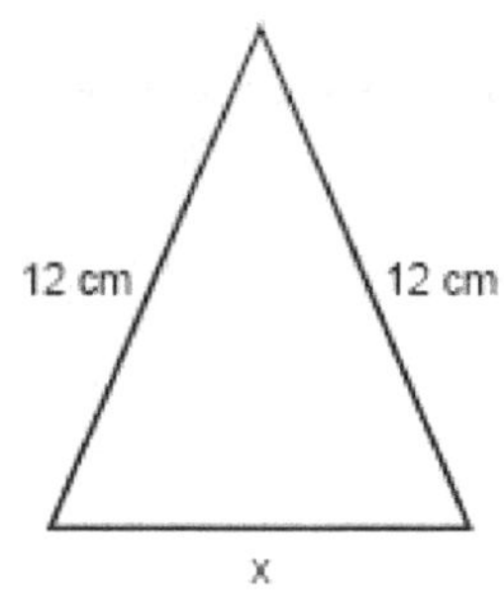

A. $8\sqrt{5}$ cm ^{2}

B. $7\sqrt{15}$ cm ^{2}

C. $7\sqrt{5}$ cm ^{2}

D. $9\sqrt{15}$ cm ^{2}

Q.15 Two cubes each of volume 64 cm³ are joined end to end. Find the surface area of the resulting cuboid.

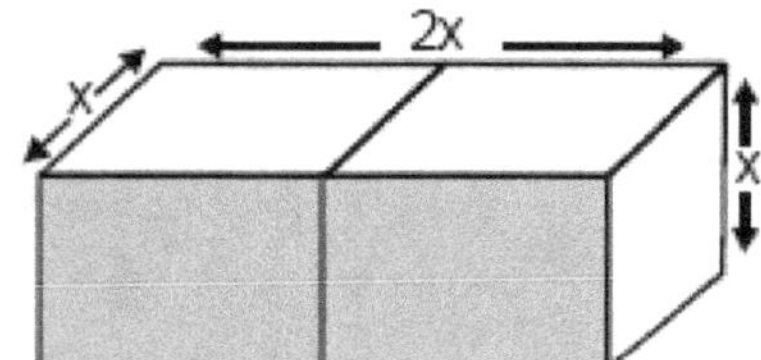

A. 150 cm ^{2} **B.** 160 cm ^{2} **C.** 180 cm ^{2} **D.** 170 cm ^{2}

Q.16 When is National Voters Day celebrated?

A. 17 December

B. 17 March

C. 21 June

D. 25 January

Q.17 When is Hindi Day celebrated?

A. 16 August

B. 14 September

C. 25 January

D. 11 July

Q.18 A person bought some eggs at a rate Rs. 5 for 3 and sold them at a rate Rs. 12 for 5. If he got Rs. 143, the number of eggs was:

A. 210   **B.** 200   **C.** 193   **D.** 195

Q.19 A reduction of 20% in the price of rice enables a customer to purchase 12.5 kg more for Rs. 800. The original price of rice per kg is (in Rs.)

A. 12   **B.** 15   **C.** 14   **D.** 16

Q.20 Pandit Harikrishna Raturi was a well known ______.

A. Writer

B. Social Worker

C. Courtier

D. Journalist

Q.21 The name Bhagat Jawahar Mal is associated with:

A. Santhal Revolt

B. Kuka Revolt

C. Naga Revolt

D. Ramoshi Revolt

Q.22 Find the square root of 15625.

[RRB/RRC Group D, 2018]

A. 125   **B.** 145   **C.** 150   **D.** 135

Q.23 In given figure AC ∥ EG, ∠DBC = 135° and ∠DFG = 145°, find the value of ∠BDF.

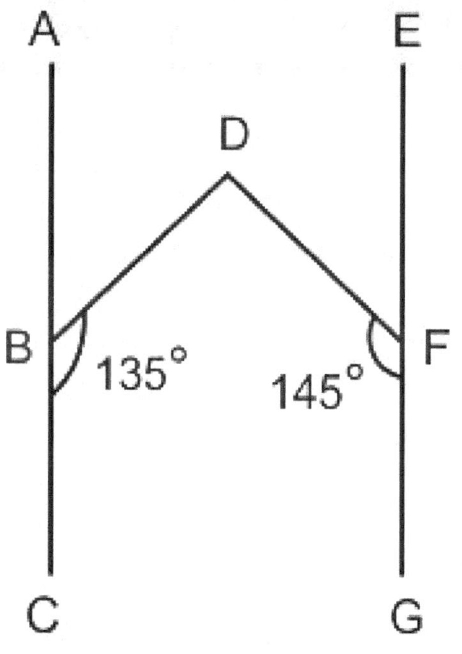

A. 60°   **B.** 70°   **C.** 80°   **D.** 85°

Q.24 "Shooting Stars" are formally known as?

A. Meteor

B. Meteoroids

C. Meteorite

D. Neutron Stars

Q.25 The country's first Super Fab Lab was launched in which state of India?

A. Karnataka

B. Tamil Nadu

C. Andhra Pradesh

D. Kerala

Q.26 The point at which all rays converge is termed as ______.

[RRB/RRC Group D, 2018]

A. Principal axis

B. Pole

C. Aperture

D. Focus

Q.27 An electric bulb of 100 W is used 8 hours per day. The energy consumed by the bulb in one day is ______ units.

[RRB/RRC Group D, 2018]

A. 800   **B.** 80   **C.** 8   **D.** 0.80

Ques (28-32):Direction: Read the passage carefully.

A recent report in News Week says that in American colleges, students of Asian origin outperform not only the minority group students but the majority whites as well. Many of these students must be of Indian origin, and their achievement is something we can be proud of. It is unlikely that these talented youngsters will come back to India, and that is the familiar brain drain problem. However recent statements by the nation's policy-makers indicate that the perception of this issue is changing. 'Brain bank' and not 'brain drain' is the more appropriate idea, they suggest since the expertise of Indians abroad is only deposited in other places and not lost.

This may be so, but this brain bank, like most other banks, is one that primarily serves customers in its neighbourhood. The skills of the Asians now excelling in America's colleges will

mainly help the U.S.A.. No matter how significant, what non-resident Indians do for India and what their counterparts do for other Asian lands is only a by-product. But it is also necessary to ask, or be reminded, why Indians study fruitfully when abroad. The Asians whose accomplishments News Week records would have probably had a very different tale if they had studied in India. In America they found elbow room, books and facilities not available and not likely to be available here. The need to prove themselves in their new country and the completion of an international standard they faced there must have cured mental and physical laziness. But other things helping them in America can be obtained here if we achieve a change in social attitudes, specially towards youth. We need to learn to value individuals and their unique qualities more than conformity and respectability. WE need to learn the language of encouragement to add to our skill in flattery. We might also learn to be less liberal with blame and less tight fisted with appreciation, especially.

Q.28 Among the many groups of students in American colleges, Asian students:

[DSSSB TGT Social Science, 2014]

A. Are often written about in magazines like News Week

B. Are most successful academically

C. Have proved that they are as good as the whites

D. Have only a minority status like the blacks

Q.29 The students of Asian origin in America include

__________.

[DSSSB TGT Social Science, 2014]

A. a fair number from India.

B. a small group from India.

C. persons from India who are very proud.

D. Indians who are the most hard-working of all.

Q.30 In general, the talented young Indians studying in America:

[DSSSB TGT Social Science, 2014]

A. Have a reputation for being hard working.

B. Have the opportunity to contribute to India's development.

C. Can solve the brain drain problem because of recent changes in policy.

D. Will not return to pursue their careers in India.

Q.31 There is talk now of the 'brain bank'. This idea:

[DSSSB TGT Social Science, 2014]

A. Is a solution to the brain drain problem.

B. Is a new problem caused partly by the brain drain.

C. Is a new way of looking at the role of qualified Indians living abroad.

D. Is based on a plan to utilize foreign exchange remittances to stimulate research and development

Q.32 The brain bank has limitations like all banks in the sense that:

[DSSSB TGT Social Science, 2014]

A. A bank's services go mainly to those near it

B. Small neighbourhood banks are not visible in this age of

multinationals

C. Only what is deposited can be withdrawn and utilized

D. No one can be forced to put his assets in a bank

Q.33 A sum of money invested at simple interest becomes 6 times of itself at 5% per annum. Find the time period.

A. 50 years   **B.** 100 years

C. 125 years   **D.** 150 years

Q.34 What is the ratio of simple interest obtained on a sum of money at a certain rate of interest for 5 years to the simple interest obtained on the same sum of money at the same rate of interest for 20 years?

A. $2:1$ **B.** $1:2$ **C.** $4:1$ **D.** $1:4$

Q.35 Radius of sphere is equal to the side of cube whose volume is 216 cubic cm. Find the surface area of sphere?

A. $144\,\pi$ square cm   **B.** $116\,\pi$ square cm

C. $242\,\pi$ square cm   **D.** $54\,\pi$ square cm

Q.36 With reference to the External debt of India, Consider the following statements:

1. Debtors can be the Union government, state governments, corporations excluding citizens of India.

2. The ratio of External Debt to GDP has been increasing steadily in the last 5 years.

Which of the statements given above is/are incorrect?

A. 1 only   **B.** 2 only

C. Both 1 and 2   **D.** Neither 1 nor 2

Q.37 With respect to direct tax proposals regarding senior citizens in the budget 2021-22, which of the following statements is correct?

A. Senior citizens aged 70 and above are exempt from paying income tax.

B. Senior citizens aged 80 and above are exempt from filing income tax returns.

C. Senior citizens aged 60 and above, whose only source of income is pension and interest are exempt from paying income tax.

D. Senior citizens aged 75 and above, whose only source of income is pension and interest are exempt from filing income tax returns.

Q.38 Who among the following was called 'Lokahitavadi'?

A. Keshub Chandra Sen

B. Mahatma Phule

C. Ishwar Vidyasagar

D. Gopal Hari Deshmukh

Q.39 Simplify:

$$\frac{1.5^3+4.7^3+3.8^3-3\times1.5\times4.7\times3.8}{1.5^2+4.7^2+3.8^2-1.5\times4.7-4.7\times3.8-3.8\times1.5}=?$$

A. 0   **B.** 1   **C.** 10   **D.** 30

Q.40 If the average of seven consecutive even numbers is 62, then the one fourth of twice of total of first and sixth number is

[Joint Entrance Examination (Polytechnic), 2018]

A. 61   **B.** 62

C. 60   **D.** None of these

Q.41 If the total of two numbers is 25 and its multiplication is 144, then their difference is

[Joint Entrance Examination (Polytechnic), 2018]

A. 4   **B.** 6   **C.** 7   **D.** 5

Q.42 In a parallelogram the side of the parallelogram is 12 cm. While the length of adjacent side is 16.66% more than the length of its adjacent side. What is the sum of squares of diagonal of the parallelogram?

A. 680   **B.** 1000   **C.** 1866   **D.** 1490

Q.43 In the given figure, AB = 6 cm, BC = 8 cm, then find the area of the trapezium ABCD.

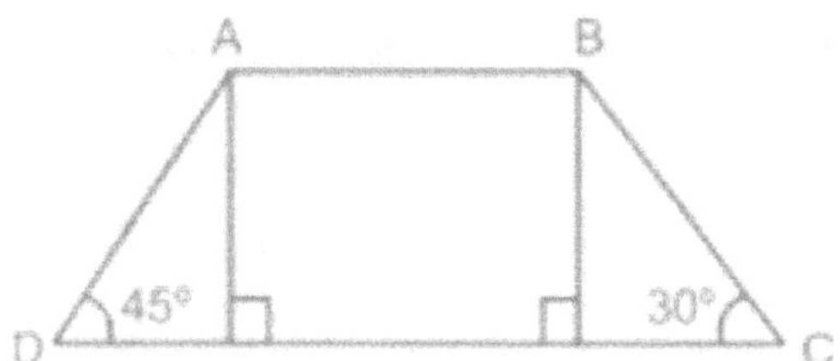

A. $\left(16 + 16\sqrt{3}\right)$ cm²   **B.** $\left(24 + 8\sqrt{3}\right)$ cm²

C. $\left(32 + 16\sqrt{3}\right)$ cm²   **D.** $\left(32 + 8\sqrt{3}\right)$ cm²

Q.44 Which of the following is not a measure of central tendency:

[UPSESSB TGT Mathematics, 2016]

A. Mean   **B.** Median

C. Mode   **D.** Standard deviation

Q.45 The mean of $1,3,4,5,7,4$ is m. The numbers $3,2,2,4,3,3,p$ have mean $m-1$ and median q then $p+q=$

[UPSESSB TGT Mathematics, 2016]

A. 4   **B.** 5   **C.** 6   **D.** 7

Q.46 The Capital of Manipur is?

A. Aizwal   **B.** Imphal   **C.** Kohima   **D.** Shillong

Q.47 If $x = 2016, y = 2015$ and $z = 2013$, then value of $x^2 + y^2 + z^2 - xy - yz - zx$ is:

A. 7   **B.** 4   **C.** 6   **D.** 2

Q.48 Direction: In the following question, some parts of the sentence may have errors. Find out which part of the sentence has an error and select the appropriate option. If a sentence is free from error, select 'No Error'.

Neither of (1)/ them (2)/ were looking for a mate. (3)/ No error (4)

A. 1   **B.** 2   **C.** 3   **D.** 4

Q.49 Which of the following parts of India receives rainfall from retreating monsoon?

[AFCAT, 2016]

A. North East India   **B.** Tamil Nadu Coast

C. Mahanadi Delta   **D.** Malabar Coast

Q.50 The Binary Star Hypothesis about the origin of the earth was propounded by:

A. H. N. Russell   **B.** R. A. Lyttelton

C. O. Schimdt   **D.** Von Weizsacker

Q.51 Match List I with List II:

List I - Land Forms		List II - Agents of Denudations	
A.	Monadnocks	I.	Wind
B.	Blind Valley	II.	Glacier
C.	Drumlin	III.	River
D.	Dreikantes	IV.	Groundwater

Choose the correct answer from the options given below:

A. A-III, B-IV, C-II, D-I

B. A-II, B-III, C-IV, D-I

C. A-I, B-IV, C-III, D-II

D. A-IV, B-II, C-I, D-III

Q.52 A shopkeeper gains 17% after allowing a discount of 10% on the market price of an article. Find his profit percent if the article is sold at a market price allowing no discount.

A. 37%   **B.** 23%   **C.** 27%   **D.** 30%

Q.53 NREGA scheme was not launched in which of the following district of Rajasthan in its first phase:

A. Jaipur   **B.** Udaipur

C. Sirohi   **D.** Dungarpur

Q.54 Harishankar Parsai, who hailed from Madhya Pradesh, was a famous writer in which branch of Hindi literature?

A. Satire   **B.** Poetry

C. Translation   **D.** Novel

Q.55 In which of the following districts of Madhya Pradesh is the 'Mahamrityunjay ka Mela' held every year?

A. Narsinghpur   **B.** Khargone

C. Sheopuri   **D.** Rewa

Ques (56-58):Direction: In the following question, the sentence is given with blank to be filled in with an appropriate word. Select the correct alternative out of the four and indicate it by selecting the appropriate option.

Q.56 The servant _____ the picture on the wall.

A. Hang   **B.** Hung   **C.** Hanged   **D.** Hunged

Q.57 She is one of the best _______ I know.

A. Teachers   **B.** Student   **C.** Doctor   **D.** Lawyer

Q.58 Soldiers are not prepared __________ that kind of attack.

A. At   **B.** By   **C.** For   **D.** About

Q.59 Consider the following statements regarding the European Union:

1. The European Union is a group of 18 countries that operate as a cohesive economic and political block.

2. The EU has developed an internal single market through a standardized system of laws that apply in all member states in matters, where members have agreed to act as one.

Which of the statements given above is/are correct?

A. 1 only   **B.** 2 only
C. Both 1 and 2   **D.** Neither 1 nor 2

Q.60 Which Organisation/Institution in its latest report named "Protecting Women's Livelihoods in Times of Pandemic: Temporary Basic Income and the Road to Gender Equality" has proposed a Temporary Basic Income (TBI) for poor women in developing countries.

A. United Nations Development Programme (UNDP)
B. Oxfam International
C. Canadian think tank Fraser Institute
D. UNESCO

Q.61 What region is also referred as the " Garden of southern India " ?

A. Western Ghats   **B.** Nilgiris
C. Cauvery Delta   **D.** Cardamom Hills

Q.62 Simplify: $y - [y - (x + y) - \{y - (y - x - y)\} + 2x]$

A. 0   **B.** x   **C.** 4x   **D.** $\frac{x}{2}$

Q.63 A and B started a business with an investment of Rs. 80000 and Rs. 60000 respectively. At the end of the year, total profit in business will be divided between them in the ratio of _______?

A. 2 : 1   **B.** 3 : 4   **C.** 2 : 3   **D.** 4 : 3

Q.64 When 50% of a number A is added to B, the second number B increase by 25%. The ratio between the numbers A and B is:

A. 2 : 3   **B.** 1 : 2   **C.** 3 : 2   **D.** 3 : 4

Ques (65-66):Direction: In the following question, a sentence has been given in Active/Passive Voice. Out of the four alternatives suggested, select the one which best expresses the same sentence in Passive/Active Voice.

Q.65 Nishu can win the prize.
A. The prize can be won by Nishu.
B. Nishu can be won by the Prize.
C. The prize can have been won by Nishu.
D. None of the above

Q.66 Do you expect your parents to come from Hyderabad today?
A. Did your parents come today from Hyderabad?
B. Is your parents expected to come today from Hyderabad?
C. Are your parents expected to come today from Hyderabad?
D. Do your parents are expected to come today from Hyderabad?

Q.67 Kautilya was the Prime Minister of which of the following Indian ruler?
A. Chandragupta Vikaramaditya
B. Ashok
C. Chandragupta Maurya
D. Raja Janak

Q.68 Find out the incorrect match-
A. Horizontal group – craft union
B. Vertical groups – corporation
C. Secondary group – corporation
D. Primary group – political party

Q.69 According to Parsons, society is a system having four basic functional prior conditions, are:
A. Adaptation, goal-orientation, integration and pattern maintenance
B. Education, socialization, social control and religion
C. Economic institutions, political institutions ideology and kinship
D. None of these

Q.70 What is the value of k for which the sum of the squares of the roots of $2x^2 - 2(k - 2)x - (k + 1) = 0$ is minimum?

[UPSC NDA, 2019]

A. -1   **B.** 1   **C.** $\frac{3}{2}$ **D.** 2

Q.71 If $|x^2 - 3x + 2| > x^2 - 3x + 2$, then which one of the following is correct?

[UPSC NDA, 2019]

A. $x \leq 1$ or $x \geq 2$
B. $1 \leq x \leq 2$
C. $1 < x < 2$
D. x is any real value except 3 and 4

Q.72 Which badminton player recently clinched the 'Indonesia Masters title'?
A. Carolina Marin   **B.** Ratchanok Intanon
C. P V Sindhu   **D.** Nozomi Okuhara

Q.73 Which Indian State/ UT has won the Khelo India Youth Games Champions trophy, 2020?
A. Haryana   **B.** Maharashtra
C. Gujarat   **D.** Karnataka

Q.74 By which process polymers are formed?
A. Condensation   **B.** Polymerization
C. Decomposition   **D.** Hydrolysis

Q.75 Who is regarded as the "Father of Modern Chemistry"?
A. Robert Boyle   **B.** John Dalton
C. Antoine Lavoisier   **D.** Dmitri Mendeleev

Ques (76-77):Direction: In the following question, out of the four alternatives, select the alternative which best expresses the meaning of the Idiom/Phrase.

Q.76 No room to swing a cat.
A. An open public area
B. To catch a cat in a closed room
C. To have a bad luck
D. To be in a very small and crowded place

Q.77 Crocodile tears
A. To feel sad for another person's misfortunes

B. To laugh so much that your eyes start to water
C. A person whose sadness is never noticed
D. Expressions of sorrow that are insincere

Q.78 The price of onions were increased by 25%. What percentage subsidy should the government provide on onions so that the effective price rise for consumers is only 10%?
A. 10%   **B.** 12%   **C.** 12.5%   **D.** 20%

Q.79 If B is 20% greater than C and 40% smaller than A then A is what percent larger than C?
A. 60%   **B.** 80%   **C.** 100%   **D.** 120%

Q.80 The 'Red Data Book' is the documentation of rare and endangered species of :
1. Animals
2. Plants
3. Fungi
A. Only 1   **B.** 1 and 2
C. 2 and 3   **D.** 1, 2 and 3

Q.81 What is the Highest Common Factor of $\dfrac{12}{17}$ and $\dfrac{15}{34}$?
A. $\dfrac{9}{68}$ **B.** $\dfrac{3}{17}$ **C.** $\dfrac{3}{34}$ **D.** $\dfrac{9}{17}$

Q.82 X and Y invested in a business in a ratio of 4 : 1. They donated 21% of a profit to an NGO and X's share is Rs. 31,600. Find the total profit.
A. Rs. 25,000   **B.** Rs. 45,000
C. Rs. 50,000   **D.** Rs. 67,000

Q.83 Who was India's first man in space?
A. Rakesh Sharma   **B.** Ravish Malhotra
C. Kalpana Chawla   **D.** None of the above

Q.84 The cube root of $.000216$ is:
A. .6   **B.** 0.06   **C.** 77   **D.** 87

Q.85 During which period bronze icons of Nataraja deity who has four hands was casted?
A. Chola period   **B.** Chera period
C. Shunga period   **D.** Pandayas period

Q.86 Name the president who was first to use the President's power to return a bill to parliament.
A. Giani Zail Singh
B. A P J Abdul Kalam
C. Sarvappalli Radhakrishnan
D. Rajendra Prasad

Q.87 Who has the distinction of serving as the Chief Justice of India, President, and the Vice president?
A. Justice M Hidayatullah
B. Justice Bhagwati
C. Justice H.J.Kania
D. Justice Mehr Chand Mahajan

Q.88 Heena and Karan together complete a work in 12 days, if Heena works alone, she completes it in 18 days. Karan alone can complete it in how many days?

A. 12 days   **B.** 36 days   **C.** 14 days   **D.** 34 days

Q.89 10 persons begin to work together on a job, but after some days, 4 persons leave. As a result, the job, which could have been completed in 40 days, was completed in 50 days. How many days after commencement of the work did the four persons leave?
A. 25   **B.** 24   **C.** 30   **D.** 20

Q.90 Teachers can remediate for the student with language difficulty by:
A. Focusing on individual progress with individual instruction
B. Providing notes that are summarized and simplified
C. Initially giving information as reading only, not writing
D. Conducting extra class for the students to 'catch up with others'

Q.91 Express X = 0.456666.... as a fraction:
A. 421900   **B.** 411990   **C.** 411900   **D.** 431900

Q.92 If $\sqrt[3]{1 + \dfrac{x}{169}} = \dfrac{14}{13}$, then x is equal to:
A. 1   **B.** 13   **C.** 27.02   **D.** 42.07

Ques (93-94):Direction: Out of the four alternatives, choose the one which can be substituted for the given word/sentence.

Q.93 An object or portion serving as a sample:
A. specification   **B.** spectre
C. spectacle   **D.** specimen

Q.94 An ability to express oneself well in speech
A. oracy   **B.** orthodox   **C.** versatile   **D.** foresight

Q.95 In a test conducted in school, 42% of students failed in math and 52% of students failed in Science. 17% of students failed in both the subjects. If 69 students passed both the subjects then determine the number of students who appeared for the test
A. 600   **B.** 500   **C.** 400   **D.** 300

Q.96 Which branch of Mathematics teaches Logical thinking and natural design?
A. Algebra   **B.** Geometry
C. Arithmetic   **D.** Trigonometry

Q.97 Consider the following statements :
$A = $ If n is even, then n^2 is even.
$B = $ If n^2 is not even, n is not even.
$C = $ If n^2 is even, then n is even.
$D = $ If n is not even, then n^2 is not even.
Which of the following statements is true?
A. B is inverse of A
B. D is contraposition of A
C. C is converse of A
D. D is converse of A

Ques (98-100):Direction: Production of paper (in lakh tonnes) by three companies X, Y, and Z over the years. Study the graph and answer the questions that follow.

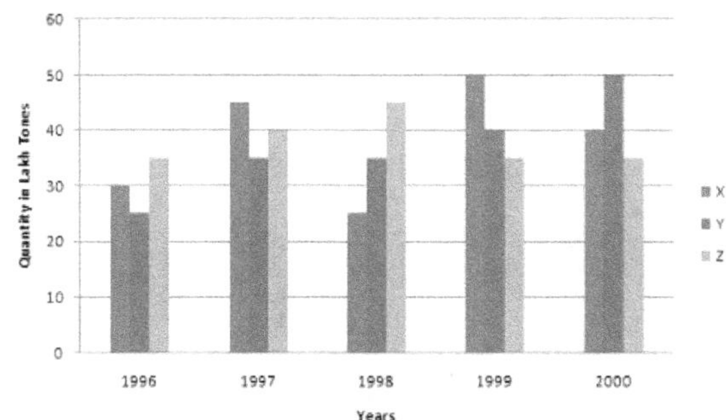

Q.98 What is the ratio of the average production of company X in the period 1998-2000 to the average production of company Y in the same period?

A. 1 : 1   **B.** 15 : 17   **C.** 23 : 25   **D.** 27 : 29

Q.99 The average production for five years was maximum for which company?

A. X   **B.** Y

C. Z   **D.** X and Z both

Q.100 In which year was the percentage of production of company Z to the production of company Y the maximum?

A. 1996   **B.** 1997   **C.** 1998   **D.** 1999

// Smart Answer Sheet //

Correct — Percentage of students who answered correctly. **Skipped** — Percentage of students who skipped.

Q.	Ans.	Correct	Skipped	Q.	Ans.	Correct	Skipped	Q.	Ans.	Correct	Skipped	Q.	Ans.	Correct	Skipped	Q.	Ans.	Correct	Skipped	Q.	Ans.	Correct	Skipped
1	C	40.19 %	1.13 %	18	D	64.02 %	1.13 %	35	A	77.46 %	0.0 %	52	D	60.96 %	1.05 %	69	A	85.48 %	0.0 %	86	B	29.93 %	4.02 %
2	D	66.12 %	1.17 %	19	D	60.38 %	1.24 %	36	C	56.37 %	1.36 %	53	A	82.02 %	0.0 %	70	C	15.53 %	3.68 %	87	A	53.45 %	1.4 %
3	B	47.7 %	1.06 %	20	A	21.55 %	3.31 %	37	D	43.2 %	1.34 %	54	A	46.02 %	1.85 %	71	C	53.4 %	1.83 %	88	B	66.34 %	1.43 %
4	A	47.69 %	1.45 %	21	B	55.32 %	1.35 %	38	D	83.46 %	0.0 %	55	D	56.4 %	1.09 %	72	B	57.67 %	1.16 %	89	A	54.5 %	1.32 %
5	C	83.01 %	0.0 %	22	A	66.18 %	1.29 %	39	C	17.14 %	4.6 %	56	B	81.47 %	0.0 %	73	B	18.33 %	4.65 %	90	A	60.35 %	1.5 %
6	A	77.52 %	0.0 %	23	C	52.24 %	1.03 %	40	A	44.01 %	1.3 %	57	A	81.62 %	0.0 %	74	B	86.84 %	0.0 %	91	C	83.1 %	0.0 %
7	B	78.3 %	0.0 %	24	A	64.55 %	1.67 %	41	C	69.91 %	1.89 %	58	C	77.16 %	0.0 %	75	C	84.59 %	0.0 %	92	D	40.77 %	1.22 %
8	C	79.05 %	0.0 %	25	D	60.92 %	1.22 %	42	A	67.42 %	1.52 %	59	B	17.69 %	3.04 %	76	D	58.87 %	1.46 %	93	D	56.19 %	1.24 %
9	A	64.83 %	1.67 %	26	D	86.91 %	0.0 %	43	D	19.06 %	3.36 %	60	A	49.77 %	1.01 %	77	D	89.91 %	0.0 %	94	A	54.48 %	1.44 %
10	A	44.44 %	1.08 %	27	D	57.06 %	1.52 %	44	D	47.39 %	1.17 %	61	C	66.94 %	1.8 %	78	B	66.75 %	1.18 %	95	D	54.53 %	1.69 %
11	D	41.34 %	1.63 %	28	C	47.72 %	1.56 %	45	D	44.68 %	1.03 %	62	C	60.28 %	1.55 %	79	C	67.58 %	1.53 %	96	B	29.69 %	4.61 %
12	D	69.44 %	1.88 %	29	A	15.88 %	4.15 %	46	B	80.77 %	0.0 %	63	D	45.23 %	1.19 %	80	D	59.7 %	1.52 %	97	A	14.04 %	4.01 %
13	D	30.37 %	4.15 %	30	D	15.51 %	4.19 %	47	A	51.99 %	1.44 %	64	B	69.97 %	1.17 %	81	C	46.63 %	1.26 %	98	C	55.78 %	1.55 %
14	D	63.29 %	1.76 %	31	C	19.18 %	3.55 %	48	C	78.06 %	0.0 %	65	A	61.91 %	1.18 %	82	C	67.09 %	1.94 %	99	D	46.88 %	1.9 %
15	B	61.03 %	1.64 %	32	A	18.67 %	3.65 %	49	B	66.99 %	1.34 %	66	C	49.07 %	1.4 %	83	A	69.4 %	1.85 %	100	A	15.97 %	3.48 %
16	D	56.53 %	1.92 %	33	B	46.56 %	1.06 %	50	A	82.0 %	0.0 %	67	C	16.45 %	3.74 %	84	B	85.82 %	0.0 %				
17	B	55.05 %	1.9 %	34	D	81.07 %	0.0 %	51	A	62.02 %	1.49 %	68	D	31.25 %	3.69 %	85	A	80.88 %	0.0 %				

//Hints and Solutions//

1. Financial Assistance to Non-School Going Disabled Children (less than 18 years) is the Financial Assistance Scheme of Social Justice and Empowerment Department of State Government of Haryana.

The Ministry of Social Justice and Empowerment is a Government of India ministry. It is responsible for welfare, social justice and empowerment of disadvantaged and marginalised sections of society, including scheduled castes (SC), Other Backward Classes (OBC), Manual Scavengers, the disabled, the elderly, and the victims of drug abuse.

Hence, the correct option is (C).

2. Iconic French filmmaker Jean-Luc Godard passed away at the age of 91 in Switzerland.

- He revolutionized popular cinema in 1960 with his debut feature 'Breathless' & stood for years as one of the world's most vital and provocative directors.
- He started his career as a film critic in the 1950s.
- In December 2007, he was honoured by the European Film Academy with a lifetime achievement award.

Hence, the correct option is (D).

3. South Africa, first time in the world, has granted a patent to an 'artificial intelligence system' relating to a "food container based on fractal geometry" innovation.

The innovation involves interlocking food containers that are easy for robots to grasp and stack.

Hence, the correct option is (B).

4. Bharat Vatwani has been awarded for Ramon Magsaysay Award, 2018.

Bharat Vatwani is an Indian psychiatrist in Mumbai. He was awarded Ramon Magsaysay Award in 2018 for leading the rescue of thousands of mentally ill street paupers to treat and reunite them with their families. Bharat Vatwani and his wife established Shraddha Rehabilitation Foundation in 1988, aimed at rescuing mentally-ill persons living on the streets; providing free shelter, food, and psychiatric treatment; and reuniting them with their families.

Hence, the correct option is (A).

5.

- 120/80 mmHg is considered to be an optimal blood pressure level.
- Blood pressure readings are expressed in millimeters of mercury (mm Hg).
- Blood pressure is measured using an instrument called a Sphygmomanometer.

Hence, the correct option is (C).

6.

- Tuberculosis is an infectious disease caused by MTB which is Mycobacterium Tuberculosis Bacteria.

- MTB is an airborne pathogen, meaning that the bacteria that cause TB can spread through the air from person to person.

Hence, the correct option is (A).

7. The word 'important' means having great meaning or lasting effect.

The word 'trivial' means of little value or importance.

Thus, we can say that 'trivial' is the opposite in meaning to the given word.

Hence, the correct option is (B).

8. The word 'move' means to cause to function.

The word 'stall' means to stop or cause to stop making progress.

Thus, we can say that 'stall' is the opposite in meaning to the given word.

Hence, the correct option is (C).

9.

- The sentence 'P' is independent of any other sentences as it is giving general information about "sometime back". Hence, 'P' is the first part.
- The noun "Professor Andrew Dessler" in the sentence 'R' refers back to the sentence 'P'. Hence, 'R' follows 'P'.
- The adjective 'introductory' in the sentence 'R' is describing the noun "course" in the sentence 'Q'. Hence, 'Q' follows 'R'.
- The sentence 'S' is concluding the sentence by mentioning for whom the course is all about. Hence, 'S' makes the last sentence.

After rearranging the sentences: Several years ago Professor Andrew Dessler created an introductory course on climate change at Texas A & M University for freshmen and sophomores.

Hence, the correct option is (A).

10. The sentence 'P' is independent of any other sentences as it is giving general information about "solving the climate change". Hence, 'P' is the first part.

The future result of the sentence 'P' is described in the sentence 'R'. Hence, 'R' follows 'P'.

The adjective 'harder' in the sentence 'R' is linked with the preposition "than" in the sentence 'Q'. Hence, 'Q' follows 'R'.

The sentence 'S' is concluding the sentence. Hence, 'S' makes the last sentence.

After rearranging the sentences: I realize that solving the climate change problem will be much harder than solving.

Hence, the correct option is (A).

11.

- The sentence 'P' is independent of any other sentences as it is giving general information about the "temperature of a layer". Hence, 'P' is the first part.

- The phrase "layer of the" in the sentence 'P' is linked with the noun 'atmosphere' in the sentence 'S'. Hence, 'S' follows 'P'.
- The adjective 'careful' in the sentence 'S' is modified by the adverb "when" in the sentence 'Q'. Hence, 'Q' follows 'S'.
- The sentence 'R' is concluding the sentence. Hence, 'R' makes the last sentence.

After rearranging the sentences: Although the temperature of this layer of the atmosphere should generally track the surface temperature, we must be careful when directly comparing the satellite measurements of temperature.

Hence, the correct option is (D).

12. The age of Guptas in Indian History is described as the Golden Age of Indian History as the age is known for extensive achievements in science, technology, engineering, art, dialectic, literature, logic, mathematics, astronomy, religion, and philosophy. This age crystallized the common elements of Hindu Culture. The age gave birth to eminent people like Kalidasa, Varahmihira, Vatsayana, AryaBhatta, Vishnu Sharma, Gautama, Patanjali etc. Since all the reasons are valid.

Hence, the correct option is (D).

13. Perimeter of the triangle $= 540$ cm

$\Rightarrow$ Semi-perimeter of the triangle, $s = \dfrac{540}{2} = 270$

$\therefore$ The sides are in the ratio of $12:17:25$.

$\therefore a = 12x, b = 17x, c = 25x$

$\therefore 12x + 17x + 25x = 540$

$\Rightarrow 54x = 540$

$\Rightarrow x = \dfrac{540}{54} = 10$

$\therefore a = 12 \times 10 = 120$

$b = 17 \times 10 = 170$

$c = 25 \times 10 = 250$

$\Rightarrow s - a) = (270 - 120) = 150$ cm

$(s - b) = (270 - 170) = 100$ cm

$(s - c) = (270 - 250)cm = 20$ cm

$\therefore$ Area of the triangle $= \sqrt{s(s-a)(s-b)(s-c)}$

$= \sqrt{270 \times 150 \times 100 \times 20}$ cm ^{2}

$=$

$\sqrt{3 \times 3 \times 3 \times 10 \times 3 \times 5 \times 10 \times 10 \times 2 \times 2 \times 5}$ cm ^{2}

$= \sqrt{10^2 \times 10^2 \times 3^2 \times 3^2 \times 5^2 \times 2^2}$

$= 10 \times 10 \times 3 \times 3 \times 5 \times 2 = 9{,}000$

Thus, the required area of the triangle $= 9{,}000$ cm ^{2}

Hence, the correct option is (D).

14. Equal sides of the triangle are 12 cm each.

Let the third side $= x$ cm.

Since, perimeter $= 30$ cm

$\therefore 12 + 12 + x = 30$ cm

$\Rightarrow x = 30 - 12 - 12$ cm

$\Rightarrow x = 6$ cm

Now, semi-perimeter $= \dfrac{30}{2} = 15$ cm

$\therefore$ Area of the triangle $= \sqrt{s(s-a)(s-b)(s-c)}$

$= \sqrt{15(15-12)(15-12)(15-6)}$

$= \sqrt{15 \times 3 \times 3 \times 9}$

$= \sqrt{5 \times 3 \times 3 \times 3 \times 3 \times 3}$ cm ^{2}

$= \sqrt{3^2 \times 3^2 \times 3 \times 5}$

$= 3 \times 3 \times \sqrt{5 \times 3}$

$= 9\sqrt{15}$ cm ^{2}

Thus, the required area of the triangle $= 9\sqrt{15}$ cm ^{2}

Hence, the correct option is (D).

15. Volume of each cube $= 64$ cm ^{3}

$\therefore$ Total volume of the two cubes $= 2 \times 64 = 128$ cm ^{3}

Let the edge of each cube $= x$

$\therefore x^3 = 64 = 4^3$

$\therefore x = 4\ cm$

Now, Length of the resulting cuboid $l = 2x$ cm

Breadth of the resulting cuboid $b = x$

Height of the resulting cuboid $h = x$ cm

$\therefore$ Surface area of the cuboid $= 2(lb + bh + hl) = 2[(2x \cdot x) + (x \cdot x) + (x \cdot 2x)]$

$= 2[(2 \times 4 \times 4) + (4 \times 4) + (4 \times 2 \times 4)]$

$= 2[32 + 16 + 32] = 2[80]$ cm ^{2}

$= 160$ cm ^{2}

Hence, the correct option is (B).

16. In India, National Voters Day is celebrated on 25 January every year. In the largest democracy like India in the world, National Voters' Day was being observed in view of the declining trend regarding voting. Mrs. Pratibha Devi Singh Patil inaugurated the 'National Voters Day'.

Hence, the correct option is (D).

17. India celebrates Hindi Diwas, also known as Hindi Day, on September 14 every year to commemorate the adoption of Hindi in the Devanagari script as one of the official languages of the nation.

Hindi Divas is celebrated on 14 September because, on this day in 1949, the Constituent Assembly of India had adopted Hindi written in Devanagari script as the official language of the Republic of India.

Hence, the correct option is (B).

18. Let the number of eggs be x

Cost of 3 eggs = Rs. 5

Cost of 1 egg = $\dfrac{5}{3} \times x$

So, CP = $\dfrac{5}{3} \times x$

Eggs sold = 5

Price at which eggs are sold = Rs. 12

So, SP = $\dfrac{12}{5x}$

Profit = SP - CP

$$143 = \dfrac{12}{5x} - \dfrac{5}{3x}$$

(For Solving, take the LCM of 3 and 5 and solve through it)

x = 195

Thus, he purchased 195 eggs.

Hence, the correct option is (D).

19. According to the question,

Let the previous rate of rice is Rs. x/kg.

Now the new rate of rice is $= x \times \dfrac{80}{100}$

$$= \dfrac{4}{5}x$$

Now in Rs. 800 the customer purchased more 12.5 kg,

$$= \dfrac{800}{\left(\frac{4}{5}x\right)} - \dfrac{800}{x} = 12.5$$

$$= \dfrac{4000}{4x} - \dfrac{800}{x} = 12.5$$

$$= \dfrac{200}{x} = 12.5$$

$$= x = \dfrac{200}{12.5}$$

= 16

Hence, the correct option is (D).

20. Pandit Harikrishna Raturi was a well-known writer.

- A book named Garhwal ka Itihas in Hindi was prepared by him.
- The English version of the book was arranged by Kirti Shah from London.
- Kirti Shah died, before the completion of the book.
- The manuscript of the book was lost by Pandit Harikrishna Raturi too.
- The book was once again written by Harikrishna Raturi in 1928 in Garhwal.
- The book Narendra Hindu law was written and published by Raturi in 1917.
- The book Garhwal Varnan was published by him in 1910.
- In June 1933, Raturi died.

Hence, the correct option is (A).

21. The name Bhagat Jawahar Mal is associated with Kuka Revolt.

- The founder of the Kuka movement was Bhagat Jawahar Mal.
- Bhagat Jawar Mal was also known as Sian Sahib. Initially, the purpose of this revolt was to purify Sikhism by removing the prevalent evils. Sian Saheb along with his disciple 'Balak Singh' formed a group of his followers. The headquarters of this party used to be in 'Hazara'.
- The Kuka Revolt also came to be known as Namdhari Movement. The Namdhari movement was founded by Balak Singh (1797–1862), who did not believe in any religious ritual other than the repetition of God's name (for which reason members of the sect are called Namdharis).
- Ram Singh, one of the famous leaders of the Kuka movement gave a call to his followers for the boycott of British goods, government schools, and government posts.
- In 2012, the Government of India released a commemorative Rs 100 coin on the completion of 150 years of the Kuka Movement.

Hence, the correct option is (B).

22. $\sqrt{15625}$

$$= \sqrt{(125 \times 125)}$$

$$= 125$$

Hence, the correct option is (A).

23. Given:

AC || EG

$\angle$DBC = 135° and $\angle$DFG = 145°

Calculation:

We construct a PQ line parallel to AC and EG

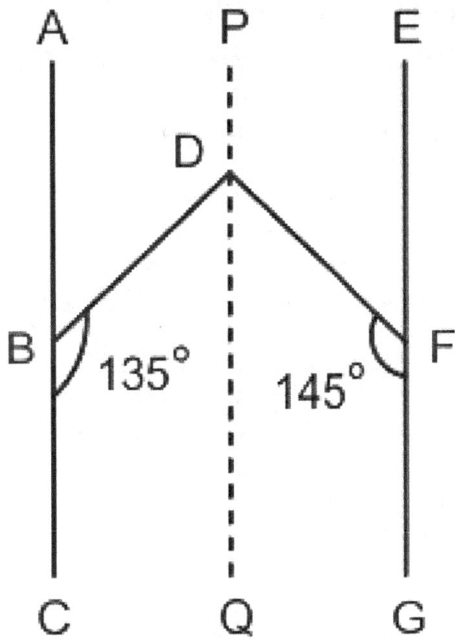

Now, AB || PQ || EG

We know that the sum of interior anngle formed on the same side of parallel lines is 180°

∠BDQ + ∠DBC = 180°

⇒ ∠BDQ + 135° = 180°

⇒ ∠BDQ = 45° -------(1)

Similarly, we have

∠QDF + ∠DFG = 180°

⇒ ∠QDF + 145° = 180°

⇒ ∠QDF = 35° -------(2)

Since, ∠BDF = ∠BDQ + ∠QDF

So on putting values of ∠BDQ and ∠QDF from -(1) & (2) we get,

∠BDF = 45° + 35° = 80°

∴ The value of ∠BDF is 80°

Hence, the correct option is (C).

24. Meteor – also known as "shooting stars" are the light phenomena which results when a small meteoroid enters the Earth's atmosphere burns up as it passes through our atmosphere and vaporizes.

Meteoroid - are fragments of a comet or asteroid orbiting the Sun or interplanetary debris.

Meteorite – is a meteoroid that survives its fall through the atmosphere and lands on the Earth's surface.

Neutron Stars - are star that have mass between 1.35 and 2.1 times the mass of the Sun.

Hence, the correct option is (A).

25.

- The country's first Super Fab Lab was launched at the Integrated Startup Complex of the Kerala Startup Mission (KSUM).

- The lab will give a major push to the hardware industry in the country and the only such facility outside the U.S.

- The Super Fab Lab will function in collaboration with the Massachusetts Institute of Technology (MIT).

Hence, the correct option is (D).

26. The point at which all the rays converge is termed focus. The straight line that goes through the center of the lens at right angles to the lens surface is called the principal axis. Pole is the midpoint of the Lens. The circular arc of any mirror is called the aperture of that mirror.

Hence, the correct option is (D).

27. Given,

Power $= 100$ w,

Time $= 8$ hours per day

We know that

$$\text{Power} = \frac{\text{Energy}}{\text{Time}}$$

Power $= 100$ w $= 0.1$ kw

$$0.1 = \frac{E}{8}$$

Energy $= 0.8$ kWh $= 0.8$ Unit

Hence, the correct option is (D).

28. Among the many groups of students in American colleges, Asian students have proved that they are as good as the whites. Asper recent report in News Week, in American colleges, students of Asian origin specially Indian origin outperform not only the minority group students but the majority whites as well and their achievement is something we can be proud of.

Hence, the correct option is (C).

29. The students of Asian origin in America include a fair number from India.

Hence, the correct option is (A).

30. In general, the talented young Indians studying in America will not return to pursue their careers in India.

Hence, the correct option is (D).

31. This idea is a new way of looking at the role of qualified Indians living abroad.

Hence, the correct option is (C).

32. The brain bank has limitations like all banks in the sense thata bank's services go mainly to those near it.

Hence, the correct option is (A).

33. Given-

A sum of money invested at simple interest becomes 6 times of itself at 5% per annum.

Let the sum $P = Rs.\,X$

Amount $A = Rs.\,6X$

Simple Interest $SI = A - P$

$\Rightarrow SI = Rs.\,(6X - X)$

$\Rightarrow SI = Rs.\,5X$

Rate $R = 5\%$ per annum

According to the formula-

$T = \dfrac{100 \times SI}{P \times R}$ [where T is time period]

$\Rightarrow T = \dfrac{100 \times 5X}{X \times 5}$

$\Rightarrow T = 100$ years

Hence, the correct option is (B).

34. Let the sum of money $P = Rs.\,A$

Let the rate of interest $R = r\%$

Case 1:

Time $T_1 = 5$ years

Simple Interest $SI_1 = \dfrac{A \times r \times 5}{100}$

$\Rightarrow SI_1 = Rs.\,\dfrac{Ar}{20}$

Case 2:

Time $T_2 = 20$ years

Simple Interest $SI_2 = \dfrac{A \times r \times 20}{100}$

$\Rightarrow SI_2 = Rs.\,\dfrac{Ar}{5}$

Required ratio $= SI_1 : SI_2$

$= \dfrac{Ar}{20} : \dfrac{Ar}{5}$

$= 1 : 4$

Hence, the correct option is (D).

35. Given:

Volume of cube is 216 cubic cm and side of cube is equal to the radius of sphere

Formula used:

Volume of cube = (Side)³

Surface area of sphere = $4\pi r^2$

The volume of cube is 216 cubic cm.

∴ Side of cube = 6 cm

Now, the side of cube is equal to the radius of sphere.

∴ Surface area of sphere = $4\pi r^2$

$= 4\pi (6)^2$ = 144 π square cm

Hence, the correct option is (A).

36. The external debt of India is the total debt the country owes to foreign creditors. The debtors can be the Union government, state governments, corporations or citizens of India. So, statement 1 is not correct.

The ratio of external debt to GDP in India varies as shown:

2016	23.4
2017	19.8
2018	20.1
2019	19.8
2020 June (Provisional)	21.8

So, It can be seen that India's External Debt to GDP ratio did not increase steadily. So statement 2 is not correct.

Hence, the correct option is (C).

37. The government has introduced various reforms in the Direct Tax System for the benefit of our taxpayers and economy. Reducing corporate tax rates, the abolition of Dividend Distribution Tax are some of the reforms the government has brought in the recent period.

In the same direction government in the budget 2021-22 has given relief to senior citizens aged 75 and above, whose only source of income is pension and interest by exempting them from filing income tax returns. Paying banks will deduct the necessary tax on their income and this will reduce the compliance burden on senior citizens.

Hence, the correct option is (D).

38. Gopal Hari Deshmukh, was an Indian activist, thinker, social reformer, and writer from Maharashtra. At age 25, Deshmukh started writing articles aimed at social reform in Maharashtra in the weekly Prabhakar under the pen name Lokhitawadi. He promoted emancipation (liberation) and the education of women and wrote against arranged child marriages, the dowry system, and polygamy, all of which were prevalent in India in his times.

He wrote against the evils of the caste system, condemned harmful Hindu religious orthodoxy, and attacked the monopoly in religious matters and rituals which Brahmin priests had through a long tradition (Deshmukh, himself, belonged to the Brahmin caste). He enunciated certain 15 principles for bringing about religious reform in Hindu society. For all his social works he came to be known as Lokhitwadi (one who works in the interest of the people).

Hence, the correct option is (D).

39.
$$\frac{1.5^3+4.7^3+3.8^3-3\times1.5\times4.7\times3.8}{1.5^2+4.7^2+3.8^2-1.5\times4.7-4.7\times3.8-3.8\times1.5}$$

$$=\frac{(1.5+4.7+3.8)\{1.5^2+4.7^2+3.8^2-1.5\times4.7-4.7\times3.8-3.8\times1.5\}}{\{1.5^2+4.7^2+3.8^2-1.5\times4.7-4.7\times3.8-3.8\times1.5\}}$$

$$\left[\because a^3+b^3+c^3-3abc=(a+b+c)\left(a^2+b^2+c^2-ab-bc-ca\right)\right]$$

$$=1.5+4.7+3.8$$

$$=10.0$$

$$=10$$

Hence, the correct option is (C).

40. Let the first of the given 7 numbers be 'm'

$$m, m+2. m+4. m+6. m+8. m+10. m+12$$

BTP.

$$\frac{(m+m+2+m+4+m+6+m+8+m+10+m+12)}{7}=62$$

or $\cdot\dfrac{(7m+42)}{7}=62$

or. $\dfrac{7(m+6)}{7}=62$

or, m $+6=62$

or, $m=62-6$

therefore.

$$m=56$$

sixth number $=m+10$

$$=56+10$$

$$=66$$

then

$$\frac{1}{4}2(56+66)$$

$$=\frac{1}{2}122$$

$$=61$$

Hence, the correct option is (A).

41. If the total of two numbers is 25 and its multiplication is 144 then their difference is

Let say two numbers are

$$A\&B$$

$$A+B=25$$

$$AB=144$$

Squaring $(A+B)$

$$(A+B)^2=25^2$$

$$\Rightarrow A^2+B^2+2AB=625$$

$$\Rightarrow A^2+B^2-2AB+2AB+2AB=625$$

$$\Rightarrow (A-B)^2+4AB=625$$

$$\Rightarrow (A-B)^2=625-4AB$$

$$\Rightarrow (A-B)^2=625-4(144)$$

$$\Rightarrow (A-B)^2=625-576$$

$$\Rightarrow (A-B)^2=49$$

$$\Rightarrow A-B=\pm7$$

Difference of numbers $=7$

Hence, the correct option is (C).

42. Given,

Length of the side of parallelogram = 12

Length of the side adjacent side of parallelogram $=12\times\dfrac{7}{6}=14$

As we know,

$$d_1^2+d_2^2=2(a^2+b^2)$$

$$\Rightarrow d_1^2+d_2^2=2(12^2+14^2)$$

$$\Rightarrow d_1^2+d_2^2=2\times(144+196)$$

$$\Rightarrow d_1^2+d_2^2=2\times340$$

$$\Rightarrow d_1^2+d_2^2=680$$

Hence, the correct option is (A).

43. Given,

AB = 6 cm, BC = 8 cm

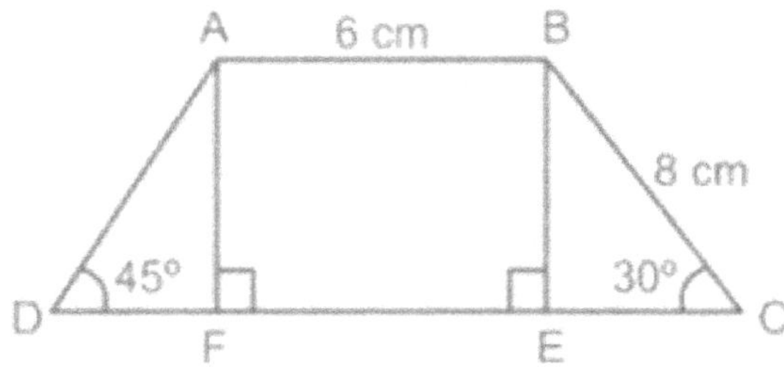

In ΔBCE:

BE = 8 sin 30° = 4 cm

CE = 8 cos 30° $=4\sqrt{3}$ cm

Since the trapezium has two parallel sides: AB ‖ CD

∴ AF = BE = 4 cm

In ΔADF:

$$\tan 45° = \frac{AF}{DF}$$

$$\Rightarrow DF = \frac{AF}{\tan 45°} = 4 \text{ cm}$$

We know that,

Area of the trapezium $= \frac{1}{2} \times$ (Sum of parallel sides) $\times$ Height

$\therefore$ Area of the trapezium $= \frac{1}{2} \times \left(6 + 6 + 4 + 4\sqrt{3}\right) \times 4$

$$= \left(16 + 4\sqrt{3}\right) \times 2$$

$$= \left(32 + 8\sqrt{3}\right) \text{ cm}^2$$

Hence, the correct option is (A).

44. Mean is the arithmetic average of a data set. This is found by adding the numbers in a data set and dividing by the number of observations in the data set.

The median is the middle number in a data set when the numbers are listed in either ascending or descending order.

MODE is the value of the observation which has the maximum frequency.

The Standard deviation is a measure of dispersion. It is the action or process of distributing thing over a wide area (nothing about central location)

$\therefore$ The Standard deviation is not a measure of central tendency.

Hence, the correct option is (D).

45. Given:
The mean of the number $1,3,5,4,7,4$ is m
The mean of the number $3,2,2,4,3,3, p$ is $m - 1$
Formula used:
Mean = Sum of all the numbers/Total numbers

Median of odd number $= \left(\frac{(n+1)}{2}\right)^{\text{th}}$ term

$$\text{Mean} = \frac{(1+3+4+5+7+4)}{6}$$

$$\Rightarrow \frac{24}{6} = m$$

$$\Rightarrow m = 4 \text{.......(1)}$$

And, Mean $= \frac{(3+2+2+4+3+3+p)}{7}$

$$\Rightarrow \frac{(17+p)}{7} = m - 1$$

$$\Rightarrow 17 + p = 3 \times 7 \text{...... (From eq (1))}$$

$$\Rightarrow p = 4$$

Arranging the given data in the ascending order then,

$2,2,3,3,3,4,4$

Here, number of terms, $(n) = 7$

Median $= \{\frac{(7+1)}{2}\}^{\text{th}}$ term $= 4^{\text{th}}$ term

4th term in the above data is 3

Median $= 3 = q$

Now, $p + q = 4 + 3 = 7$
Hence, the correct option is (D).

46.

- The official language of Manipur is Manipuri.
- Capital: Imphal.
- State animal: Sangai.
- State bird: Mrs Hume's pheasant.
- State tree: Toon.
- State flower: Shirui lily.

Hence, the correct option is (B).

47. Given,

$$x = 2016, y = 2015 \text{ and } z = 2013$$

Then,

$$x - y = 2016 - 2015 = 1$$

$$y - z = 2015 - 2013 = 2$$

$$z - x = 2013 - 2016 = -3$$

$$\therefore x^2 + y^2 + z^2 - xy - yz - zx$$

As we know,

$$(a - b)^2 = a^2 - 2ab + b^2$$

Now, in the given equation, numerator & denominator multiplied by 2, we get

$$= \frac{1}{2}(2x^2 + 2y^2 + 2z^2 - 2xy - 2yz - 2zx)$$

$$= \frac{1}{2}(x^2 + y^2 - 2xy + y^2 + z^2 - 2yz + z^2 + x^2 - 2zx)$$

$$= \frac{1}{2} - [(x - y)^2 + (y - z)^2 + (z - x)^2]$$

$$= \frac{1}{2}[1 + 4 + 9]$$

$$= \frac{1}{2} \times 14 = 7$$

Hence, the correct option is (A).

48. The error lies in the third part of the sentence. The subject here is "neither of them" which is singular; thus, the singular verb "was" should be used with it.

Hence, the correct option is (C).

49.

- Retreating monsoon is also known as Northeast Monsoon.
- The travelling of the Northeast monsoon from land to the sea leads to the rainfall along the Coromandel Coast.
- North-east monsoon is commonly known as "October heat".

- Tamilnadu and Andhra Pradesh experience heavy rainfall during this season.
- The name Northeast monsoon derives from the direction in which it travels, not related to the North-East states of India.
- Malabar Coast is a region of the southwestern coastline of the mainland Indian subcontinent.

Hence, the correct option is (B).

50. The binary star hypothesis about the origin of Earth was given by Russel in 1937. R.A. Lyttelton worked on and improved upon theory.

Hence, the correct option is (A).

51.

Landforms	Agents of Denudations
Monadnocks	• Monadnock, isolated hill of bedrock standing conspicuously above the general level of the surrounding area. • Monadnocks are left as erosional remnants because of their more resistant rock composition; commonly they consist of quartzite or less jointed massive volcanic rocks. • In contrast to inselbergs (island mountains), a similar tropical landform, monadnocks are formed in humid, temperate regions.
Blind Valley	• Blind valley is a narrow, deep, and flat-bottomed valley that has an abrupt ending.
Drumlins	• Drumlins and Eskers are both hilly glacial landforms. However, they differ in shape. • Eskers are narrow, long, winding hills that were deposited by streams underneath the glaciers. • Drumlins, in contrast, are oval egg - like hills featuring a steep slope at one end and a gentle incline at the other.
Dreikantes	• A Dreikanter is a type of ventifact that typically forms in desert or periglacial environments due to the abrasive action of blowing sand. • Dreikanters exhibit a characteristic pyramidal shape with three wind-abrased facets. The word Dreikanter is German for "three-edged."

Hence, the correct option is (A).

52. Let the cost price $= Rs.\ 100$

$\therefore$ Selling price $= Rs.\ 117$

$\therefore$ Marked price $= \dfrac{117}{90} \times = Rs.\ 130$

Profit percent on selling at the marked price

$= \dfrac{130-100}{100} \times 100 = 30\%$

Therefore, the total profit percent at marked price will be 30%.

Hence, the correct option is (D).

53. NREGA scheme was not launched in the Jaipur district of Rajasthan in its first phase.

In order to address the migrant crisis during the corona period, the government has allocated an additional fund of Rs. 40,000 crore for MGNREGA, as part of the stimulus package under Atma Nirbhar Bharat Abhiyan.

Mahatma Gandhi National Rural Employment Guarantee Act 2005 (MGNREGA):

- NREGA provides 100 days of guaranteed employment to the poor families of the country under the MGNREGA act 2005.
- Initially, it was launched in 100 districts of the country, including six districts of Rajasthan namely Udaipur, Sirohi, Dungarpur, Jhalawar, Karauli, Banswara.
- Later in 2008, it was extended all over the country.
- It was renamed MGNREGA on 2 October 2009.

Hence, the correct option is (A).

54. Harishankar Parsai, who hailed from Madhya Pradesh, was a famous writer in Satire.

- Nithalle Ki Diary, Apni Apni Bimari, and Do Naak Vale Log are some of his notable writings.
- He won Sahitya Akademi Award in 1982, for his satirical work "Viklaang Shraddha ka daur''.

Hence, the correct option is (A).

55. In the Rewa district of Madhya Pradesh, the 'Mahamrityunjay ka Mela' is held every year.

- There is a temple of Maha Mrityunjay in Rewa.
- The fair is held every year on Basant Panchami and Shivratri.
- Bhairavnath of Bhagat Panchami is a famous Shiv Temple in Devtailab Birsinghpur.

Hence, the correct option is (D).

56. Hang means kill (someone) by tying a rope attached from above around their neck and removing the support from beneath them (often used as a form of capital punishment).

Forms- Hang, Hanged, Hanged.

He was hanged for murder.

Hang- to have been suspended in the air or placed on a wall

Forms- Hang, Hung, Hung.

He hung up his coat.

Hence, the correct option is (B).

57. After the phrase 'one of the', a plural noun is used. Hence, 'teachers' is the only suitable choice for this blank.

Hence, the correct option is (A).

58. 'For' is the most appropriate choice of preposition here as 'prepare for' means to make plans for a future event.

Hence, the correct option is (C).

59. The European Union is a group of 28 countries that operate as a cohesive economic and political block.

- So statement 1 is not correct.

19 of these countries use EURO as their official currency.

9 EU members (Bulgaria, Croatia, Czech Republic, Denmark, Hungary, Poland, Romania, Sweden, and the United Kingdom) do not use the euro.

The EU grew out of a desire to form a single European political entity to end centuries of warfare among European countries that culminated with World War II and decimated much of the continent.

The EU has developed an internal single market through a standardized system of laws that apply in all member states in matters, where members have agreed to act as one.

- So statement 2 is correct.

Hence, the correct option is (B).

60. United Nations Development Programme (UNDP) in its latest report named "Protecting Women's Livelihoods in Times of Pandemic: Temporary Basic Income and the Road to Gender Equality" has proposed a Temporary Basic Income (TBI) for poor women in developing countries.

- International Women's Day is observed on 8th March every year.
- MHRD remembered the women of history who have made significant contributions in the past and planted a sapling in memory of Gaura Devi, a Chipko Activist.

Hence, the correct option is (A).

61. The Cauvery Delta region is also known as the 'Garden of Southern India'.

Cauvery river also known as Dakshin Ganga is one of the major rivers in the south Indian region. On its course to Bay of Bengal, Cauvery gets branched into many distributaries forming many fertile deltas. It is for this reason that Cauvery is also known as the "garden of southern India".

Hence, the correct option is (C).

62. Follow the rule of 'VBODMAS'

Step 1: Solve the expression below bar

y-[y-(x+y)-{y-(y-x+y) }+2x]

Step 2: Solve () bracket

y-[y-(x+y)-{y-(2y-x) }+2x]

y-[-x-{y-2y+x}+2x]

Step 2: Solve {} bracket

y-[-x-{y-2y+x+2x}]

y-[-x-{-y+3x}]

y-[-x+y-3x]

Step 3: Solve [ ] bracket

y+4x-y

4x

Therefore, correct answer is 4x.

Hence, the correct option is (C).

63. Given:

Investment of A = Rs. 80,000

Investment of B = Rs. 60,000

Time of investment = 1 year

Ratio of their profit = Rs. 80,000 : Rs. 60,000

$\Rightarrow 4 : 3$

∴ The required ratio will be 4 : 3

Hence, the correct option is (D).

64. Given:

50% of a number A is added to B.

The second number B increase by 25%.

When 50% of one number is added to a second number, the second number increase to 25%.

Let one number be 'x' and the second number be 'y'.

According to the question,

$$\Rightarrow 50\% \text{ of } x + y = \left(\frac{125}{100}\right) \times y$$

Solving the equation,

$$\Rightarrow \left(\frac{50}{100}\right) x = \left(\frac{5}{4}\right) y - y$$

$$\Rightarrow \frac{x}{2} = \frac{y}{4}$$

$$\Rightarrow \frac{x}{y} = \frac{1}{2}$$

Hence, the correct option is (B).

65. The given sentence is of active voice and it uses a modal verb. The structures for active/passive voices for modal verbs are:

Active: Subject + modal verb + verb (Ist form) + object

Passive: Object + modal verb + be + verb (IIIrd form) + by + subject

So, with the help of the above structures, we can convert the given sentence into passive voice:

The prize can be won by Nishu.

Hence, the correct option is (A).

66. The given sentence is in the active voice. It is in interrogative form of present tense. The structures for active/passive voices are:

Active: Do/does + subject + verb (Ist form) + object?

Passive: Is/are/am + object + verb (IIIrd form) + by + subject?

So, based on the above structures, we can convert the given sentence into passive voice:

Are your parents expected to come today from Hyderabad?

Hence, the correct option is (C).

67.

- Kautilya was an Indian statesman and philosopher, chief advisor, and Prime Minister of the Indian Emperor Chandragupta Maurya, the first ruler of the Mauryan Empire.
- Kautilya was also known as Chanakya and Vishnugupta.
- He also authored Arthsahstra.

Hence, the correct option is (C).

68. The incorrect match is: Primary group – political party

Sorokin, an American sociologist, has divided groups into two major types – the vertical and the horizontal. The vertical group includes persons of different strata or statuses. But the horizontal group includes persons of the same status.

Social groups include two or more people who interact and share a sense of unity and common identity. Primary groups are small and characterized by close, personal relationships that last a long time. Secondary groups include impersonal, temporary relationships that are goal-oriented.

Hence, the correct option is (D).

69. According to Parsons, society is a system having four basic functional prior conditions, are adaptation, goal-orientation, integration and pattern maintenance.

Talcott Parsons viewed society as a system. He argued that any social system has four basic functional prerequisites: adaptation, goal attainment, integration and pattern maintenance. In order to survive, social systems must have some degree of control over their environment.

Hence, the correct option is (A).

70. We know that,

If α and β are the roots of the quadratic equation, $ax^2 + bx + c = 0$. Then,

$$\alpha + \beta = -\frac{b}{a} \text{ and } \alpha \times \beta = \frac{c}{a}$$

The given equation is,

$$2x^2 - 2(k-2)x - (k+1) = 0$$

By comparing the given equation with the quadratic equation, $ax^2 + bx + c = 0$. We get, $a = 2, b = -2(k-2)$ and $c = -(k+1)$

Let α and β be the roots of the equation $2x^2 - 2(k-2)x - (k+1) = 0$

$$\Rightarrow \alpha + \beta = -\frac{-2(k-2)}{2} = k - 2$$

$$\Rightarrow \alpha \times \beta = \frac{-(k+1)}{2}$$

As we know that, $\alpha^2 + \beta^2 = (\alpha + \beta)^2 - 2\alpha\beta$

$$\Rightarrow a^2 + \beta^2 = (k-2)^2 + (1+k)$$

$$\Rightarrow a^2 + \beta^2 = \left(k - \frac{3}{2}\right)^2 + \frac{11}{4}$$

So, the minimum value of $a^2 + \beta^2$ is found when $k - \frac{3}{2} = 0 \Rightarrow k = \frac{3}{2}$.

Hence, the correct option is (C).

71. The given equation is:

$$|x^2 - 3x + 2| > x^2 - 3x + 2$$

Case-1: If $x \geq 0$

$$\Rightarrow x^2 - 3x + 2 > x^2 - 3x + 2$$

∴ No real value of x satisfies the above equation.

Case- 2:- If $x < 0$

$$\Rightarrow -(x^2 - 3x + 2) > x^2 - 3x + 2$$

$$\Rightarrow x^2 - 3x + 2 < 0$$

$$\Rightarrow (x - 1)(x - 2) < 0$$

$$\Rightarrow 1 < x < 2$$

Hence, the correct option is (C).

72. Ratchanok Intanon, the Badminton player of Thailand, defeated Spain's Carolina Marin in the women's singles final match of the Indonesia Masters tournament in Jakarta, held recently. This is her second win in the Indonesian Masters event after her triumph in 2010.

Ratchanok Intanon became world champion in women's singles in 2013 and became the first Thai player to become No.1 in women's singles. Carolina Marin is the present Olympic Champion and three-time World Champion.

Hence, the correct option is (B).

73. The Team of Maharashtra dominated the Khelo India Youth Games by clinching the overall trophy for the second time with a huge haul of 256 medals, including 78 gold and 77 silver. Last year, Maharashtra topped the table with 228 medals. The trophy was presented to Maharashtra by the Chief Minister of Assam Sarbananda Sonowal in the presence of Union Sports Minister Kiren Rijju, during the closing ceremony.

The second place was bagged by the state of Haryana with 200 medals and Delhi with 122 medals. Khelo India Youth games has been organised in Assam's Guwahati for the last 13 days.

Hence, the correct option is (B).

74. Polymerization is a process through which a large number of monomer molecules react together to form a polymer. The macromolecules produced from a polymerization may have a linear or a branched structure. They can also assume the shape of a complex, three-dimensional network.
Hence, the correct option is (B).

75. Antoine Lavoisier was a French chemist who is popularly considered as the "Father of Modern Chemistry" mainly due to the central role he played in the 18th-century chemical revolution and he had a large influence on both the history of chemistry and the history of biology.
Hence, the correct option is (C).

76. The idiom "no room to swing a cat" means a place is very small and crowded. used in reference to a very confined space.

Example:

It was described as a large, luxury mobile home, but there was barely room to swing a cat.

Hence, the correct option is (D).

77. Crocodile tears (or superficial sympathy) are a false, insincere display of emotion such as a hypocrite crying fake tears of grief.

Hence, the correct option is (D).

78. Let the initial price of onions be Rs. 100

$\Rightarrow$ Price of onions after 25% rise = 100 + 100 $\times$ $\dfrac{25}{100}$ = 125

$\Rightarrow$ Final price after government subsidy = 100 + $\dfrac{10}{100}$ $\times$ 100 = 110

$\Rightarrow$ Subsidy to be provided by government = 125 – 110 = 15

$\Rightarrow$ Subsidy in percentage = $\dfrac{15}{125}$ $\times$ 100 = 12%

Hence, the correct option is (B).

79. Let A, B and C have the value of a, b and c respectively

As B is 20% greater than C

$\Rightarrow$ b = 1.2c

Also, B is 40% smaller than A

$\Rightarrow$ b = 0.6a

From above two relations:

1.2c = 0.6a

$\Rightarrow$ a = 2c

$\Rightarrow$ $\dfrac{a}{c}$ = 2

$\Rightarrow$ A is double of C

$\therefore$ A is 100% larger than C

Hence, the correct option is (C).

80. A Red Data Book contains lists of species whose continued existence is threatened. Species are classified into different categories of perceived risk. Each Red Data Book usually deals with a specific group of animals or plants and fungi. They are now being published in many different countries and provide useful information on the threat status of the species.

Hence, the correct option is (D).

81. Formula Used:

HCF of fraction $= \dfrac{HCF\ of\ Numerator}{LCM\ of\ Denominator}$

HCF of $\left(\dfrac{12}{17}\right)$ and $\left(\dfrac{15}{34}\right)$ $= \dfrac{3}{34}$

$\therefore$ The required answer is $\dfrac{3}{34}$.

Hence, the correct option is (C).

82. Given:

X and Y invested in a business in a ratio of 4 : 1.

They donated 21% of a profit to an NGO

and X's share is Rs. 31,600

Let total profit is Rs. x.

Donated to NGO = 21% of x

Remaining profit = Rs. (x - 21% of x)

$= \dfrac{79x}{100}$

According to the question,

$\Rightarrow \left(\dfrac{79x}{100}\right) \times \left(\dfrac{4}{5}\right)$ = 31,600

$\Rightarrow$ x = $\dfrac{(31,600 \times 100 \times 5)}{(79 \times 4)}$

$\Rightarrow$ x = Rs. 50,000

$\therefore$ Required total profit is Rs. 50,000.

Hence, the correct option is (C).

83. Rakesh Sharma was the first man in space.

Wing Commander Rakesh Sharma, AC (born 13 January 1949) is a former Indian Air Force pilot who flew aboard Soyuz T-11 on 3 April 1984 as part of the Soviet Interkosmos programme. He is the only Indian citizen to travel in space, although there have been other astronauts with an Indian background who were not Indian citizens.

Hence the correct option is (A).

84. $(.000216)^{\frac{1}{3}} = \left(\dfrac{216}{10^6}\right)^{\frac{1}{3}}$

$= \left(\dfrac{6 \times 6 \times 6}{10^2 \times 10^2 \times 10^2}\right)^{\frac{1}{3}}$

$= \dfrac{6}{10^2}$

$= \dfrac{6}{100}$

$= 0.06$

Hence, the correct option is (B).

85. During Chola period bronze icons of Nataraja deity who has four hands was casted.

As the cosmic ecstatic dancer, Nataraja is a depiction of the Hindu god Shiva. Its best known expressions were emerged in the chola period made up of bronze of variou heights typically less than four feet.

Hence, the correct option is (A).

86.

- A P J Abdul Kalam was the first to use the President's power to return a bill to parliament. (Suspensive Veto)

- President Giani Zail Singh exercised a pocket veto to prevent the Indian Post Office (Amendment) Bill from becoming law.

- Zail Singh was the President of India from 1982 till 1987.

- A pocket veto allows a president to exercise power over a bill by taking no action.

- Zakir Husain Khan was the third President of India.

- Zakir Husain Khan was also the Vice President of India from 1962 to 1967.

- Sarvappalli Radhakrishnan served as the first Vice President of India (1952–1962)

- He was the second President of India (1962–1967).

- Dr. Sarvepalli Radhakrishnan was nominated 27 times for the Nobel Prize.

- Rajendra Prasad was the first President of India.

Hence, the correct option is (B).

87.

- Mohammad Hidayatullah (17 December 1905 – 18 September 1992) was the eleventh Chief Justice of India serving from 25 February 1968 to 16 December 1970, and the sixth Vice-President of India, serving from 31 August 1979 to 30 August 1984.

- He had also served as the Acting President of India from 20 July 1969 to 24 August 1969 and from 6 October 1982 to 31 October 1982.

- He is regarded as an eminent jurist, scholar, educationist, author, and linguist.

Hence, the correct option is (A).

88. Given:

Number of days taken, if Heena and Karan work together = 12 days

Heena alone completes the work in 18 days.

Let the number of days taken by Karan to complete work be x.

Work done in 1 days by Heena $= \left(\dfrac{1}{18}\right)$

Work done in 1 day by Karan $= \left(\dfrac{1}{x}\right)$

Work done in 1 day when both work together $= \left(\dfrac{1}{12}\right)$

According to question:

$$\left(\dfrac{1}{18}\right) + \left(\dfrac{1}{x}\right) = \dfrac{1}{12}$$

$$\Rightarrow \dfrac{1}{x} = \dfrac{(3-2)}{36} = \dfrac{1}{36}$$

$\Rightarrow x = 36$ days

$\therefore$ Karan completes the work in 36 days.

Hence, the correct option is (B).

89. Given:

Number of persons = 4

Initial time to complete the work = 40 days

Final time to complete the work = 50 days

Total work done = Number of persons × Time taken

Total work = 10 × 40 = 400 units

Let 4 persons leave after x days

So, remaining persons will complete the work in (50 – x) days

Total work = (10 × x) + 6(50 – x)

= 10x + 300 – 6x

= 4x + 300

Now, according to question,

400 = 4x + 300

$\Rightarrow$ 4x = 100

$\Rightarrow$ x = 25

$\therefore$ The four persons will leave after 25 days

Hence, the correct option is (A).

90. Individualized Instruction: Instructions of teaching materials should be based on the principle of self-placing. It should be the educational ability of the child and then match the learning materials with that ability. They can learn better if teaching is adapted to the needs of these children.

Benefits of individualized instruction:

- It helps them to gain self-confidence as learners.

- It brides language learning gaps by focusing on individual progress.

- Opens up students to engage more with their teachers.

- It offers freedom to students to work at their own pace.

Thus, we conclude that teachers can remediate for the student with language difficulty by focusing on individual progress with individual instruction.

Hence, the correct option is (A).

91. Given,

X = 0.456666.... ....(i)

Multiply by 100 in equation (i)

100X = 45 + 0.6666.... ......(ii)

Multiply by 1000 in equation (i)

1000X = 456 + 0.6666.... ......(iii)

Subtract equation (ii) from equation (iii)

900X = 411

∴ X = 411900

Hence, the correct option is (C).

92. Given,

$$\sqrt[3]{1 + \frac{x}{169}} = \frac{14}{13}$$

$$\Rightarrow 1 + \frac{x}{169} = \frac{2744}{2197}$$

$$\Rightarrow \frac{x}{169} = \left(\frac{2744}{2197} - 1\right)$$

$$\Rightarrow \frac{x}{169} = \frac{547}{2197}$$

$$\Rightarrow x = 42.07$$

Hence, the correct option is (D).

93. The correct answer is the specimen.

An object or portion serving as a sample is the **specimen.**

Specimen: something used as a sample (of a group or kind of something, especially an object to be studied or to be put in a collection)

Example:

The gorgeous football player is a specimen of the perfect man.

Hence, the correct option is (D).

94. The correct answer is 'oracy'.

An ability to express oneself well in speech is **oracy.**

Oracy: the ability to express oneself fluently and grammatically in speech.

Example: Infant teachers will be urged to concentrate on reading, writing, oracy, and numeracy.

Hence, the correct option is (A).

95. Given,

Percentage of students who failed math = 42%

Percentage of students who failed science = 52%

Percentage of students who failed both = 17%

⇒ Percentage of students who passed both = (100 – 42 – 52 + 17) % = 23%

Let total number of students be $'x'$

23% of $x = 69$

$$\Rightarrow \frac{23x}{100} = 69$$

$$\Rightarrow x = 69 \times \frac{100}{23} = 300$$

∴ Total noumber of students who appeared for the test is 300.

Hence, the correct option is (D).

96. In the development of a particular branch of mathematics, the mathematician is chiefly concerned with a logical rigorous treatment of the subject matter, whereas the teacher is usually concerned with its psychological organization and presentation. It is the curriculum organizer who is called upon to integrate the two approaches.

Main branches of Pure mathematics:

- Algebra: Algebra is first accepted as a branch of mathematics. It is a kind of arithmetic where we use unknown quantities along with numbers. These unknown quantities are represented by letters of the English alphabet such as X, Y, A, B, etc., or symbols. The use of letters helps us to generalize the formulas and rules that you write and also helps you to find the unknown missing values in the algebraic expressions and equations.

- Geometry: It is the most practical branch of mathematics that deals with shapes and sizes of figures and their properties. The basic elements of geometry are points, lines, angles, surfaces, and solids.

- Trigonometry: Derived from Greek trigōnon, "triangle" and metron, "measure", it is a branch of mathematics that studies relationships between side lengths and angles of triangles.

- Calculus: It is a branch of mathematics concerned with instantaneous rates of change and the summation of infinitely many small factors.

- Statistics and Probability: The branches of mathematics concerned with the laws governing random events, including the collection, analysis, interpretation, and display of numerical data.

Hence, the correct option is (B).

97. Mathematical reasoning is a topic of mathematics which deals with truthfulness and falsehood of a statement. A statement is a sentence which is either true or false, but can not be both at the same time. There are certain terms that are frequently used in mathematical reasoning:

- Inverse: The conditional statement " $\sim p \to \sim q$ " is called the inverse of the conditional statement " $p \to q$ ", where $(\sim p)$ and $(\sim q)$ means 'not p ' and 'not q' respectively. For example, if ' n is not even, n^2 is not even' is the inverse of 'if n is even, n^2 is even."

- Converse: The conditional statement " $q \to p''$ is called the converse of the conditional statement $^xp \to q''$. Example, 'if n^2 is even, then n is even' is the converse of 'If n is even, then n^2 is even'.

- Contrapositive: The statement $''(\sim q) \to (\sim p)''$ is called the contrapositive of the statement $p \to q$. For example, 'If n^2 is not even, then n is not even' is contrapositive of 'If n is even, then n^2 is even'

Hence, the correct option is (A).

98. Average production of company X in the period 1998-2000

$$= \left[\frac{1}{3} \times (25 + 50 + 40)\right]$$

$$= \left(\frac{115}{3}\right) \text{ lakh tons.}$$

Average production of company Y in the period 1998-2000 =
$$\left[\frac{1}{3} \times (35 + 40 + 50)\right]$$

$$= \left(\frac{125}{3}\right) \text{ lakh tons.}$$

Required ratio = $\dfrac{\left(\frac{115}{3}\right)}{\left(\frac{125}{3}\right)}$

$$= \frac{115}{125} = \frac{23}{25}$$

$\therefore$ Required ratio is $\dfrac{23}{25}$.

Hence, the correct option is (C).

99. The average production for company $X = \left[\frac{1}{5} \times (30 + 45 + 25 + 50 + 40)\right]$

$$= \frac{190}{5}$$

$$= 38$$

The average production for company $Y = \left[\frac{1}{5} \times (25 + 35 + 35 + 50 + 40)\right]$

$$= \frac{185}{5}$$

$$= 37$$

The average production for company $Z = \left[\frac{1}{5} \times (35 + 40 + 45 + 35 + 35)\right]$

$$= \frac{190}{5}$$

$$= 38$$

$\therefore$ Average production of five years in maximum for both the companies X and Z.

Hence, the correct option is (D).

100. The percentage of production of company Z to the production of company Y for various years are:

For 1996

$$= \left(\frac{35}{25} \times 100\right)\%$$

$$= 140\%$$

For 1997

$$= \left(\frac{40}{35} \times 100\right)\%$$

$$= 114.29\%$$

For 1998

$$= \left(\frac{45}{35} \times 100\right)\%$$

$$= 128.57\%$$

For 1999

$$= \left(\frac{35}{40} \times 100\right)\%$$

$$= 87.5\%$$

For 2000

$$= \left(\frac{35}{50} \times 100\right)\%$$

$$= 70\%$$

Clearly, this percentage is highest for 1996.

Hence, the correct option is (A).

// Notes //